MW00780001

PROMOTING SUSTAINABLE LOCAL AND COMMUNITY ECONOMIC DEVELOPMENT

American Society for Public Administration
Book Series on Public Administration & Public Policy

Editor-in-Chief
Evan M. Berman, Ph.D.
National Chengchi University, Taiwan
evanmberman@gmail.com

Mission: Throughout its history, ASPA has sought to be true to its founding principles of promoting scholarship and professionalism within the public service. The ASPA Book Series on Public Administration and Public Policy publishes books that increase national and international interest for public administration and which discuss practical or cutting edge topics in engaging ways of interest to practitioners, policy-makers, and those concerned with bringing scholarship to the practice of public administration.

Promoting Sustainable Local and Community Economic Development,
Roland V. Anglin

Government Contracting: Promises and Perils, William Sims Curry

Managing Public Sector Projects: A Strategic Framework for Success in an Era of Downsized Government, David S. Kassel

Organizational Assessment and Improvement in the Public Sector,
Kathleen M. Immordino

Major League Winners: Using Sports and Cultural Centers as Tools for Economic Development, Mark S. Rosentraub

The Formula for Economic Growth on Main Street America, Gerald L. Gordon

The New Face of Government: How Public Managers Are Forging a New Approach to Governance, David E. McNabb

The Facilitative Leader in City Hall: Reexamining the Scope and Contributions, James H. Svara

American Society for Public Administration
Series in Public Administration and Public Policy

PROMOTING SUSTAINABLE LOCAL AND COMMUNITY ECONOMIC DEVELOPMENT

ROLAND V. ANGLIN

CRC Press
Taylor & Francis Group
Boca Raton   London   New York

CRC Press is an imprint of the
Taylor & Francis Group, an **informa** business

CRC Press
Taylor & Francis Group
6000 Broken Sound Parkway NW, Suite 300
Boca Raton, FL 33487-2742

© 2011 by Taylor and Francis Group, LLC
CRC Press is an imprint of Taylor & Francis Group, an Informa business

No claim to original U.S. Government works

International Standard Book Number: 978-1-4200-8810-6 (Hardback)

Library of Congress Cataloging-in-Publication Data

Anglin, Roland, 1959-
    Promoting sustainable local and community economic development / Roland V. Anglin.
        p. cm. -- (American Society for Public Administration book series on public administration & public policy)
    Includes bibliographical references and index.
    ISBN 978-1-4200-8810-6 (hardcover : alk. paper)
    1. Community development. 2. Economic development. I. Title. II. Series.

HN49.C6A55 2011
338.9'27091732--dc22   2010026746

Visit the Taylor & Francis Web site at
http://www.taylorandfrancis.com

and the CRC Press Web site at
http://www.crcpress.com

Contents

Preface xi

Acknowledgments xv

About the Author xvii

Introduction xix

1 What Is Community Economic Development? 1
The CED Intermediaries 9
Expanding Capital Access 11
Support for Community Economic Development 14
Summary 15
Endnotes 18

2 Searching for Sustainable Community Economic Development 23
What Can Be Done? 26
Rethinking People and Place Development 28
Putting People First 29
Livable and Sustainable Communities 32
Brownfield Redevelopment 33
Reusing Steel from Automobiles to Build Affordable Housing 34
Summary 36
Endnotes 37

3 Public Sector Innovation and Community Economic Development 39
Leadership and Innovation 41
Community Economic Development Capacity 46
Community Building and Development 50
Assets and Agency 52
Changing Strategies in Workforce Development 53
School Reform for Sustainable Community Economic Development 55
The Role of Higher Education 56

Summary 57
Endnotes 57

4   Locally Based Community Economic Development Institutions:
A Base for Innovation **61**
Community Development Corporations 62
Government Support 62
    Community Reinvestment Act 64
    The Low Income Housing Tax Credit 69
    New Markets Tax Credit Program 71
The Management Challenge 74
The Unity Council: Connecting Transit-Oriented Development to
Community Economic Development 75
The Mountain Association for Community Economic Development:
Bridging the Regional Divide 76
    Preserving Individual Assets 79
    Research and Policy 80
Summary 80
Endnotes 83

5   The Role of Community Economic Development Intermediaries **87**
Expanding the Supply of Capital: Public Sector Support of
Community Development Finance 88
Building Capacity on the Community Side 90
    NeighborWorks America 91
Building Strong Communities 93
    The Local Initiatives Support Corporation 94
    Connecting the Basics 95
    Enterprise Community Partners 96
Experimentation and Innovation 97
    Regional and Local Intermediaries 98
    Neighborhood Partnership Inc.: Less Is More 98
Summary 100
    Institutional Strength Conditions Innovation and Policy
    Leadership 100
    CED Intermediaries Augment the Field by Routinizing the
    Development Process 101
    Linking Mainstream Markets and CED 102
    Leading the Way for Sustainable Community Economic
    Development 102
Endnotes 103

6   Community Building and Development **105**
Are Community Development and Community Building Different? 106

Reintroducing Old Friends 106
Planning, Information Management, and Development........................109
Neighborhood Security and Community Economic Development......... 111
Weed and Seed 112
    Partnering with Weed and Seed, LISC's Community Safety
    Initiative 114
Gang Diversion: Homeboy Industries... 114
Developing Youth/Youth Developing Communities............................ 116
    YouthBuild 116
Arts and Culture..121
    Turning Graffiti into Art: The Mural Arts Program in
    Philadelphia..122
Food and Community Development 124
Summary..125
Endnotes..127

7   Assets and Agency 133
Individual Asset Building 135
    Individual Development Accounts..135
    Hidden Gold: Earned Income Tax Credits 138
    Access to Credit for Self-Employment and Human Capital
    Development 140
Collective Asset Building..144
    Stabilizing the Commons 144
    Operation Neighborhood Recovery 145
    Financing Innovation 146
    What Can Be Done Nationally: The National Community
    Stabilization Trust 147
Summary..148
Endnotes..150

8   Innovations in Community-Based Workforce Development 155
Sectoral Employment...157
    Second Chance, Inc..159
Career Ladders..160
    Temporary Staffing..161
Network Building...162
Partnerships with Community Colleges 163
Summary..164
Endnotes..166

**9   Reforming Schools and Strengthening Community Economic
Development 167**
Linking Community Building and Education....................................168

Lincoln, Nebraska: Leadership Makes a Difference 170
Smart Education Systems 172
Chicago: Logan Square Neighborhood Association.......................172
Parent Involvement and Organizing 174
Linking Community Economic Development and Educational Reform . 174
Community Economic Development Partnerships for Educational
Reform...177
Enterprise Community Partners and New Compact School 179
Summary..180
Linking Schools to Community 180
Linking Education and Development...181
More Effective Mobility Policies 182
Endnotes...182

10 Higher Education as a Partner in Development................................185
Successful University–Community Partnerships 186
Building Community Capacity 187
The University as Developer...190
Knowledge Generation, Geographical Information Systems, and
Community Economic Development 192
Minnesota 3D 192
The Special Role of Community Colleges as CEDIs..............................195
Summary..196
Effective Partnerships 197
Public Sector Support 197
Endnotes...197

11 Looking Forward: Promise and Hope...199
Addressing the Organizational and Institutional Challenge.................... 200
Expanding the Planning and Implementation Capacity for Innovation ...203
Modeling Innovation...205
Community Development.. 206
Local School Reform 207
Assets and Agency 207
Workforce Development.. 208
Sustainable Development.. 208
Public Sector Involvement in Sustainable Community
Economic Development...209
Summary..209
Endnotes...210

References **211**
Resource Guide **231**
    Further Reading: Public Sector Innovation...............................231
    Further Reading: Sustainable, Community, and Economic
    Development 234
    Community Economic Development Institutions and Stakeholders........239
        The Public Sector Institutions, Strategies, and Programs 239
        Community Economic Development Support, Advocacy and
        Learning Resources...241
        Asset Building and Community Development 246
        Workforce Development..250
        Higher Education and Community Economic Development 251
    Community Building/Development..253
        Arts and Community Economic Development............................253
        Education Reform and Community Development 254
        Community Organizing Groups 254
        Crime Prevention...255
        Youth Development 255
    International CED...257
Index **261**

Preface

Revitalizing central business districts and attracting new businesses to improve local economies suffering decline define the parameters of local economic development in the United States. Of course the underlying argument is that growing local economies through corporate attraction or supporting local entrepreneurs results in jobs. In reality, this simple, enduring calculus is never enough to address the multiple and often complicated challenges of unemployment and concentrated poverty.

Local economic development strategies and tools such as tax increment financing, tax abatements, Business Improvement Districts, and enterprise zones have their place. These strategies, however, are not the focus here. Over the last 40 years, conventional public management thought on place and people revitalization has greatly expanded to include strategies and tools that rebuild communities and neighborhoods along with rebuilding central business districts. These emerging strategies and tools combine traditional incentives for economic development with institutional arrangements that share the responsibility for development beyond the business community.[1]

The difference between what is now termed community economic development (CED) and traditional local economic development practice is the priority placed on community involvement in economic development partnerships between the private sector and government. Innovation and innovative practices are often found in government support for organizational arrangements that promote cooperation and diffusion of benefits to communities outside the central business district. Increasingly, local economic development now incorporates policies geared toward developing the primary unit of place: the local community or neighborhood. Neighborhoods with a good quality of life, good housing, and productive people are the foundation of place and regional development.[2]

The accomplishments of community economic development are significant. In aggregate, the field is a leader in producing affordable housing, training the unemployed, and providing capital and advice for low-income people seeking to escape poverty through self-employment.[3] This ongoing work, in concert with other development policies, has helped many nonurban and urban places return to economic viability.[4]

As the globalization of capital proceeds, an increasing number of communities, states, and regions not normally placed in the distressed category will need the lessons learned by CEDs over the years to adjust to changing economic and demographic circumstances.

A good example is the current immigration pattern to the United States, which is changing the face of nonurban communities all over the country. This pattern runs counter to previous waves of immigration, which saw cities as ports of entry to the rest of the country. Immigrants are passing over cities to find opportunity in suburban and rural communities.[5] These communities face age-old problems of unemployment, crime, and concentrated poverty, with few roadmaps to guide public managers and other stakeholders.

Managing the effects of physical blight and concentrated poverty is no longer unknown to public policy. This is not to say that we can eliminate poverty or physical blight, which America seems to be unwilling to admit to as a nation. We constantly look for the "magic bullet" or the comprehensive solution to place decay and poverty. There is no such solution, but we do have partial solutions that can be applied and connected in a thoughtful fashion.

I wrote this book for all who wish to see strong local neighborhoods and communities. Serving in multiple roles as a practitioner and applied academic has given me a unique vantage point from which to see community economic development practices grow over time in size, scale, and impact. Its accomplishments are often underrated and its ability to solve the problems of poor communities is sometimes clouded by outsized expectations. I hope this book serves as a reference for elected and administrative leaders needing to survey the breadth of innovative place and people development practices. Although it is not a "how to" book, the lessons and examples are presented at both a general and a textured level so that practitioners, public managers, and others can see innovative ways to change, influence, and, I hope, improve the economic development process. A Resource Guide is included at the end of the book for readers who may want a more expansive understanding of community economic development. Knowledge about the field—and what works—is growing, but not always publicized and accessed by a general audience. The section's goal is to provide a wide range of thought, best practices, and strategies, including a compilation of leading national and international organizations, programs aimed at poverty reduction and community economic development, as well as a national and international bibliography on innovative efforts to build communities and economic opportunity.

Endnotes

1. Kromer (2009); also Feehan and Feit (2006).
2. Florida (2005); Kanter (1995); Kotkin (2007).

3. Vidal and Keys (2005); Ferguson and Dickens (1999); United States Congress. Millennial Housing Commission (2002).
4. Bennett and Giloth (2007); *Businessweek* (2003); Giloth (1998); Kromer (2000).
5. See Singer (2009) for a good overview of immigration trends.

Acknowledgments

I want to thank the American Society for Public Administration and Taylor & Francis for the opportunity to participate in this book series. The series editor, Evan Berman, has been a tremendous colleague, providing advice and direction at just the right points. I thank him for his patience as I went through the process of discovering my voice.

My immediate family, Dale, Lena, and Micah Anglin, gave me the unconditional love and energy to just write. There are many others to thank, although it is impossible to mention everyone. The short list includes Ronald Berkman, Gordon Clark, Marlene Cohen, Joel Kassiola, Gary Orfield, Michael Preston, the late Archibald Singham, and Bernard Silberman, all wonderful teachers and scholars. Robert Curvin led the Ford Foundation's Urban Poverty Program in the 1990s. I was a member of the unit and learned many things about community development and community economic development from Bob Curvin. He is a gifted manager and is no less a gifted teacher. My extended family and friends, Blossom Anglin-Brown, Leslie Anglin, Craig Brown, Christine Barnett; friends, Diana Bermudez, Anne Chien, Henry Coleman, Linetta Gilbert, Norm Glickman, Andrew Foster, Alan Rosenthal, Ian Shearn, James Spencer, Carl Van Horn, and Cliff Zukin, all provided fellowship and support over the years.

The Ford Foundation helped to support this book in two important ways. I was fortunate to work at the institution from 1991 to 1998. There is no better place to learn all aspects of community economic development while making a difference in this world than the Ford Foundation. Some years after my departure, I received support to examine models for leadership development in the field of community economic development. That research helped influence and forward this study in many ways. Although I am grateful for my experience with Ford, this book does not represent the institution's views or policy in any way. I learned much from working with Kiran Cunningham (who read an early draft of this book) and Hannah McKinney on the City Halls and Equity project for the National League of Cities. Our conversations greatly influenced how I now think about the role of the public sector in community economic development.

Support for this work also came from Dean James Hughes of the Edward J. Bloustein School of Planning and Public Policy at Rutgers University. He has played a major part in building a strong institution that values equally theoretical and applied scholarship on important questions of public policy and planning. Willa Speiser helped shape my words and focus my voice on this and many other projects. Many research assistants helped gather the information in this volume: Janine White, Stephen Van Maren, Tim Nordin, Diana Won, Jane Hand, Victoria Gilbert, Thomas Arndt, Kenya Crumel, Marissa Meyers, Emily Guskin, Nagla Bedir, Christopher Jones, and Allison Harris. Dahk Muhammad helped prepare the manuscript. All are thanked, but special dedication and thanks go to Claudius and Gwendolyn Anglin. They taught me the necessity and responsibility of leaving the world better than you found it. I can only hope that they are pleased.

About the Author

Roland V. Anglin's career spans over 20 years of working in the public, educational, and philanthropic sectors. In all his professional positions, Anglin has focused on promoting economic and community development in and for marginalized communities. Currently, he is faculty fellow at the Edward J. Bloustein School of Planning and Public Policy, Rutgers University, and directs the Initiative for Regional and Community Transformation (IRCT), which is housed at the school. The IRCT is a national initiative whose mission is to support the transformation of marginalized communities and people in urban and rural places through applied research and program management.

Dr. Anglin began his academic career at Rutgers University. There he examined issues related to economic development and growth management. During this time, he published some of the seminal work on citizen attitudes toward sprawl development. In 1991 he was recruited to the Ford Foundation, where he spent eight years. He served first as the program officer responsible for community development. Subsequently, he was asked to become deputy director for Community and Resource Development, which is part of the Asset Building and Community Development Division.

After leaving Ford, Dr. Anglin went to the Structured Employment Economic Development Corporation (Seedco), a national community development intermediary. At Seedco, Dr. Anglin was the senior vice president responsible for building the capacity of community-based housing organizations in 23 cities partnering with Seedco.

Since returning to academia, Dr. Anglin has pursued an active research agenda and has managed many demonstration initiatives for philanthropy, state governments, and national associations. Dr. Anglin received his doctorate from the University of Chicago.

Introduction

To say that the last 60 years or so have seen a momentous change in the world economy is like saying the Beatles changed the world of popular music. It has been said, and said many times. Globalization is an imprecise term, but however it is defined, it encourages a tilt toward regional markets challenging the fixed boundaries of nation-states. The technological integration of world markets and rapid capital deployment can democratize economic development in some cases. In others, however, these trends weaken the ability of local places to manage investment and development.[1]

If the inability to control local economic circumstances is not enough, increasing metropolitan development patterns that dominated the physical landscape in the United States after World War II are exacting great economic and environmental costs. In the process, unplanned growth is limiting efforts at place-based development. Metropolitan development, where huge tracts of land are consumed for low-density living, has encouraged significant population shifts away from central cities, leaving reduced tax bases in core cities to support critical public services and amenities.[2] For nonurban places the impact is no less dramatic. Initially, development in rural and suburban places brings investment and jobs. Over time, the influx of people brings "diminishing returns" such as increased traffic, degradation of the environment, and other effects of high-density living layered on places with limited infrastructure.[3]

In many instances, population movement away from central cities correlates with concentrated urban poverty. The urban poor, who in past generations used cities as staging areas for upward mobility, found this role all but gone in the latter half of the twentieth century.[4]

Yet even as local communities face significant challenges in their ability to remain economically viable, it is unlikely that they are going to lose their relevance in public and economic affairs despite periodic calls for public policy to encourage population dispersal to growing regions.[5] Communities, neighborhoods, and cities will remain important. If nothing else, these are places people call home, not to mention that enormous capital and human investment remain in these places.[6]

Despite the economic and demographic realities that communities and neighborhoods face, the future is not preordained. Many cities and communities have found ways to improve key policies and enhance their local economies and quality of life. Much of this improvement is due to support or leadership from the public sector working cooperatively with other stakeholders.[7] As Cunningham and her colleagues note in their book, *Tapping the Power of City Hall to Build Equitable Communities:*

> A new wave of innovative leadership is emerging in cities across America. This group is concentrating on solutions rather than problems, building coalitions rather than winning confrontations. They are using this pragmatic approach to tackle the persistent and difficult problems of poverty, inequalities and racism endemic to urban America. In doing so, they are making their cities more livable for residents and more attractive to people who want to invest there.[8]

Business Attraction Is Not Enough

In the years following the Industrial Revolution, standard operating policy saw states and localities respond to adverse economic conditions by competing to provide industry with financial incentives and constructing local or state economic development bureaucracies.[9] In many instances, these organizations are little more than civic or state boosters. Economic development departments emphasize their state or city's cosmopolitanism (or lack of it), inexpensive utility rates, low taxes, stable politics, and, for those with right-to-work laws, nonunionized labor. The pure form and structure of these policies have changed only slightly over the years and, in fact, continue to command the lion's share of attention in economic development practice.

Such policies constitute a negative-sum game where the aim is to lure industry from other cities and states. The fact that these types of policies are pervasive does not make them right or appropriate in all cases. Study after study shows that fiscal incentives are a small part of the decision making in plant or office relocation. Firms are probably going to establish a branch office or plant in a community without government incentives if that community is the first choice based on criteria other than incentives.[10]

Relocation policies are a well-used regional and local economic development strategy; however, they do not aim at changing structures and institutions that impede economic, social, or political equity, which is a core goal of CED policies.[11] Community economic development, and its values and practices, are indeed important strategies to help forge a stronger base for addressing key challenges going forward such as (1) development that protects the environment while opening opportunities for the poor to build wealth and opportunity, and (2) assisting in the larger project of strengthening the economic competitiveness of cities and regions.

Public Sector Leadership and Innovation

Some of the most important public sector innovations are not the result of improvements in the administrative activities of government.[12] Rather, significant policy outcomes are often a function of governance arrangements in which government is part of a wider policy network that might include nonprofits, interest groups, the private sector, and citizens.[13] This amalgam of governance arrangements and public leadership forms the framework that drives innovation in the effort to reduce poverty and rebuild cities and neighborhoods.[14]

Innovation here does not entail dramatic shifts in strategy and practice; rather it encompasses incremental improvements and approaches in policy and outcomes.[15] This view runs counter to prevailing conceptions of ossified bureaucracies and stale administrative practices. My view of government practice does not deny the limitations of bureaucracy but argues that we have to take an expansive view of how government operates over time. As the main provider of financial support, and its incomparable ability to convene, the public sector—that is, government—is pivotal.

Efforts by the city of Chicago to reinvent itself are a prominent example of public sector leadership and coordination around regional and community development. Thirty years ago, Chicago was written off as a casualty of Rust Belt decline coupled with the corrosive effects of decades-old racial and ethnic cleavages that left groups contesting over a shrinking pie.[16] The city was surrounded by some of the nation's fastest-growing counties and communities. These rapidly expanding communities did not see their fate connected to the city of Chicago resulting in negative-sum economic development policies that further hastened the Windy City's decline. Innovation and change came with the election of Richard M. Daley, whose father had presided over the city's fortunes in a much different era and manner.[17]

Daley the younger changed the narrative of Chicago by pursuing strategies that improved the quality of life as the base for economic revival.[18] He planted trees to beautify Chicago's communities and parks. Public art became a staple feature of city life. Figure, I.1 shows some of the many examples of public art that dot the Chicago landscape. Daley also moved to manage racial and ethnic fault lines by engaging community leaders and supporting citywide economic restructuring, community-based economic development, and educational reform. The second Mayor Daley also pursued opportunities to form institutional relationships with surrounding municipalities on a host of public policies.[19] These included planning for housing development and improving the region's air and water quality.[20]

Today, Chicago is far from the Rust Belt basket case of earlier decades. The same can be said of cities such as Pittsburgh, Cleveland, and New York, all once written off as repositories of the poor with no economic future. These cities engaged in similar processes using public leadership and stakeholder engagement to come back from the edge of the abyss through forging collaborations key to each city's future.[21] Collaborative engagement does not guarantee economic prosperity. All of the mentioned cities still struggle with economic relevancy and concentrated poverty, but the tools now exist to help them go beyond simple stalemate and paralysis.[22] What are the tools?

Some of the tools are *institutional*. We now have effective ways to organize key sectors, including economically marginalized communities, to act collectively on local and community economic development, workforce development, and now education reform.[23]

Other tools are *strategic policies*. Chicago's significant attempt at school reform through elected school-based management comes to mind. Federal policies such as the Community Reinvestment Act and the Community Development Financial Institutions Act are strategic efforts to provide the capital investment needed to reinvigorate depressed communities. The Brownfield Redevelopment Act helped define a new strategic direction in economic development policy when resources were made available to clean up parcels of land contaminated by past industrial uses that now can be used productively for housing and economic development. The Department of Housing and Urban Development's Community Outreach Partnership grants encouraged productive relationships among colleges and universities and their surrounding communities.

The list of federal, state, and local policies to help community and economic development in various forms is substantial. Government, along with engaged community interests in both the nonprofit and the private sectors, has jointly developed institutional components, strategies, and policies that are developing people and places.[24] The evolution of cooperation and sometimes conflict among these key sectors created a community economic development system complete with norms, core strategies, and centerpiece institutions.[25]

Whole neighborhoods ravaged by economic dislocation and change have become viable communities once again through the use of public sector strategies designed to provide development capital, support for housing development, and workforce development for the unemployed. There is no better example of this than the revival of the South Bronx.

When President Jimmy Carter visited the South Bronx in October 1977, the community was unarguably an American disaster. Redlining, population flight, and poverty left it without much investment and social capital. High crime and constant torching of buildings for insurance terrorized the remaining residents trying to live a safe, secure life.

Carter's visit was a clear message to America: the nation had to do better. In the next few years, the federal government and city government worked together. The relationship was fraught with national and local political pressures, but the result was that in 1986 Mayor Edward Koch announced a billion-dollar investment in redeveloping housing in the South Bronx. The problem was how to accomplish this. Private developers could have been used, but strong community feelings about being used and taken advantage of in the past made that a less-than-viable option. City administrators and politicians made a bold decision: the public sector decided to rely on community groups, many without any development experience.[26]

Figure I.1   Examples of Chicago's public art. Courtesy of Dale Robinson-Anglin.

Over the next 15 years, the city, philanthropists, and nonprofit support intermediaries worked tirelessly to develop the capacity of these groups to build housing.[27] In the process, the groups not only built housing but also reignited local housing and labor markets. New York City used what it was learning in the South Bronx to commit $4 billion over a 10-year period, using community-based developers to rebuild housing in other communities. Today the South Bronx is not perfect, but it is an example of what public-sector commitment and innovation can accomplish in bringing a community back from near oblivion.

The innovations that led to renewed viability in places such as the South Bronx over the last 40 years may not necessarily lead to sustainability without further innovation and learning. The world does not stand still. This book argues that community economic development, the set of practices that brought the South Bronx back, is a significant public sector–supported innovation.[28] Economic change and metropolitan development patterns are limiting the field's practices and outcomes. This does not mean we should find a different vehicle to address existing trends. Far from it.

Reflection and Learning

We should continue to reflect on the knowledge accumulated thus far and use it to inform our response to the immense challenges facing communities in the near and long term.[29] Major lessons are waiting to be harvested and used to promote more effective community economic development practices. Silo thinking, however, dominates approaches to poverty alleviation, upward mobility, and economic development. This limits the possibility for broader learning and change. Important publicly supported innovations are emerging in workforce development, economic development, youth development, education, neighborhood security, and new fields such as sustainable development. These are distinct fields of practice, but they directly affect the possibilities for community economic development.

The framework that can inform policy and practice, though, is either absent or in the beginning stage of development. This book is first and foremost an effort to show that we can build a framework for addressing emergent questions of place and people policy by looking at innovative practices that enhance the effectiveness of community economic development.

Endnotes

1. A number of studies look at the continuing impact of globalization on places and people; Barnes and Ledebur (1998); Friedman (2000, 2007); Kanter (1995); Sassen (2006); and Teaford (2006) offer an overview of the key issues.
2. Flint (2006).
3. Anglin (1990).
4. Lemann (1992); Wilson (1996).
5. Dreier et al. (2004); Shuman (1998); and Williamson, Imbroscio, and Alperovitz (2002) all make trenchant arguments for the importance of local places and economies. Borts and Stein (1964) and Peterson (1985), on the other hand, make the argument that places are not sacrosanct. People have to move when places lose their economic function.
6. Dreier et al. (2004); Garmise (2006).
7. Feiock, Steinacker, and Hyung (2009); Gazley (2008); Barlow (2003); Greasley and Stoker (2008).
8. Cunningham, Furdell, and McKinney (2007, p. 1). I would also extend their point to nonurban settings. Many of the same problems, with some qualifications for context, are facing rural communities and small cities.
9. Eichner (1970); Goodman (1979); Harrison and Kanter (1978); James (1984); O'Neill (2006); Thomas (1975).
10. Markusen (2007).
11. For a very good and succinct definition of CED, see the Canadian Centre for Community Renewal (http://www.cedworks.com/CEDdefinition.html) (accessed July 17, 2008). See also Simon (2001).

12. The Ash Institute for Democratic Practice, with its Innovation in American Government Award, has been the leader in defining and chronicling public sector innovation in the United States and, increasingly, the world. See http://ashinstitute.harvard.edu/. See also Altshuler and Behn (1997); Carty (2003); and Walters (2001). See Calestous and Lee (2005) for a discussion of international development and poverty drawing on the innovation and learning literature.
13. Agranoff (2003); Nambisan (2008); General Accountability Office (2007a); Morse, Buss, and Kinghorn (2007); Snyder and de Souza Briggs (2003); and Silverman (2008).
14. Cunningham, Furdell, and McKinney (2007).
15. See Osborne and Gaebler (1999) and Rivlin (1992) on this trend. With states and localities working with fewer resources but with no less demand from the public, many public managers have found innovative ways to provide public goods, including privatization, public/private partnerships, and the increased use of nonprofits. See Borins (1998); Hula and Jackson-Elmoore (2000); Salamon (1995); and United States Congress, Joint Economic Committee (1993) for a look at what some are terming the rise of the "joined government." See Alford and Hughes (2008) and Perri 6 (2004).
16. Teaford (1993, pp. 211–212).
17. See, for example, Cohen and Taylor (2000) for a balanced view of Daley senior.
18. One might argue that Richard M. Daley presaged the "creative economy" discussion made popular by Florida (2008).
19. In 1997, Mayor Richard M. Daley played a leadership role in convening the Metropolitan Mayors Caucus (MMC) to deal with issues of regional concern in the Chicago metro area including air quality. Many major metropolitan regions across the country, including the Chicago metropolitan areas, have to satisfy federal air quality standards. The Chicago area was found to be in violation of EPA's National Ambient Air Quality Standards (NAAQS) for ozone. At the time, the Caucus numbered 270 municipalities in the six-county region. The Caucus explicitly linked clean air and economic development and made the former a top priority. The MMC established the Clean Air Task Force to build the capacity of local governments to define and implement workable strategies for improving the region's air quality and to support economic development goals. The Task Force created the Regional Clean Air Dialogue in March 1999 that provided a mechanism for a wide range of input, including federal, state, and local governments, the business and civic community, and environmentalists. The Task Force has developed strategies for local governments to reduce emissions. These initiatives include encouraging public transportation fleets using alternative fuels, constructing a network of alternative fueling stations throughout the region, conducting a six-county lawnmower buy-back program, switching to low volatile organic compound (VOC)-emitting paints and coatings, and converting public lawns back to native species of grass. The work of the Task Force evolved into the "Clean Air Counts" campaign, which is winning national awards for its unique and effective partnership (http://www.cleanaircounts.org/). (accessed July 21, 2008)
20. Case material for the Chicago discussion was distilled from the following: *New York Times* (1990); Staples (1996); D. Johnson (1999); Belluck (1999); Almer (2000); Saulny (2007); *New York Times* (2007); D. Johnson (2008); also Project for Public Spaces (2001); and *The Economist* (2008).

21. See Gottlieb (1994) on this point. Cunningham, Furdell, and McKinney (2007) and Henton, Melville, and Walesh (1997) provide examples of regional and local leaders trying to define new ways to cooperate and implement strategies to encourage upward mobility for the least fortunate.

22. Another caveat. Here the focus is on institutional and strategic innovation. There are still and will always be problems of implementation. Implementation challenges can be found in the examples used throughout this book. This does not diminish their worth or impact; in fact one of the subtle arguments made here is that public policy is interactive and institutions learn what works by groping toward increased impact over time. However, without a cutoff point, it becomes difficult to tell if a policy is successful. In a dynamic system such as the American political economy, there is almost always a point where a perceived or real policy problem disappears or is redefined. The point where death or redefinition occurs is context-specific and best left to policy historians to determine.

23. Feiock, Steinacker, and Hyung (2009).

24. Gazley (2008); Weber and Khademian (2008).

25. Vidal and Keys (1999); Walker and Weinheimer (1998); Ferguson and Dickens (1999).

26. Herbers (1983) and Gonzalez (1993) for background on how New York City decided to rely on local groups.

27. My discussion of the South Bronx case does not do justice to what really is a remarkable achievement by government at all levels. Jill Jonnes (2002); Grogan and Proscio (2001); Orlebeke (1997); and Worth (1999) present the story in all its rich complexity and detail.

28. It is difficult to see a body of practice as an innovation, especially an innovation inspired by the public sector. But one only has to reach back 40 years to see that no such thing as community economic development existed at that time. Development was hierarchical and often defined by powerful interests (see Caro, 1974). The result, in the urban context, was the destruction of viable neighborhoods in the immediate post-World War II period with no say, no vehicle to contest public sector policies such as urban renewal. It was because of significant battles by ordinary citizens to resist destruction of their communities, not only through urban renewal but also through the expansion of the interstate highway system, that the public sector began to value "voice" in public sector planning. The battle for political rights and economic inclusion in the 1960s and 1970s by African Americans and other marginalized groups further cemented the need for an institutionalized community voice in planning and development.

29. Neustadt and May (1986) remains an important work detailing the need for learning in the public sector through the history.

Chapter 1

What Is Community Economic Development?

Community economic development is an important tool for place and people revitalization in the United States.[1] Encompassing a range of activities, institutions, and policies, it seeks to improve the quality of life and promote economic opportunity for low-income people.[2] Viewed as a process, community economic development helps residents engage in mobilizing and building assets that will improve their individual and collective future. Such assets include public and private investment, philanthropic investment, human capital, social networks, natural resources, cultural traditions, and community leadership.

That communities can coordinate and use their assets for economic development is a function of their ability to make collective decisions (social capital), stock development experience, and access external assets that can augment their own over time.[3] This chapter presents an overview of the field and its component institutions.

The presence (or absence) of strong institutions determines the pace of development, in any context. As the World Bank's 2003 World Development report states about institutions:

> They are the rules and organizations, including informal norms, that coordinate human behavior. They are important for sustainable and equitable development. When they function well, they enable people to work with each other to plan a future for themselves, their families, and their larger communities. But when they are weak and unjust, the result is mistrust and uncertainty. This encourages people to take rather than "make," and it undermines joint potential.[4]

The term *community economic development institutions* (CEDIs) is used to reflect the great range of locally based organizations involved in community economic development. Table 1.1 provides a summary of widely used CEDIs. Over the years, the public sector has supported the efforts of CEDIs to coordinate and implement economic development initiatives. CEDIs attempt to overcome market failure and nonmarket barriers to general economic development.[5]

CEDIs are typically community-based (or community-focused) organizations whose mission is the physical, social, and economic development of people and places. There are primary CEDIs that directly address workforce skills development and wealth building. As Table 1.1 shows, there are also community development organizations that build the networks, social capital, human capital, and quality of life that improve the chances that CEDIs will achieve their goals in any given community.[6]

Community economic development cannot happen without community development. Both are inextricably linked. They often have different primary goals, but one overarching goal: the development of economically marginalized people and places. Table 1.2 presents the major categories of CED institutions.

Community development corporations (CDCs) are perhaps the best-known primary CEDIs.[7] CDCs are resident-controlled community corporations that overcome the perceived and real lack of organization in poor communities by planning and directing local economic initiatives and programs.[8]

Before the advent of the modern community development corporation in the mid to late 1960s, the voice of less privileged communities was often overridden in the name of banishing blight and urban renewal.[9] Communities were acted on and not consulted, which led to significant demands for community representation and voice. CDCs evolved to directly engage in housing and economic development, but

Table 1.1 Selected Types of Community Development and Community Economic Development Institutions

Community Development Institutions	Primary Community Economic Development Institutions
Faith institutions	Community development corporations
Settlement houses	Community development intermediaries
Youth serving agencies	Community development financial institutions
Family development organizations	Community colleges
Arts and culture organizations	
Community organizing groups	

Source: Author's compilation.

Table 1.2   Community Economic Development Institutions by Type and Function

CEDI Primary Function	Type of CEDI			
	Community Development Corporations	Community Development Intermediaries	Community Development Financial Institutions	Community Colleges
Business development	2	2	3	2
Housing and commercial space development	3	3	2	1
Microbusiness lending	2	2	3	4
CED organizational and technical assistance	2	3	3	2
Workforce development	2	2	2	3
*Other community development programming	3	3	3	2

Source: Author's compilation.

1 = Limited involvement in service provision or financial support.

2 = Some involvement in service provision or financial support.

3 = Strong involvement in service provision or financial support.

4 = Not applicable.

* Community development programming includes the provision of social services such as child care, substance abuse counseling, and activities such as community organizing for local school improvement, crime reduction, and financial literacy.

when firmly rooted in the community, they represent the community's interest in the larger economic development process.[10]

As with all classes of organizations, CDCs vary in size: there are big CDCs (500 or more employees), mid-sized CDCs (200 or more), and small CDCs (10 employees or less). The majority of CDCs average fewer than 20 employees.[11] Walker and Weinheimer, in their landmark study, found that CDCs are most effective in communities where there is a set of community resources and networks with which they can partner to accomplish the complex tasks necessary for community economic development.[12] But the determining factor of CDC effectiveness, as noted by Twelvetrees in his comparative analysis of the CDC model, is organizational leadership. The words from his study still ring true:

> The quality of a CDC's leadership determines more than anything else its success.... Usually that leadership is the leadership of the chief executive officer....Funding agencies with which I was in contact often implied that they gave or withheld funds...on the basis of their estimation of the quality of the top leadership...the leaders of successful CDCs have a strong vision of what they want to see happen, are passionately concerned about quality, monitor each part of the organization closely enough to know when a problem is about to occur...intervene personally if necessary, to make something work which is about to fail, establish appropriate political support and exploit that support to the full, though this can be done in many different ways.[13]

A good example of a CDC with effective leadership is La Casa de Don Pedro, in Newark, New Jersey. La Casa de Don Pedro, Inc. (known generally as La Casa) was founded in 1972 by 10 concerned Puerto Rican parents who sought to find hope for their children and their community in the aftermath of the 1968 Newark civil disturbance.[14] From the start, La Casa made an effort to assist a predominantly Latino community link to and get resources from the larger society for community and economic development.

Although La Casa started out serving a mostly Latino community, a significant portion of its client base is African American.[15] La Casa's mission was and still is to provide for the well-being of low- and moderate-income families by helping them break the financial and psychic hold of poverty through fostering self-sufficiency and empowerment, regardless of ethnicity. This mission connects the programs in La Casa's five corporate divisions (and three affiliate entities), which serve over 36,000 Newark residents. The five divisions are Early Childhood Development, Youth and Family Services, Personal Development, Community Improvement and Community, and Economic Development.

Child care is crucial to La Casa's effective work in a community with a high number of working families. To meet the need for quality preschool education, the organization runs a Newark Board of Education certified prekindergarten program funded through the State of New Jersey's long-running effort to equalize educational opportunities. Using state-of-the-art facilities and staffed by certified teachers (many of whom are supported and mentored through a teacher certification process), the program provides free bilingual education and related services to children ages three and four (see Figure 1.1).

Through the Youth and Family Services Division, children and teens between the ages of five and seventeen participate in after-school and summer programs designed to provide a motivating environment for learning, recreation, cultural enrichment, and leadership development. The division also offers youth and family counseling, parent literacy courses, and a full-time bilingual domestic violence program. The Personal Development Division and Hispanic Women's Resource Center have emerged as leading statewide resources for occupational training and job development, as well as education geared toward publicly assisted adults and

Figure 1.1   La Casa de Don Pedro child facility. Photo courtesy of La Casa de Don Pedro

recent immigrants. Through GED and ESL classes, immigration services, and courses on workplace fundamentals, La Casa assists new immigrants and women toward self-sufficiency.

One of La Casa's central tools is the Community and Economic Development Division, a major housing rehabilitator and developer in the Newark's North End. La Casa's role as developer is complementary to its mission of community development and neighborhood empowerment. All of its housing developments flow from neighborhood plans that La Casa develops and updates in partnership with residents and other stakeholders. La Casa also has generated several subsidiaries that enrich the quality of life and opportunities in this area, including Don Pedro Development Corporation, the organization's real estate and commercial development arm; LC Home Builder, a for-profit construction company; and La Olla, a catering business specializing in breakfast and lunch meals for early childhood education centers in and around Newark. These subsidiaries support program activities, create employment opportunities, and assist the other divisions through internally generated revenue (see Figure 1.2 for a sample of La Casa's housing projects).

La Casa has gone through its share of cycles of growth and decline, although it has emerged as a strong community institution. Leadership counts, but strategy and performance count even more. La Casa had to become embedded in the state and local community economic development system in New Jersey to survive as an organization. The organization built a reputation for delivering quality services and projects. In time, its reputation allowed it to move to the top of the queue when state and local government wanted a stable local partner to implement programs and projects. This reputation for delivery allows La Casa to navigate a challenging local political environment with a level of integrity and independence. Regrettably, CDCs are not always able to resist being drawn into the political process in a way that preserves their independence and legitimacy in the community.[16]

Even a strong organization such as La Casa is bound by the limits of its budget, which now stands at $16 million a year (FY 2009–2010). But that figure could change just as fast as the next national or state fiscal crisis or shifts in the funding priorities of the philanthropic community. Ray Ocasio, the executive director of the organization, put it clearly to me when he said, "As good as we are, we still survive with the help of local foundations, and the revenue from our development projects and project based funding from government. This forces us to be entrepreneurial. We can never stand pat."[17]

What is the difference here? Why is this organization, now a community institution, not likely to disappear even in tough times? Many things factor into the strength and longevity of any institution. First, La Casa has gone through points in time where it did not look as if it were going to survive. As with any private or nonprofit institution, the survival of the organization depends on the board, the stewards of the organization. In rough times, the board managed to keep the organization going until it found a good leader. Ocasio, a nonprofit executive with vast experience working in international development, city government, and for

Figure 1.2   La Casa de Don Pedro housing project. Photo courtesy of La Casa de Don Pedro

the CED intermediaries, may not be the norm. His outlook on building a strong lasting organization, though, should be the norm.

Ocasio has built a strong board that works productively with him as the executive director but challenges him where necessary and appropriate on questions of strategy and operations. He has put together a team of individuals who are competent and committed to the work. Talent is valued and nurtured in an organizational environment that is dynamic and at times demanding. As we move to a community economic development paradigm that values sustainability, the lessons of encouraging organizational longevity will be just as important as helping poor communities achieve financial and environmental sustainability.

The CDC model is now well established; however, the model works best when there is a supportive infrastructure including local and state government and foundations working in concert to (1) create a transparent, routinized financial support base, (2) encourage an environment of learning from challenges and best practices beyond the local environment, and (3) develop a culture of accountability that is shared by nonprofit CDCs, their community stakeholders, and resource providers.[18]

In terms of strategic direction, CDCs accomplish much if they pursue clearly directed strategies such as housing development at the beginning of their life cycle.[19] CDCs need the revenue generated by real estate development to build a base of organizational expertise and success. Real estate development can be a significant element in financial sustainability for this class of organization, if, as Bratt and Rohe observe, the developments are managed well.[20] CDCs blessed with good leadership and support from the resource environment can often take on challenges beyond housing, such as workforce development, business development, and community organizing.

By any measure, La Casa is a high-capacity CDC and CEDI that has developed many units of housing, but it is also an organization that has managed to do a variety of other things even with budget limitations. Important research, done by Melendez and Servon, shows that this is not uncommon.

As a group, CDCs engage in a wide range of community development activities, but they have been accused of narrowing their missions to focus on affordable housing while other problems in a distressed community go begging. Recent analysis does not bear out that contention. As Melendez and Servon note,

> [C]ontrary to expectations based on the literature, the data suggest that specialization in housing production and activities is not associated with a less diverse program portfolio. In all activities except incubator programs, large and medium producers with housing activities have a higher index of nonhousing activities than nonhousing producers or medium producers with few housing programs. In fact, medium housing producers with housing activities exhibit the highest scores in three of the four nonhousing activities categories. The data…also suggest that the portfolio of nonhousing producers is somewhat less diversified than

that of housing producers and that housing production might actually be the foundation for a more diversified community development portfolio. These findings clearly contradict the contention that housing specialization is associated with less engagement in other community development activities.[21]

The key to the effective use of CDCs in economic development is recognizing that they cannot do everything, nor should they be expected to replace government or the private sector. CDCs can be important community intermediaries in ways that are unique and irreplaceable. CDCs can focus the community voice for planning and development and host community development programs that augment community economic development.[22] As useful as they have become to the public sector, CDCs are only one piece of the puzzle.

The CED Intermediaries

Community development intermediaries arose to support the capacity-building (organization, technical, and access to capital) needs of community-based development organizations. The major national community development intermediaries, such as NeighborWorks, the Local Initiatives Support Corporation, and Enterprise Partners, have proven effective not only in growing the capacity of local organizations but also in becoming forces for quality assurance so that CEDs can argue for continued support from the public sector and philanthropy. The intermediaries have also become thought leaders and policy advocates when necessary to expand the impact of CEDs through government policy. Although the three large intermediaries have made significant contributions to community economic development, local and regional intermediaries such as state associations of CDCs and support collaborations have played similar roles in relation to their national counterparts at a different level.[23]

One example of a local and regional CED intermediary trying to push the field forward is the Atlanta Neighborhood Development Partnership (ANDP). The Atlanta Neighborhood Development Partnership began in 1989 as a project of the Atlanta Economic Development Corporation, the Metropolitan Atlanta Community Foundation (MACF), and the Atlanta Chamber of Commerce Housing Resource Center. The partnership's mission is to contribute to the revitalization of Atlanta's neighborhoods by focusing private and public resources on building affordable housing directly or through building the capacity of CEDIs.

For many years, ANDP was recognized for its effectiveness in building affordable housing and the organizational capacity of CEDIs, but it also operated in a context similar to that of many other major American cities. Atlanta's metropolitan fringe experienced rapid expansion, while the core central business district and neighborhoods declined. The problems brought by sprawl development are myriad:

rising housing costs in fast-growing communities, long journeys to work, traffic jams slowing travel to a crawl, and the flight of taxable revenue making it difficult for the city to maintain its social and economic infrastructure. All of these factors conspired to push Atlanta's core neighborhoods into steep decline.[24]

In 1998 the Metro Atlanta Chamber of Commerce approached ANDP and suggested that ANDP lead a public/private effort to attract middle-income households back to Atlanta.[25] After collecting data and talking to stakeholders, ANDP developed a report called "Resettling Atlanta—The Mixed Income Housing Initiative." The report became part of an ongoing campaign to educate the public on the necessity to attract the middle class back to the city while maintaining affordable housing opportunities.

In 2001 ANDP established the Mixed Income Communities Initiative (MICI) to address the growth and development needs of the city of Atlanta and its surrounding region.[26] To work, the strategy would need to appeal to the wider metropolis, not just the poor and advocates for the poor. Housing, as they came to learn, was the great leveler. Both urban and metro Atlanta faced housing challenges. ANDP used its development experience and financing to help infill developers and suburban towns plan and build affordable housing, but with a twist: mixing in affordable units.

ANDP provided many county development offices with technical assistance to learn how to "make the numbers work" and produce affordable housing. ANDP's strategy with MICI and its regional work is to use its credibility as an effective community economic development intermediary to participate in and shape various metropolitan planning initiatives.

ANDP also appealed to prominent developers, arguing (through the use of demographic and market data) that the urban core is economically viable. At a microlevel, ANDP works with the city of Atlanta and metropolitan planning and administrative agencies to review and change small policies that make a big difference in encouraging mixed-income development, such as removing obsolete building ordinances and reviewing other regulations limiting density.[27]

By pursuing these and other strategies, such as employer-assisted housing, land banking, and inclusionary zoning, ANDP has tried to advance neighborhood revitalization in the context of regional development. ANDP knows that mixed-income communities cannot be promoted through government fiat. As it says, "Rather than curtail growth into the suburbs, our task is to retool our regulations and policies so that the private sector can serve an enormous, unmet demand."[28]

It takes nothing away from CDCs (and other locally based CEDIs), which are on the frontlines, to say that the growth and evolution of the CED intermediaries at all levels is one of the most important innovations encouraged by the public sector over the past 40 years. Their presence has really defined a body of work that is now an industry with roles, norms, and expectations. Because of the intermediaries, the public sector can turn to CED with more than a passing expectation that it can play an effective part in economic development. Increasingly, local jurisdictions rely on either local or national intermediaries (or some combination thereof) to manage the neighborhood revitalization process, confident that the intermediaries have the expertise to accomplish much when conditions allow.

Expanding Capital Access

Lack of capital and access to capital prevent meaningful wealth building and economic development. Community development financial institutions (CDFIs) directly address this problem through different institutional forms. Community development credit unions (CDCUs), for example, have been around for decades, and their goal is to help low-income residents living in a defined area save for major purchases such as a house, a car to get to work, or investment to start a micro- or small business. Often CDCUs are the only avenue for low-income members to obtain reasonably priced loans, financial education, and counseling. CDCUs are cooperatively owed and governed.[29] They can be freestanding or hosted by a faith institution, CDC, or a community development loan fund.

The main limitation to the community credit union model is the transaction costs involved in servicing small accounts in low-income communities. Often the host organization has to subsidize their efforts to keep them operating. They are not the tool for every circumstance, but the credit union movement has proven an important CED institutional strategy for building individual and collective wealth.

Community development loan funds aggregate capital from institutional (including government) and individual investors to lend to nonprofit housing developers such as CDCs and to small-scale businesses in low-income communities. Like CDCUs, community development loan funds can be freestanding or hosted by an organization with community economic development goals. Community development loan funds (CDLFs) operate on market principles. Their capital is often borrowed at a low cost and lent out at a higher rate to cover the loan fund's operation. Loan funds try to keep their interest rates low or at least competitive with market rates.[30]

The Self-Help loan fund located in Durham, North Carolina, is recognized as unique and innovative. Started in the early 1980s to provide management assistance to worker-owned businesses, Self-Help began making loans to small businesses and home mortgages in a matter of years after its founding. Steady growth in the lending capacity and a creative approach to community development lending allowed it to attract support from local and national philanthropy. In the 1990s it received an appropriation from the North Carolina General Assembly. In total, it has invested over $5.6 billion in loans to low-income borrowers (84 percent of their portfolio), many of whom are people of color (46 percent) or women (42 percent).[31] Self-Help makes loans to a variety of community economic development efforts, including financing charter schools and other community facilities.

Self-Help has become an important regional lender in North Carolina (it also has offices in California and Washington, DC). Beyond that, Self-Help's success as an innovative CEDI has allowed it to play an important role in national policy discussions affecting CED in much the same way as the community development intermediaries. The example of Self-Help is powerful; a Treasury official brought up the organization's work in the 1998 reauthorization of the Community Development Financial Institutions Fund, a major federal effort to grow the capacity of CDFIs and the community development finance:

> I can testify from some personal observation about the impact. I recently visited Self-Help of North Carolina, which operates a credit union and a venture capital fund. The CDFI Fund's February 1997 $3-million investment in Self Help has already enabled Self Help to effectuate $24 million in home mortgages and commercial lending transactions. I saw firsthand how a young man who had been running a marginal fresh fish business in Durham, North Carolina was able to get a $1,000 micro-loan from Self Help to buy a fish fryer and thereby offer a fast food menu to his customers. This fellow had been selling fresh fish off the back of a truck with his father and they decided to open a store. They found out they couldn't sell much fresh fish without attracting customers in, and with the aid of this $1,000 loan they got into the fast food business. His business began to grow and now he employs two full-time and two part-time workers. He has expanded by buying another fryer and a stove, and now he wants to borrow $15,000 more from Self Help to buy a refrigerated truck that will enable him to pick up his own fish. This is only one example, and a small one; of how much difference even a very small loan can make for a small business entrepreneur with the creativity and drive to be financially successful. That is one of the things that CDFIs can do very well.[32]

What has happened since that 1998 hearing is a profound growth in appreciation for CDFIs as an effective CED strategy, in no small part due to the efforts of Self-Help and other CDFIs. As the 2007 testimony of the CDFI Fund's leadership summarized to Congress:

> CDFI Program awardees are having significant impact in the communities they serve. As a steward of taxpayer dollars, making this impact is of the utmost importance. ... In FY 2005, the most recent year for which data is available, 186 CDFI Program awardees reported leveraging their awards with $1.4 billion in private and non-CDFI Fund dollars. These CDFIs reported that their financing helped to...create or maintain nearly 14,000 full-time equivalent (FTE) jobs, and develop or rehabilitate nearly 27,000 affordable housing units....These new jobs, along with the increase in residential housing and commercial real estate, result in an increase in tax revenue (consisting of federal, state and local income taxes, and social security taxes), reduce the amount

of state unemployment benefits paid out, and increase the amount of local property taxes.[33]

Related to CDLFs are microenterprise funds, which offer more flexibility to low-income entrepreneurs. Many such funds provide loans of under $13,000 and understand that losses will be high if intensive management is not provided with the loan. There is belief that self-employment can be a significant antipoverty strategy if done correctly. The example of the entrepreneur selling fish from the back of a truck, then getting a loan to move the operation to a store is one that we all want to see. But the reality is that some significant portion of those microbusinesses will fail.[34] That is just the nature of small and microbusiness. The point is not to retreat, but to build strong management assistance programs that help entrepreneurs as Self-Help and other CDFIs have done. But the question remains: at what point does public policy balance the use of microenterprise as an antipoverty strategy against the inherent challenges of self-employment? The question is revisited in Chapter 7.

Community development banks and community development venture capital funds are at the other end of the size and scale spectrum. Both aim at economically revitalizing lower-income communities through supporting (lending to) projects or businesses with a significant level of scale thus creating jobs or building capital projects. Community development venture capital funds assume that there are market imperfections in capital-starved communities.

Good ideas for profitable businesses and projects exist, but capital and management experience from the venture capitalist side can make the difference in profitability or failure. Community development venture capital funds don't target communities to concentrate resources (as do many community development banks); rather they seek to achieve broad place and people development goals. Such a fund might help an entrepreneur in Detroit who wants to reopen a defunct steel mill but with a scaled-down purpose such as steel fabrication. The resulting jobs help workers in a distressed city, but there is no expectation that those hired must come from the place where the factory is located.

Community development banks such as South Shore Bank in Chicago (which now has affiliates in other parts of the country) do exactly what their name implies: they are banks, they take deposits from the general public and investment from investors then lend to credit-worthy projects in their target community. Make no mistake: South Shore has to provide a return to its investors while satisfying its community economic development mission of developing its target community.[35]

The community development bank model has proven helpful in stabilizing communities that are on the brink of being overwhelmed by concentrated poverty. However, even balanced assessments of the South Shore model (and by extension, community development finance) caution:

> Herein lies a fundamental problem. Shorebank's distinctive approach is derived from the discovery that providing credit alone is insufficient for solving the problems of low-income communities. …This is not a world where large numbers of qualified credit-starved individuals are waiting in line. Consequently, a successful development program must be multi-pronged and proactive.[36]

No amount of access to capital will help communities under the crush of entrenched poverty without interventions that augment the possibilities of economic development. These interventions include lowering crime rates, building a good community workforce, and establishing effective schools. This caution is often ignored in the headlong rush to create small businesses or develop the next financing mechanism for helping the poor through entrepreneurship. Often we ignore the basics, such as the development of people, because it is a complex and frustrating undertaking that takes time and patience.

Institutions of higher education play an important role in community economic development, as we show.[37] All are not CEDIs. Most universities have some functional relationship to the local and community economy, but only one class of higher educational institution has a mission that incorporates workforce development and economic development.

Community colleges can make a strong argument for being viewed as CEDIs. They train students in vocational skills needed to power the local economy. Some urban and rural community colleges are embedded in challenging circumstances and do a terrific job of educating individuals with limited preparation for the workforce. Community colleges often work with local employers, tailoring their curricula to the needs of the local economy. Innovative community colleges, such as Los Angeles Trade Technical, realize they have a clear link to community economic development and capitalize on that link by hosting a dedicated program to train individuals to be community economic development practitioners.[38] Given their students, the institution can well claim to be among the few dedicated training institutions that help low-income and moderate-wage individuals become community economic development professionals.

Support for Community Economic Development

Support for community economic development began with a few national and local foundations along with the federal government in the 1960s. Now, support for community development and community economic development is ensconced in philanthropic giving and public sector support. National data for community development and community economic development expenditures are not pinpointed in a way that gives an accurate figure either for philanthropy or the public sector.

Painting a clear picture of federal government support for community economic development is like Hercules cleaning the Augean stables. There is no firm definition of CED in the federal budget and so no clear point of entry for culling expenditures and no clear end. There is fulsome support for programs that affect CED. Table 1.3 gives a snapshot of federal programs that have a direct impact on community economic development as defined in this study.[39]

The best estimate for philanthropy comes in a Foundation Center study of grants to the social justice field from 2002 to 2006. The Center, which is the organization that assembles data for the field of philanthropy, reported that economic and community development captured the largest share of social justice grant dollars (30.5 percent), followed by human and civil rights (13.8 percent) and health care access and affordability (13.4 percent). Total grant-making for the period came to $2.3 billion, therefore economic and community development received about $702 million.[40]

Foundation support for the field is varied. Increasingly, local community foundations and United Ways are sharing the burden of supporting CED initiatives previously funded by national foundations. This trend is expanding understanding of the field at the local level and ensuring that such efforts can become institutionalized.[41]

Some philanthropic support goes to the community development intermediaries, CDFIs, and public/private partnerships at the local level. One good example of how philanthropy provides support is through program-related investments (PRIs), which are essentially low-interest loans with a long repayment period to CDFIs. A foundation will typically give a nominal-interest loan to a CDFI, which then loans the principal at a higher rate. The PRI allows the CDFI to build capacity, while still lending at favorable terms to low-income borrowers or for CED projects. The most valued feature of foundation support comes through their ability to provide core support for organizations. Operational support is the most difficult support to come by, but it allows an organization to plan and acquire the personnel needed to build the organization's infrastructure. This is unlike project support, which assumes some level of capacity and readiness to do the work.

Philanthropy has played a significant role in building and promoting the field of community economic development, but philanthropic resources should be thought of as research and development support for innovation in CED. Foundations cannot support CED initiatives over time and hope to make an impact. That is the role of the federal government.

Summary

Community economic development has evolved primarily, but not exclusively, as a place-based strategy. Development outcomes have been measured by building affordable housing, starting businesses, and creating jobs: all things that lead to economic development in a geographically defined place. Community economic development

Table 1.3 Selected Federal Programs Supporting Community Economic Development[a]

Program	Type of Support	Summary	Authorizing Federal Agency
Assets for Independence Program	Grant	Supported savings for low-income individuals	Health and Human Services
AmeriCorps/Vista	Grant	Engaging citizens in community service; helpful to supplement talent for local CEDIs	The Corporation for National and Community Service
Brownfields Redevelopment Program	Grant	Reclaiming land contaminated by industrial use	Environment and Protection Agency and Housing and Urban Development
Community Development Block Grants	Grant	General support for local community development activities	Housing and Urban Development
Community Development Financial Institutions Fund	Grant/Tax Credits	Supporting individual and collective asset building	U.S. Treasury
Community Outreach Partnership Center Program	Grant	Engaging colleges and universities in community and economic development	Housing and Urban Development
Community Reinvestment Act	Private Sector Commitments	Engaging private sector in community economic development	Office of the Comptroller
Earned Income Tax Credit	Tax Credit	Refundable tax credit designed to increase the income of low-income wage earners	U.S. Treasury

Program	Type	Description	Agency
Low Income Housing Tax Credit	Tax Credits	Expands the supply of affordable housing through market incentives	Housing and Urban Development
Rural Housing and Economic Development	Grant	Supports capacity building for rural housing and economic development	Department of Housing and Urban Development
Rural Cooperative Development Grants	Grant	Encourage the growth and capacity of rural development cooperatives	U. S. Department of Agriculture
Rural Business Opportunity Grants	Grant	Promotes sustainable economic development in rural communities through provision of training and technical assistance for business development, entrepreneurs, and economic development officials	U.S. Department of Agriculture
Home Investment Partnership Program	Grant	Supports state and local partnerships with local nonprofit groups to build, buy, or rehabilitate affordable housing for rent or homeownership	Housing and Urban Development
Weed and Seed	Grant	A community-based strategy to prevent, control, and reduce violent crime, drug abuse, and gang activity through a comprehensive multiagency approach to law enforcement, crime prevention, and community revitalization	Department of Justice
YouthBuild	Grant	Supports nonprofit organizations to assist high-risk youth to learn housing construction job skills and complete their high school education.	Formerly HUD now Department of Labor

Source: Author's compilation.

[a] Every CEDI mentioned in this study has received one or more of these grants on an ongoing basis or has been the beneficiary of tax credits and CRA.

and CEDIs have done a very good job in these areas, often acting as the public sector's main development partner in marginalized communities (see the discussion of the South Bronx experience in the Introduction to this book). In this respect, community economic development is an important institutional innovation in which government has partnered with the private and nonprofit sectors to develop policy networks and strategies to reduce poverty and build wealth in low-income communities.[42]

Collaboration is an integral part of community economic development. ANDP shows that any region needs a coordinating force to help steer the change conversation at different moments and levels. Through its support role for CDCs, ANDP can not only improve performance and development on the ground but can also shape the regional conversation through its role as respected convener of the public and private sector.[43]

Endnotes

1. Community economic development, as a term and then as a set of policies, first appeared in the late 1960s in response to the "urban crisis," which encompassed a range of problems, including declining central city economies, rising juvenile delinquency, racial discontent, unemployment, and concentrated poverty. As a strategy, community economic development attempts to increase the political power of poor and minority residents through a collective voice in addition to building an economic base through small enterprise development and workforce preparation. O'Connor (2000) and Sviridoff et al. (2004) provide a good layered analysis of the social conditions and responses that lead to community economic development as a policy innovation.

2. In simple terms, economic development is the productive joining of capital, labor, and technology to assure wealth creation and the positive well-being for a nation, region, city, and even community. Thus economic development and community economic development are closely related. The consequential difference is that community economic development focuses on key issues that economic development finds difficult to address, such as inequities brought about by market failure, economic obsolescence, weak institutions, and the lack of plural networks that link capital, labor, and technology. Of course there are nonmarket barriers such as racial and ethnic exclusion that also make community economic development an important adjunct of economic development.

3. Simon (2001); Ramsay (1996); also Nowak (1998).

4. World Bank (2003, p. 37).

5. Simon (2001, Chapter 2).

6. Ferguson and Dickens (1999, pp. 4, 5).

7. It should be noted that there is not a strict demarcation in the form and function of CEDIs. Some CEDIs can be both community development financial institutions (CDFIs) and community development corporations (CDCs) at the same time. The important thing is not the label but the actual function. See also Ferguson and Dickens (1999, p. 6).

8. CDCs are very much in keeping with de Tocqueville's (1945, p. 198) observation about civic life and how problems get addressed in the United States:

   In no other country in the world has the principle of association been more successfully used or applied to a greater multitude of objects in America...the same spirit pervades every act of social life. If a stoppage occurs in a thoroughfare and the circulation of vehicles is hindered, the neighborhood immediately form themselves into a deliberative body; and this extemporaneous assembly gives rise to an executive power which remedies the inconvenience before anybody has thought of recurring to a preexisting authority superior to that of the persons immediately concerned.

9. Caro (1974).
10. Simon (2001, pp. 14–19).
11. Mayer (1984, pp. 12–19).
12. Walker and Weinheimer (1998).
13. Twelvetrees (1996, p. 105).
14. http://www.lacasanwk.org/. (accessed July 21, 2008)
15. The present executive director and the board have embraced this as an opportunity by putting African Americans on the board and cementing ties to the broader African American community. La Casa's leadership does not engage in the ethnic power struggles that have limited the effectiveness of other CDCs in places where new people are coming to the community in greater numbers. The difference is that La Casa's leadership recognizes that struggling over ethnic succession is a quick way for an institution to lose relevance.
16. Silverman (2009).
17. Ocasio (2008).
18. Vidal and Keys (2005).
19. CDCs often live their organizational existence in compressed cycles of birth, growth, steady state, decline, and resurgence depending on board and executive leadership. In this regard, they are not that different from most nonprofits.
20. Bratt and Rohe (2007).
21. Melendez and Servon (2007, p. 268).
22. Mayer (1984, Chapters 2–4).
23. There is one class of CEDIs that does not get the same recognition that the mainstream intermediaries receive. CEDIs that specifically target minority groups and marginalized communities, such as the Urban League, the National Council of LaRaza and First Nations, are important players in workforce development and economic development. Although they often labor in the shadow of others, their work is no less important and the public sector has long recognized their ability to deliver specialized services to their target communities.
24. Metropolitan Area Research Corporation (2003).
25. The Chamber's charge to ANDP was to take the lead on addressing the need of the city of Atlanta to attract 65,000 new "middle income residents" back to the city over a 10-year period and satisfy the need of approximately 25,000 new homes in that same period for these residents in order to keep Atlanta competitive with other similarly placed cities in the United States. The need was identified by a 1997 study done by McKinsey and Company for the Renaissance Commission formed by then Mayor Bill Campbell following the Summer Olympic Games. The goal of the Renaissance Commission was to determine how Atlanta could transition into a world-class city as it entered the twenty-first century.

26. The initiative was largely envisioned as far back as 1998, but it did not come to be firmly recognized as MICI until 2000, when the Atlanta Neighborhood Development Partnership began assembling a team of stakeholders and experts from business, non-profits, government, and academia.

27. See "Making the Case for Housing Choices and Complete Communities: The Next Generation" (http://www.andpi.org/mtcng.pdf). (accessed July 23, 2008)

28. See Atlanta Neighborhood Development Partnership (http://www.andpi.org/mici.htm). (accessed August 4, 2008)

29. Brookings Institution, Community Development Credit Unions: An Emerging Player in Low Income Communities. http://www.brookings.edu/articles/2001/09metropolit anpolicy_tansey.aspx. (accessed August 4, 2008)

30. It is important to note that CDLFs are not lenders of last resort. Their role is to build a functioning, sustainable, capital market in and for low-income communities. Risk must be, and should be, accounted for in their loan products. To expect anything less is to ask CDLFs to be granting programs, which is unsustainable in the long-term.

31. http://www.self-help.org/about-us/impact-1. (accessed July 24, 2008)

32. H.R. 3617—Reauthorization of the Community Development Financial Institutions Fund, Wednesday, June 17, 1998. http://commdocs.house.gov/committees/bank/hba49352.000/hba49352_0.HTM. (accessed August 5, 2008)

33. Testimony of Kimberly A. Reed, Director, Community Development Financial Institutions Fund, U.S. Department of the Treasury, Before the House Appropriations Committee, Subcommittee on Financial Services. March 1, 2007. http://www.ustrea s.gov/press/relea ses/hp286.htm. (accessed August 7, 2008)

34. Microbusiness or microenterprise is often put in the same category as self-employment. Some define it as an enterprise with five or fewer employees with an initial capitalization of $35,000 or less. Defined as the latter indicates that the majority of the American economy is built on microenterprise. The Association for Enterprise Development reports that there are 23,000,000 such enterprises representing 18 percent of private sector employment and 87 percent of businesses. I am not disputing the figure, but the definition seems to replace the "small business" category that we are all familiar with in the popular imagination and public policy. This adds a level of category creep that dilutes the concept of microenterprise and its original aim, which was its ability to reduce poverty and build assets not only abroad but in the United States. See http://www.microenterpriseworks.org/. (accessed August 19, 2008)

35. See Kerwin Tesdell and Charity Shumwa, *Investing for Social Good: Community Development Venture Capital,* Federal Reserve Bank of San Francisco, http://www.frbsf.org/publications/community/investments/0311/article1f.html. (accessed August 20, 2008)

36. Taub (1994, p. xiii).

37. Maurrasse (2001).

38. See http://www.lattc.edu/dept/ta50/home.htm. (accessed August 20, 2008)

39. This table is based on numerous interviews with urban and rural CEDIs and culling the programs they most commonly mentioned as important to their work.

40. See Foundation Center, Social Justice Grantmaking II. http://foundationcenter.org/gainknowledge/research/pdf/socialjustice2009_highlights.pdf. (accessed September 3, 2008)

41. R. Cohen (2003), Mayer (1994).

42. Berry, Portney, and Thomson (1993); Dionne (1998); Ferguson and Dickens (1999); Walker and Weinheimer (1998); and Walker (2002).
43. Support for this point can be found in Safford (2009), a very important work. Using sophisticated network analysis he shows that social linkages and networks are key to place and regional economic resurgence.

Chapter 2

Searching for Sustainable Community Economic Development

Government and philanthropic efforts to support place-based development have been stymied by trends and policies encouraging the dispersal of people from the urban core.[1] Referred to as sprawl development, this population pattern consumes large rural tracts, contributes to long journeys to work, and takes a heavy toll on the environment. Sprawl development is a trend that correlates with the concentration of poverty in the United States. Table 2.1 provides a snapshot of people and place poverty from 1990 to 2008.

Poverty in America is increasingly concentrated in isolated older urban areas and suburban and rural enclaves.[2] As the middle class escapes to lower-tax, higher-service communities, residents of poor places have decreasing access to the social and economic benefits of living in mixed-income places.[3] Concentrated poverty is not simply the result of market forces, however. It is the result of public policies in areas such as transportation, tax policy, and housing, all interacting with market trends and individual choice to create a physical and social landscape increasingly divided along lines of income and race.[4]

Table 2.1 Poverty of People, by Residence: 1990 to 2008 (Numbers in Thousands)

Year	Inside Metropolitan Statistical Areas		Inside Principal Cities		Outside Principal Cities		Outside Metropolitan Statistical Areas /15	
	Poor	Percentage	Poor	Percentage	Poor	Percentage	Poor	Percentage
2008	32,570	12.9	17,222	17.7	15,348	9.8	7,259	15.1
2007	29,921	11.9	15,983	16.5	13,938	9.0	7,355	15.4
2006	29,283	11.8	15,336	16.1	13,947	9.1	7,177	15.2
2005	30,098	12.2	15,966	17.0	14,132	9.3	6,852	14.5
2004	NA	NA	NA	NA	NA	NA	NA	NA
2003	28,367	12.1	14,551	17.5	13,816	9.1	7,495	14.2
2002	27,096	11.6	13,784	16.7	13,311	8.9	7,474	14.2
2001	25,446	11.1	13,394	16.5	12,052	8.2	7,460	14.2
2000	24,603	10.8	13,257	16.3	11,346	7.8	6,978	13.4
1999	25,278	11.3	13,404	16.5	11,874	8.3	7,513	14.3
1998	26,997	12.3	14,921	18.5	12,076	8.7	7,479	14.4
1997	27,273	12.6	15,018	18.8	12,255	9.0	8,301	15.9
1996	28,211	13.2	15,645	19.6	12,566	9.4	8,318	15.9
1995	28,342	13.4	16,269	20.6	12,072	9.1	8,083	15.6

1994	29,610	14.2	16,098	20.9	13,511	10.3	8,449	16.0
1993	29,615	14.6	16,805	21.5	12,810	10.3	9,650	17.2
1992	28,380	14.2	16,346	20.9	12,034	9.9	9,634	16.9
1991	26,827	13.7	15,314	20.2	11,513	9.6	8,881	16.1
1990	24,510	12.7	14,254	19.0	10,255	8.7	9,075	16.3

Source: U.S. Bureau of the Census, Current Population Survey, Annual Social and Economic Supplements.

Note: For information on confidentiality protection, sampling error, nonsampling error, and definitions, see http://www.census.gov/apsd/techdoc/cps/cpsmar09.pdf. Footnotes are available at http://www.census.gov/hhes/www/poverty/histpov/footnotes.html.

What Can Be Done?

Breaking down the cumulative effects of racial and ethnic exclusion, especially when all are now self-generating in disadvantaged communities, is difficult. Crime, family dissolution, bad schools, criminal gangs, and teenage childbearing can all be traced, in large measure, to the lack of economic opportunity in many communities and the inability to escape these problems by simply moving.[5]

Essentially, community economic development principles and values posit that local collective action is a necessary precursor to overcoming political and social constraints on economic development.[6] Collective action is difficult in the best of circumstances.[7] Community economic development relies on local institutions to organize wealth-building programs and strategies for people and places.

Skeptical voices maintain that recent community-based development practices support the production of affordable housing over other important elements of community economic development.[8] They argue that the field has attained a measure of success, but at the expense of community involvement and community action.[9] These latter values were central to the community building and development groups that emerged in the late 1960s and early 1970s and now do the work of community economic development.

These skeptical voices also say that increasing professionalization and concentration on the technical aspects of affordable housing production have encouraged the evolution of organizations that are not in tune with the long-term interests of the communities they purport to serve. This leads to the conclusion that government and philanthropy should re-evaluate community economic development as an antipoverty strategy.[10] Maybe.

The larger implication of the criticism holds that community-based economic development organizations (as a class, and notwithstanding the notable exception) should be organizing poor communities to press government for additional expenditure and attention to poor communities. Starkly put, one side argues that self-help (with assistance from government) is the right development path toward economic and political self-determination. The other side, the community organizing argument, says government should be held accountable for what it should be doing in the first place (providing services and opportunity). In reality, the poles are not that different in what they want to see happen in poor communities, nor are the strategies incommensurate. Yet adherents often and mistakenly pose both approaches as incommensurate.

Still others take community economic development to task for resembling the boy with his finger in the dyke that is about to burst. In this case the metaphor refers to two ongoing trends: development away from central cities and the globalization of capital. These voices charge that community economic development is an anachronism that gives false hope to communities marked by concentrated poverty.

David Rusk, in his 1999 book, *Inside Game/Outside Game: Winning Strategies for Saving Urban America,* questions the impact of community development corporations. Retrospectively looking at one of the first and most visible of such organizations, the Bedford Stuyvesant Restoration Corporation, Rusk, a former mayor of Albuquerque, writes 27 years after the organization's founding:

> I will concede that, to some degree, Restoration's efforts contributed to the revival of downtown Brooklyn. Nevertheless, the hard fact remains: the Bedford Stuyvesant community is poorer today than when Restoration began. And, with a rising concentration of poverty, falling relative incomes, and slowly declining real buying power, Bedford Stuyvesant's capacity to be, in Bobby Kennedy's words, an "avenue of opportunity" (much less a place of pleasure and excitement) grows less and less with each passing decade. If Bedford Stuyvesant Restoration Corporation, the vanguard, is failing as a neighborhood anti-poverty program, are other community development Corporations that followed faltering as well? Or was Restoration's failure really an exception to a general pattern of success?[11]

Rather than try to rebuild the economic base of these communities, Rusk and others hold that public policy should encourage the regional dispersion of the poor. Much better to limit the negative effects of concentrated poverty by opening up the suburbs for the poor so they can gain access to good jobs and schools.[12]

This is a solid point, but we need to be careful about what measures we use to hold strategies and community institutions accountable. No local organization can significantly move the needle on poverty in a community (Bedford-Stuyvesant) that would be called a small city anywhere else in the country.[13] The economy is simply too large, complex, and open.[14]

It is true that in the beginning of the community economic development movement, exuberance gave way to overreaching. There were many pronouncements that poverty would be banished; time has taught us that those pronouncements were premature. CEDIs should be measured by more circumspect measures that reflect society's overall investment in reducing poverty and promoting economic development. Although this investment is significant, it is not enough to ask individual organizations to consistently make a difference in local economies, much less the difficult challenges of individual behavior resulting as a byproduct of poverty.

Yet the larger point that Rusk and others argue is valid. Of course public policy should encourage open access to housing, jobs, and good schools through inclusionary zoning and other dispersal strategies. It is not a point needing much debate. Promoting dispersal policies as a top-shelf antipoverty strategy should be done with caution.

Government attempts to desegregate by race and income class have been contentious and the outcomes very mixed. Even the most celebrated case of inclusionary zoning, the Mt. Laurel decisions by New Jersey's state supreme court to get the state's growing regions, communities, and towns to take on a "fair share" of housing the poor, has met with intense political resistance. The Mt. Laurel process is now more a stylized dance than substantive progress in meeting the court's original intent.[15]

Waiting for government-sponsored desegregation by race and class to make a dent in concentrated poverty is simply no policy at all and risks keeping generations of people in poverty. That is politically and morally unacceptable. It is much better to fight the battle on many fronts, making sure that communities can still function as staging areas for upward mobility through effective development policies.[16] However, we will not get far by arguing that poverty can be addressed by one or even two strategies.

Rethinking People and Place Development

Community economic development has in recent years gone through a sustained period of self-examination and has identified some of the trends that limit its impact. At points, this self-examination has been pushed by voices from outside community economic development such as journalists and academicians.[17] What has happened is the steady incorporation of new ideas that take the criticisms into account.[18]

One strand of discussion has encouraged community economic development to find ways of integrating its core competencies, which are place and people development, with active engagement in changing or at least mitigating the land-use policies that limit its effectiveness as a field.[19] Essentially, can community economic development find a place in the "smart growth" dialogue that is relevant and productive for both fields?[20]

Another way of thinking says that rather than pursuing the explicit goal of reigniting community economies—which is less feasible today than when it originated 40 years ago—the aims should be (1) to concentrate on building the workforce skills of people so that they have choices to stay or leave their communities, and (2) to comprehensively develop places of opportunity by helping to reform schools and encouraging home ownership and business development.[21] Again, the focus, goes the argument, should be more on the individual, but not to the exclusion of place development.[22]

Calls to link metropolitan development to place-based development are emerging as an important direction for community economic development.[23] Building sustainable communities in a metropolitan context has many meanings, but the primary definition here is encouraging the development of human settlements that (1) are dense, compact, and walkable; (2) encourage reasonable journeys to work and public transportation access for the poor searching for jobs, good housing, and reasonably priced opportunities to shop; and (3) generate economic activity that can support a good quality of life for residents.[24]

Sustainable economic development also means using the assets of existing settlements, communities, and neighborhoods to refashion them into places of opportunity so that existing residents can live productive lives in these communities or move to other communities if they so choose.[25] In this respect, the existing values of community economic development are still relevant; these values can be reduced to the following:

- Community economic development begins with resident mobilization for change and economic self-sufficiency.
- Community economic development's main goal is to build wealth for poor people and poor places through the coordination of social, political, and financial capital and harnessing the talent and commitment of community residents.

In practice, these values and principles provide a base for the multiple goals of community economic development policy over the last 40 years. Going forward, public policy toward building sustainable communities in a metropolitan context must incorporate places of local and regional opportunity where:

- Public policy gives priority to using or reusing existing assets such as land, buildings, and other resources to base development that is sustainable over time.
- The economic base of the community is diverse and open and promotes access to social and economic integration in and to a wider city and regional economy.
- Public policy helps communities gain access to resources to support functioning schools, health care, employment, neighborhood security, transportation linkages to jobs, and a good quality of life such as parks and recreation and a healthy environment.
- Development incorporates a range of capable institutions (e.g., churches, associational groups, the public education system, higher education, and the public and private sectors) that can contribute to community building and sustainable community economic development.
- Development leads to residents exercising bounded choice (i.e., choice exercised within the limits of income, education, and cultural affinity) in residing, or not residing, in the community.

Putting People First

The key to an effective, sustainable place-based strategy is to develop people to the point where they have the choice of staying in their community or going elsewhere. Developing the physical place needs new thinking to assure that it is a viable and sustainable place to live so that people are not limited to slums.[26]

It is not easy to equally value the development of people and place in one organization or strategy. One organization that has created some innovative linkages between people and place development is Isles Inc., a community-based nonprofit in Trenton, New Jersey. Founded in 1981, Isles is unique in that it defines itself as a "nonprofit community development and environmental organization" with a mission to "foster more self-reliant families in healthy, sustainable communities."

Isles addresses key aspects of people and place development in a strategic way that does not spread the organization thin. One key strategy focuses on youth. The Isles Youth Build Institute (IYI) is a school and training center for individuals ages 16 to 24 who have struggled in conventional school settings. Many of the young people have gone through the justice system and are looking for ways to re-enter mainstream society.

The IYI provides a supportive environment to help the young people make personal progress through training in construction, computer technology, and office administration. Through the Youth Build model (examined in Chapter 5 in greater detail), young people improve themselves through rebuilding their community, building and rebuilding houses in and around Trenton.

IYI is not just a program; it is a school where students earn a state-recognized high school diploma while learning life skills and leadership. Isles helps students decide on careers, finding jobs or pursuing higher education through an intensive case-management process. Isles also supports family development through its Parents Empowering Parents (PEP) effort. The PEP program offers parents intensive two-month (more if necessary) peer training and group counseling to support healthy parent–child interactions.

Isles does this programming very well, but so do other CEDIs. What is unique and innovative about Isles is that it recognizes in all its programs the value of environmental sustainability and the need to connect people development to trends in the region. That includes housing development and rehabilitation work.

Most CEDIs have a set catchment area. Isles has accumulated vast development experience, so much so that is has been able to become a regional developer, including suburbs surrounding Trenton. Adhering to a mixed-income model of development, Isles has been able to help many jurisdictions diversify their housing and income mix by building affordable housing. Isles is known for building "green" affordable housing in high-density, walkable communities throughout the Trenton region.[27] This type of mixed-income development promotes long-term community sustainability, affordability, and racially integrated communities.

Did Isles start out to be this regional CEDI? No; in fact, as Martin Johnson, one of the founders of the organization, recounts:

> Isles looked to the Healthy Cities movement in Europe and Canada to devise ways to assess neighborhood and city "health." When we did that, vexing questions kept arising: even though Isles developed hundreds of homes, nurtured many family self-help successes, and spent millions to redevelop Trenton communities, the population of the city kept shrinking. Working-class families continued to flee to the suburbs, leaving behind increasingly concentrated poverty. In fact, the suburbs around the city were witnessing white flight out to the even further

exurbs. Could we be winning and losing at the same time? We were successful at the community development game, but our work was growing more difficult as overall neighborhood deterioration worsened. Once we mapped the regional social and economic forces fueled by sprawl, we were surprised. It was as if we were making waves at the local level, but the tide was heading out. Not only was our community development work not addressing the core forces of sprawl, but sprawl was undermining the important community work we had accomplished. And community residents were weighing in: 85 percent of the roughly 300 families that came to us annually to buy a home sought homes *outside* of Trenton.[28]

This is much the same dynamic and outcome that concerns Rusk. Rather than cast it as an either/or circumstance, Isles went into "discovery" mode and sought out new ways to carry out its mission. As Johnson notes, it came up with a strategy to turn itself into a "regional CDC" containing the following goals:

- Understand the limits of community development-type projects. Self-help development projects are important and are undermined if poverty is concentrated and other systemic reforms are not achieved.
- Improve research capacity to better understand the limitations of any place-based development strategy, not just symptoms.
- Challenge racial and income segregation, especially in growing communities. Build affordable housing in places with the greatest social, educational, and economic opportunities within a region.
- Address public policy through collaboration with advocacy organizations. Tax, housing, regional governance, and other issues are best addressed by statewide policy changes, and CEDIs can lend voice and support to those specializing in policy advocacy on these issues.
- Connect to the suburbs. Many older suburban municipalities face the same issues as core inner cities. Some growing suburbs face labor shortages or scarcity in affordable housing. These challenges present opportunities to engage in constructive conversations with different types of suburban settlements.
- Link working families with educational, economic, and employment opportunities within a region. Support lower-income families who seek a greater voice and choice in moving to communities where opportunities—with good jobs, schools, and lower taxes—are available.
- Remain engaged in inner-city investment and revitalization by supporting public transit, open spaces, and biodiversity, all of which help cities develop into healthy places to live, work, and play.[29]

The Isles case is an important example on a number of fronts. Not only is the organization's work on the ground guided by value principles to develop people and place, but it has also played a leadership role in its surrounding region on issues of tax-base sharing and land-use planning.

Livable and Sustainable Communities

As Isles shows, community-based economic development has started to incorporate concepts such as "livable" and "sustainable" as pivot points for development thinking even while continuing the core work of developing people in place. There is no single way to pursue livable sustainable communities, and in fact the field is in a much-needed period of sorting out new paths. But we can discern overlays of what locally sustainable development in the context of an advance economy might mean.

This overlay defines locally sustainable development as the use of natural, economic, political, human, and social capital with attention to the ability of future generations to benefit from these resources.[30] The discussion centers on how to effectively use or reuse natural or man-made assets in a way that allows good stewardship of the environment while generating income and livelihoods.[31]

Much has been made of the "green economy" and "green-collar jobs." Some define green-collar jobs as "blue-collar work force opportunities created by firms and organizations whose mission is to improve environmental quality."[32] Examples of green-collar jobs include recycling and reuse, hazardous material cleanup, building retrofits to increase energy efficiency and conservation, housing deconstruction, solar installation, urban agriculture, and manufacturing that does not degrade the environment.

Many of these jobs have limited educational requirements and are viable alternatives to (not replacements for) vanishing manufacturing jobs. Proponents maintain there is a path for career development in the green economy that not only provides a livelihood but is also a way for people to build wealth and assets to help them to move out of poverty.[33]

Advocates for livable and sustainable communities see their goals advanced by activities such as brownfield redevelopment, transit-oriented development, community gardens, urban agriculture, and urban open space preservation programs.[34] Livability speaks to two broad strands of thought. The first is the "new urbanism," which encourages compact, pedestrian-friendly, dense development. Livability also incorporates long-standing arguments in the economic development literature that encourage policies to reduce crime, improve schools, and build parks and other amenities in poor neighborhoods.

We should be careful about the promise of livability and sustainability to truly change the fortunes of the poor and build assets. But use of these concepts, both as an analytical frame and as a practical guide for development, should not be dismissed as a path to invigorate community economic development. Let's look at some examples of how livability and sustainability can help improve CED practice.

Brownfield Redevelopment

Brownfields are industrial and commercial facilities where redevelopment is difficult due to perceived or real toxic waste contamination. Located in every state in the nation, brownfield parcels can range from old leather-tannery buildings with pools of toxic waste in back to the corner gas station with underground storage tanks.[35] For many years, brownfields were nearly undevelopable. Fear of liability and costly cleanups stalled reuse of these parcels. In the 1980s and 1990s, mayors and other local officials realized the vast potential of bringing brownfields back on the tax rolls and pushed the federal government to adopt policies that would make redevelopment possible.

The Small Business Liability Relief and Brownfields Revitalization Act authorizing the U.S. Environmental Protection Agency's (EPA) Brownfields Program is largely responsible for making once-shunned properties economically viable. The EPA's Brownfields Program funds assessment and cleanup of sites. There is a revolving loan fund for actual development in addition to support for job training in toxic waste remediation. Where once there was little support for brownfields reuse, there are now other state and federal programs that complement the EPA such as the HUD Brownfields Program.

This funding stream and attention to brownfields has helped CEDIs make such development a central part of their efforts both in terms of reclaiming land and job training. Two examples serve to illustrate the power of brownfields development. One project illustrates how a Chicago community was able to reclaim a contaminated parcel and turn it into a community facility. The other example shows how brownfields development can be used for workforce development.

North Lawndale is one of those Chicago neighborhoods with a rich history that can be seen when one looks closely at the magnificent gray stone buildings dotting the community. It was first settled by immigrants from Czechoslovakia in the late nineteenth and early twentieth centuries; Jewish immigrants succeeded the Czechs in the 1920s, and African Americans came in the 1960s. Now 98 percent black and with a median income of $18,000, North Lawndale struggles to be once again a community of opportunity. The Lawndale Christian Development Corporation (LCDC) is a key institution trying to make that happen. In 2001 the LCDC and the North Lawndale community cut the ribbon on the North Lawndale Family Resource Center, a day care center employing 50 people and serving the educational needs of the community's children. The Resource Center sits atop the site of an old auto repair shop, which itself sat atop a site that had seen its share of industrial use.

The Family Resource Center is now a community asset, but to get to that point much had to be done. The LCDC and the Illinois Facilities Fund (a nonprofit CDFI) initiated the project in 1998 as a result of community desire for quality day care for working families. The LCDC and the Illinois Facilities Fund approached the city with a proposal to develop the brownfield parcel on which the day care center now sits. Using EPA resources, the city remediated the site and got a release from liability from the state of Illinois. With that release, LCDC was able to get private financing and support from Chicago's CDBG program. North Lawndale received a new community asset, day care for working families, because the public sector (at all levels) and the nonprofit community were able to work with available resources.[36]

Brownfield development can encompass job training. In 2002, the EPA provided a grant to STRIVE, a nationally known workforce development intermediary. The grant enabled STRIVE to work with CEDIs such as the St. Nicholas Neighborhood Preservation Corporation in Brooklyn, New York. The partnership with CEDIs trained low-income residents in environmental remediation (e.g., lead abatement and asbestos removal). It is an ongoing program, and many of the trainees have found jobs in environmental remediation paying upward of $16 an hour. STRIVE and partners such as St. Nicholas provide wraparound services to trainees so they enter the workplace with "soft skills" training and knowledge of financial management for when they start earning a paycheck.[37]

Reusing Steel from Automobiles to Build Affordable Housing

Brownfields redevelopment is a key strategy for reclaiming an important asset now in short supply: urban land.

In a rural context, the work of the North Carolina Community Development Initiative (or simply "the Initiative" as it has come to be known in North Carolina) in engaging the concept of sustainability is instructive. Like ANDP, the Initiative is a financial and technical assistance intermediary chartered to expand the capacity of CEDIs, most of them rural organizations. Born in 1994, the organization has established itself as a national model for building the capacity of young rural development organizations with a combination of patient assistance and firm standards that encourage organizational progress and effectiveness.

Like many other regional community economic development intermediaries of its kind, the Initiative is also a developer. The Initiative's work has been so important to building the development infrastructure of North Carolina that it has been included as a line item in the state for much of its existence. Through changing party leadership and shifting priorities, the Initiative has endured in the state budget, steadily growing from a base of $1 million to now over $6 million per year. This is almost unheard of in a field where government support for the work of community economic development is patchwork and negotiated from year to year.

Although the Initiative's work in directly building homes or helping local CEDIs has been noteworthy, it is the organization's receptivity to new ideas and innovations that marks it as a learning organization. Recently, it has partnered with the state's environmental community to rethink and develop new experiments in "green building." The Initiative joined with a conservation effort called Land for Tomorrow, a statewide partnership of citizens, businesses, interest groups, and local governments that was successful in convincing the general assembly to provide $200 million a year for five years to protect the state's land and water resources.[38]

Participation in this effort led the Initiative to start thinking strategically about providing "conservation-based affordable housing" to low-income communities that will include green technologies, passive solar energy, dual-flush toilets, and fabrication of nontraditional building materials. As Abdul Rasheed, the CEO of the Initiative, said in a 2008 interview,

> We're trying to move from just getting people into a house to getting people into a smart house. ...We're making every concerted effort now to bring those technologies to low-income communities based on our ability to afford the technology....If we don't do it now, as this curve moves, to come back and try to reinvest and re-establish these principles as we have done historically would be a shame on us that know better during this generation.[39]

Using a variety of federal and local tax incentives and state grants, the Initiative is helping some of its rural CEDIs build energy-efficient homes using steel recycled from automobiles. In a short time, a nonprofit development system for fabricating and developing affordable housing centering on recycled steel has emerged. One of the Initiative's grantees, the UDI Community Development Corporation, a CDC with over 40 years of experience, formed Carolina Steel Construction LLC to manufacture steel studs and steel framing fabricated from melted-down automobiles. The company sells these products to developers of commercial and residential real estate, with a priority for developers of affordable housing. Carolina Steel manufactures and assembles galvanized steel studs, framed wall panels, and roof trusses, and ships the products directly to job sites for new home construction. Revenues go back to UDI for use in its broader mission of community development.[40]

The Initiative helps to develop the end use of the steel framing through its EnviroSteel project, and finances the production of homes using Carolina Steel's products. The initiative also supports its grantee CEDIs to produce land-use and architectural plans to comply with local ordinances.

Steel-framed homes are more durable and less prone to fire damage and natural disasters. The project is an experiment and the Initiative admits that it is still early to tell if consumers in rural markets will accept this type of home, even with subsidies. But the Initiative's receptivity and willingness to go beyond its standard work and standard partnerships illustrate my earlier point about modeling.

Summary

The convergence of efforts against urban sprawl and a refocus on building the skills and assets of poor people and enhancing the sustainability and livability of poor communities is producing a new way of practicing community economic development. Practitioners steeped in urban, rural, and community economic development are making headway into the sustainability realm through linking place and people development in fairly opportunistic ways.

The examples in this chapter show a level of innovation and creativity, but not so much that any are off the charts for those looking to learn from or replicate these efforts. We should not forget that innovation and sustainability start from one basic platform: an organization that is internally strong and driven by principles that support institutional longevity and strength. We see that with Isles and the North Carolina Community Development Initiative: two different organizations with the same compelling internal force to improve and change when necessary. From that base of institutional strength, organizations can branch out and adapt to the times.

The EPA's Brownfields Program shows that the public sector can change the development dynamic and shape an entirely new conversation on the reuse of a scarce resource: land. None of the examples points to a clear road to help community economic development transition to sustainable development. Perhaps that is not necessary. Perhaps the key is a willingness to explore new ideas and programs, with the following guiding principles:

- CEDI institutions must become knowledge-seeking and -creating institutions in order to assess and manage rapidly shifting trends and markets. Information is key in the knowledge economy, and its impact is no different for CED.
- Public policy, although always important to CED, is an even more important force in keeping CED relevant. Policies must productively link different communities in a region and encourage regional thinking and action on workforce development systems, tax-base sharing, and the deconcentration of poverty.
- CEDIs can and must develop strategies to address sustainable development, not in ways where development is an "add-on" but rather where it is an important way of doing business.
- CEDIs have to define a level of accountability and impact that makes their in-place work more definitive and with clear effect to assure continued reliance on them by the public sector as an antipoverty strategy. Institutional longevity and capacity are just as important a part of defining sustainable community economic development as concerns for the environment.

The next chapter explores key issue areas where we need to see innovations to further promote sustainable community economic development.

Endnotes

1. See Bradbury, Downs, and Small. (1982), Flint (2006), and Orfield (2002) for detailed analyses of how government policy has contributed to urban decline.
2. Jargowsky (1997). To be sure, Jargowsky (2003) found significant reductions in the number of people living in high-poverty urban neighborhoods; first-ring older suburbs actually experienced a parallel rise in high-poverty neighborhoods, which points to the conclusion that poverty is shifting through the metropolis.
3. Orfield (2002); Jargowsky (1997).
4. Bullard (2007); Orfield (2002); Wagner (2005).
5. Wilson (1996); Ferguson and Dickens (1999, pp. 15–20).
6. Simon (2001, Chapter 3).
7. Olson (1965); Reisman (1990).
8. Rusk (1999); Stoecker (1997).
9. Stoecker (1997).
10. Stoecker (1997). Although Green and Haines (2008) don't argue that professionalization is negative, they do present a balanced view of professionalization in the community economic development field. It is natural that professionalization becomes a point of tension when the partnership between government and nonprofits deepens and the former comes to rely on the latter to deliver services. Nonprofits have to increase along a continuum of ability to ensure continued partnership with government. See Geoghegan and Powell (2006) for a comparative case of professionalization of community development institutions in an international context.
11. Rusk (1999, p. 36).
12. Rusk (1999) is most emphatic on this point, but so is Orfield (2002).
13. The population for Bedford-Stuyvesant is approximately 125,000 people. See the Furman Center for Real Estate and Urban Policy (at New York University) community profile, http://furma ncenter.org/fil es/203.pdf. (accessed September 3, 2008)
14. Ferguson and Dickens (1999, pp. 19–20) make a similar point.
15. Anglin (1994); *New York Times* (2001b).
16. Hughes (1994).
17. Lemann's (1994) journalistic piece questioning the fundamental usefulness of community economic development sent shock waves through the field. Although we can argue with many of Lemann's interpretations of the field, he served a productive purpose in starting a public dialogue on antipoverty strategies such as community economic development.
18. See Pitcoff (1998).
19. Greenstein and Sungyu-Eryilmaz (2004); Silberstein and Maser (2000).
20. Karlinsky (2000).
21. Pitcoff (1996, 1997); Taveras (1998).

22. See Wachter, Penne, and Nelson (2000) for a summary set of conference proceedings for a meeting that brought together an important cross-section of thinkers on regional, people, and place development. The conference and the proceedings remain a seminal force in forging the new consensus mentioned in the text.
23. Katz (2003); see also Kotkin (2007) and Hall (2008).
24. Garmise (2006, p. 3).
25. *New Urban News* (2000).
26. Garmise (2006).
27. Isles ensures that all its real estate projects meet exceptional standards of energy efficiency, indoor air quality, sustainability, and resource efficiency.
28. M. Johnson (2005).
29. These points are excerpted from M. Johnson (2005). Minor changes have been made to reduce length but not substance.
30. This is similar to the widely accepted definition of sustainable development developed by the Bruntland Commission, a United Nations process begun in 1983. The official name, United Nations World Commission on Environment and Development, was convened to study the increasing degradation of the human and natural environment along with ways to stop these trends. See United Nations General Assembly (1987) for the recommendations.
31. United Nations General Assembly (1987).
32. Pinderhughes, Green Collar Jobs.
33. In December 2007, Congress passed the Green Jobs Act of 2007 creating a pilot program between the U.S. Department of Labor and the U.S. Department of Energy.
34. Calthorpe (1993).
35. The EPA estimates there may be over 600,000 of these sites in the United States. The Department of Defense is a major owner of brownfields sites and it has identified over 14,000 sites on military installations requiring some level of cleanup.
36. Material for this case comes from Environmental Protection Agency, Abandoned Lot to Family Resource Center—Partnering for Education in Chicago. http://www.epa.go v/brownfields/success/ ss_chica.pdf. (accessed September 3, 2008)
37. Environmental Protection Agency, Brownfields Environmental Job Training Programs Lead to New Lives for Graduates. http://epa.gov/brownfields/success/brooklyn_ny_ ss.pdf. (accessed September 4, 2008)
38. North Carolina Community Development Initiative (2009).
39. Grizzard (2008).
40. http://www.udicdc.org/. (accessed September 4, 2008)

Chapter 3

Public Sector Innovation and Community Economic Development

The preceding chapter noted the emerging consensus linking sustainable development to place and people development in a metropolitan context, a link that is also important in renewing and augmenting community economic development.[1] This chapter takes into account this emerging consensus and identifies categories or points of learning and innovation that would improve the development of people and places.

Public sector innovation, narrowly defined, is a change that improves the effectiveness of policy or strategy in any given issue arena. Public sector innovation is better examined as an evolutionary process in which change does not have to come from one government agency or one level of government.[2]

In *Transforming Public Leadership for the 21st Century*, Ricardo S. Morse, Terry F. Buss, and Morgan C. Kinghorn address public sector innovation, reframing the concept of public leadership. They use the phrase "intraorganizational leadership" to define the traditional hierarchical way organizations are viewed and function. The authors contrast this with the "interorganizational" form of public leadership wherein organizations form networks that work together to promote the public good and, yes, innovation.

Morse, Buss, and Kinghorn (2007) note that globalization has played a significant role in bringing about the shift in perspective. According to them, the global breaking down of political and organizational boundaries has made it more necessary for actors from different sectors to coordinate their efforts. The authors explain that the "public leadership process...extends beyond public organizations and beyond formal leaders. It reflects the realities of a 'shared power world' where governance is the product of many organizations—not just government."[3]

Government action and functioning are now embedded in policy issue networks where various institutional actors, such as elected officials, public agency leaders, think tanks, and practitioners of all stripes define problems and solutions over time.[4] Those who are part of a policy issue network interact at conferences, belong to peer groups, testify before Congress, state legislatures, and city councils, and are often called upon to write the rules for pending legislation at all levels.[5]

Community economic development can be said to have a policy network that includes government, CEDIs, intermediary organizations, and the private sector. Suggestions and examples for innovation can come from anywhere in the policy issue network and after a period of testing can translate into routine operation through public policy.[6]

Table 3.1 summarizes the major public sector innovations at the federal level in both community economic development policy and the broader policy environment.

The rise of charter schools as an alternative to the "one size fits all" approach to public education in the United States is a good example of an idea started in the policy environment, then brought into the public arena. Parents, local community groups, and educators in places such as Chicago, New York, and Minneapolis in the 1960s and 1970s started "alternative schools" to provide choice to parents and children hoping that a tailored curriculum would appeal to students.[7] Public sector innovation, although difficult to define, can be recognized through the following:

■ An idea, strategy, or program leads to measurable improvement in policy outcomes on a scale beyond just one jurisdiction, neighborhood, or city. In short, scale matters.
■ Public sector financial support is important to the inception or continuation of the innovation.
■ Innovation is multidirectional: the origin of change can come from outside of government and then be adopted on a wider scale, or it can come from local, state, or federal policy that encourages change throughout the policy network.
■ Time is linked to innovation. Innovation can take years to unfold and make an impact, but the opposite also is true; innovations can last a short time (for any number of reasons, including timing and cost) and disappear. The question is how much we can learn from the innovation's impact and the potential to change outcomes at some later date.[8]

Innovation in the public sector has been helped along in recent years by the federal devolution begun in the 1970s (and greatly expanded in the 1980s and beyond) that dispatched increased responsibilities to states and local governments.[9] An important literature has developed focusing on studying the aftermath of devolution and efforts to reinvent government in the late decades of the twentieth century. With states and localities working with fewer resources but with no less demand from the public, many public managers found innovative ways to provide public goods, including privatization, public–private partnerships, and the increased use of nonprofits.[10]

Broadening the scope of public leadership and management becomes the means to understand how policy networks within and across fields can promote and sustain innovation in community economic development.[11]

Leadership and Innovation

Leadership has become central to the discussion of economic prosperity in a time of increased turbulence and change. Often subsumed under the rubric of globalization and regionalization, these economic changes are undermining local and regional economies even while bringing many benefits to the national economy in the process. As a consequence, local governments and communities are finding it difficult to maintain a level of control over their economic destiny..

The dominant theme in the literature describing innovative public leadership is the attenuation of natural leadership skills such as the ability to (1) articulate a vision, (2) communicate with a wide and varied set of stakeholders, and (3) facilitate collective action.[12] I say "attenuation" because in the past, a local community with stable institutional economic relationships did not demand that public managers appeal in any substantive way to leaders and forces outside their political jurisdictions. In fact, the academic literature supported the view that economic competition for population and taxable assets framed the negative-sum world of local elected officials and public managers.[13]

Contemporary public managers have to use a wide array of skills to convince companies that their community is worthy of investment; they also have to work in concert with other jurisdictions in the emerging regional economy on issues of land use and economy development. Lastly, there is a growing acceptance that economic development, not the simple attraction policies that dominated an earlier era, has to be expanded and linked squarely with efforts to reduce poverty and inequity.[14]

Perhaps the most expansive example of public sector innovation in more than a generation to reduce poverty and build wealth in poor communities is what New York City has undertaken.

In 2006, the city's mayor, Michael R. Bloomberg, put together a Commission for Economic Opportunity composed of 32 civic leaders from the private, nonprofit, and public sectors to recommend poverty-reduction strategies and programs to improve economic opportunity for poor New Yorkers. Supported by the staff work of nonprofit and academic institutions, the Commission conducted focused work groups on several areas inextricably linked to poverty such as education, job growth, health and housing, and workforce development.[15]

Table 3.1 Public Sector (Federal) Innovation and Community Economic Development

		1960s	1970s	1980s	1990s	2000+
Policy Problem		Urban unrest born of limited attention by local governments to the needs of marginalized communities Limited economic development opportunities in marginalized communities Beginning of post-WWII economic restructuring	Unrest in marginalized communities partially based on rising expectations Increasing economic opportunity Economic restructuring	Concentrated poverty in marginalized communities; place revitalization Economic restructuring	Concentrated poverty in marginalized communities; place revitalization Economic restructuring	Concentrated poverty spread beyond core urban areas to communities in wider metropolis Advancing globalization Building linkages and networks to create communities of opportunity in place of concentrated poverty Climate change
Policy Environment		Strong economy for most of the decade; inflation in the latter part of the period due to increased military spending	Slowing economy ("stagflation") Strong public backlash against the perceived over-attention, by the public sector, to marginalized minority communities resulting in lessened attention to rural and urban poverty	Weak economy Acceleration of economic change (e.g., industrial economy to an information-based economy)	Strong economy for most of the decade	Strong economy for first part of the decade Limited concern and attention to CED policy problems for most of the decade

Policy Environment	Public focus and attention to urban and rural poverty. Significant migration of African Americans, Appalachian whites, and Latinos to central cities	Devolution of responsibility from the federal level to states and localities. Slowing economy marked by high inflation	Continued backlash. Rise of the "entrepreneurial state"; public sector focus on market-based solutions to place revitalization	Beginning discussions of the "stakeholder" society and asset building as an antipoverty strategy in a regional context	
Public Sector CED Innovation	Special Impact Program (SIP) legislation sponsored by Sen. Robert Kennedy (D.-NY) and Sen. Jacob Javits (R.-NY) support the creation of nine community-based organizations charted to promote economic development	Federal support for CED and CEDIs; efforts to connect the work of CEDIs to federal programs and agencies impacting CED. Passage of the Community Development Block Grant, which focused myriad housing and economic development programs into one block grant so state and localities could access support. Beginning of the federal, private sector, and philanthropic support of financial and technical assistance intermediaries. Community Reinvestment Act	Passage of the Low Income Housing Tax Credit under the Tax Reform Act of 1986	Strong political support for CED experimentation. "Reinvention" of Housing and Urban Development. Weed and Seed HUD Community Builders Community Outreach Partnership Program. Hope IV; Enterprise Zones; Community Development Financial Institutions Act; YouthBuild; AmeriCorps	Local CED stakeholders exploring concepts such as sustainable development and asset-based development to improve CED; community development moves to incorporated educational reform as part of development agenda

Source: Author's compilation.

The Commission's recommendations resulted in the creation of the Center for Economic Opportunity, a public–private partnership responsible for funding experimental antipoverty programs across the city. Started with the help of public and private funds, "the Center for Economic Development works with City agencies to design and implement evidence-based initiatives aimed at poverty reduction."[16]

The city as leader of the initiative committed to funding and raising $150 million per year for an Innovation Fund. The Center provides city agencies annual support to implement asset-building initiatives through the Innovation Fund.[17] Since 2006, the Center for Economic Opportunity has worked with other city agencies to implement a wide array of community and economic development programs.

One of the more innovative programs currently being implemented is the Conditional Cash Transfer (CCT) program. CCTs are gaining a following in antipoverty policy circles worldwide.[18] The programs provide straight cash to recipients only if they perform a pre-agreed action that, theoretically, will help them get out of poverty. Essentially, CCTs use the economist's touchstone of "rationality" to get people to do the "right thing." As an example, with a CCT program, the public sector will transfer benefits (cash) to parents who get their children a full course of vaccinations or keep their children in school. Some CCT programming goes further to reward parents for increased achievement in schools.

New York's Center for Economic Opportunity is testing three models of conditional cash transfer, all supported by private philanthropy and public resources. One such experiment, the Opportunity NYC Work Rewards program, tries to increase workforce participation and savings. Using an existing HUD program called the Family Self-Sufficiency (FSS) program (discussed in more detail in Chapter 7), which establishes a matched savings account for public housing residents, the Work Rewards program adds cash bonuses on top of matched savings for sustained employment. Public housing residents can also receive cash bonuses for completing education and training courses while employed. The program also partners with and supports CEDIs in communities with high numbers of Work Reward participants to do the type of intensive case management that public housing authorities probably cannot do because of time and cost limitations.[19] Other interesting interventions include the following:

- *Office of Financial Empowerment (OFE).* OFE, which resides in the Department of Consumer Affairs, supports asset building, financial education, and protection from predatory practices for low-income New Yorkers through various projects.
- *Prepopulated Earned Income Tax Credit (EITC) Forms.* The EITC is one of the most important antipoverty tools that we have as a nation. It is a progressive tax credit that gives money back to low-wage earners through the income tax system, up to a threshold. Low-income wage earners underutilize the tax. The New York City Department of Finance took the unparalleled

step of searching previous federal tax information to identify New Yorkers eligible for the Earned Income Tax Credit. The agency then used that information to fill out and mail amended tax returns so people could claim their credits.

- ■ *Community-Based Organization (CBO) Outreach Program.* The CBO Outreach program recruits job seekers from high-poverty areas for placement by the City's Workforce 1 Career Centers.[20]
- ■ *Alternative Measurement of Poverty.* The federal poverty measure does not accurately reflect the number of poor Americans. The Center for Economic Opportunity developed an alternative poverty measure based on recommendations of the National Academy of Sciences. The new measure accounts for geographic variation in the cost of living and the real value of government interventions.
- ■ *City University of New York (CUNY) Prep.* CUNY Prep offers out-of-school youth full-time study focused on GED completion and preparation for college admission. Rigorous academic standards, high-quality instruction, a supportive community, and college orientation distinguish CUNY Prep from other GED programs.
- ■ *Healthy Food Policies.* Working with small, ubiquitous Latino grocery stores, locally called bodegas, New York City is expanding access to healthy foods in targeted low-income communities, including a campaign to promote the consumption of low-fat milk and fresh fruits and vegetables. In addition, the city is expanding vending cart permits to expand the presence of Green Carts, which sell only fruits and vegetables, in high-poverty neighborhoods.
- ■ *City University of New York Accelerated Study in Associate Programs (ASAP).* CUNY ASAP provides academic and economic support to help accelerate the number of low-income students completing an associate's degree.
- ■ *Sector-Focused Career Centers.* The sector-focused initiative creates job-placement and training centers focused on specific industries with excellent salary growth potential and a need for new employees.
- ■ *Young Adult Internship Program (YAIP).* YAIP provides disconnected youth ages 16 to 24 with paid internships, employment and education placement assistance, and follow-up services.
- ■ *The Million Trees NYC Training Program.* The jobs program offers professional training with a focus on forestry and horticulture to young adults disconnected from schools or careers. Through this paid on-the-job training program, participants cultivate job skills preparing them for the available green jobs that involve tree planting, pruning, and stewardship.[21]

New York is without question a unique place given its size, public sector administrative capacity, and nonprofit capacity. It would be a mistake to try and replicate the entirety of the New York effort, especially because much of it is still being tested. But the Center for Economic Opportunity is already generating learning for other jurisdictions to consider and use in their own efforts at building places of economic opportunity.[22]

The range of strategies in the New York example illustrates public sector support for the existing community economic development network. But without directly saying so, the effort is also embracing conceptions of sustainable community economic development (see the example of the Million Trees NYC Training Program).

The extent to which community economic development capacity, community building, access to capital, workforce development, education reform, and higher education can learn from, and collaborate around, the principles of sustainable community economic development brings us closer to articulated places of hope and opportunity. The rest of this chapter presents the categories that are central to building a framework for increased impact in community economic development and poverty reduction. No one theory allows me to define these as the right categories. I wish there were such a theory. The categories are a derivative amalgam of practitioner and academic discussions presented thus far. My goal is to present important examples and evidence that the categories lead in a public policy direction worth taking.

Community Economic Development Capacity

A rich set of activities and relationships now exists that we can call a community economic development network (see Table 3.2). Community economic development capacity focuses on building the organizational and institutional ability to (1) plan and execute development projects of scale and (2) effectively implement and manage human development programs. Community capacity in large part is defined by the presence and strength of community organizations that can train people, build homes, and implement various human development programs.

Organizational strength and effectiveness, although central to community economic development, are difficult to achieve and they remain the Achilles heel of the field. A number of CEDIs operate outside the norms of good organizational practice. Accounting is haphazard. Boards are weak and lack the diverse skills needed to guide an organization. Many are frustrating places to work because their leaders are unable to nurture talent. Many do not have systems in place to connect with and listen to their constituents.[23]

Social and economic development needs organization, but it also demands the presence of specialized skills geared toward advancing strong enduring organizations, otherwise known as leadership. Leadership skills are not technically based. These skills encompass intangibles such as proposing a vision and a set of goals for people to follow, building the architecture of an enduring organization that is transparent, and putting in place ethical values that prevent diversion of resources meant for the community. Some leadership skills can be taught and some are innate.

Experience tells us that for any community to develop and prosper, a plural base of strong organizations needs to be present. Unfortunately, the evolution of community economic development has seen the uneven development of ground-level CEDIs.[24] At the center of this challenge is the failure of many CEDIs to practice "stakeholder community development." Stakeholders include any institution or individual having a latent or expressed interest in the organization accomplishing its mission and goals.[25]

In stakeholder community development, CEDIs both recognize the value of stakeholders in their work and develop the capacity of those stakeholders to act as stewards of their institution. Stewards work for the long-term health of an institution and do not see it as something to be mined for personal gain and discarded when convenient; they add value to the institution instead of taking it away. There are many kinds of stakeholders in a CEDI, including staff, board members, community residents, and resource providers. Each kind faces unique challenges in acting on its stake in the CEDI. Firm, even inflexible, standards are necessary for increasing accountability.

Stakeholder accountability is the base for an enduring community institution but also for an institution that is a base from which to promote innovation and change in the community. The fact that many CEDIs have limited organizational capacity does not make the community-based economic development model a failure; in fact, the argument can be made that building out organizational capacity in poor communities is fundamental no matter what strategy is tried. As messy and nettlesome as it is, the public sector and society broadly don't have much choice but to strengthen community-based organizations. Not to do so limits the collective well-being. Public policy needs strong community-based organizations to perform key development and programmatic roles. How to do that effectively is still a difficult problem.

The question is, who should hold CEDIs and other nonprofits accountable for becoming stakeholder organizations? Ideally, community vigilance and the fact that CEDIs are creatures of our tax laws would prevail, but the reality is that resource providers must take the larger share of this burden.[26] For the community economic development field, national intermediaries such as LISC, Enterprise Foundation, and NeighborWorks America are other important means of promoting standards and building effective organizations. Government (federal, state, and local) and the growing use of performance-based contracting are other elements. In addition, over the past 20 years or so, community development financial institutions, local community economic development partnerships (usually composed of the public sector, philanthropy, and some private sector actors, such as banks), have grown in significance and reach and should play an important role in improving accountability.

Despite the limitations of locally based CEDIs, the regional and national infrastructure that has grown to support these organizations and to carry out direct development is a significant innovation. The infrastructure that has emerged over the last 20 years is very different from past efforts to encourage community-based economic development. The intermediaries now possess important tools to routinize

Table 3.2 The Community Economic Development Network by Jurisdiction and Sector

	Public Sector	Private Sector	Voluntary and Nonprofit Sector	Trends, Challenges, and Opportunities
National	Federal agencies (e.g., Department of Housing and Urban Development; Department of Agriculture; Economic Development Administration; Department of Justice; Department of Transportation; Department of Commerce; the Department of the Treasury; Department of Health and Human Services; government-sponsored enterprises (GSEs); Federal Home Loan banks; elected officials	National banks; mortgage industry; pension funds	National foundations; national community development intermediaries; national community development financial institutions; national field associations affecting CED	Globalization of capital; market-based solutions to public policy problems; government devolution; immigration; advances in the use of information technology
State	State departments of commerce and community affairs; state housing mortgage finance agencies; state agencies (e.g., social services, education, workforce development, housing); elected officials	Regional banks	Regional community development support partnerships; regional community development financial institutions; regional workforce development partnerships	Increased responsibility for regional community and economic development; immigration; advances in the use of information technology

| Local | Local community and economic development departments; elected officials; local, public, and charter schools | Local banks; local corporations working in market-based partnerships with community economic development institutions or providing philanthropic resources | Local philanthropy; local community development support intermediaries; local community development financial institutions; United Ways; workforce development organizations; community colleges, four-year public and private colleges; community-based organizations addressing various facets of people and place development | Concentrated poverty; capital transiency leading to limited "anchor corporations"; local philanthropy and capital formation; advances in the use of information technology |

Source: Author's compilation.

and improve the local development process, including time-tested capacity building programs, their ability to generate financing for community-based projects, and their own projects. In addition, CDFI and CED intermediaries are leading the way in the field, adjusting to changing needs. The partnership among CDFI and CED intermediaries and the communities in which they work is creating some of the most effective examples of place and people development within a regional frame.[27]

Community Building and Development

Community building and development precede community economic development in that the former's goals are to (1) build strong community institutions and initiatives that can promote economic and social mobility, (2) ensure a safe physical environment so families and children can thrive, and (3) encourage community definition of interests, goals, relationships, and institutions to promote them.

Community development appears again on the U.S. policy landscape as a strategy in the late 1960s as a response to the "urban crisis."[28] The urban crisis encompassed a range of problems specific to the marginalization of African Americans who moved to America's cities in successive waves beginning in the early twentieth century. To a lesser extent, the policy response also sought to address the problems of Appalachian whites who moved from declining rural areas in Kentucky and West Virginia in the 1950s and 1960s and the problems of Latino migrants from Mexico and Puerto Rico during the same period (see Table 3.1).

Forced into overcrowded conditions and lacking political and economic power, African Americans and others endured communities that can only be described as places of stagnation and limited opportunity. The national response, much of it framed under the banner of the Great Society championed by then-President Lyndon Johnson, was far-reaching. Some responses argued for youth and educational programs to address rising delinquency in urban ghettos. Others promoted job training, access to capital, and entrepreneurial training to encourage economic development.[29]

Political participation was not sought for the sake of participation, but for the public goods that groups received by competing in the political system. Thus when Johnson implemented his War on Poverty, the twin pillars of change rested on political and economic empowerment.[30] Over the years since the Great Society, community development and community economic development became so conflated that, recently, many practitioners have started to use community building to signal the importance of dedicated initiatives that do not necessarily have economic development as an end.

Practices such as community organizing to promote voice on garbage pickup, crime in the community, or initiatives such as family support programs that provide parenting skills and youth development all contribute to economic development.

Primarily, their goal is to build the type of community strength and cohesion that can be used to promote collective action in addition to family and individual self-sufficiency.

There is a need to highlight community building and community development, as distinct from community economic development. Yet their conceptual difference from each other is less clear. As I interpret community development and building, the aim is to construct a human and community infrastructure that is resilient and strong enough to participate in the larger political and economic mainstream.

Communities, especially poor communities, have to be organized for internal change and development to participate in building a sustainable regional economy. Communities possessing a strong level of internal cohesion and a history of collaboration (especially centering on development and direction of the local economy) are more likely to attract public and private investment. Building the infrastructure, the capacity, of a community is the most critical component of sustainable community economic development.

Building community capacity is not the work of one CEDI nor is it the work of one strategy. Colleges and universities can be an important tool in community capacity building (see Chapter 10). Through the HUD Office of University Partnerships (OUP), this role has been supported with the emergence of interesting examples of key community institutions helping people help themselves. An initiative that serves the Native American community is instructive here.

The College of Menominee Nation (CMN), a college located on the Menominee Indian Reservation in Wisconsin, has received three grants in the last decade under the OUP's Tribal Colleges and Universities Program (TCUP). With two campuses, one in Keshena and one in Green Bay, CMN serves four Native American nations of northeastern Wisconsin along with neighboring non-Indian communities. OUP funding has contributed to its efforts to expand and improve its facilities and provide a wealth of community services to the local population. In 2001, CMN used its TCUP grant to build additional classroom space, necessary to accommodate its steadily increasing student population.[31]

This initiative engaged the local community by involving a variety of partners, including Menominee Tribal Enterprises and the Community Development division of the Menominee Indian Tribe of Wisconsin. The College's Youth Options program was a third partner, working with the Menominee Indian School District to provide training in construction as part of a transition program for students from high school to college.[32]

Most recently, CMN received a Tribal Colleges and Universities Program grant from HUD in 2008 to complete the second phase of the construction of a library. All of these efforts help the college to better serve the needs of its population of more than 500 students per semester, especially low-income students and those with disabilities.[33] Faculty, staff, and community members also benefit from the various expansion projects in that they allow the college to better serve its students and surrounding community.

CMN also supports a wide variety of community services to expand educational and training opportunities for the local population. Although the Menominee Nation has historical ties to the logging industry, it has in recent years sought to widen its economic base to meet current demands in the information-based economy. The college plays a key role by offering a variety of programs in math and science and reaching out to involve local residents as students. For young people who are not yet ready for college-level math and science courses, CMN offers a one-year program that prepares them in algebra, biology, computers, and other related subjects.

CMN's efforts also extend beyond having local young people attend the college as matriculated students. They include a variety of other opportunities for community members to gain access to educational opportunities. For example, residents can participate in noncredit workshops with qualified instructors.[34] Topics of current workshops include résumé writing, leadership in the workplace, team building, archaeology, elder computer training, and interviewing skills.[35]

A more extensive program, the Transportation Alliance for New Solutions, involves CMN and the Wisconsin Department of Transportation in training the underemployed so that they can work as laborers and then apprentices in the road-building industry. This free 120-hour program is a public–private partnership that focuses especially on women and minorities, helping them gain full-time employment in the skilled trades related to highway construction. CMN's Education Outreach Department then continues to support the program's graduates by helping them find jobs, achieve further training, and gain access to community resources.[36]

As an additional aspect of community involvement, the college also has a Sustainable Development Institute. As mentioned earlier, the Menominee Nation has long been centrally involved in the logging industry, so this effort seeks to promote its forest management efforts through education, research, and community activities. CMN offers a variety of courses in this field, including a required course for all students, along with academic programs in Sustainable Development and Sustainable Forestry. Furthermore, organizations, internships, and projects provide students with the opportunity to gain both theoretical and practical experience in this field.[37]

Assets and Agency

One of the central reasons for the rise of community economic development was lack of access to capital by marginalized communities. For much of the twentieth century, many communities, especially communities of color, were excluded from capital markets because of factors outside the normal risk profile associated with lending. Lack of capital limited the ability of many middle-class communities of color to leverage the equity in their homes for self-employment, upkeep, and the intergenerational transfer of wealth.

The impact on poor communities of color (and rural communities) was even more destructive. If one cannot borrow to secure a mortgage because lenders decide a certain community is not worthy to invest in, based solely on race, then over time capital flight is sure to follow, leaving that community an economic wasteland.

The Community Reinvestment Act (CRA) of 1977, for example, was designed to ensure that financial institutions invest in the neighborhoods where they do business. An earlier piece of legislation, the Home Mortgage Disclosure Act of 1975, requires depository institutions to collect information on mortgages so that regulators and the public can determine if these institutions are serving the housing needs of communities and neighborhoods in their service areas.[38]

CRA investment has been used primarily, but not always, as a tool to provide more affordable housing. There are other areas where access to capital is an important precursor to development. Asset-building policies, such as the Community Development Financial Institutions Fund (which is part of the U.S. Treasury), have come to prominence in the last 17 years. This policy and program support, in part, a vast array of CDFIs such as community development credit unions that can "bank the unbanked" in this country, and community development capital venture funds that back development projects of scale where mainstream venture funds might not take the risk.[39]

The rise of the asset-building movement has dramatically focused the economic development side of community economic development in ways that bode well for building an architecture of finance in and for poor people and places.[40] Asset building, as we see from the New York example, has also become the frame and end goal for public sector poverty reduction policy.[41]

Changing Strategies in Workforce Development

The link between workforce development and community economic development is ubiquitous. As a nation, we have tried many experiments in "manpower development," many with limited success.[42] As Mueller and Schwartz note regarding the learning:

> First, strategies typically focus on one aspect of the employment problem, under the assumption that this is key to setting other changes in motion. Whether it be physical proximity to jobs, job search assistance, or tax costs, such a narrow focus, reflected also in inflexible program rules, precludes linkages concerned with other aspects of the employment issue and fruitful collaborations across agencies and stakeholders…in the end, success is too often defined…as employment, even when the jobs obtained may not pay enough to move workers out of poverty.[43]

The public and nonprofit sectors learned important lessons from the early manpower experiments and efforts to manage the aftermath of the Personal Responsibility and Work Opportunity Reconciliation Act of 1996 (which changed the workforce landscape) that are now informing innovations in community-based workforce development programs.[44]

Here is how one CEDI is addressing the complex issues surrounding workforce development. The Regional Economic Development Institute (REDI) is a "career and technical education" research, training, and technical assistance center located at the Los Angeles Trade Technical College mentioned earlier. REDI strives to "strengthen the regional economy through the design, delivery, and dissemination of state-of-the art workforce development, vocational, and basic skills education and training programs." The program attempts to "re-engineer" public education (K–16) to match high-demand industries and jobs to California's unemployed and underemployed.[45]

REDI consists of a group of workforce partnerships among industry, labor, community groups, and the government that focus on linking low-income people to higher-wage job opportunities, with the goal of creating a high-skilled workforce in Los Angeles.[46] It aims to strengthen the competitiveness and profitability of its industry partners while at the same time creating a useful educational experience resulting in careers with livable wages.

The program distinguishes itself from other workforce programs because it is focused on "regional and sector-based economic development goals and strategies" as opposed to individual participant success. It also wants to revitalize communities "disconnected from the regional economy" by both developing economic opportunities and providing educational services. REDI attempts to bring together a diverse set of faculty members to teach a broad range of technical, business, and other skills that will help students gain a foothold in their future careers.

The program emphasizes growth in high-wage and high-growth sectors, the attainment of universal skills, curricula created by industry forces, educational pathways in high-wage careers, and a focus on the disadvantaged. REDI is made of four distinct operating units: Research and Development, Workforce Solutions, Career and Technical Education, and Community Enterprise Development.

First, the Research and Development Unit evaluates best practices and innovations from the California community college system as well as community colleges throughout the country. It creates regional economic and labor market studies that explain needs and opportunities in a changing marketplace. The Research and Development Unit also creates the job-training materials and provides technical assistance to faculty members and administrators in the public school system.

Next, the Workforce Solutions Unit ensures that workplace skills are taught in the training program; these skills include workforce literacy, technology, business leadership, organizational effectiveness, and diversity. The organizers attempt to develop and adapt the program as the industry itself changes, ensuring that the program stays up to date in a constantly changing workplace.

The Career and Technical Education Unit creates curricula to meet all levels of industry needs, from "entry level to executive level." Training for entry-level jobs is full time and "fast track," incorporating basic, technical, and soft skills. Skills learned in training are universal and can be applied to any career, including workforce literacy, technology, problem solving, teamwork, and basic math and English. Still, training programs are "tailored to the unique requirements of industry and of the individual student."

Once students complete the training, they are offered work experiences and apprenticeships that are coupled with counseling services so that trainees are supported throughout the experience. These positions are in several high-demand industries, including energy, utilities, hospitality, and logistics. Those who already have established positions in the workforce attend training sessions for the chance to increase their understanding of advances in the industry, keep up with changes, and adapt their skills. Often, these programs are offered both online and in person so that working people can easily learn while keeping a job. In addition, students can complete four-year degrees at participating colleges.

School Reform for Sustainable Community Economic Development

School reform affects community economic development on several fronts: government, the private sector, and nonprofit developers have learned that building or rebuilding homes in economically challenged communities can only accomplish so much.[47] The economic mix of a community is central to building a place of opportunity. Without good schools, it is difficult to attract lower-middle-income to middle-income residents who often possess the social capital necessary for community leadership.

Educational reform is also crucial for helping existing residents climb the ladder of upward mobility the traditional way through the acquisition of basic skills. The link between education reform and community economic development is perhaps the most recent and difficult link in this book because (1) the definition of basic skills has changed for entrance into the knowledge economy and (2) the challenges brought to school doors by students and parents are significant.[48]

The challenges of implementing transformative education reform in poor communities take many forms. Some of the current trends include viewing schools as human development vehicles for students, their families, and the community at large.[49] As such, so-termed community schools offer access to the knowledge assets of a school (the library), medical clinics, job training, and other services. Educating children is still dominant in this model, but the school's role as a focal point in the community is used to good end. Another model sees parents and other community stakeholders organizing to improve the administrative and educational outcomes of local schools.[50]

Charter schools have made inroads in urban communities as an alternative and some CEDIs have chosen to host charters.[51] But CEDIs, especially CDFIs, have found a niche financing charter schools. Still another model sees developers and some CEDI intermediaries getting directly involved through partnership with community institutions and residents in improving local school administration. We are still at an early stage of assessing the success and impact of many of these models and ultimately it might not make sense to choose a winner among any of the models.

The Role of Higher Education

Review the history of community economic development, and colleges and universities turn up as important change agents, especially in rural communities. The Morrill Act of 1862, which created land grant colleges and universities, had a lot to do with developing this early role. Through the years, public-supported institutions of higher education have played an active role in everything from developing community leaders to dispatching extension workers to help local farmers.

This traditional role has not changed, and in fact has deepened. Publicly supported institutions such as community colleges mirror many community economic development principles in their missions and are important partners with other community-based development institutions.

Private higher educational institutions, especially those in urban settings, have found it necessary to become immersed in community economic development out of self-interest. Landlocked, so to speak, these institutions have been reaching out, trying to improve their surrounding communities for rational institutional reasons. As the community goes, so do they. Many such institutions are involved in improving primary and secondary education for children in their surrounding community. Some colleges and universities have become active developers, buying real estate and rebuilding housing directly or in partnership with a CDC.[52]

Take the example of the Alabama A&M University Community Development Corporation (AAMU CDC), which closely collaborates with Alabama A&M University.[53] The AAMU CDC was incorporated in 1999 as "an independent, private not-for-profit entity that focuses on affordable housing development and neighborhood revitalization."[54] Its mission is to work with citizens and local governments to revitalize neighborhoods and build viable and successful communities.

In addition to its revitalization, renovation, and construction projects, the AAMU CDC also operates a Homebuyers Education Club that helps community members by providing them with homeownership and credit counseling services. From 2001 to 2004 the AAMU CDC worked with Madison County, Alabama's Cooperative Extension System, and the university itself to provide after-school tutoring and mentoring for public school students struggling academically.

Core funding comes from several sources: Alabama A&M University provides a quite significant 50 percent of funding, followed closely by the city of Huntsville, with 40 percent of the support.[55] Recently, the CDC has embarked on a new project, the construction of low- and moderate-income housing close to the university that promises to substantially improve the community both socially and economically. The mixed-income project will attract middle-income professionals by providing access to high-quality, reasonably priced homes.

Construction on the homes began in August 2008 and is expected to reach completion by summer 2011. RBC BANK and the Federal Home Loan Bank of Atlanta (which is subsidizing mortgages through down payment assistance) are financing the $1.6 million project. Additionally, AAMU CDC will provide social services to residents, including child care services in conjunction with the Alabama A&M University Child Development Center, after-school tutoring and mentoring for older children in a partnership with the Bo Matthews Center of Excellence, employment opportunities for adults through West Corporation, a call center, and career counseling provided by the Madison County Skills Center.

Summary

These are the categories, the components, of sustainable community economic development. Sustainability is defined as: (1) any strategy or component that focuses its attention on preserving natural assets but with due attention to livelihoods and poverty reduction, and (2) the ability and coherence of any category and strategy to sustain institutional attention to people and place development over time. The goal is not to find all the components in one place or strategy. Rather, the task is to present examples of promising strategies with many of the categories naturally woven into community economic development practice.

Categories where innovations are sought recognize the critical importance of balancing people and place development in one overarching framework. The framework cannot be seamless, nor can it promise predictable results. What it seeks to do is lift up interesting work in the field that can get us to better outcomes in the effort to reduce concentrated poverty and encourage places of opportunity.

Endnotes

1. Linking environmental stewardship to helping the poor might seem a stretch, but not so when considering that sprawl development is (1) depleting land and other resources while (2) helping to deplete fiscal support for the communities left in the wake of sprawl development and (3) depleting the social and public capital sprawl-affected communities need to remain politically and economically viable.

2. Reference to policy issue networks is best understood in the context of the agenda-setting literature, although innovation is not the central force driving that body of work. See the important work of Kingdon (2003); also see Howlett (1999).
3. Morse, Buss, and Kinghorn (2007, p 5).
4. Gazley (2008).
5. Carayannis and Campbell (2007); Organisation for Economic Co-operation and Development (1999); H. Brown (2007); Baumgartner and Jones (1991).
6. Liou and Stroh (1998); Vidal and Keys (2005); Bingham, Nabatchi, and O'Leary (2005).
7. P. M. Brown (2006).
8. Elements of these definitions can be found in Donahue (2005); Bourn (2006); Kamarck (2003); Armstrong and Ford (2002); and Walters (2001).
9. Osborne and Gaebler (1993); Rivlin (1992). The role and perception of the public sector has shifted over the past 40 years. From the expansiveness of the Great Society and the belief that the public sector could change the fortunes of poor places and people, the perception of government shifted to one of public caution and disbelief in the government's ability to do anything consequential. The media and political discourse support this corrosive doubting of government's ability to play a role in positive change much beyond the most elemental duties. It does not help the progovernment argument when elected officials and public managers provide fodder for the media with acts of poor management or judgment born of human frailty. The reality is that government accountability, effectiveness, and productivity are improving, spurred on by trends such as the "reinventing government" movement, performance management, increasing professionalization of the civil service, and the vast improvement in information technology and management.
10. Borins (1998); Hula and Jackson-Elmoore (2000); Salamon (1995); United States Congress, Joint Economic Committee (1993).
11. Alford and Hughes (2008).
12. Cunningham, Furdell, and McKinney (2007); Henton, Melville, and Walesh (1997); Kanter (1995); and Safford (2009).
13. Tiebout (1956).
14. Cunningham, Furdell, and McKinney (2007, pp. 1–35).
15. http://www.nyc.gov/html/ceo/html/about/commission.shtml. (accessed October 8, 2008)
16. http://www.nyc.gov/html/ceo/html/about/about.shtml. (accessed October 8, 2008)
17. Initially, the Innovation Fund included approximately $60 million in city funds, approximately $42 million for the Child Care Tax Credit, over $11 million in city education funds, and approximately $7 million in state and federal funding.
18. Brière and Rawlings (2006).
19. Like many of the other Center for Opportunity programs, this effort is being evaluated through random assignment methodology. The New York City's "CBO Outreach" pilot recognizes the built capacity of New York's CEDIs to access jobseekers. Working with these organizations has led to an aggressive job-matching program with New York City employers. The effort is showing promising results in getting jobs for hard-to-place low-income individuals. Again, the effort is promising but needs more time for a significant evaluation of impact.
20. http://www.nyc.gov/html/sbs/wf1/html/home/home.shtml. (accessed October 8, 2008)

21. These descriptions are excerpted and fuller details can be found at http://www.nyc.gov/html/ceo/html/programs/programs.shtml. (accessed October 8, 2008)
22. One important byproduct is that Mayor Bloomberg and mayors from other major cities are now pressing for a national innovation fund, modeled after New York's, that would set a national strategic vision nationwide for achieving measurable results in reducing poverty. "Mayor Bloomberg Announces Major Progress For New York City Anti-Poverty Strategy Under Center For Economic Opportunity," http://www.ny c.gov:80/portal/site/ nycgov/menu item.c0935b9 a57bb4ef3daf 2f1c701c789a 0/index.jsp?page ID=mayor_p ress_releas e&catID=1194&d oc_name=http%3A%2F%2F www.nyc.g ov%2Fhtml%2Fom% 2Fhtml%2F200 9a%2Fpr179-09.html&cc=un used1978&rc=1194&ndi=1. (accessed October 8, 2008)
23. Bratt et al. (1995, Chapter 3).
24. The General Accountability Office (2007a) makes this general point in relation to all nonprofit organizations in their role as proxies for the public sector.
25. Anglin (2000).
26. For a discussion on CEDI accountability, see Simon (2001, pp. 199–230).
27. See Vidal and Keyes (2005) for support of my argument here.
28. "Community development" is an umbrella term for a set of strategies that promote (1) collective and individual voice in any given national, regional, and local political system; (2) social, cultural, and economic advancement by and for a group of individuals defined by a physical place; and (3) strong social networks that produce trust, reciprocity, and ultimately collective action.
29. Johnson's antipoverty ideas were an amalgam of existing policy theories regarding poverty. Many argued that the problem rested on lack of education and training for existing jobs; others argued that lack of place economic development was the main challenge. Still another side of the equation was the realization by Johnson and his administration that political empowerment was inextricably linked to poverty. In essence, Johnson argued that one of the major problems of poor America was nonparticipation in the political process (and for African Americans, the historical exclusion from the process).
30. The clearest evidence of Johnson's desires was Title VII of the 1964 Economic Opportunity Act (EOA). The Act required local government and the community agencies with which they worked to encourage the "maximum feasible participation of the poor" in the development and operation of community-based poverty programs. Called "community action," the federal government strongly encouraged the participation of low-income individuals in all facets of policy and program development. The Office of Economic Opportunity, which implemented EOA, represented a new way of the federal government addressing local problems. Before the EOA, the federal government respected state and local government prerogatives by sending resources for programs through them. The EOA authorized funds directly to qualified Community Action Agencies, which caused a great uproar and scaling back of the EOA and the OEO. By then, the organized role of communities could not be excised from government policy toward poor and marginalized communities.
31. http://www.oup.org/grantee/orgDetail.asp?orgid=358&myHeadID=TCUP&yr=2001 (accessed June 19, 2009).
32. http://www.oup.org/grantee/AbstractDetail.asp?Abstract=1868&Program=TCUP (accessed June 19, 2009).

33. http://www.oup.org/grantee/orgDetail.asp?orgid=358&myHeadID=TCUP&yr=2008 (accessed June 19, 2009).

34. http://www.menominee.edu/01/CommunityServices/EducationOutreach.html (accessed June 19, 2009).

35. http://www.menominee.edu/01/CommunityServices/EO_Workshops.html (accessed June 19, 2009).

36. http://www.menominee.edu/01/CommunityServices/EO_TRANS.html (accessed June 19, 2009).

37. http://www.menominee.edu/01/CommunityServices/SDISustainability.html (accessed June 22, 2009).

38. The act required depository institutions and their subsidiaries to provide the total number and dollar amount of mortgages that originated and were purchased in the local market by census tract.

39. http://www.cdvca.org/. (accessed June 22, 2009)

40. See Shapiro and Wolff (2001) for a range of arguments supporting the importance of assets as the base of an antipoverty policy.

41. Asset building, economic opportunity, and wealth building are synonyms for the same underlying quest to help the poor achieve economic self-determination.

42. Mueller and Schwartz (1998).

43. Mueller and Schwartz (1998, pp. 42–43).

44. See Giloth (1998, pp. 1–13).

45. http://www.lattc.edu/dept/lattc/REDI/about.html. (accessed June 23, 2009)

46. See Harrison and Weiss (1998) for a well-reasoned discussion of the value of what they call "citizen-neighborhood-college-employer networks" (p. 35).

47. Khadduri, Schwartz, and Turnham (2007) and Chung (2002).

48. Duncan and Brooks-Gunn (1997) and Harrison and Weiss (1998).

49. Abrams and Gibbs (2000); Crowson and Boyd (2001); Dryfoos (1995); O'Looney (1996); and Warren (2005).

50. Comer (1991), Shirley (1997), and Payne (2008).

51. P. M. Brown (2006).

52. Maurrasse (2001).

53. http://www.aamucdc.org/funds.html. (accessed June 24, 2009)

54. http://www.knowledgeplex.org/news/2972661.html. (accessed June 24, 2009)

55. http://www.aamucdc.org/funds.html. The remaining 10 percent of assistance comes from the Structured Employment Economic Development Corporation (Seedco), a New York-based CED intermediary, Madison County, HUD, the Federal Home Loan Bank of Atlanta, Fannie Mae, and Am South Bank. (accessed June 24, 2009)

Chapter 4

Locally Based Community Economic Development Institutions: A Base for Innovation

Community economic development institutions (CEDIs) are organizations whose central mission is building the individual and collective assets of poor communities so residents can enter the economic mainstream. By definition, community economic development institutions reside in a community or a place. Community development corporations (CDCs) are the best-known subset of CEDIs, but they are not the only organizations whose mission is centrally or partially economic development. Some Urban Leagues across the country are CEDIs, and so are many YMCAs, United Ways, and Mutual Housing Associations, not to mention a legion of community-based or community-centered organizations with no concrete label that do the work of community economic development.[1]

I focus attention on CDCs here because they were the first publicly supported organizational innovation to challenge the traditional economic development paradigm giving voice and representation to poor communities. In addition, CDCs are now widely accepted and supported across the political spectrum.[2] Supported first by philanthropy and then the public sector, community development corporations evolved to build a representative voice in many aspects of development while implementing self-help projects, primarily economic development, in poor communities.[3]

CDCs represent an important advance and reflect recognition that the voice and interests of poor people and places are central to the development process. CDCs can be valuable tools in combating place and people poverty, especially when used in partnership with government and the private sector, but their role as development agents has to evolve to stay relevant in today's environment. Can CDCs go beyond the fact that they were once innovations holding the promise of economic inclusion for marginalized groups, or have they outlived their time?

Community Development Corporations

The first publicly supported CDCs came about as a result of an amendment to the Economic Opportunities Act that created the Special Impact Program (SIP) and Title VII funding.[4] CDCs grew in number and effectiveness in the post-Great Society period as a result of federal support of local government efforts at community economic development, the rise of national and local intermediaries that provide financial and technical assistance to community-based development organizations, and the increasing role of the private sector in supporting CED projects.[5]

There is no universal legal definition for CDCs. By mission and convention, CDCs are place-based nonprofit organizations that provide leadership in revitalizing economically challenged communities. That they work in a specific place with core representation from the community is an important way in which CDCs are distinguished from other CEDIs and nonprofits.

Often residents, congregations, and other community stakeholders start a CDC as a vehicle for physical development. Averaging fewer than 10 employees, CDCs typically help to coordinate community planning and act as developers of affordable housing and commercial development. CDCs often venture into job creation directly through equity stakes in franchises or small businesses. Some CDCs also provide a variety of social services to their target area.[6]

There is no solid data on the number of CDCs in the United States, partly because the definition of a CDC is so fluid. Melendez and Servon (2007) compiled perhaps the best database on community-based development organizations (housing, economic development, and workforce development being central to their programmatic offerings). They estimate that approximately 8,358 CDCs operate across the country in urban and nonurban areas.[7]

Government Support

The system that has slowly but steadily evolved to support CEDIs and CDCs is nothing short of remarkable, yet it is patched together like a quilt. Much of this support is channeled through local governments and sustains many community development activities and CEDIs across the nation.

Federal and local governments have supported CEDIs and their community economic development work for many years, primarily through the Community Development Block Grant (CDBG) funds administered through the Department of Housing and Urban Development. As Quigley points out, CDBGs "are...the backbone of all federal expenditures on urban and regional development activities, constituting more than half of all these expenditures."[8]

The Housing and Community Development Act of 1974 is the authorizing legislation for the CDBG program. When it was passed, the Act folded a number of categorical housing programs (the remnants of Urban Renewal) and Model Cities into a block grant for local jurisdictions to choose how to rebuild blighted communities and neighborhoods.[9] Today, this grant program is the closest thing we have to a national community development policy (see Figure 4.1 for CDBG expenditures from 1980–2009).[10]

CDBG grants to state and local jurisdictions are determined by a mathematical formula made up of community need measures such as the extent of poverty, population, age of housing and overcrowding, and declining population growth. CDBGs are appropriated annually, then allocated between state and local jurisdictions called "nonentitlement" and "entitlement" communities. Entitlement communities are cities of 50,000 or more people and urban counties with a population of 200,000 or more. States distribute CDBG funds to nonentitlement localities

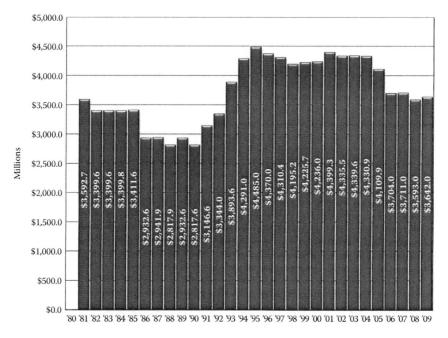

Figure 4.1 Community Development Block Grants expenditure (1980 to 2009).

that are not qualified as entitlement communities. To receive CDBGs, jurisdictions prepare detailed plans demonstrating that:

- Seventy percent of CDBG funds will be used for activities benefiting low- and moderate-income individuals.
- Resources will be targeted toward the elimination of slums or blight.
- Low- or moderate-income individuals are part of the implementation and governance process.

Table 4.1 shows the range of activities funded by the Community Development Block. These activities go beyond just the work of CEDIs and CDCs, and take into account a range of community development and community economic development activities taken on by state and local government.

Usually, local planning or economic development offices administer CDBG grants. CEDIs are given yearly operational or project support carved from CDBGs that varies widely from jurisdiction to jurisdiction. Some cities allocate small amounts of operational support to support a number of CEDIs, whereas other jurisdictions are strategically opting to choose performing CEDIs and provide them with enough operational resources to accomplish their mission.

It is tempting to argue for government efficiency by supporting the model where star performers are rewarded or a metric using cost/benefit analysis. The reality is that CDBG grants for CEDIs are often grafted onto local ward and neighborhood politics. Mayors and city council members often support organizations with thin capacity because the local organization is an adjunct of their electoral enterprise or supporting the CEDI is seen as responsive to community needs. The complications of democratic politics cannot be ignored, nor should we automatically make this a negative scenario.

One jurisdiction's inefficient spread of resources is another jurisdiction's attempt at building the capacity of locally based development organizations to address community problems. The two poles, although nuanced, should be judged in any given situation by the underlying development strategy employed by the jurisdiction.

Community Reinvestment Act

Arguably, the Community Reinvestment Act of 1977 (CRA), administered by the Office of the Comptroller of the Currency (OCC), is the most innovative and effective public policy constituted to redirect private investment back to urban and rural areas. Estimates are that since 1977, CRA has leveraged six trillion dollars for projects (many conceived and implemented by CDCs) in moderate- and low-income minority communities.[11] Figure 4.2 provides a breakdown of CRA obligations from 1996 to 2007.[12]

Table 4.1   FY 2008 CDBG Accomplishments

Eligible Activity	*Households Assisted*
Homeownership Assistance (Not Direct)	512
Construction of Housing	2,157
Direct Homeownership Assistance	4,009
Rehabilitation: Single-Unit Residential	109,965
Rehabilitation: Multi-Unit Residential	14,317
Public Housing Modernization	4,313
Rehabilitation: Other Publicly Owned Residential Buildings	282
Energy Efficiency Improvements	2,745
Acquisition for Rehabilitation	1,853
Rehabilitation Administration	7,943
Lead-Based Paint/Lead Hazard Test/Abatement	764
Residential Historic Preservation	394
Total Households Assisted	**149,254**
Eligible Activity	*Jobs Created/ Retained*
Acquisition of Real Property	1,378
Public Facilities and Improvements (General)	2,948
Clearance and Demolition	9
Relocation	0
Privately Owned Utilities	293
Rehabilitation: Publicly or Privately Owned Commercial/ Industrial	138
Nonresidential Historic Preservation	0
Commercial/Industrial Land Acquisition/Disposition	123
Commercial/Industrial Infrastructure Development	6,847

(continued)

Table 4.1 (*Continued*)   FY 2008 CDBG Accomplishments

Eligible Activity	Jobs Created/ Retained
Commercial/Industrial Building Acquisition, Construction, Rehabilitation	428
Other Commercial/Industrial Improvements	465
Direct: Financial Assistance to For-Profit Businesses	14,014
Direct: Technical Assistance	3,278
Microenterprise Assistance	1,776
CDBG Nonprofit Organization Capacity Building	5
CDBG Assistance to Institutions of Higher Education	21
Total Jobs Created/Retained	**31,723**

Eligible Activity	Number of Persons Benefiting	Persons for Whom Services Were Available
Operating Costs of Homeless/AIDs Patients Programs	460,344	0
Public Services (General)	7,745,942	26,781,497
Senior Services	1,300,572	0
Services for the Disabled	116,459	0
Legal Services	41,327	77,552
Youth Services	1,233,661	0
Transportation Services	1,246,349	341,411
Substance Abuse Services	27,695	4,751
Battered and Abused Spouses	128,212	0
Employment Training	145,328	143,328
Crime Awareness/Prevention	43,316	5,203,941
Fair Housing Activities	99,420	967,945

Table 4.1 (*Continued*)   **FY 2008 CDBG Accomplishments**

Eligible Activity	Number of Persons Benefiting	Persons for Whom Services Were Available
Tenant/Landlord Counseling	56,990	0
Child Care Services	80,608	0
Health Services	600,308	774,571
Abused and Neglected Children	57,109	0
Mental Heath Services	81,587	0
Screening for Lead-Based Paint/Lead Hazards Poisoning	687	0
Subsistence Payments	22,717	0
Total Persons	13,488,631	34,294,996
Rental Housing Subsidies (HOME Tenant-Based Rental Assistance)	1,304	0
Security Deposits	2,752	0
Total Households	**4,056**	**0**

Eligible Activity	Number of Persons Benefiting	Number of Persons for Whom Facilities Were Available
Public Facilities and Improvements (General)	1,163,989	5,023,543
Senior Centers	170,364	0
Centers for the Disabled/Handicapped	22,852	0
Homeless Facilities (Not Operating Costs)	165,881	0
Youth Centers/Facilities	52,418	0
Neighborhood Facilities	223,904	2,031,594
Parks, Recreational Facilities	173,138	3,316,856

(continued)

Table 4.1 (Continued)   FY 2008 CDBG Accomplishments

Eligible Activity	Number of Persons Benefiting	Number of Persons for Whom Facilities Were Available
Parking Facilities	45,308	35,803
Solid Waste Disposal Facilities	0	23,269
Flood and Drainage Facilities	17,159	163,521
Water/Sewer Improvements	25,065	1,029,991
Street Improvements	150,688	2,642,562
Sidewalks	359,029	2,802,171
Child Care Centers/Facilities for Children	8,562	0
Tree Planting	0	476,813
Fire Stations/Equipment	3,954	724,878
Health Facilities	126,491	386,854
Abused and Neglected Children Facilities	5,955	0
Asbestos Removal	0	951
Facilities for AIDs Patients (not operating costs)	0	0
Total Persons	**2,714,757**	**18,658,806**

Source: Department of Housing and Urban Development

The CRA requires that banks and other deposit-taking financial institutions be held accountable for how well they make the effort to and, in fact, commit, capital to low- and moderate-income communities. Laggard financial institutions can find their applications to the OCC for geographic expansion held up by challenges from community groups or regulators.

Originally fought by banking interests on the grounds that CRA was forcing them to invest in unprofitable communities, banks found the opposite.[13] They found that working with CDCs and other community-based development institutions lowered their risk because they were partnering with these organizations to build affordable housing or make loans for economic development.[14] Banks found that money could be made in neighborhoods once thought marginal. Before the recent meltdown in the financial markets, banks had acquired an expertise in

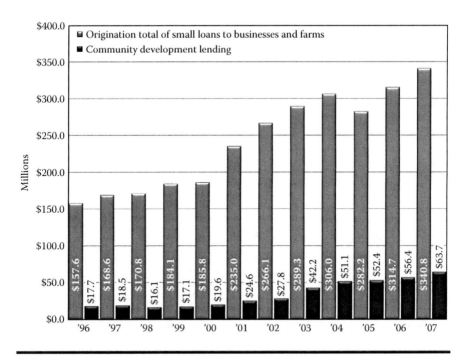

Figure 4.2   Community Reinvestment Act obligations (1996 to 2007).

moderate- and low-income communities, so much so that they were executing deals well beyond their CRA obligations.[15]

Many banks started their own bank CDC, which is different from the standard definition of a CDC. In the 1990s, when banks began expanding their experience in "new markets," they competed to find "bankable" economic development and housing deals in communities that were off limits in the 1980s. These bank CDCs were subsidiaries encouraged by the CRA rules to bring the financing and development in-house to make sure that deals were "flowing," satisfying their CRA obligations and making money. This is not a negative reflection. In fact, these bank CDCs had to partner with actual community-based development organizations to build housing and start businesses. Many CDCs and CEDIs were able to establish track records with major banks under this win–win regime that carried the relationship, in some cases, well beyond the need to use CRA as the "stick," especially when the New Markets Tax Credit came on the scene.

The Low Income Housing Tax Credit

The Low Income Housing Tax Credit (LIHTC) is similar to and often used in conjunction with the CRA. It allows for the flow of mainstream capital to asset-poor communities for affordable housing development. It is a dollar-for-dollar credit to investors in the development of low-income rental housing and was created as part of the Tax Reform Act of 1986.

The LIHTC program authorizes state housing credit agencies (HCAs) to award federal tax credits to developers of affordable rental housing.[16] The tax credits are then used by developers to raise equity financing for real estate projects. Equity capital generated from the tax credits lowers the debt load on LIHTC properties, making it easier to offer affordable rents. In turn, investors receive a dollar-for-dollar reduction in their federal tax liability. Figure 4.3 provides a dollar value for the tax credit from 1987 to 2007.[17]

The LIHTC proved an important tool for community economic development, especially the housing end of it.[18] The LIHTC is not without its detractors. Some observers argue that the tax credit is an effective but inefficient way to encourage affordable housing. Transaction costs are high in the application and administration of the credit. Then again, at the pinnacle of its use, the credit gave well-above market rates of return to individual investors in tandem with tax relief.[19] That has since changed, but concern remains with critics asking, "Why not support the production of affordable housing through direct expenditures?"

Others in the civil rights community argue that the credit is responsible for enforcing racial and economic segregation. Essentially, they maintain that the credits are used to build affordable rental housing in already segregated urban

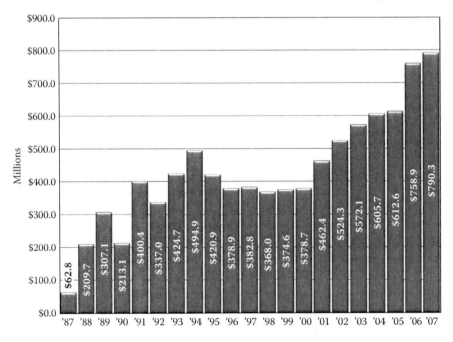

Figure 4.3   Low Income Housing Tax Credits (1987 to 2007).

communities. In this respect, the LIHTC might violate the nation's fair housing laws. There is no denying that LIHTCs are used to develop housing in racially segregated communities, but the credits are not a causal factor; rather, they are correlative.[20]

The questions about the LIHTC are fair and well placed. Administration and ease of use have dramatically improved over the years, indicating that administrators and Congress heard the criticisms, learned, and improved the tool.[21] Yet even with past and present criticism the LIHTC has accomplished something beyond questions of efficiency, effectiveness, and equality.[22]

In the 1980s, newly emerging community economic development intermediaries such as the Local Initiative Support Corporation and the Enterprise Foundation (now Enterprise Community Partners) were able to quickly expand and grow thanks to their ability to (1) understand the complicated features of the program, (2) bundle projects for investors, and (3) help CDCs complete the projects, once funded, through organizational and technical assistance. The Tax Reform Act and the LIHTC were responsible for the development of the field of community economic development in a way unmatched by any other public policy.

The LIHTC not only brought mainstream capital to bear in low-wealth markets but also bolstered the fortunes of young institutions in the community economic development network at a time when direct expenditures for CDCs were being withdrawn.[23] Community economic developers grew to use the LIHTC and CRA in tandem to reshape the urban and rural landscape in ways unimagined at the beginning of the economic development movement. Do we still need a low-income tax credit? We still need some version of the tax credit for a very practical reason: tax expenditures have proved to be a very good way to link community economic development to mainstream markets and vice versa. There is tremendous long-term benefit to that. The more mainstream markets know and feel comfortable investing in low-income communities, the more community economic development can achieve one aspect of sustainability. So the issue is not whether the tool should survive, but how to improve its effectiveness and efficiency.[24]

New Markets Tax Credit Program

On December 21, 2000, shortly before he left office, President Bill Clinton signed the bipartisan-supported Community Renewal Tax Relief Act into law. The Act included two initiatives, the New Markets Tax Credit (NMTC) and the New Markets Venture Capital programs. The NMTC program is administered through the U.S. Department of Treasury's Community Development Financial Institutions (CDFI) Fund. Unlike previous legislation passed to increase affordable housing units within distressed communities, NMTC seeks to raise business activities in distressed communities (including urban and rural communities).

The program allows taxpayers to receive tax incentives (credit against their federal income tax) for making equity investments into certain community development entities (CDEs). CDEs must then invest "substantially all" (85 percent) of those investments made by investors (such as banks and individuals) into businesses in low-income and underserved communities. Table 4.2 summarizes the allocation rounds of the New Markets Tax Credit from 2003 to 2008.

The NMTC program allows investors to purchase stock or capital interest in qualified CDEs. CDEs subsequently make businesses investments in low-income communities. The primary goal of NMTC is to create jobs in low-income areas and promote economic development. In addition, investors receive a tax credit, claimed over a seven-year period. The first three years, investors receive credit on 5 percent of the original investment amount, annually. The next four years, investors receive credit on 6 percent of the original investment amount. The credit provided to the investor totals 39 percent of the cost of the investment. Supporters of the program believe that by increasing the capital base in low-income communities, the tax credit will enable CDEs to lend and invest more, to attract additional outside capital, and to bring even more private-sector activity into low-income areas.

Table 4.2   New Markets Tax Credit 2003–2008

NMTC Allocation Rounds	Allocation Year	Original Allocation Years	Amount Allocated ($) (in Billions)
Round 1	2003	2001–2002	2.5
Round 2	2004	2003–2004	3.5
Round 3	2005	2005	2.0
Round 4	2006	2006	4.1
Round 5	2007	2007	3.9
Round 6	2008	2008	3.5
Total			19.5

Source: Table and notes taken from General Accountability Office (2007b).

Notes: The amounts available to be allocated in Round 4 and Round 5 were increased by $600 million and $400 million, respectively, because of increased NMTC allocation limits targeted toward the GO Zone. Congress initially only authorized NMTC allocation authority through 2007. However, the Tax Relief and Health Care Act of 2006 (Pub. L. No. 109-432) extended NMTC allocation authority for one year (through 2008) with an additional $3.5 billion of NMTC allocation authority.

To qualify as a CDE, the organization must demonstrate a primary mission of serving low-income communities or low-income persons. CDEs must also maintain accountability to residents of low-income communities through representation on a governing board or advisory board. Eligible CDEs can include for-profit community development financial institutions (CDFIs), for-profit subsidiaries of community development corporations, Small Business Administration-approved New Markets Venture Capital companies, and Specialized Small Business Investment Companies.[25]

Use of the New Markets Tax Credit has led to significant economic development projects in low-income communities.[26] In Missouri, for example, a group of businesses teamed up to finance the renovation of an old U.S. Customhouse and Post Office in St. Louis. Altogether, the Trust for Historical Preservation, the Enterprise Social Investment Corporation (ESIC), Bank of America, and the Missouri Development Finance Board used Historic and NMTC tax credits to fund the construction and remodeling of the historic building. The National Trust's CDE made a tax credit equity investment of $25.5 million (which combined federal, state, Historic, and New Markets tax credits), and ESIC CDE made a first mortgage loan of $8.2 million.[27] In the end, the 242,000-square-foot building created approximately 1,458 construction jobs, 850 permanent jobs, and about $8 million in state and local tax revenue.

In another instance, Bethel New Life, a faith-based community development corporation located on the West Side of Chicago, was awarded $4 million in tax credits in the first round of New Markets Tax Credit (NMTC) allocations.[28] Bethel used these tax credits to expand its housing development program while also increasing its investments in commercial projects to expand its development efforts and enhance the financial sustainability of its various real estate developments.

The NMTC funds allowed Bethel to include more financial partners in its efforts to bring new investment dollars into the lower-income African American home community. Bethel allocated the funds with 57 percent going toward establishing a revolving construction loan fund for affordable home-ownership housing, enabling Bethel to expand its construction of single-family homes from 14 to 50 annually.

The commercial development is a 23,000-square-foot green building near a transit spot with six commercial storefronts, including an employment center for Bethel and a day care center for over 100 children. It replaced a "rundown, neglected corner."[29] Even though funders had turned Bethel down for financing before, due to the building's location and funding uncertainty for the employment center and the day care, the NMTCs allowed Bethel to get construction financing. This, in turn, gave it the ability to create a more flexible interest-only loan at a lower interest rate, which lowered the costs of operating the day care and employment center during the building's initial years of operation.

Is the New Markets Tax Credit effective? The available evidence suggests that the credit is an effective tool. A 2007 Government Accountability Office (GAO) assessment reported that banks and individuals comprise the largest proportion of investors, which by January of the assessment year stood at $12.1 billion in credit authority. The majority of investment in low-income communities had been used for either commercial real estate rehabilitation or new commercial real estate construction. In looking at the total view of the NMTC, the GAO concluded:

> The results of our survey and statistical analysis are consistent with the NMTC program increasing investment in eligible low-income communities by the investors that participate in the program and with this investment coming primarily from funds shifted from other uses. Such a shift would be one indicator that the NMTC program is effective because the NMTC sought to increase investment in eligible low-income communities. An estimated 64 percent of the NMTC investors reported that they increased the share of their investment budget for low-income communities because of the credit.[30]

The Community Development Block Grant, the Community Reinvestment Act, the Low Income Housing Tax Credit, and the New Markets Tax Credit are not the only funding streams supporting the work of CEDIs. They remain, however, the most used and flexible means to support the work of community economic development, especially in the context of the United States, where public policy is filtered through the lens of how it affects markets and politics. Whatever the limitations of this body of policies, they have been immensely important to the ongoing project of people and place development.

The Management Challenge

Building strong community organizations takes time and effort. The difficulties in building a plural base of community leaders who understand nonprofit management have produced uneven patterns of strength in the CDC model. Part of the problem is the attractiveness of community-based economic development as a public policy strategy. Who can argue with a strategy that is market-oriented and based in conceptions of self-help along with structured connections to the political and economic mainstream?

After the initial experiments in the 1960s, there were low barriers to entry for communities wanting to start a CDC. Funders and other stakeholders tacitly encouraged the growth in these organizations until it became obvious that many were not performing well.

CDC growth in the 1990s and beyond presents a conundrum for funders: the funding community (defined as philanthropists and the public and private sectors) realized that the increasing number of CDCs diluted available resources, thereby creating weak organizations. Funders were unwilling to tell poor, often minority communities that starting a CDC may not be the best strategy for every community.

The management challenge is ongoing.[31] As the field evolves, local governments, philanthropists, and community development intermediaries are encouraging self-reflection, pushing for increased attention to building the capacity of community leaders who can not only organize communities but also build and manage strong organizations.[32]

Locally based CEDIs are evolving, changing their organizational forms and strategies to manage challenges in their communities such as welfare reform and decentralized development that has dispersed talent and capital away from the urban core.[33] In both rural and urban contexts, CEDIs are adjusting and can play an innovative role in making poor places in any region more competitive and improving the quality of life.[34]

The Unity Council: Connecting Transit-Oriented Development to Community Economic Development

One key to continued innovation is to seek the benefits of comparative advantage. This may mean that CEDIs should be less focused on development and play more of a leadership and planning role in their communities. It may also mean that CEDIs become more focused on knowledge creation, defining and stating the problems for the larger world. Future innovation by CEDIs should not be one-dimensional; rather, it should include a full panoply of choices that will allow them to act in many different ways and partner with other members of the community economic world to accomplish similar goals. The following discussion highlights two CEDIs that are trying innovative strategies within a regional frame while still maintaining a core set of place-based strategies.

The Unity Council, a CDC formerly known as the Spanish Speaking Unity Council, recognized that the status quo was not viable for a community marked by 70 percent poverty. At the end of the 1980s and into early 1990s, the Unity Council, like many of the early CDCs supported by the SIP and Title VII funds, was struggling. Once an established community institution building affordable housing for seniors and others and providing a range of social services for residents of the Fruitvale section of Oakland, California, it went through a period of extended decline beginning in 1982.

The organization had gone through a period of leadership turbulence when, in 1989, the board asked Arabella Martinez, its founding director, to return as executive director. Martinez, one of the seminal thinkers and practitioners in CED, realized that the landscape had changed.[35] CDCs practicing CED had to find new ways of doing their craft.

The organization's opportunity for renewal and continued relevance presented itself in 1992 in the form of a proposed Bay Area Rapid Transit (BART) multi-level parking facility adjacent to the BART stop in Fruitvale. The Unity Council opposed the facility and pressured state and local government to rethink the best use of the land. In 1992, the Unity Council was granted $185,000 in Community Development Block Grant (CDBG) funds to study and propose alternative uses of the site.

Working with the National Transit Access Center at the University of California–Berkeley, the Unity Council held a community design symposium that lifted up the idea of a multipurpose transit village that would economically revitalize the community and build more affordable housing.[36] The community vetted the plans and in 1996 the City of Oakland passed a zoning ordinance that created a new transit village zone, which allowed higher-density, mixed-use development. By 1997, working with BART, the Unity Council and its development corporation, the Fruitvale Development Corporation (FDC), gained site control through a land swap to build its parking facility near the station. In 1997, the Fruitvale Transit Village broke ground, and in 2003 the project was complete.

Now fully built, the transit village is a 257,000-square-foot complex with an active, retail-lined connector between the BART station and the neighborhood's primary retail artery. An attractive pedestrian street and plaza serve as a center for community activity. The complex includes 47 units of mixed-income housing, 114,000 square feet of community services (clinic, library, senior center) and office space (including the Unity Council's headquarters), and 40,000 square feet of neighborhood retail (shops and restaurants), including a convenience store, bank, and a number of restaurants. See Figures 4.4a and 4.4b.

Transit-oriented development is not going to solve all the problems of the Fruitvale community.[37] It is, however, creating the reality that the community is worth investing in and that there are natural advantages for residents and potential residents who want direct access to their jobs in San Francisco. The central role of the Unity Council in building this development platform has helped to encourage mixed-income development in a depressed community in the core of the region and illustrates the innovative way a CDC can play a role in promoting sustainable development.

The Mountain Association for Community Economic Development: Bridging the Regional Divide

CEDIs and CDCs are rooted in place, and there is little evidence that their work in neighborhoods will be eclipsed any time soon. The question is how CEDIs that have been tethered to one place will survive now that their underlying function is changing. Rural CEDIs (this is where labeling is important) have never been

Figure 4.4a   The Fruitvale Transit Village.

that tied to a discrete geographic area. For rural CEDIs, the challenges of shifting capital and people have been occurring for some time. Complicating this long-term dynamic are the deeply entrenched pockets of poverty found in many rural settings where low-paying, natural-resource-extractive industries dominate.[38] They can provide some lessons; in fact, at least one rural CEDI is providing many innovative lessons on how to thrive in this new economic environment.

The Mountain Association for Community Economic Development (MACED) was founded in 1976 to serve the most disadvantaged low- and middle-income residents of Kentucky and central Appalachia, with a primary focus on the 51 Appalachian counties of eastern Kentucky. Like many nonprofits, MACED has gone up and down in strength and accomplishment over the years, but it has maintained its focus on economic development.

Figure 4.4b   The Fruitvale Transit Village.

The challenges facing eastern Kentucky and central Appalachia today are daunting and complex. The regional economy was built on coal mining and logging, both extractive industries that create significant environmental destruction and economic dependency. Coal remains a major force; however, it is declining as a share of the regional economy. Employment in Kentucky's coal industry decreased from 35,000 jobs in 1980 to 15,010 in 2006, although there has been a recent upward trend.

The regional economy has made a transition over the last decade to low-wage service jobs and transfer payments as the economic base for families and communities.[39] The sum total is a region defined by a complex set of challenges, including declining natural-resource-based extractive industries, environmental degradation (particularly due to mountaintop removal during coal mining and significant timber harvesting), and high rates of poverty.

MACED views the economic and ecological challenges of the central Appalachian region as an opportunity to diversify the regional economy to provide wealth-building opportunities for local people and protect the natural environment. Terming its policy "regional sustainable development," MACED and its partners are organizing to stop mountaintop removal and working with state governments to look beyond the usual industrial recruitment strategies to implement regionally sustainable development strategies.[40]

Important to MACED's vision of sustainable development are (1) strengthening private and nonprofit enterprises working to make renewable energy, sustainable forestry, and other sectors successful; (2) bringing capital investment to sustainable economic development enterprises; and (3) improving state and local policies that build wealth and protect the environment.

MACED's primary method of investing in communities is through its Business and Enterprise Development Program. This program builds financial assets, creates quality jobs, and develops entrepreneurial capacity in economically distressed communities. MACED offers three tools to assist in this goal:

Microloans provide capital and access to technical assistance needed for low-income people to be self-employed or generate supplementary income. Loan amounts range from $1,000 to $35,000.
Targeted enterprise loans strengthen key business fields that provide needed community benefits such as community services (focusing on child care and health care), natural resources, and cultural assets. Loan amounts generally range from $35,000 to $700,000.
Economic development business loans create quality jobs for low-income people and diversify the local economy by funding the expansion of small businesses or start-ups. Loan amounts typically range from $35,000 to $700,000.

In addition, MACED helps sustain and grow enterprises by combining its investment capital with technical assistance to increase the capacity of entrepreneurs. MACED focuses its attention on one-on-one technical and financial management support and uses its loan products as tools to help ensure managed growth.

Preserving Individual Assets

MACED launched the Common Cents Financial Initiative in 2007 to combat predatory payday lending in rural eastern Kentucky and central Appalachia. Payday loans, or paycheck advances, are small, unsecured short-term loans that are intended to bridge the borrower's cash-flow gap between paydays. The region is filled with predatory lenders who provide expensive financial services that strip hundreds of millions of dollars a year from families. Payday lending is a significant predatory lending practice in rural America, with estimates that Americans lose $3.4 billion dollars a year to this practice. Financially distressed individuals turn to payday lenders as a last resort, pay high fees, and find themselves in a continuing cycle of debt rollovers, which results in fees that are equal to the original loan amount within three months.

The Save It! Loan is a 10-month term loan at 18 percent interest with a savings component that results in an additional 50 percent of the amount borrowed going to the borrower with an optional employer match. Loan amounts range from $250 to $750 based on the borrower's income. These loans are offered to low-income working people through regional employers. MACED has built an online application system that makes the process easy for the borrower and lending institution. Loan proceeds are deposited directly into a bank account or via a stored value card to allow people without bank accounts to borrow funds and begin to use financial services. Financial education is provided to employees of all participating employers through direct mail, the Internet, and a free phone-based counseling service.

Research and Policy

MACED sees itself as a knowledge-creating institution that conducts research to remove the barriers that hinder sustainable economic development strategies and make government a more effective partner in promoting development that works for the region. The organization does that by conducting research, developing policy proposals, and promoting policy change through advocacy, communications, and alliance building. Central to this work is the High Road Initiative, MACED's partnership with Kentuckians for the Commonwealth (KFTC).[41]

MACED is ahead of the curve; more important, it is illustrating that CEDIs can be innovative in defining new directions and work for CED. MACED recognizes that it has to continue doing its core work, which is economic development. But specifically targeting and segmenting its work in economic development, then using research to spot trends, allows it to be more effective. MACED's explicit approach keeps a strong development focus but equally values knowledge building for policy change and advocacy, which marks it as a leadership organization showing the field how to adjust to the emerging limitations of place.

Can urban CEDIs use some of the lessons of MACED? Without question, the focus on knowledge building can help urban CEDIs strategically find new opportunities and creatively shape public policies and advocacy in more effective ways than we currently see in the CED field.

Summary

Community economic development, while incorporating markets as a core principle of development, also tries to democratize development. CED does not try to replace other forms of economic development. That core mission is still an innovation in the context of the American political economy. Community economic development principles allow ordinary people to legitimately challenge the privileged position of business, but with a viable alternative to simple stalemate and conflict: partnership with capital and the public sector in the direction of economic development that is beneficial for all.[42]

The work of any CEDI or CDC, in isolation, cannot reignite the fortunes of a sagging region, but building community capacity is a crucial first step in getting poor communities back in the economic mainstream and creating the possibility of sustainable development. The examples I have highlighted thus far show that there are very diverse ways and steps to create the spark for economic regeneration. There are several specific lessons for innovation:

- *Public sector support drives innovative community economic development.* Although public funding of community economic development is myriad and sometimes fragmented, there has been convergence on support for development and public policies that link mainstream markets to poor communities. A counterargument questions the "marketization" of poverty. In other words, why not directly support poverty alleviation programs through grants? [43] The type of massive investment needed to make communities viable after they have fallen into economic disrepair (if we are speaking about a national place revitalization policy) is politically beyond the public sector's ability. History has shown that the public sector has a short window of concentrated investment and only then after a crisis. Sustained support can only be expected if there are policies that help poor communities and people participate in mainstream housing, capital, and labor markets. The Low Income Housing Tax Credit, New Markets Tax Credit programs, and the Community Reinvestment Act are helpful innovative tools that have directed productive investment back to capital-starved communities. These tools are innovations; however, they should not be viewed as static. Rather, their basic form should be updated and improved in keeping with the needs of the CEDI network.
- *Competent leaders and managers drive innovation and success.* Examples of innovation and innovative CEDIs rest on the presence of competent managers. Much is made of the charismatic leader in CED, but the organizations that survive and contribute to innovation are those whose leaders and managers possess some combination of (1) experience, (2) knowledge of economic and real estate development, (3) a willingness to take informed risk, (4) passion for methodically changing the fortunes of economically challenged places and people, and (5) recognition that building a lasting organization is just as important as innovative programming.[44]
- *Community development corporations are an important innovation, but...* Continued innovation, given the changed environment, is contingent on partnerships that find their base in shared economic interests. That is where public policy can continue to find incentive-based policies encouraging market participation by poor communities. Another imperative is the present need

to improve the internal management and cross-organizational collaborations by CDCs and CEDIs. Many CEDIs are small and without much capacity. Although public policy can discourage the existence of weak organizations by limiting funding, other ways can be found to support the CEDI model.

■ *Nontraditional partnerships help expand the possibility of program innovation.* The Unity Council's Fruitvale BART transit-oriented project illustrates this. The Unity Council initially fought the Bay Area Rapid Transit District project in its community, but it was nimble enough to see an opportunity and make a case not only to BART but also to local government, the community, and eventually the federal government that they could all partner to help improve the community and also help BART. Not an easy task, but with patience and planning, they were able to bring a now nationally recognized project into reality. Most important, the Unity Council did not take on face value the notion that transportation was not part of community economic development. Rather, the organization assessed its assets broadly and began the process of sustainable development.

■ *Community-generated knowledge to inform public policy is key to innovation.* Changing circumstance is more a part of CED than ever before. CEDIs must aggressively pursue knowledge and collect data that can be used to manage change. MACED illustrates that CEDIs need not become research organizations to use (or generate) applied research to help chart their programmatic course and influence important public policies affecting the quality of life in their communities. For the most part, CEDIs should partner with responsive community colleges, universities, and applied research organizations to produce information that can improve local and regional CEDI programs.

■ *Geographic boundary is not destiny.* MACED helps us understand that boundaries need not be fixed. Although a multicounty organization, MACED has a constituency base that it serves. There is no reason not to call an organization a community economic development institution as long as that organization has a plan for effectively serving multiple territories where low-income, blighted communities exist.

As the organizational form that evolved from community economic development principles, the community development corporation is an important vehicle that mirrors the reality of economic development in a representative democracy: a thousand voices and volunteers cannot accomplish development. But we should not be blind to the need to rethink and change geographic conceptions of community if the times and context warrant.[45]

Community economic development is now an important part of our national framework for dealing with distressed places and marginalized people. As some of the examples presented in this chapter illustrate, the field is evolving, and taking on new challenges. CEDIs can and do work with diverse partners and strategies to move toward sustainable community economic development.

Endnotes

1. Mutual Housing Associations are generally nonprofit, 501(c)(3) partnership organizations that develop, own, and manage affordable housing. Mutual housing is membership-based, composed of residents and other stakeholders. A representative board of directors governs the association. See Simon (2001, Chapter 8) for a good discussion of CEDI institutions.
2. The term CEDI is used here to encompass all community-based development organizations. Where appropriate, CDCs are mentioned specifically.
3. Other examples of organizing community voice for community economic development include the Alaska Native Corporations, which represent the community and economic interests of Alaska's indigenous people. Chartered under the 1971 Alaska Native Claims Settlement Act, the Alaska Native Regional Corporations (Alaska Native Corporations or ANCSA Corporations) provided for the establishment of 13 regional corporations to administer land and surface rights claims. These corporations have developed into significant vehicles for place and people development in Alaska. The idea that a specialized community economic development corporation is important for community self-determination is also taking hold in Indian Country (see Henson (2008) on this point).
4. Public Law 89-794, 89th Congress, H.R. 15111, November 8, 1966, "Economic Opportunity Amendments of 1966," Part D—Special Impact Programs, sec. 131(a), (5).
5. Grogan and Proscio (2001); Liou and Stroh (1998); Vidal and Keys (2005); Sviridoff et al. (2004).
6. Simon (2001, p. 119).
7. Urban CDCs work in targeted neighborhoods (averaging about 10,000 people). Rural CDCs sometimes take the form of areawide organizations with affiliates in different communities. See Dangler (2007).
8. Quigley (1999, p. 49).The Housing and Community Development (HCD) Act of 1974 is the authorizing legislation for Community Development Block Grant. See Buss, Redburn, and Guo (2006); Rich (1993); and United States Congress (2005) for an overview of the strengths and challenges of the Community Development Block Grant.
9. It is almost quaint to remember that the CDBG program was considered an innovative attempt to rationalize an often-conflicting set of urban development programs in addition to superseding the old revenue sharing model of federalism. See Rich (1993).
10. FY 1981–FY 2006: Appropriations levels include funding for grants to both entitlement communities and to states for distribution to nonentitlement communities, under both the CDBG Small Cities Program and under what then became the state-administered program for nonentitlement communities. Appropriations levels exclude supplemental appropriations made in response to presidentially declared disasters. All the data for the figure can be found at: http://www.nemw. org/NEMWAppropsFacts _CDBGFormulaG rants1206.pdf, also FY2007-2010: http://www.nlihc.org/det ail/ article.cfm?article_id=6034&id=46. FY 1996-FY 1997 has different values shown at: http://archive .gao.gov/paprpdf1/159061.pdf. (accessed November 15, 2008)
11. This figure comes from the National Community Reinvestment Coalition (http://www. ncrc.org/) (accessed November 20, 2008). The National Community Reinvestment Coalition stated, "Since the passage of CRA in 1977, lenders and community

organizations have signed CRA agreements totaling more than $6 trillion in reinvestment dollars." This advocacy report also has facts in support of CRA scattered throughout it such as the Harvard study, *The 25th Anniversary of the Community Reinvestment Act: Access to Capital in an Evolving Financial Services System*, demonstrates that without CRA, home purchase lending to LMI borrowers and communities would have decreased by 336,000 loans from 1993 through 2000.

12. Data for this figure was compiled from the following sources: http://www.ffiec.gov/craadweb/national.aspx; http://www.ffiec.gov/hmda/pdf/08news.pdf; http://www.ncrc.org/images/stories/era/cra%20toolkit_v8_remarks_joint_statement.pdf. A good source for further research on CRA rules and regulation is: http://www.community-investmentnetwork.org/cra-information/introduction-highlights. (accessed November 21, 2008)

13. Immergluck (2004, pp. 238–240).

14. Schwartz (1998).

15. It was inevitable that CRA and other efforts to promote investment in low- and moderate-income communities would draw fire from those looking for someone or something to blame for the disintegration of the housing market in 2008. Financial institutions made substantial loans to individuals in poor communities under the general rubric of CRA mandates. When banks found that they could make significant profits in financially marginal communities, many relaxed underwriting standards, putting many people into predatory loan situations. This was not the fault of the legislation but rather the overexuberance by financial institutions hoping to maximize profit. For years, the community economic development community had railed against the relaxed standard that promised more minority homeownership but in reality stripped equity from already economically strapped communities and people. See Immergluck (2004) on the preceding points.

16. The Internal Revenue Service allocates tax credits to state HCAs after they submit qualified allocation plans (QAPs). States set specific allocation criteria for awarding tax credits through the QAPs setting priorities for housing for low-income households. Nonprofit and for-profit developers apply for the tax credits to build and rehabilitate affordable rental housing. Tax credits are used to help cover the cost of rental units for qualified low-income households.

17. Data for this figure can be found at: http://www.danter.com/taxcredit/stats.htm. As the notes for the source table document: (accessed November 22, 2008)

Not every LIHTC dollar is allocated every year. Those dollars not allocated in a given year are allowed to carry over to the next year, hence the higher amounts allocated in some years. In addition, some dollars not allocated, as well as allocations for units that are not placed in service, are placed in a national pool and redistributed to the states. The average allocation per low income unit has increased significantly, from $1,823 in 1987 to $10,586 in 2007. This increase is most reflective of the increase in land acquisition and development costs. It is worth noting that the increase in allocations since 2001 is primarily a result of increasing the per capita rate on which allocations are based.

To note on Tax Credit Allocation Calculations: "Until 2000, each state received a tax credit of $1.25 per person that it can allocate towards funding housing that meets program guidelines. The per capital allocation was raised to $1.50 in 2001, to $1.75 in 2002, and adjusted for inflation beginning in 2003. These tax credits are then used to leverage private capital into new construction or acquisition and rehabilitation of affordable housing." http://www.danter.com/taxcredit/about.htm (accessed November 22, 2008); "For the calendar years beginning in 2005, the credit ceiling is the greater of $1.85 multiplied by the state population or $2,125,000." http://www.aarp.org/research/housing-mobility/affordability/fs74r_lihtc.html. (accessed December 2, 2008)

18. McClure (2000).
19. Stegman (1991).
20. See Porter (1995).
21. Jackson (2007).
22. The efficiency versus equality questions surrounding CDBG and also the LIHTC are reminiscent of earlier concerns best captured in the work of Okun (1975).
23. The time period here begins in the early 1980s and lasts to the mid- to later 1990s.
24. See the work of the Millennial Housing Commission (2002) on the future of tax credits in affordable housing and by extension CED.
25. U.S. Treasury, http://www.cdfifund.gov/what_we_do/programs_i d.asp?programid=5. (accessed December 2, 2008)
26. Rubin (2007).
27. Armistead (2005).
28. Nelson (2005).
29. Ibid., p. 51.
30. General Accountability Office (2007, p. 4).
31. Bratt et al. (1995).
32. Anglin (2004).
33. Hula and Jackson-Elmoore (2000) and Wright, Ellen, and Schill (2001).
34. Henton, Melville, and Walesh (1997).
35. See Carlson and Martinez (1988) for support of my view of Martinez as a reflective practitioner.
36. The Unity Council was awarded a $470,000 Federal Transit Administration (FTA) planning grant for predevelopment activities, including economic, traffic, and engineering studies of the area (see http://www.unitycouncil.org/fruitvale/index.htm).
37. See Cervero (2004). Transit-oriented development (TOD) is often defined as higher-density mixed-use development within walking distance of transit stations. This innovative form of development seeks to create compact, attractive, walkable, sustainable communities that provide residents with readily accessible housing and transportation choices. Transit-oriented development is the direct opposite of sprawl development, where dwelling patterns and lifestyles are heavily dependent on the automobile.
38. Duncan (1986 and 1992); Freudenburg (1992).
39. The statistics are revealing. Kentucky's median household income lags behind the rest of the nation, and within the state's Appalachian counties it amounts to 56 percent of the national average. The percentage of children in poverty remains high at 33 percent in the 40 core Appalachian counties in eastern Kentucky (2005). In 2000, one in five children lived in a household with no working parent. The Appalachian Regional Commission has designated 34 of Kentucky's 51 Appalachian counties as distressed, meaning that income is less than two-thirds the U.S. market income and poverty and three-year unemployment rates are at least 150 percent of the U.S. rate.

40. Justin Maxon, executive director, Mountain Association for Community Economic Development, in discussion with the author. Mountaintop removal is a relatively new variation on traditional coal mining that began in Appalachia in the 1970s. The process involves using dynamite to clear mountaintops. Dynamiting blasts away as much as 800 to 1000 feet of mountaintop, and the waste is then dumped into nearby valleys and streams. The debris compromises air quality and drinking water supplies, and the result is severe compromise of the surrounding communities, which also have to contend with continual blasting from mining operations.
41. See http://www.highroadinitiative.org/ (accessed December 3, 2008)
42. Simon (2001, Chapter 2). Use of the term the "privileged position" is used in the same spirit articulated by Lindblom (1977) in his classic work.
43. Harvey (2005); Kuttner (1990).
44. Anglin (2000); Zdenek and Steinbach (2000).
45. Simon (2001, Chapter 3).

Chapter 5

The Role of Community Economic Development Intermediaries

Community economic development is now composed of a set of intermediaries that support the development of poor communities. Some of these intermediaries developed to build the capacity of community economic development institutions of various kinds. CEDIs such as community development financial institutions (CDFIs), some of which predate the development of a formal community economic development field, work with locally based development organizations. Their primary mission is to provide affordable capital to poor communities for mortgages, investing in small businesses, and community facilities.

National, regional, and local community economic development intermediaries assemble private and public capital for the field, advocate for policies that improve outcomes, and publicize the accomplishments of the system as a whole. The public sector, philanthropy, and the private sector find it is easier to make large grants or loans to one agent that can distribute resources rather than dealing with a number of organizations.

The intermediaries—whatever the focus, organizational support, or financial services—all developed with the direct and continued involvement of the federal and local government. The public sector innovation here is the federal government's leadership in supporting an extended web of stakeholders such as philanthropists, interest groups, and community-based economic development practitioners, all struggling to find various ways to build organizational and financial capacity in distressed communities. The strength of this system is its unparalleled capacity to mobilize capital for all manner of economic development activity.[1]

As a class of organizations, the intermediaries represent a response to a pressing need to rationalize and increase the impact of CEDIs and build the larger field of community-based economic development. The intermediaries, at all levels, have become important thought leaders for the field, often gathering information on trends and challenges from stakeholders in the community economic development system, then implementing new programs to increase the sustainability and relevance of the field.

Although the community economic development intermediaries have accomplished a great deal, they, like their community-based partners, are seeking continued relevance and impact in a changing environment. In this chapter I make several arguments:

- The evolution of the intermediaries over the past 25 years or so is perhaps the most advanced accomplishment that can be attributed to public sector involvement.
- Community economic development intermediaries, although born in a time that stressed local focus and action, have shifted to new thinking and practices to manage regional and local challenges facing marginalized communities. Their role is now central to the future ability of community economic development to affect poverty and place revitalization in the context of regional development.

Expanding the Supply of Capital: Public Sector Support of Community Development Finance

Community development financial institutions have been serving low-income communities as intermediaries for many years. Community development credit unions, for example, have been serving communities in the United States and abroad for decades.[2] The South Shore Bank on the South Side of Chicago became a contemporary model of how a community-based financial institution can reverse the financial disinvestment of community through the provision of patient capital and technical assistance.[3]

In 1992, presidential candidate Bill Clinton used a visit to South Shore Bank to declare his intention to create 100 community development banks similar to his host and support over 1,000 microlenders. President Bill Clinton's administration moved quickly to work with stakeholders in the CDFI movement to implement his promise. The result was a legislative proposal to create the Community Development Financial Institutions Fund, which sought to increase the number and capacity of organizations providing capital to poor communities. Approved by Congress in September 1994, the CDFI Fund's mission is to promote economic revitalization and community development through investment in and assistance to community development financial institutions.[4] The fund accomplishes its mission in several ways:

1. Directly investing in CDFIs that provide loans, investments, financial services, and technical assistance to underserved populations and communities
2. Providing tax credits to community development entities (CDEs) through its New Markets Tax Credit (NMTC) Program, which then allows them to attract investment from the private sector and reinvest this capital in low-income communities
3. Providing incentives for banks to invest in their communities and in other CDFIs through its Bank Enterprise Award (BEA) Program
4. Through its Native Initiatives, by taking action to provide financial assistance, technical assistance, and training to Native CDFIs and other Native entities proposing to become or create Native CDFIs.

The CDFI Fund has experienced success in its short life. It has helped create or expand the capacity of 1,000 CDFIs and awarded over $900 million in investment and support resources to community development organizations and financial institutions. Figure 5.1 shows the CDFI Fund expenditures from 1995 to 2009.[5] The New Markets Tax Credits program is even larger, allocating some $16 billion by 2008.[6]

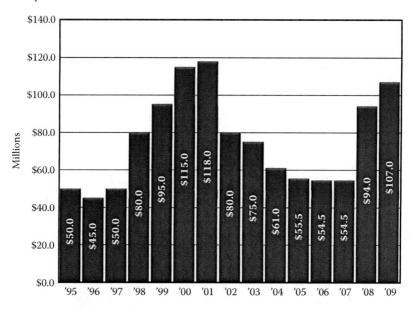

Figure 5.1 Community development financial institutions (1995 to 2009).

The varied types of organizations invested in by the CDFI include community development credit unions, banks, bank CDCs, community development venture funds, and CEDIs with the capacity to absorb and use the fund's resources.

The CDFI Fund, which now incorporates the private sector as an active partner, is much different from previous government efforts to increase access to capital, many of which rested on supporting lending to small business through the Small Business Administration. Now the CDFI Fund supports an infrastructure encompassing a broad range of community economic development segments, including supporting entrepreneurs and community facilities such as charter schools, mortgages, and supermarkets.

But just how does the CDFI Fund make an impact on the ground? The work of Coastal Enterprises Incorporated, headquartered in Wiscasset, Maine, is one of many innovative examples of what capital access can do for a community. Chartered in 1977, this rural CDC's mission is to serve Maine's poor rural communities. It is also a CDFI. Over the years, this organization has built a strong portfolio of housing and economic development projects, including equity investments in companies that provide jobs in Maine.[7]

Coastal Enterprises' work helping fishermen along the Maine shoreline is notable. Fishing is a capital-intensive industry, and for small-scale fishermen, the capital requirements of this seasonal industry can be onerous. Add to that the fact that overfishing has left the area with thinning fishing stock, threatening to wipe out the livelihoods of these fishermen. Through the New Markets Tax Credit, Coastal Enterprises was able to greatly expand its capacity not only to assist with the capital needs of the small-scale fishing industry but also to explore ways to make the industry sustainable in the face of government regulation of overfishing.

Through a subsidiary, CEI Capital Management Group, Coastal Enterprises used part of its $129,000,000 in New Markets Tax credits to leverage private capital to build a 56,000-square-foot facility called the Gulf of Maine Research Institute. The institute, now in its last phase of development, will be home to government agencies, nonprofits, marine biologists, and fishermen, all searching for new and innovative ways to sustain the ecology of the Gulf of Maine along with sustaining the 25,000 fishing jobs that depend on the ecosystem. The institute will be an economically self-sustaining incubator of ideas and projects all forged in a shared physical place and between stakeholders who often don't see common interests.[8]

Building Capacity on the Community Side

The CDFI side of the intermediary equation has come a long way very fast. CDFI intermediaries benefit from the discipline of the market in their operation and lending in the community economic development field. The intermediaries that sprang up to build the capacity of people and organizations such as CDCs operate in a different framework, where the measure of accomplishment is less clear. National, regional, and local community development intermediaries such as NeighborWorks America, Local Initiatives Corporation (LISC), and Enterprise Partners are chartered to build organizational capacity.[9]

Both LISC and Enterprise Community Partners also receive federal resources to help support the operations of CDCs through the National Community Development Initiative (NCDI), now called Living Cities.[10] NCDI was formed in 1991 by eight private foundations and financial institutions with the goals of (1) assisting in the development and effectiveness of local systems that support community economic development, and (2) increasing the availability of long-term financing for CEDI projects.

NCDI's purpose was to strengthen the capacity of community-based organizations engaged in community economic development activities with operating support, training, technical assistance, and project financing. The intermediaries have to match every federal dollar they receive with at least three dollars of private funding. Congress authorized HUD to join the initiative in 1994.[11] NeighborWorks is a creation of Congress and has a line item in the federal budget.

The intermediaries, at all levels, have become important thought leaders for the field, often gathering information about trends and challenges from stakeholders in the CED system, then implementing new programs to increase the sustainability and relevance of CED. The intermediaries serve their local CDC partners and occupy an independent role as institutional leaders in the field of community economic development. Increasingly, the national, regional, and local intermediaries are playing a direct development role to increase the pace of local development when local organizations cannot complete projects because of limited capacity.

Building capacity, or helping communities pursue economic development, is an extremely complicated proposition. The capacity-building intermediaries serve their local community partners and occupy an independent role as institutional leaders in the field of community economic development.

NeighborWorks America

The Neighborhood Reinvestment Corporation (NRC), which officially changed its name to NeighborWorks America (NWA) in 2005, is a national nonprofit CED intermediary organization created by Congress in 1978 to provide financial support, technical assistance, and training for community-based revitalization.[12] The fact that a quasi-governmental organization exists to assist directly in community and economic development is not only an innovation but also reflects an evolving view that communities and neighborhood need significant support in order to revitalize.

Local NWA programs work with the national program's five core elements: fixed boundaries, resident-majority boards of directors, bank commitments, enhanced code enforcement, and a high-risk loan fund. Local NWA offices, however, have expanded the products and services they make available. In addition to their traditional home improvement and purchase loans, most also offer mutual housing, home ownership education and counseling, multifamily development, small business loans, and assistance with down payment and closing costs. NWA's national office focuses largely on building capacity at the local level, because local offices shape much of the development work.[13] Figure 5.2 shows the flow in the NeighborWorks system (driven by NRC) from congressional appropriation to the production of housing and implementation of economic development projects.

NWA maintains a full complement of leadership and organizational training programs for organizations in and out of the network. These training programs are perhaps the most comprehensive in the field, offering a range of topics from organizational budgeting to board and staff training. One of the areas covered in the training is community building and organizing. Even though the ultimate goal is building affordable housing and generating economic development, NWA feels strongly that its local development partners must be relevant and sensitive to the needs of the communities they serve.

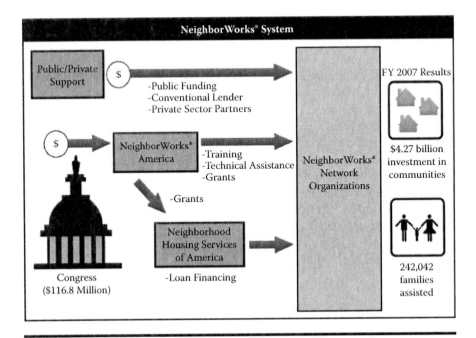

Figure 5.2 The NeighborWorks System 2008. (Source: http://www.nw.org (accessed December 22, 2008).)

Building Strong Communities

An interesting, innovative example of what local organizations can accomplish under the umbrella of an intermediary such as NeighborWorks can be found in the community organizing work of the Lawrence CommunityWorks (LCW), a CDC located in Lawrence, Massachusetts. CommunityWorks has embarked on an effort to promote civic engagement using a strategy called "network organizing."[14]

Network organizing is a variant of social network theory that views social relationships as a series of nodes and ties. Nodes are the individual actors within the networks, and ties are the relationships between the actors. Many kinds of ties connect the nodes. A social network is, simply, a map of all of the relevant ties between the nodes being studied. The network can also be used to determine the social capital of individual actors. Social network theory says that the attributes of individuals are less important than their relationships and ties with other actors within the network.

A significant ongoing challenge to CED work is that community-based institutions working on the ground, such as CDCs, often do not have the resources to engage their residents, that is, to do community organizing. This presents an ironic situation in which community-based developers are sometimes at odds with the community that they purport to serve.

The question is and has always been how to pay for community organizing when it is not one of the items that can be supported over time. Most CEDIs grab resources from different funding streams to incorporate community organizing in their operations, rendering the impact of this important function sporadic and uneven. This is why the work of LCW is interesting, especially given that the CEDI is part of a larger intermediary network. It is thinking creatively about a barrier to effective CED work, using a relatively low-cost way of forging community connections that can ultimately strengthen development.

Lawrence CommunityWorks has mobilized local residents in order to expand beyond its initial function of developing affordable housing.[15] Specifically, LCW uses network theory to connect people to each other in the effort to break down the barriers that prevent residents from actively engaging in their communities. Executive Director Bill Traynor describes LCW's network as an "environment of connectivity." He sees it not as an organization but as a "bundle of thinking, language, habits, value propositions, space and practice—all designed to comprise an environment that more effectively meets people where they are and offers myriad opportunities and levels of engagement."[16]

This approach has indeed allowed LCW to be an active, engaged, and effective community organization. Various programs provide multiple ways for community members to get involved. Some of these include the NeighborCircle campaign, which builds relationships among neighbors in diverse sections of the community in order to promote local change. Participants host dinners for residents to give them a chance to have conversations that lead to direct action. These circles often lead to Property Improvement Committees (PICs) that work on local issues. Another project, the five-month PODER Leadership Experience for resident leaders, teaches participants how to develop their own powers and learn new skills.[17]

LCW's organizing effort is quite unusual and thoughtful. The fact that the effort can thrive is partially a result of its being embedded in a larger intermediary framework that encourages experimentation. No doubt LCW's organizing work will filter beyond the NWA network and make its way to the broader field of community economic development, but the point is that regional cohesiveness and competitiveness will only come about through microlevel connections that produce effective community change. Individual community organizations cannot do this alone. Community economic development intermediaries can support the type of networks that produce locally connected organizations, which in turn, can more effectively carry out economic development.

The Local Initiatives Support Corporation

The Local Initiatives Support Corporation came into being in 1979, when federal funding for community development, which had been increasing for a decade, began to decrease after a backlash against federal efforts that supported community development and individual mobility. Although the Nixon administration, coming into office in 1969, had helped begin a new federal view of cities and distressed communities by questioning the basis for government intervention in social problems, funding for community development continued under the Nixon administration.[18] President Jimmy Carter initiated significant cuts in many community economic development programs.[19]

By the time Ronald Reagan was elected in 1980, a clear trend had developed. The Reagan administration cut the vestiges of community economic development programs and pushed more functional responsibility for all areas of government to the states. In response to devolution of federal support for CED, the Ford Foundation, who had played a significant role in supporting the evolution of community economic development, initiated internal discussions about creating an independent means of financial support for the field.[20]

In January 1979, the Ford Foundation's Division of National Affairs produced a discussion paper titled "Communities and Neighborhoods: A Possible Private Sector Initiative for the 1980s."[21] The paper also underscored that local CDCs themselves would need to work toward financial viability through fund-raising with government, foundation, and financial institution sponsors and noted,

> Most important…the impact of the Center should extend far beyond local community organizations and foundations. By making community groups into partners of commercial developers, or into competent developers themselves, the Center could indirectly make the expenditure of local public and private funds more rational and effective…

these resources are essential to neighborhood revitalization, and community organizations that blend professional competence with a strong constituency can have an important impact on their use.[22]

In October 1979, LISC was incorporated as a private nonprofit corporation with an initial endowment of $9.35 million. The Ford Foundation provided the largest share, a $4.75 million, three-year grant.[23] By 2008, LISC operated 30 urban and rural programs and was considered a significant force in community economic development. LISC estimates that since 1980 it has invested $8.6 billion in community development activities that leveraged additional private and public sector resources for a total of $25.3 billion in investment.

The numbers tell an important story yet mask another story: the evolution of an institution whose core programs rest on physical development but whose strength over the years has allowed a level of experimentation that touches all aspects of community economic development. LISC has tried programs supporting neighborhood security, family self-sufficiency, neighborhood leadership development, organizational capacity building, and community organizing. Some of these efforts yielded learning that strengthened the organization's core functions locally, whereas others did not pan out. But lessons were learned and captured and used to improve the organization and the field.

LISC, like other institutional components of community economic development, is adjusting to changing field dynamics. During the late 1980s and much of the 1990s, the organization encouraged its CDC partners to focus on housing production to alleviate widespread homelessness and housing blight. LISC has evolved to recognize that it has a central role to play in regional development, saying that "[s]timulating local economic activity, which incorporates connecting our targeted neighborhoods to the regional economy and beyond, is another important goal."[24]

Connecting the Basics

Through its work with CDCs, LISC maintains that it can be an important part of regional and local development through support of commercial revitalization, financing charter schools, child care facilities in low-income communities, and workforce development.

LISC's interest and support of workforce development is a key acknowledgment that housing, economic development, and workforce development are inextricably linked and that a central task of community economic innovation is getting all three to work in a connected fashion. With its Centers for Working Families (CWF), Chicago's LISC office is helping low-income families retain jobs and financially plan for the future by teaching them how to manage their money.[25] The program began in Chicago, where 12 CDCs in various Chicago neighborhoods are currently running CWFs.[26] CWFs get their funding from HUD and various foundations.[27]

The emphasis of each center varies based on the community served, but each CWF offers three integrated core services: workforce development, income supports, and financial and asset-building services. Each center has a financial counselor and an employment specialist. These professionals provide employment services and assistance with accessing public benefits; many also offer free tax preparation services.

The MacArthur Foundation has funded CDCs to manage centers for working families as part of its effort to work with LISC on the New Communities Program, which it defines as a comprehensive approach for neighborhoods that invests in people and places through a variety of partners. The CWFs, strategically located in diverse communities with large concentrations of working-poor families, close to residents of NCP neighborhoods, serve a population whose median annual household income is $10,800 to $39,000.

More than two dozen organizations are replicating the CWF concept in cities such as New York, Baltimore, Atlanta, Indianapolis, Albuquerque, San Antonio, and Minneapolis–St. Paul.[28] The popularity and expansive reach of the CWFs suggest that the network which created them has played a significant role in allowing CDCs to reach more people in innovative ways.

The fact that LISC is leading this effort points to several important innovations. For one, the experiment in promoting workforce development is an important strategy shift, indicating recognition that housing is not enough to move individuals and families out of poverty. Not least among the innovations is the evolution of an organization's more encompassing vision of community economic development.

Enterprise Community Partners

The Enterprise Foundation, now called Enterprise Community Partners, emerged from the vision of the late James Rouse, a successful developer of large-scale housing and retail developments who had a strong interest in helping people and communities overcome poverty. In 1982, he founded and began raising capital for a nonprofit organization, the Enterprise Foundation, as a means for repairing inner cities by building "decent housing in decent neighborhoods for everyone."[29]

By the end of its first year of operation, Enterprise was working with nonprofit housing developers in six cities. Today, Enterprise operates in 17 regional offices offering services to a network of approximately 2,200 nonprofit and government-sponsored organizations in 800 cities, towns, and Native American reservations. Any nonprofit organization, public housing authority, or Native American tribe with the mission of revitalizing local communities may join the Enterprise network without cost.

Enterprise offers diverse program services, including a community safety program, the Enterprise Women's Network, the Community Employment Alliance, and child care services. Enterprise's large network and broad range of services limit its ability to provide direct capacity-building assistance to its members. Instead, it makes extensive use of local partners and community development alliances. In an approach similar to the one LISC has used, Enterprise established the Enterprise Social Investment Corporation (ESIC), an adjunct organization that sells low-income housing tax credits. This venture has raised more than $3 billion from the private sector to fund new construction or to rehabilitate roughly 70,000 low-income rental units.

Enterprise includes several major social venture subsidiaries and related organizations. Enterprise Mortgage Investments Inc. provides long-term mortgages to developers of affordable multifamily housing. Enterprise Homes Inc. directly develops affordable homes for ownership and rental in the mid-Atlantic region. The Enterprise Loan Fund raises local funds from socially responsible investors (willing to lend and accept a lower than market rate for their financing) to provide low-cost financing for nonprofit affordable housing developers. Enterprise Housing Financial Services provides financial products to nonprofits for acquiring, developing, and rehabilitating affordable housing for low- and moderate-income families.

Experimentation and Innovation

Similar to LISC, Enterprise Partners acts a vehicle for community economic development experimentation, and innovation can take place even if the outcomes are less than clear. No better example of this can be found than Enterprise Partners' involvement in the Neighborhood Transformation Initiative (NTI) demonstration in Baltimore's Sandtown–Winchester neighborhood.

In 1990 Baltimore was a city on the ropes (and arguably remains so today): high crime rates, rampant unemployment, and physical blight marked this city, which was and is famous for its row homes. The mayor at the time, Kurt Schmoke, formed a partnership with Enterprise (then the Enterprise Foundation) to work simultaneously to overhaul all of the neighborhood's dysfunctional systems (schools, health care, jobs, safety, and housing) in the belief that each system would strengthen the community as a whole. Interestingly, the initiative focused on reforming the public systems affecting the community, which is a different outlook than the "community as the problem" view often grafted onto poor communities. But the NTI also broke new ground in including city government at the outset, hoping for true change and sustainability.

Enterprise played multiple roles in the initiative, from technical assistance broker, staff for actual projects in the community (coordinated through the Neighborhood Transformation Center), and aggregator of financial resources to cheerleader to many communities, including the philanthropic community.

The NTI continues, but the effort is much more circumspect and focused. More than $100 million of public money have been invested over the years for job training, building housing, community organizing, economic development, and school reform. System change has occurred in areas such as public safety and school reform, but, as with many of these efforts, a change in administration brought a shift in priorities and a scaling down of public sector interest, although not complete withdrawal.

Some ask what has been accomplished by such a heavy investment, but that is the wrong question. Many important lessons have been learned from the Sandtown–Winchester effort, including the fact that a national intermediary can play a direct role in leading a comprehensive neighborhood-based initiative and experience success if the effort and measure of success are circumspect.[30]

Regional and Local Intermediaries

Since the early 1980s, some cities and regions have created their own intermediaries intended to improve the capabilities and accomplishments of targeted CEDIs. These organizations generally are known as community development partnerships (CDPs). Like national intermediaries, they provide centralized distribution of funds and technical assistance to CEDIs. One key difference between the regional/local intermediaries and their national counterparts, however, is that most local partnerships focus on the organizational development of CEDIs rather than on specific projects. Local and regional intermediaries have made deliberate efforts to increase the ability of neighborhood organizations to be more effective agents of community economic development.

Many local partnerships receive support from LISC or Enterprise, and some are even managed by local LISC or Enterprise offices. CDPs typically encompass a collection of local funders serving as an intermediary force. They assemble financial resources and coordinate an array of support services to CEDIs, including the provision of core organizational support in return for organizational progress and impact and serving as information clearinghouses and advocates.[31]

The CDP concept places a premium on the ability of local leaders to assess the capabilities of local nonprofits and provide CDCs with a more centralized mechanism to build their relationship with funders. The main benefit of CDPs to CDCs is that they can focus on cultivating just one relationship with local funders and focus their energy on actual development.[32]

Neighborhood Partnership Inc.: Less Is More

The Cleveland Neighborhood Progress (NPI) is an example of a collaborative that fosters innovative community economic development. Founded in 1988, the NPI works as an umbrella organization that distributes grants and support to CDCs and nonprofits in Cleveland and assembles finance capital for CDCs and projects they undertake that local CDCs are unable to pursue due to project size or complexity.

NPI works with various partners and funders to enhance the city's CED network. Its partners include the City of Cleveland, Cleveland Housing Court, First Suburbs Consortium, Cleveland Neighborhood Development Coalition,

Enterprise Community Partners, Cleveland State University, and Case Western Reserve University.[33]

Cleveland's robust capacity-building system has helped strengthen the city's exceptionally active and engaged CED system. Intermediaries have been influential in this city, which is the only one in the country where Enterprise and LISC work in the same market.

NPI was one of the first intermediaries, local or national, to recognize that human capital in the community economic development field needed to be addressed in order to keep it vibrant and relevant. To do this, NPI provides operating support for a carefully chosen set of CDCs while providing organizational development assistance to strengthen the organizations so they can more successfully engage in community economic development.

NPI's leadership is very aware that Cleveland's core neighborhoods are important in encouraging an economically vibrant region, especially given the uphill climb of a metropolitan area that lost population (–1.6 percent) from 2000 to 2006 and had been only growing marginally (2.2 percent) from 1990 to 2000. NPI's strategy, with the encouragement of local funders, is to build strong local neighborhood organizations that are making measurable change in their communities.

The Strategic Investment Initiative provides funding to six CDCs picked through a competitive application progress; all are concentrating on one individual neighborhood and must show change in property values, home ownership, and occupancy rates, and additional increases in private investments to receive continued funding. The criteria for choosing the CDCs are worth summarizing because they embody a coherent strategy for making Cleveland, not just one neighborhood, more competitive in the region. The core elements of the Strategic Investment Initiative are as follows:

- *Focuses on broad market outcomes rather than housing production.* The Initiative seeks to alter a neighborhood's quality of life so it can compete for population growth and investments in regional markets.
- *Focuses on specific geographic areas.* The six CDCs target their planning and investment, focusing on a small number of blocks with high-value assets such as proximity to a major employment center, historic architecture, or superior views.
- *Comprehensive plans.* With NPI's assistance, CDCs involve residents in developing land-use surveys, real estate project plans, marketing strategies, and other quality-of-life initiatives.
- *High-impact anchor projects.* Each Strategic Investment Initiative neighborhood contains a large-scale "anchor project" in its focus area designed to lend weight and credibility to the prospect of significant economic development.
- *Model blocks that complement anchor projects.* Physical improvements on selected blocks near anchor projects include home repairs, landscaping, streetscape improvements, and new green spaces.

- *Supports land acquisition and vacant/abandoned properties.* NPI helps CDCs acquire vacant property for Strategic Investment Initiative projects.
- *Supports comprehensive amenities and services through strategic partnerships.* CDCs create new collaborations with nontraditional partners to address factors other than physical development that enhance neighborhood attractiveness, such as schools, safety, parks, health, jobs, and other quality-of-life issues.
- *Encourages significant attention to marketing and market competitiveness.* NPI commissioned market research studies and provided marketing training to help funded CDCs define their market niches and marketing strategies.
- *Supports dedicated staffing.* Adopting a venture capital model, NPI and local Enterprise Partners staff work collaboratively with CDCs on all aspects of their initiative. Each CDC has a full-time Strategic Investment Initiative manager, who plans, organizes, and advocates for projects in focus areas.[34]

The Initiative is well under way, and time will judge the outcomes and overall success of the Initiative. What NPI has done is to follow a strategy of supporting a core set of CDCs with the capacity to plan and mount expansive projects that revitalize their neighborhoods. Rather than support all CEDIs, NPI concentrates resources with the hope of creating neighborhoods of choice by stimulating market recovery and improving the quality of life.

Summary

The challenges facing America's regions, cities, communities, and neighborhoods are daunting by any measure. The organizations, strategies, and policies needed to improve development policies and actual development are now emerging. The overriding force in all of this is the presence of institutions that can not only mediate common cleavages such as wealth and power, government and civil society, and race and ethnicity, but also bind them together in such a way that sustained attention can be focused on community and local development.

It would have been unthinkable 30 years ago that the United States would have a set of financial and capacity-building intermediaries that wield significant influence in Congress, state capitals, and city halls and are reshaping the local landscape through aggregation of resources and informing public policy. It is worth summarizing the lessons from these important institutions.

Institutional Strength Conditions
Innovation and Policy Leadership

The intermediaries are in a position to do two things that push the field forward: (1) increase the professional and technical expertise of the existing practitioners (such as the efforts of NeighborWorks America) to be more innovative, and (2) increase the programmatic effectiveness and diversity of the field through experiments of scale. Learning from experiments such as the Chicago project, Sandtown–Winchester, Neighborhood Progress in Cleveland, and many others, can be used to inform field practice or change public policy when appropriate. No other set of CED actors can do this in such a directed manner. Ultimately, this is all "usable" knowledge that helps the field establish that working regionally means developing locally.

CED Intermediaries Augment the Field by Routinizing the Development Process

At the beginning, community economic development was a collection of practitioners and organizations trying different local experiments, some successful and others not. The national intermediaries are able to use their reach and experience to assemble the best information about what types of housing and economic development strategies and programs make economic sense. This programmatic learning reduces the transaction costs associated with development and establishes development standards across jurisdictions.

This capacity now allows the intermediaries to partner with government and the private sector, using not only their investment capital but also their significant knowledge of markets (such as inner-city housing markets) not well understood by the mainstream. A good example of how this knowledge promotes innovation can be seen in the participation of both LISC and Enterprise in the New York City Acquisition Fund.

Established in 2006, the New York City Acquisition Fund created a private sector lending market to address a critical public sector challenge, promoting affordable housing development in a competitive market.[35] Like many other cities, the supply of New York City-owned land for affordable housing is nearly exhausted. Small developers and nonprofit developers cannot effectively compete in the private market for developable land to build affordable housing. This $230 million fund finances the purchase of land and buildings for affordable housing by using innovative private financing that allows small developers and nonprofit organizations to compete in New York City's tough real estate market.

Supported through a collaboration of the city's leading financial institutions, 10 national philanthropies, and the City of New York, the Fund encourages banks to offer credit to smaller and nonprofit developers by shielding bank investments from the highest-risk loans within the Fund. Foundation contributions of $33 million and city funds of $8 million take the riskiest positions and are combined with $192.5 million in bank investments. Managers of the Fund work directly with the intermediaries, who provide financing and technical assistance to small and nonprofit developers to build up a pipeline of good projects resulting in affordable housing. LISC and Enterprise, though, play an important role not only in "deal flow" but also in ensuring that projects actually come to fruition.

Linking Mainstream Markets and CED

One of the major accomplishments of the community economic development intermediaries has been to aggregate capital from resource providers such as foundations and the public sector. But perhaps a greater accomplishment has been to smooth the way for private sector organizations to once again invest in neighborhood markets that have fallen on difficult times. The Low Income Housing Tax Credit has gone a long way in encouraging the public/private link, but there are other important connections. LISC, for example, has worked with the real estate industry through Social Compact (a nonprofit research firm funded by real estate and financial companies) to gather demographic and economic data about communities underserved by retail and the food services industry. Using this data, LISC and Social Compact have been able to build the knowledge base for private, public, and nonprofit investment resulting in new supermarkets and retail shops in over 100 underserved communities.[36]

This effort provides a way for the retail shopping industry to feel comfortable approaching and working in inner-city markets. The result is that many communities now have access to supermarkets that sell fresh food at reasonable prices and retail shopping that can serve the day-to-day needs of community residents without the residents traveling long distances. Strategies of this type help make communities viable in the context of regional development rather than being labeled as uncompetitive places.

Leading the Way for Sustainable Community Economic Development

The regional and national community economic development intermediaries recognize that they need to link their current programs and initiatives to sustainable community economic development.[37] In a number of instances, they have devoted substantial resources to supporting alternative educational models in poor communities, green building techniques for affordable housing, linked workforce development efforts, and initiatives that support wealth building for poor communities and people. The intermediaries are also using their substantial political clout to represent the interests of poor communities in the corridors of power as national and local decisions are made about the future of community economic development policy. As development decisions are increasingly made at a regional level, the intermediaries are poised to be an effective voice for continuing attention to the needs of poor people and places.

Endnotes

1. Simon (2001).
2. Tansey (2009).
3. Taub (1994).
4. Placement of the CDFI Fund in the Department of the Treasury was an important signal that community development finance was a priority for the Clinton administration.
5. See http://www.cdfifund.gov/. The figure was constructed from yearly expenditures not found in a single place on the site. (accessed January 6, 2009)
6. See http://www.cdfifund.gov/ for documentation of these figures. The New Markets Tax Credit (NMTC) Program allows investors to receive a credit against their federal income taxes for making "qualified" equity investments in what are called Community Development Entities (CDEs). A CDE must (1) be a domestic corporation or partnership at the time of the certification application; (2) demonstrate a primary mission of serving, or providing investment capital for, low-income communities or low-income persons; and (3) maintain accountability to residents of low-income communities through representation on a governing board of or advisory board to the entity. Qualified equity investment must be used by the CDE to provide investments in low-income communities. The credit provided to the investor totals 39 percent of the cost of the investment and is claimed over a seven-year credit allowance period. In each of the first three years, the investor receives a credit equal to 5 percent of the total amount paid for the stock or capital interest at the time of purchase. For the final four years, the value of the credit is 6 percent annually. Investors may not redeem their investments in CDEs prior to the conclusion of the seven-year period. (accessed January 6, 2009)
7. See http://www.ceimaine.org/ for a full description of Coastal Enterprises. (accessed January 6, 2009)
8. http://www.ceimaine.org/. (accessed January 6, 2009)
9. It is important to note that all of the capacity-building intermediaries, national, regional, and local, have always provided financial services, and many have received CDFI status and investment.
10. http://www.livingcities.org. (accessed January 7, 2009)
11. The program was enacted as Section 4 of the HUD Demonstration Act of 1993 (P.L. 103-120) and amended in the 1997 Emergency Supplemental Appropriations Act (P.L. 105-18).
12. Neighborhood Reinvestment changed its name to NeighborWorks America in April 2005. Neighborhood Reinvestment Corporation remains the legal incorporated name, as stated in the 1978 statute. The board of directors approved the name change in September 2004, to align the Corporation with NeighborWorks organizations and all of the other components in the overall NeighborWorks system.
13. See www.nw.org. Understanding the NW network gets somewhat complicated. There are dedicated NW affiliates that provide housing counseling and development assistance to residents. These offices also act as local intermediaries to build the capacity of local CDCs or CDC-like organizations. In addition some high-capacity CDC organizations work under the banner of NWA in various states and localities. These network organizations receive grants, technical assistance, and access to financing for their projects. Participation in the NWA network does not stop them from working with other intermediaries. (accessed January 8, 2009)

14. http://www.lcworks.org/. (accessed January 16, 2009). See also DeFilippis and Saegert (2007) for an additional analysis of LCW.
15. See www.nw2.org/WinningStrategies. (accessed January 16, 2009)
16. See ibid.
17. See ibid.
18. See O'Connor (2000) and Carlson and Martinez (1988).
19. See Carlson and Martinez (1988); see also Cuciti and Kaplan (1986).
20. See Ford Foundation (1979).
21. Ibid.
22. Ibid, pp. 12–13.
23. Of the initial 19 first-round recipients, 9 operated in Chicago, Boston, New York, and Philadelphia—cities that have continued to serve as important hubs of LISC activity. Soon after announcing the first-round recipients, LISC established a small number of program areas on which to focus; all had existing private-sector resources and a group of promising CDCs engaged in activities. Thus, a fundamental tenet of LISC was working with promising CDCs with strong ties to the community. See also Liou and Stroh (1998).
24. See www.lisc.org. (accessed January 17, 2009)
25. In Chicago, CDCs had already been engaging in this type of work before LISC/Chicago launched the CWF initiative in January 2004 with a grant from the Casey Foundation. LISC had formed a network of employment centers through various CDCs, but it wanted to extend its support to families who had an income but were still financially vulnerable as a result of low wages and rare benefits. Because this network was already in place, CWFs were able to form, from existing job resource centers, a social services program and a vocational program. This example is just one of many where CDCs were already running workforce development programs within their communities, but plugging into a network helped them to expand their reach and engage in more innovative efforts to help neighborhood residents.
26. See http://www.lisc-chicago.org/directory.aspx?pointer=5666. (accessed January 17, 2009)
27. Martinson and Holcomb (2007).
28. Annie E. Casey Foundation (2007).
29. See http://www.enterprisecommunity.org/. (accessed February 10, 2009)
30. Brown et al. (2001).
31. See Ford Foundation (1987).
32. Ibid.
33. For funding, NPI works with a variety of public and private organizations. These include Charter One Bank, the City of Cleveland Department of Community Development, the Cleveland Foundation, Enterprise Community Partners, the George Gund Foundation, the Mandel Foundation, Saint Luke's Foundation of Cleveland, and the Surdna Foundation.
34. See http://www.neighborhoodprogress.org/. (accessed February 10, 2009)
35. http://www.nyc acquisitionfund.com/. (accessed February 11, 2009)
36. McLinden (2006).
37. http://www.lisc.org/se ction/goals/eco nomic; http://www. enterpr isecommu nity.org/ programs/gre en%5F communities/. (accessed January 17, 2009)

Chapter 6

Community Building and Development

Community building and development are important tools used the world over to fight poverty.[1]

> Many observers have noted the long community-building traditions that undergird local revitalization or "development" efforts in the United States as well as other parts of the globe. From the richness of Native American cultures to the utopian communities pursued by religious reformers or other European settlers, from social clubs and mutual aid societies organized by successive waves of immigrants to the self-help organizations created by descendants of African slaves, every major group and region of the country has roots that go deep.[2]

Community economic development functions best when community building and development exist and productively operate in a neighborhood or community. Only then can poor communities use social capital or the presence of dense social networks to even attempt the type of collective decision making necessary to improve their circumstances. This chapter defines community building and development, then discusses its role in promoting sustainable community economic development. My central argument is that community building and development are important processes in promoting community economic development, but only if narrowly defined. Without a clear view of how community building and development help community economic development, we risk reducing them as a force conceptually and programmatically.

Are Community Development and Community Building Different?

In the last decade, much effort has been put into discussing community development versus community building versus community economic development, so much so that a discussion is necessary here. The meaning of each has been blurred to the point that they need distinction to show their importance to the immediate project: understanding and presenting the innovations that promote sustainable community economic development.

Community building and development aim at producing a community with an expressed interest in, and action toward, wealth building. Gibson and his colleagues (1997) observe that community building works by "neighbors learning to rely on each other, working together on concrete tasks that take advantage of new self-awareness of their collective and individual assets and, in the process, create human, family, and social capital that provides a new base for a more promising future and reconnection to America's mainstream."[3]

But note the definition of community development in a United Nations document authored a generation ago:

> Community Development means the process by which the efforts of the people themselves are united with those of governmental authorities to improve the economic, social and cultural conditions of communities, to integrate these communities into the life of the nation and enable them to contribute fully to national progress. The distinctive features of community development programmes are the participation by the people themselves in efforts to improve their level of living with reliance as much as possible on their own initiative.[4]

One is hard-pressed to see the conceptual difference. Both value community advancement through neighbors working to address common concerns such as neighborhood beautification projects, youth development programs, and crime reduction initiatives. Community-building advocates, though, distinguished themselves from the overreliance on housing development that has come to be associated with community development in the United States. In short, the practical use of the term many be skewed, but the conceptual underpinning is not.[5]

Reintroducing Old Friends

In their seminal work, *Urban Problems and Community Development,* Ferguson and Dickens (1999) comment,

> Community development should be a much broader idea and have a more comprehensive agenda than any one class of institutions can

manage (or lead) alone. By the definition that we propose, community development subsumes the work of community development corporations (CDCs) and community building and comprehensive community initiatives (CCIs), in addition to other asset-based development initiative…it also subsumes the education, health care, and community-building aspects of local human service provision by nonprofits and for profit organizations and government.[6]

How and why did we see a divergence of thought? One key reason is the evolution of the community development corporation (CDC). For some, CDCs have been welcomed as a way of anchoring the field to a tangible delivery and implementing force. For others, CDCs present limitations, not the least of which is that it is a competing policy choice for those who believe that direct pressure on government to promote redistributive policies trumps all other development strategies.

There were other reasons for separating functions. CDCs evolved as a hybrid nonprofit form combining social development, advocacy, and economic development. The multifunction CDC was not financially sustainable, especially when government reduced support in the 1980s.[7]

Separation of thought may have resulted from the unsustainability of the CDC model, but funders and government had already learned by the 1980s that one agency trying to do many things was a recipe for disaster at worst and limited impact at best.[8] This is why government and foundation policy over the years moved toward support of projects and organizations that produced tangible outcomes such as housing.[9]

The focus on housing development since the 1980s, at least for CDCs, also brought a certain rigor and need for practitioners adept at the technical practices of construction to the diminution of the other goals of community development such as building community voice and individual and family development. In the mid-1990s, practitioners and funders, concerned over the emphasis on housing production and the ascendancy of technical skills for practitioners, went in another direction, supporting experiments in community building and comprehensive community development hearkening back to the multifunctional CDCs of the past.[10]

The community-building movement argued the necessity of bringing community residents back into the equation by supporting the development of social capital as the key end goal, which sets the stage for collective action and voice on other issues. The new community building, so defined, produced less than fulsome success. As de Souza Briggs points out

> Many saw, in the community building movement, a chance to renew the case that capable communities with real influence over resources are much more likely to be healthy and productive than are communities that are mere targets for decisions made and capacity developed elsewhere.…But the proverbial honeymoon for community building,

if there was one, would prove short-lived, at least in the U.S. The new wave led to a mix of success and failure, learning and frustration, in part because the local projects were often conflict ridden, whether because of divisions internal to participating communities, a clash of expectations with funders and regulators, or both....And given all the investments of time, money, and reputation, the failures were often hard to acknowledge—and even harder to discuss openly. All of these factors inhibited learning that might strengthen the field of community development.[11]

de Souza Briggs's point is not that community building and development are unattainable. Building or developing community may be a function of focus; he goes on to note that the

[T]ensions and trade-offs demanded by community building's *political influence and resource mobilization* agenda become clearer in light of community's building's second agenda, which seeks productive action to generate tangible outcomes—healthier children, safer streets, better employment, beautified surroundings, and more—through collective action, close to the ground.[12]

The lesson here is that moving a community building/development, indeed any community agenda, means focus must be narrowed to the point of concentrating on doing one or two things well. It is important to start with something concrete and attainable that demonstrates a tangible benefit to residents. This does not mean narrowing the effort to one thematic or functional area. Community building and development encompass a wide variety of activities that touch on the human condition, including livelihoods, arts and culture, youth development, and family development. These all are necessary and must connect to be effective in community development, but the question must always remain: how do these independent fields contribute to community economic development?

Working on a clear challenge builds and strengthens community building and development or augments community networks while building external networks.[13] But it is through the actual work of social and economic change that sustained community capacity is built to (1) implement projects of scale and (2) augment community influence and voice.

Public sector innovation in this arena is measured by the formal and informal structures that policy creates to allow for networked community building and development. In sum, community building and development that assist CED can be found in a program or initiative that (1) builds sustained attention to addressing a specific social, economic, or cultural challenge and (2) creates the opportunity to build trust and exchange relationships that can be carried over to other issue areas and concerns.[14]

The examples of innovative community building and development discussed in this chapter follow a simple formula. Each example comprises an issue area that directly helps community and economic development. The examples show the work of government, communities, and organizations striving to implement community and city planning, reduce crime, develop youth, create community art, and find alternative food sources. In the process, relationships emerge that build effective community and individual voice. In the end, community capacity is expanded and used for community economic development.

Planning, Information Management, and Development

There are many barriers to community economic development. Some are standard, such as access to capital, or limited community capacity. Others are less apparent and rest not only within the community but also with the larger administrative structure of local government.

At the extreme, some cities have less than up-to-date information on lots and properties in their jurisdiction. This is not simply an issue of identifying real estate ownership. It is not easy in most cities to get real-time, cross-agency information that identifies properties or property owners at risk of abandonment or foreclosure, but it is possible through the inexact art of matching delinquent water bills, utility bills, and property taxes. With this information, city planners and managers can spot trends and fashion policies to address the problem.

Increasingly, information technology and management are enhancing government effectiveness and in the process making government a better partner in community economic development. Although there are many examples of information technology changing public sector practice, New York City has long used COMSTAT, or COMPuter STATistics, as a performance measurement and management tool for fighting crime. The New York City Police Department (NYPD) uses Geographical Information Systems (GIS) to map crime in command districts throughout the city. In weekly meetings, senior NYPD officials meet with local precinct commanders to discuss elevated crime levels and problem neighborhoods identified by the maps and data.

Precinct commanders then deploy resources designed specifically to address problem points in a community. Commanders are asked hard questions about strategies and are held accountable for improving outcomes. The reduction of New York City crime rates using COMSTAT, combined with techniques such as community policing, have given crime-ridden neighborhoods in the Bronx, Brooklyn, and Queens new hope. These communities were given a chance, over the last decade and more, to go beyond a singular focus on crime toward working to rebuild homes and start new businesses and focus on improving schools in their communities.

Other jurisdictions are now using COMSTAT, and cities such as Baltimore, where COMSTAT originated, have extended the reach of GIS and the performance-management process to all major city departments. The Baltimore example, called CitiStat, uses mapped data as a foundation of city decision making. As much as it is feasible, real-time agency data is translated into performance measures, which are then used in mayoral decision making.

Line agencies meet every two weeks to report on target problems pinpointed by the maps and data. Although CitiStat is meant to be an accountability device, agencies are assisted in their efforts to address key challenges, which are broken down into short- or long-term frames.

Performance is keenly watched and assessed, but CitiStat was conceived as a way to change the culture of city government, making it more responsive and effective. CitiStat, which won Harvard University's Innovations in American Government Award, has demonstrably improved government performance.[15] Crime has been reduced, and strategies such as government outsourcing are now used as key responses to the CitiStat process. Code enforcement, a stable tool in fighting neighborhood blight, has been streamlined and made more effective in securing abandoned homes.[16]

None would claim that CitiStat has led to the rebirth of Baltimore. The networked system, though, has established a visible effective statement that the city is using information technology, planning, and management to improve the basics of service provision. At a symbolic and substantive level, CitiStat sends the message that Baltimore is attempting to modernize and increase its investment attractiveness for capital and people.

In isolation, CitiStat is an important governance innovation that affects community economic development. And although CitiStat is helped by citizen input, it is not meant to be a community development process. On the other side of the equation in Baltimore, a data-driven process called the Baltimore Neighborhood Indicators Alliance (BNIA) assists community development. BNIA is an umbrella group for a number of city and community stakeholders that devise indicators for community "health" in many forms.[17] Stakeholders include CDCs, neighborhood watch groups, faith institutions, and local philanthropy, all acting as both a steering committee and consumers of the data-driven indicators produced by BNIA.

The data and indicators are wrapped into a system called Vital Signs for Baltimore. BNIA collects the data and constructs the indicators based on the input and direction of their stakeholders. The BNIA process helps community stakeholders develop a long-term vision and tools, plans, and strategies to accomplish the vision. After implementing their plans, community residents and institutions continually assess the impact on their quality of life.

Much like CitiStat, those implementing strategies derived from the indicators calibrate the collection and use of data to reflect changing circumstances. Community residents and organizations use the indicators to track progress from their strategies and to become better consumers and users of data. In the end, the goal is to construct a usable and appropriate accountability system. But who are community stakeholders holding accountable?

In some instances, the BNIA is an accountability system for the nonprofit and voluntary sectors in Baltimore. Productive questions reduce the "slack" in any sector, especially a sector where the measures of success are often fluid. But community organizers also use the neighborhood-indicators process to work with government and the private sector to improve goods and services for the community. In addition, the fact that BNIA is an alliance means that knowledge and social capital are shared and built across neighborhoods and communities.

The BNIA and CitiStat processes work in tandem where appropriate. Data that are shared back and forth do not violate respective roles and interests. In both instances, significant community development knowledge and social capital are generated, which translates into active collaboration and learning. Again, BNIA is not a panacea that is likely to return Baltimore to economic vibrancy on its own. Baltimore has its share of politics and divisiveness that slow community and economic development, but this data-based management and planning regime (including CitiStat) has proved an important intervention and a lesson for other communities on how to coordinate city administrative reform and community development simultaneously.

Neighborhood Security and Community Economic Development

Public sector and philanthropic attention to community and economic development in the early 1960s began with concerns about ineffective schools and youth crime. Population shift to cities after World War II exacerbated existing overcrowding, residential segregation, and youth unemployment, creating a problem with juvenile delinquency. Popular social theory of the time blamed what we now call the concentration of poverty and community disorganization for youth crime. If communities had strong institutions that could provide structure (youth development programs, effective schools) and opportunity (job training), the level of juvenile delinquency would recede: so the theory went.[18] The institutional analysis and prescription would find its way into public policy and, ultimately, support for the rise of community development corporations and various types of CEDIs.[19]

Today, community safety challenges eclipse older conceptions of juvenile delinquency. As much as changing economic fortunes, both the business and the use of drugs have ravaged inner-city communities, and, increasingly, older suburbs and rural areas, Gangs now degrade the quality of life and sense of hope for the vast majority of law-abiding citizens residing in gang-infested communities. And, to be sure, the gangs of today are nothing like their 1950s and 1960s predecessors, popularized and even romanticized in *West Side Story* and *Grease*.[20]

The challenge now, similar to the 1960s, is to expand the internal and institutional organization and access to opportunity of poor communities. Now, however, communities face the presence of strong, pervasive gang organizations (many of them transnational) that have taken hold and made many communities unsuitable for economic investment. What is interesting about current efforts is the extent to which they have learned lessons from the past. Even conservative administrations voicing tough law-and-order platforms have come to recognize the importance of community building and development in the tough struggle to mitigate the problems of gangs and drugs.

Weed and Seed

The fury of destruction released by the introduction of crack cocaine in the mid-to-late 1980s led then-President George H. W. Bush to propose a demonstration program in 1991 called Operation Weed and Seed. The goals of the program were and remain ambitious: target high-crime neighborhoods and control violent crime, drug trafficking, and drug-related crime through intensive police presence and action.[21] The federal government provides support for targeted communities to bolster community involvement in crime reduction and youth development, the underlying public policy philosophy being that targeted areas can be best revitalized by "weeding" out violent offenders, drug traffickers, and other criminals from the targeted area and "seeding" the area with human services and neighborhood revitalization efforts.[22]

Following the April 1992 disturbances in Los Angeles, the demonstration program became a full-fledged program resting in the Department of Justice administered by the Executive Office for Weed and Seed (EOWS), now the Community Capacity Development Office (CCDO).[23] In full form, Operation Weed and Seed sees the federal government working with state and local governments, nonprofits, and the private sector to reduce crime and revitalize communities. Figure 6.1 shows expenditures for Weed and Seed from 1991 to 2009.[24]

Partnership is central to the process.[25] Each Weed and Seed site has a steering committee chaired by the U.S. attorney for the site's district.[26] Steering committee members often include representatives from key local, state, and federal agencies, business leaders, CDCs, and community residents. To receive funding, Weed and Seed sites submit a plan covering the following:

- Specifying a comprehensive multiagency strategy to manage and prevent violent crime, drug trafficking, and drug-related crime in targeted neighborhoods.
- Coordination and integration of existing federal, state, local, and private sector initiatives that have proven to maximize crime reduction.
- Mobilizing community residents to partner with law enforcement to remove violent offenders and drug traffickers from their neighborhoods.

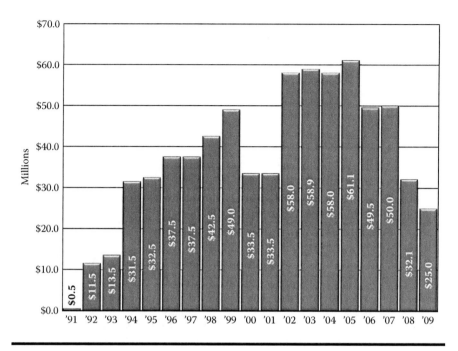

Figure 6.1   Weed and Seed expenditures (1991–2009).

■ Strategies to seed social services and economic development to ensure long-term change and a higher quality of life for residents.[27]

Weed and Seed sites are encouraged to establish a "Safe Haven," a multiservice center, often housed in a school or community center, where many community services are offered. The impact of the program is most felt in its ability to directly attack the social challenges preventing economic development. One example of this is employing hard-to-reach youth in three Pittsburgh, Pennsylvania, neighborhoods: Garfield, Larimer, and East Liberty. Each neighborhood received a $43,700 grant from Weed and Seed to implement a crime prevention initiative through job training and placement. That is not a lot of money.[28] The initiative, however, created a workforce development collaborative (encompassing more than a dozen local organizations) that is taken "on the road," blanketing the Garfield, Larimer, and East Liberty neighborhoods. Two longtime community-based organizations, the Bloomfield-Garfield Corporation (BGC) and the Eastside Neighborhood Employment Center (ENEC), lead the collaboration effort, using their extensive knowledge of the neighborhoods to adapt programs for youth and the unemployed. ENEC, for example, uses a mobile computer lab to tailor training and informational sessions directly to targeted residents in the three communities.[29]

Partnering with Weed and Seed, LISC's Community Safety Initiative

The utility and sheer necessity of community safety as a predecessor to community economic development has not escaped the formal CED system. Shortly after the birth of Weed and Seed, the Local Initiatives Support Corporation began working with the Department of Justice to partner and use LISC's existing local system as a way to maximize the impact of the program. LISC's Community Safety Initiative (CSI) builds partnerships between police and community development corporations (CDCs) in troubled neighborhoods to address issues of crime.

CDCs and police departments often exist in close proximity in crime-challenged neighborhoods, but it is not a given that they will collaborate on solutions given differing organizational cultures. CSI tries to overcome these challenges through strategic partnerships, in many cases brought together by a Weed and Seed program.

LISC's multidimensional role varies according to circumstance. With its local CDC partners, it can use its expertise and financing to renovate blighted buildings formerly used for crime. LISC also provides local Weed and Seed sites with local project coordinators who help translate site partner ideas into actual projects. The coordinators also serve as the liaison between police and community members.[30] And in an attempt to encourage the diffusion of innovation, LISC sponsors cross-site sharing conferences and conference calls.

As part of their involvement in Weed and Seed, LISC's CSI is now active in more than 20 sites in nine jurisdictions across the country, including Los Angeles, Richmond (California), Kansas City (Kansas and Missouri), Boston, the Bronx (New York), Cincinnati, Toledo (Ohio), Canton (Ohio), Seattle, and multiple cities in Rhode Island.[31]

LISC's CSI Weed and Seed partnerships have seen significant reduction in crime, turning lawless places into livable communities. Although this is not the silver bullet for crime reduction and community security in troubled neighborhoods, it is a significant policy innovation by the public sector (working with other stakeholders) that recognizes the need for community building and development to begin before community economic development can be realized.

Gang Diversion: Homeboy Industries

Another unique community security program is Homeboy Industries. Located in Los Angeles, it is specifically a gang-diversion program. The group grew out of a previous effort called Jobs for a Future, or JFF, which was created in 1988 by a Jesuit priest named Father Gregory Boyle. It began within his parish but quickly gained momentum and soon expanded into its own facility. Starting with a small bakery in a dilapidated warehouse, the program began employing local youth.[32] This concept was later replicated with the establishment of a tor-tilla stand, and before long the group was providing employment and training in food service to scores of former gang members. In 2001, the organization became an independent nonprofit group and later established its headquarters in downtown Los Angeles.[33]

Its motto is as simple as it is profound: "Jobs Not Jails." It also likes to say, "Nothing stops a bullet like a job." The group seeks to take people who may have felt they had no legitimate way to make an honest living and turn them into pro-ductive members of society.

To accomplish this goal, Homeboy Industries has started a whole host of innova-tive in-house business enterprises that act as springboards for eventual employment beyond Homeboy Industries. The group now operates Homeboy Silkscreen, which prints logos on clothing and provides embroidery services; Homeboy Maintenance, which provides landscaping and maintenance services; Homeboy Merchandise, which sells T-shirts, mugs, tote bags, and mouse pads with the Homeboy logo; and, more recently, Homegirl Café, a dedicated catering kitchen.

Gang-diversion programs, through workforce development, are nothing new; this program is not just a jobs program, however, but also a community-embedded effort that redirects the outlook of gang members through intensive education and community service. A more holistic approach to gang diversion includes basic assis-tance with food, clothing, and shelter, but the program also offers aggressive educa-tion programs, job placement, and health care.

Homeboy currently engages in computer-training programs as well, offering the technological skills required for success in the twenty-first-century job market. In many cases, the individuals receiving this training have had little or no expo-sure to computers. In addition, the organization has funded training programs for green jobs, specifically by teaching people how to become solar panel installers.[34] Homeboy has also pioneered efforts for tattoo removal. Often the main barrier to members leaving a gang or finding legitimate work is the tattooing of gang insignia on their skin. Through advances in laser removal technology, the group can fund the removal of a moderate-sized tattoo for as little as $125.

This effort might seem to be singularly geared toward community economic development, but it is more. These businesses give former gang members something to do and develop particular skills while weaning them from one all-encompassing (albeit negative) culture to mainstream culture and mores. Aside from business and workforce development, the other means by which Homeboy prevents the growth of gang activity reflect the new realities of today's gangs.

As a result of the decline in average age of new gang members, the target popula-tion is much younger than had been the case previously. Groups such as Homeboy Industries must now engage teens and even preteens in order to prevent them from joining a gang. Early on, Homeboy Industries tries to instill a work ethic and a hopeful attitude toward achieving legitimate success. Interestingly, many of the most effective voices within such organizations are former gang members. Often, they are the ones who have seen the pitfalls of the gang lifestyle, turned their lives around, and have come to be the most outspoken opponents of gangs. They can speak with the passion and conviction that others who have not been exposed to the tragedies of a gang lifestyle cannot.

Developing Youth/Youth Developing Communities

All young people need community support, guidance, and opportunities to build a positive role for themselves in their communities and beyond. Future Farmers of America, 4-H Clubs, Future Business Leaders of America, and Boys and Girls Clubs all teach community values, leadership, and other important life and citizenship skills. Although not as in vogue as they were 60 or so years ago, they still stand out as exemplary youth development vehicles. Kids in poor communities need this type of vehicle just as much or even more to impart leadership skills that can help build their community.[35]

Unfortunately, youth development in poor communities has become an ameliorative strategy helping to reclaim kids from the criminal justice system instead of helping them avoid the system in the first place. That said, youth development, however constituted and whatever the end goals, is important in promoting community economic development.

YouthBuild

YouthBuild is a great example of linking community building and development to community economic development, getting youth involved in community and economic development. It was begun in New York City's East Harlem during the 1960s by community activists distressed by the limited opportunities for young people to develop into productive citizens. Over time the idea emerged that youth are a key resource in the physical revitalization of their communities and that in the process they can learn citizenship and actual life and work skills.[36]

Over the years, the core idea that youth should be engaged in rebuilding their community survived mainly through the determination of Dorothy Stoneman, a teacher turned community organizer. Stoneman grew the idea through a series of successive New York-based youth development programs mostly funded by New York City government. In 1988, Stoneman and her organization, Youth Action, received a small grant from the Ford Foundation to take the idea of youth involvement in community building and development national. Eventually, the idea spread to other cities, morphing into YouthBuild USA, an intermediary promoting the integrity of the YouthBuild model.

YouthBuild USA (YBUSA) really got up and running in the early 1990s with programs in 14 cities. Shortly thereafter the power of the idea was recognized by the Department of Housing and Urban Development when it funded local

CEDIs to host YouthBuild programs through an amendment to the National Housing Act.[37] YouthBuild USA maintains the integrity of the model through program-development assistance, networking, and access to support beyond HUD resources.[38] Figure 6.2 details spending for YouthBuild from 1993 to 2008.[39]

YouthBuild USA helps low-income youth work toward their GED while obtaining hands-on construction skills by building affordable and low-income housing. YouthBuild USA has aided in the development of more than 226 local YouthBuild programs across communities. With much of the 6- to 24-month program sponsored by community and faith-based nonprofit organizations, youth are encouraged to participate in leadership development and community service activities.[40]

Evaluations of the YouthBuild USA model have consistently found positive outcomes from public investment in this program. For example, one study (Cohen and Piquero, 2008) conducted an outcome and cost–benefit evaluation of the YouthBuild Offender Project. In 2004, the Department of Labor funded YBUSA to implement their intervention targeting youth offenders re-entering their communities. YBUSA awarded grants to 31 local sites. The Cohen and Piquero (2008) study was limited to the sites that had fully implemented the intervention.

Within a sample of 388 youth offenders from across the YouthBuild sites they found evidence of reduced recidivism and improved educational outcomes

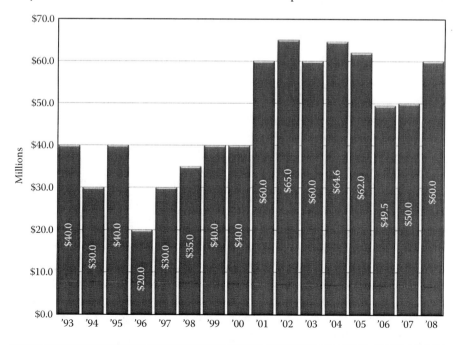

Figure 6.2 YouthBuild expenditures (1993–2008).

compared to similar cohorts. Cohen and Piquero also found evidence consistent with a positive cost–benefit ratio, in which every dollar spent on the YB Offender Project produces a social return on investment between $10.80 and $42.90. In addition, it is estimated that benefits to society range between $134,000 and $536,000 per participant, while only presenting a cost to society of about $12,500.

YouthBuild does make a difference in communities in which it is used as a strategy, but how? In 2002, the Prudential Foundation offered a $1 million grant to YouthBuild USA to organize the development of new YouthBuild programs in Newark, New Jersey, and Jacksonville, Florida. In Newark, YouthBuild USA and the Prudential Foundation collaborated with the community to create a new program in Newark's Central Ward, while establishing several goals for success. During the summer of 2003, the program recruited its first class of trainees. Over 250 youth and young adults between the ages of 16 and 24 applied; the first group of 70 trainees began orientation in September 2003.

In light of the fact that 76 percent of YouthBuild Newark's student body has at some point been involved with the criminal justice system and faced incarceration, the majority are considered to be "re-entry" students.[41] As a result, YouthBuild Newark has formed partnerships with YouthBuild USA, the U.S. Department of Labor (DOL), and the New Jersey Juvenile Justice Commission (JJC) in order to provide tailored re-entry services to its clients. The organization offers counseling services, including but not limited to case management, individual and family counseling, group counseling, substance-abuse prevention and treatment, and child care services. In addition to the services offered at YouthBuild Newark, many clients receive support through additional programs offered by referrals to partnering agencies.[42] Through the organization's cooperative work in conjunction with all levels of the legal system, many personnel of the justice system have begun to view YouthBuild Newark as a productive option for the re-entry population. Through community service activities, such as learning how to register to vote, participating in Newark Municipal Council meetings, and attending relevant events in the community, participants learn the value of civic activism and the individual roles they can play in rebuilding their own neighborhoods.[43]

In order to divide the program to provide entry/re-entry points for individuals who cannot afford to pass all segments consecutively, the YouthBuild Newark Program is scheduled in three phases.[44] After Mental Toughness, the first phase is focused on basic education to plant the foundation of essential academic and skills coursework, such as reading and math, construction fundamentals, and personal enrichment. For their initial assessment, students take The Adult Basic Education (TABE) locator test, which allows program directors and instructors to determine a student's approximate grade level for math and reading.

A student with a low score on the entry exam will undergo rigorous remedial education prior to entering the high school equivalency preparation program. When the student exits or graduates from the program, the test is again used to document the growth and progress made. Construction Fundamentals allow for basic skills building without the time constraints and pressures of an actual worksite, and Personal Enrichment groups students together to discuss their development and overall success. Through classroom and hands-on lab instruction, students develop general construction skills in a reasonably paced, structured atmosphere that allows for "making beginner's mistakes" in a less-pressured and constrained job setting.[45]

YouthBuild Newark runs a high school equivalency program for young adults in the program. The GED curriculum at YouthBuild Newark follows the New Jersey Core Content Curriculum Standards (NJCCCS) required by all New Jersey public schools. Through the program, students are expected to think critically about the material and gain familiarity with subject matter that could appear on tests.[46] In preparation for solving the questions on the high school equivalency exam, students primarily do problem-based work.

At the second phase, students begin to prepare for their careers and life after YouthBuild Newark.[47] While students prepare for their GEDs in the classroom, they build low-income and affordable housing at the construction site. During on-site skills training, participants gain exposure to the holistic process of construction from the initial process of cost analysis and developing a projected work schedule to the later stages of installing various appliances, making repairs, and painting walls, ceilings, or trim.[48] Students develop their job-readiness skills and build confidence in their skills sets through reviewing possible careers in construction, as well as exploring options in higher education. Instructors try their best to integrate the academic curriculum into the skills learned on the work site and needed in the construction industry, as well as other employment fields. For students who complete their high school equivalency requirement earlier, YouthBuild Newark offers an advanced curriculum.

Most students are introduced to the National Center for Construction Education and Research (NCCER), a not-for-profit education foundation whose mission is to address the critical worker shortages in the construction industry. Through its standardized craft training programs, NCCER allows participants to gain valuable knowledge through its curriculum of smart home, voice systems, fiber optic networking, copper networking, job search, and retention techniques, especially concerning the telecommunications industry.[49] The end of the second phase usually culminates in most students taking the GED exam. In order to give students a greater responsibility for the development of new students, current students provide coaching and involve themselves in the selection and preparation of new YouthBuild Newark members.

During the third, and final, phase, the Graduate Services Coordinator oversees students' preparation of college entrance exams, preapprenticeship programs, and searches for jobs and careers.[50] In order to facilitate the transition to full-time employment or higher education, strategies to support graduates include job placement assistance, counseling, refresher training, and transportation assistance.[51]

YouthBuild has become an important evidenced-based effort at youth crime prevention in New Jersey. The attorney general has started the Governor's Youth Crime Prevention Initiative, which uses YouthBuild programs as a key intervention.

Figure 6.3   Then-New Jersey Attorney General Anne Milgram announcing support to state's YouthBuild program: October 2009.

The Youth Crime Prevention Initiative provided increased support for existing programs in Newark, Trenton, Paterson, and Camden. Figure 6.3 (bottom) shows then-Attorney General Anne Milgram announcing the pilot in October 2009. This pilot is an example of cross-networking sectors, ideas, and programs that only enhance the impact of community development as a precursor to community economic development.[52]

Arts and Culture

The importance of the arts and cultural development in community building and development is not seriously contested, nor is it contested for community economic development. Examples of the power of the arts as a development device are just too numerous to deny the impact.[53]

The effect of arts in community development can be measured in many ways. Cultural production can bring in revenue through tourism, for example. In 2007, the city of New York brought in over $30 billion in revenue from tourism thanks to the density of its cultural institutions, including Broadway shows and museums. The role of public art has been central to Chicago's recent effort to brand itself as a livable city.

Use of art by the public sector as an economic development strategy has transformed abandoned buildings and vacant lots, often viewed as symbols of decay, into productive attractions. For years, the city of North Adams, Massachusetts, struggled in the aftermath of the closing in the mid-1980s of two major employers, Sprague Electric and General Electric, and with them the disappearance of 3,600 manufacturing jobs.

In 1999, after much planning (through the administrations of two governors), the Massachusetts Museum of Contemporary Art (Mass MoCA) opened as a mixed-use cultural and commercial center, reusing 27 abandoned factory buildings in downtown North Adams. Both public and private resources went into this adaptive reuse project, transforming a once-depressed town.[54] North Adams is now a destination for visitors, creating jobs and vibrancy that continues to extend development benefits.

Among many other such examples of the arts acting as an anchor for economic development are the New Jersey Performing Arts Center in Newark, the Broward Center for the Performing Arts in Fort Lauderdale, Florida, and the Mesa Arts Center in Mesa, Arizona. Yet we know that art is more than cultural economic production. Arts and culture are the grounding forces that transmit history, values, and vision for the future in all communities.

Developing a cultural base for social change in marginalized communities featured prominently at the beginning of the modern community development movement. The Community Arts Movement, the Black Arts Movement, and other similar efforts sought to infuse racial and community pride, and encourage social change through cultural production.[55] Many of the early CDCs and CEDIs had signature arts programs that tried to fuse community building and action for community education and change.

Today many of those community-based arts efforts have waned. Some have survived and have formally evolved a link to economic development. In doing so, they constantly face the challenge of using the community building and development force of arts and culture and making it relevant to the economic development needs of poor communities.

The work of Manchester Bidwell Corporation (MBC), located in the Manchester community in Pittsburgh, is perhaps one of the best illustrations of managing the tension well. MBC defines itself as a multiservice CEDI whose mission is to "reshape the business of social change through the arts, entrepreneurship, and community partnerships; and preserve, present, and promote jazz."[56]

Started by an extraordinary social entrepreneur named William Strickland, MBC is an internationally recognized example of a CEDI using the arts to base social and economic development.[57] Since 1968, MBC has provided arts education linked to job training and economic development to thousands of adults and youth in the Pittsburgh region. MBC and its subsidiary, Bidwell Training Center (BTC), provide career training for approximately 200 adults (predominantly low-income) per year in southwestern Pennsylvania. Additionally, BTC serves approximately 400 adults per year through literacy, General Education Diploma, and other human development programs.[58]

Students can earn a diploma in the culinary arts, concentrating in classic cuisine fundamentals and the importance of management skills while getting hands-on experience in a fully equipped professional kitchen. The office technology major emphasizes business instruction and extensive hands-on training on modern computers. The horticulture technology major provides core instruction in agriculture/horticulture and develops a background in the plant sciences while making connections to critical environmental issues. Instruction takes place at the Drew Mathieson Center, which is one of region's best educational greenhouses.[59] The center is the home for BTC's Horticulture Technology Program and boasts four gutter-connected, high-tech greenhouses with integrated classroom and lab components. It offers an applied learning experience for students aspiring to careers in landscaping or running a retail or wholesale floral shop.[60]

Turning Graffiti into Art: The Mural Arts Program in Philadelphia

Sometimes art, or what one person perceives as his or her art, can have a negative effect on economic development. Already burdened by heavy job and population loss in the 1980s and the ensuing decades, the prevalence of graffiti in Philadelphia telegraphed the message, "This is a city out of control." The city tried a number of things, including supporting an Anti-Graffiti Network made of community-based organizations. In 1984 the city started the Mural Arts Program (MAP) as a component of the Anti-Graffiti Network.[61] It hired a muralist to reach out to graffiti writers in an effort to turn a negative into a positive through constructive mural painting.

The city, in a bold move, used the Mural Arts Program to build a support structure for these mostly young graffiti artists to develop their skills and change their outlook on Philadelphia. Often, those who "tag" publicly visible property with spray paint do so to claim territory for a gang. Others who engage in the act are merely youth with few outlets for their artistic talents. The program's founder and current executive director, Jane Golden, saw an opportunity to clean up the image of Philadelphia while empowering aspiring artists who would otherwise have no legitimate market for their talents. The program helped instill an ethic that they could be part of the solution to Philadelphia's challenges.

In 1996, the City of Philadelphia folded the Anti-Graffiti Network into the Mural Arts Program to form a nonprofit organization, the Philadelphia Mural Arts Advocates, which raises money for various support programs. The Mural Arts Program is now one of the nation's largest public arts initiatives of its kind. The mission is arts education, promoting public art collaborations, and increasing public access to art. The program's goals, in partnership with communities, grassroots organizations, city agencies, schools, and philanthropies, are to:

■ *Develop* sustainable partnerships with community organizations in order to create murals reflecting the community's culture, history, and vision.
■ *Catalyze* community development, neighborhood activism, and civic pride.
■ *Foster* youth development through experiential art education and mentorship with professional artists.
■ *Support* artists and artisans in sharing their talents and experiences with youth and communities in Philadelphia.
■ *Use* the power of art and the mural design process as tools for community engagement, blight remediation, beautification, demonstration of civic pride, and crime prevention.[62]

The Mural Arts Program has produced well over 3,000 murals and educated more than 20,000 youth from economically challenged circumstances. Creating public art with over 2,500 mural sites in Philadelphia, and 150 to 200 new sites per year, MAP has had a visible impact on Philadelphia neighborhoods.[63] Private citizens and public leaders alike have largely been receptive to the idea driving MAP, and what started as a loosely knit effort is now an indispensable social program within the Philadelphia Department of Recreation.

In addition to merely removing unsightly graffiti that contributes to unpleasant cityscapes, the concept of painting over it with attractive and positive images has had innumerable social benefits for the young men and women (particularly low-income minorities) looking to express their creativity. More recently, MAP has formalized the training of muralists. MAP now offers after-school workshops in mural painting and community engagement with young people from around the city. These workshops enhance MAP's mission of partnering with community residents, community-based organizations, the public sector, and others to use the arts as a development device. With aggressive programs for teaching how to carry out mural arts projects, these workshops get kids off the streets and serve to overhaul the look and feel of Philadelphia.

Food and Community Development

"Food is at the very foundation of community development." That quote, from Will Allen, a 2008 recipient of a MacArthur "genius grant," sums up his philosophy and the philosophy of his community-based organization, Growing Power, in Milwaukee, Wisconsin.[64]

In 1995, Will Allen was helping neighborhood children with a gardening project. He had done many things in his life, including professional basketball and various corporate stints. He felt the tug and power of farming and imagined the possibility of what it could do to help inner-city communities counter limited access to fresh foods, obesity, and a disconnect with the work ethic that successful farming demands.[65]

That gardening project would grow to an inner-city farming enterprise that now includes over 10 greenhouses producing a variety of vegetables, greens, and herbs. Growing Power's land is the only place zoned as farmland in Milwaukee. Growing Power also has a 40-acre farm in Merton, a nearby town, and has gardens in neighborhoods all around the city.[66] It runs a world-class composting operation that turns urban and rural waste into fertilizer. The organization's aquaculture operation, which raises tilapia and Great Lakes perch, is in the forefront of the "urban aquaponics" movement.

Growing Power is not a small precious innovation. The organization produces a significant volume of food for sale and distribution to upscale restaurants in Milwaukee and Chicago that want fresh organically produced food.[67] Growing Power's mission and methods set it apart and qualify it as a community development innovation. Growing Power focuses on educating young people about the virtues of hard work and giving them a sense of purpose so they can avoid gangs. Working with the school system, each year Growing Power brings in scores of young people, many of them minority and immigrants, for six-week intensive courses covering sustainable farming, entrepreneurial skills, and good eating habits. Many of the teenagers stay on for internships or volunteer at Growing Power, cementing the lessons learned in their initial exposure. Some of the young people have gone on to operate small farms or to work for Growing Power.

Interestingly, Growing Power makes this all work in an urban environment on land that may have been contaminated in the past. It works with area universities to test the soil to make sure that it is not contaminated. Again, with the help of universities, it has pioneered the use of small spaces and low-cost farming technologies, such as using raised beds, aquaculture, vermiculture, and heating greenhouses through composting to produce food year-round.[68] Many see its aquaculture work as an opportunity to grow a sustainable industry in Milwaukee. Growing Power has also partnered with local organizations and activities such as the Farm-City Market Basket Program, which provides a weekly basket of fresh produce grown by members of the Rainbow Farmer's Cooperative to low-income urban residents at a reduced cost.

Community gardens and urban agriculture are becoming more than isolated experiments. Concerns about food safety and the industrialization of food production that has undermined the availability of nutritious food has spurred a movement encompassing many mainstream communities and poor communities.[69] But beyond food concerns, urban farming and urban gardens are becoming a viable strategy for urban communities to reclaim people and promote collective action on other important challenges in their community.[70]

Summary

Community building and development are not in short supply in the United States. The examples in this chapter represent just a few resourceful efforts. Community economic development is a difficult undertaking, and without attention to shoring up the other elements of people's lives, it is a nonstarter. Central to shoring up community or the people side of things is the attitude and willingness of local government to show tangible leadership in the larger process of city transformation.[71] For example, CitiStat is more than a GIS, numbers-counting exercise. It is a clear statement, now over two mayoral administrations, that reforming city government to pick up garbage, reduce crime, and improve major services to the public is a precondition to both the survival of Baltimore as an economic force in its region and a signal to its neighborhoods that government will not abandon them.

Communities understand when government is making an investment, and it need not be more than what government should be doing as a matter of course. It just has to do it well and effectively. But the BNIA process shows another side of the transformation to sustainable communities: communities have to find ways of organizing more effectively and efficiently, not only to articulate demands to city governments but to organize to do what they can for themselves.

The BNIA is a good example of putting in place a deliberative process of planning, coordinating, and building social capital between government and community and also between community and community. The key is that all the actors have individual community goals to satisfy through the planning process. This does not mean that those goals are always attained, but there is an umbrella structure that can provide communities with the crucial knowledge and assistance they need to make informed decisions about a range of community development issues. This is community organizing, community building, and community development, but with a structure that applies knowledge to address key issues such as housing abandonment and access to health care. The old adage "knowledge is power" still applies in community building and development.

An important key to sustainable community economic development is how we address youth development. This does not mean that we neglect family development and building wealth as other features of people and place development. The reality, however, is that the needs of youth exert an inordinate force in the development of neighborhoods and communities. It is no accident that most if not all of the innovative community building and development examples in this chapter eventually focus on helping youth find their way in life. As a nation, we either do it at the front end or spend much time and many resources at the back end trying to clean up the problems of wayward youth.

The good news is that as a nation we have found ways to link community building and development to youth development. The Weed and Seed approach, for example, is a layered effort that recognizes that development of any kind is not going to occur without a secure community. That is an important policy statement and philosophy that puts in perspective an often-ignored reality about development. While recognizing that drug dealers and other offenders need to be vigorously prosecuted, the effort builds social capital between the authorities and community and then within community networks around development projects.

Homeboy Industries links the notion of job development and workforce development and brings it in-house so to speak. Using what might be called a "training business" model, Homeboy Industries focuses on locally relevant enterprises not only to provide livelihoods but also to build an alternative lifestyle to gang culture in Los Angeles. Looking in from the outside, it is easy for us to ask, "Why not leave gangs?" The truth is that gangs dominate poor communities because they provide a continuum of life stages and opportunity for members, from community, social capital, leadership development, and livelihoods. Using the key focus of jobs, Homeboy Industries provides a coherent alternative than may look simple but is calibrated to divert gang members to more productive pursuits.

YouthBuild started out as a progressive way to get youth involved in community development. In today's urban environment it is shaping up to be an extraordinarily effective way to manage the challenges of re-entry after youth leave the juvenile justice system. From providing a trade that will always be in demand to providing a workable way to provide remedial education to ex-gang members, YouthBuild is proving to be an important intervention.

One product of YouthBuild does not often come to the surface in the numbers. In Newark, program operators related a story that they thought ordinary, but is extraordinary in its impact. They spoke of members of the Crips and the Bloods, two well-known national gangs, self-organizing to go bowling in Essex County on

Friday nights. YouthBuild did not organize or sanction the activity, but after going through the program together, the youth got to know each other outside their often-violent roles as gang members. They were able to form bonds of respect and affection. Although a great example of developing social capital, this should also be processed as an example of the possibility of what can happen when youth are extracted from the unfortunate norms that exist in most urban communities today.

We need to remember that although these young people have experienced the worst of life, they can be reclaimed. YouthBuild, the Bidwell Training Center, the Mural Arts Program, Growing Power, and many more show us that there many ways to help youth and build community at the same time. The important thing, in all the examples, whether they touch on workforce development or economic development or sustainability, is they all offer interconnected ways to improve the economic circumstance of people, places, and regions.

Endnotes

1. http://web.worldbank.org/WBSITE/EXTERNAL/TOPICS/EXTSOCIALDEVE LOPMENT/EXTCDD/0,,menuPK:430167~pagePK:149018~piPK:149093~the SitePK:4301 61,00.html. (accessed February 9, 2009)
2. de Souza Briggs (2007, p. 4).
3. Gibson, Kingsley, and McNeely, (1997, p. 3).
4. United Nations (1959, p. 2). A generation ago, community development gathered force as a strategy, internationally, with the emergence of many new nations after World War II. Community development was seen as an adjunct to nation building. Communities and villages in these new nations undertook projects such as building schools, digging wells in rural communities, establishing cooperative credit unions, and constructing local governance systems such as village councils, all under the rubric of community development and with the support of international multilateral and bilateral aid. Thus community development was defined more as a set of activities with the goal of human improvement rather than a fully defined strategy in any one functional area.
5. Ferguson and Dickens (1999, introduction).
6. Ibid., pp. 3–4.
7. Sviridoff and Ryan (1996); also Carlson and Martinez (1988). On reflection, it was perhaps too much to ask any one organization to fulfill these many roles, especially if there were other agencies in the community that could share the burden. The multi-function CDC that touched every aspect of human development became a rare bird and along with that the separation of the social development, voice/advocacy, and economic development, at least in the American community development context.
8. Ford Foundation (1979).
9. The early community economic development movement struggled with economic development efforts. Much like the broader economy, shifting economies troubled the fragile efforts of small- to medium-size efforts of emerging CEDIs. Many CEDI workforce development efforts succeeded, but these efforts became specialized, transformed by the availability of federal funds into solely workforce development organizations.

CEDIs, such as CDCs, did perform well in the area of housing development (Carlson and Martinez 1988; Halpern 1995). With the advent of the Community Reinvestment Act and the Low Income Housing Tax Credit, coupled with the reduction of government support that came in the 1970s and early 1980s, housing development became the significant area of work for Community Economic Development (United States Congress).

10. Sviridoff and Ryan (1996); Brown (1996).
11. deSouza Briggs (2007, p. 7).
12. Ibid, p. 21.
13. See Chaskin (2001) and de Souza Briggs (2007).
14. Though I try to use them consistently here, the reader should note that a reference to community development or community building is all part of one underlying conceptual and administrative framework.
15. Perez and Rushing (2007).
16. CitiStat has also led to collaboration between the Department of Solid Waste, Health Department, Department of Transportation, and Department of Housing and Community Development called Cleanstat. Cleanstat's goals are to improve Baltimore's quality of life by targeting graffiti removal, cleaning up abandoned lots, and recycling solid waste. Citizen complaints drive the process and agency managers have to report on reducing public nuisances.
17. http://www.bnia.org/. BNIA is part of a national movement seeing neighborhoods and communities use data to base community-based planning. See http://www2.urban.org/nnip/. (accessed February 10, 2009)
18. Lewis (1996, p. 95) sums the argument very well.
19. Magat (1979, pp. 119–122).
20. The reader is encouraged to see a quite revealing short film produced by the New Jersey Institute for Social Justice (http://www.njisj.org/action/support.php#2) chronicling the voices of gang members in Newark, New Jersey. The film provides a direct and unvarnished portrait of why gangs now proliferate in many communities. (accessed February 25, 2009)
21. http://www.ojp.usdoj.gov/ccdo/ws/welcome.html. (accessed February 25, 2009)
22. Ibid. The "weed" portion of the effort is not without controversy. Coupled with stiff drug dealing and possession laws that were passed in the 1970s, the conviction of "extracted" drug offenders has surely contributed to the enormous swelling of this nation's prison population. We now have a problem of these ex-offenders returning to the same communities in which they committed crimes without much ability to earn livelihoods. See Clear (2007) on this point.
23. The Weed and Seed Program has no formal authorization. In July 1992, the attorney general established the Executive Office for Weed and Seed in the Department of Justice although budgetary authority comes under the Department of Commerce, Justice, and State, the Judiciary, and Related Agencies Appropriations Act, 1995 (P.L. 103-317) and succeeding appropriations.
24. The Weed and Seed figure was constructed using the following sources. It is important to note that "Since 1994, in addition to appropriated funds, the U.S. Department of Justice has allocated $9 million annually in Asset Forfeiture Funds for Weed and Seed-related task forces administered through the Drug Enforcement Administration, the Federal Bureau of Investigation, and other DOJ law enforcement agencies." http://www.ncjrs.gov/pdffiles1/175685.pdf. See

also: FY 2000-FY 2001: http://thomas.loc.gov/cgi-bin/cpquery/?&sid=cp106Q
uAhF&refer=&r_n=hr680.106&db_id=106&item=&sel=TOC_171804&;   FY
2002, FY 2004: http://ftp.resource.org/gpo.gov/bills/110/hr108ih.txt; FY 2003:
http://www.spaceref.com/news/viewsr.html?pid=7759; FY 2005: http://www.calinst.
org/pubs/cjs06s.htm; FY 2006-FY 2008: http://reentrypolicy.org/announcements/
presidents_budget_released; FY2009: http://thomas.loc.gov/cgi-bin/query/F?c111:4:./
temp/~c111GCoq91:e180527. (accessed March 4, 2009)
25. Communities interested in becoming Weed and Seed Communities (WSCs) must
    submit a Notice of Intent to the U.S. Attorney's Office (USAO). WSCs must be devel-
    oped in partnership with many local organizations to reduce crime and improve the
    quality of life in a community primarily through the redeployment of existing public
    and private resources into the community.
26. The U.S. Attorney's Office is key to the process, often facilitating the coordination of
    federal, state, and local law enforcement in local plans and strategies.
27. http://www.ojp.usdoj.gov/ccdo/ws/welcome.html. (accessed February 25, 2009)
28. Martinac (2009).
29. See ibid. ENEC also plans career fairs in conjunction with other CBOs including:
    Brothers and Sisters Emerging; Wireless Neighborhoods; East Liberty Concerned
    Citizens Council; Carnegie Library of East Liberty; West Penn Hospital; UPMC;
    Garfield Jubilee Association; Eastminster Presbyterian Church; East Liberty
    Development, Inc.; Kingsley Association; and the Community College of Allegheny
    County.
30. http://www.lisc.org/section/goals/healthy/safety. (accessed February 8, 2009)
31. Ibid.
32. http://www.homeboy-industries.org/history.php. (accessed March 4, 2009)
33. It has received government support from agencies ranging from the Office of Juvenile
    Justice and Delinquency Prevention located in the Department of Justice to the
    National Endowment for the Arts for its literary magazine.
34. To read the full article about this aspect of Homeboy's job training, see Jordan (2009).
    http://online.wsj.com/article/SB123457326090086555.html. (accessed March 5,
    2009)
35. M. Guajardo, F. Guarjardo, and Casaperalta (2008). (accessed March 9, 2009)
36. http://www.youthbuild.org/site/c.htIRI3PIKoG/b.1240601/k.C3BC/History.htm.
37. The National Affordable Housing Act, Title IV, Subtitle D, 42 U.S.C. 8011, as
    amended; Housing and Community Act of 1992, Section 164, Public Law 102-
    550. YouthBuild's statutory authority has been transferred to the U.S. Department
    of Labor.
38. In addition to providing local programs with guidance in implementation and staff
    training, YouthBuild USA advocates raise funds from corporations, individuals, and
    foundations such as the Bill and Melinda Gates Foundation, Home Depot, and Bank of
    America.
39. Funded by more than $700 million in federal funds since 1994, YouthBuild is also
    funded by donations from corporations, foundations, and individuals, as well as state
    funding. http://www.youthbuild.org/site/c.htIRI3PIKoG/b.1223923/k.C7D6/About_
    Us.htm. A detailed breakdown of donation amounts and funders can be found at: http://
    www.youthbuild.org/site/c.htIRI3PIKoG/b.1247793/k.CF27/Partners.htm#federal; FY
    1993: http://www.youthbuild.org; FY 1996: http://www.openplanner.org/node/637;
    FY 1997: http://fhasecure.gov/sec4.cfm; FY 2000-FY 2004 (FY 2001 and FY 2002 are

reported different here than on the spreadsheet, I used the numbers from the GAO Web site listed last below). http://www.hud.gov/offices/cpd/economicdevelopment/ programs/youthbuild/qfacts.cfm; FY 2006: http://www.ssireview.org/site/printer/full_ scale_ahead/; FY 2007: http://www.youthbuild.org/site/apps/nlnet/content2.aspx?c=h tIRI3PIKoG&b=1306513&ct=2343143; FY 2009-2010 http://www.youthbuild.org/ site/apps/nlnet/content2.aspx?c=htIRI3PIKoG&b=1306513&ct=6989909; A good graph of annual funding which was used to find FY 1998, FY 1999, FY 2001, FY 2002, FY 2004 and estimate FY 2005 is on page 8 of the GAO document (which also has other good graphs and information on the program) at: http://www.gao.gov/new.items/ d0782.pdf. (accessed March 10, 2009)

40. YouthBuild USA. (2008). *About YouthBuild*. Retrieved 5/4, 2009, from http://www. youthbuild.org/site/c.htIRI3PIKoG/b.1223925/k.DF42/Programs.htm. (accessed March 10, 2009)

41. http://www.youthbuildnewark.com/re-entry/. (accessed March 10, 2009)

42. http://www.youthbuildnewark.com/counseling/. (accessed March 10, 2009)

43. http://www.youthbuildnewark.com/leadership-development/. (accessed March 10, 2009)

44. www.youthbuild.org/atf/cf/%7B22B5F680-2AF9-4ED2-B948-40C4B32E6198%7D/Newark%20Trimester%20plan.pdf. (accessed March 10, 2009)

45. http://www.youthbuildnewark.com/construction-training/. (accessed March 10, 2009)

46. http://www.youthbuildnewark.com/education/. (accessed March 10, 2009)

47. www.youthbuild.org/atf/cf/ %7B22B5F680-2A F9-4ED2-B948-4 0C4B32E6198%7 D/Newark%20Trim ester%20plan.pdf. (accessed March 10, 2009)

48. http://www.youthbuildnewark.com/construction-training/. (accessed March 10, 2009)

49. http://www.youthbuildnewark.com/credentialing-activities/. (accessed March 10, 2009)

50. www.youthbuild.org/at f/cf/%7B22B5 F680-2AF9-4E D2-B948-40C 4B32E6198%7 D/Newark%20 Trimester%2 0plan.pdf. (accessed March 10, 2009)

51. http://www.youthbuildnewark. com/graduate-services/. (accessed March 10, 2009)

52. Office of the Attorney General, "Attorney General Announces Major Funding for Education and Job Training Programs $6.25 million in state and federal money for YouthBuild programs," http://www.nj.gov/oag/newsreleases09/pr20091021a.html. (accessed October 21, 2009) A small bit of transparency for the reader: the author has been chosen to lead a team of researchers evaluating the effects of this recent enhancement of New Jersey's YouthBuild programs. This fact does not cast doubt on my objective use of YouthBuild as an example given many past evaluations that have documented its effectiveness.

53. www.usmayors.org/maf/documents/20081215-Arts.pdf. (accessed March 12, 2009)

54. Condon (2003).

55. See, for example, http://www.communityarts.net/ and http://www.englis h.illinois. edu/ma ps/blackarts/blac karts.htm. (accessed March 12, 2009)

56. See http://www.manchesterbidwell.org/ and http://www.manchesterguild.org/About_ mcg.htm. (accessed March 13, 2009)

57. http://www.bill-strickland.org/. Among other awards, Strickland has won the MacArthur Foundation's "Genius" award (1996), which gives an unrestricted five-year grant totaling $500,000. (accessed March 12, 2009)

58. http://www.manchesterbidwell.org/. (accessed March 15, 2009)

59. The 40,000-square-foot complex is located on the BTC campus and was established to support training in the plant sciences. See http://www.manchesterbidwell.org/. (accessed March 16, 2009)

60. BTC also has a slew of health majors including health unit coordinator, medical coder, pharmacy technician, and chemical laboratory technician. These majors provide a firm footing for graduates looking to break into unique niches in the health care industry.

61. http://www.muralarts.org/. (accessed March 16, 2009)

62. Ibid.

63. At the time of writing (2009), the Mural Arts Program works with a $4.4 million budget. The organization employs 165 muralists on a contractual basis, turning former criminals into entrepreneurial freelance artists.

64. *Christian Science Monitor* (2009).

65. Guiding all his efforts is the recognition that the unhealthy diets of low-income, urban populations, and such related health problems as obesity and diabetes are largely attributable to limited access to safe and affordable fresh fruits and vegetables.

66. The group also has operations in Chicago, including urban farms in Grant and Jackson Parks.

67. The store at Growing Power's Milwaukee farm is the only place for miles around that carries fresh produce, free-range eggs, grass-fed beef, and local honey. Even in winter, customers find the shelves stocked with fresh greens.

68. Vermiculture uses a variety of worms to break down organic material for composting. Using millions of pounds of food waste, his farm produces endless compost piles, which are then enriched by thousands of pounds of worms, essential to producing high-quality fertilizer.

69. There is a history of CEDIs (such as the Watts Labor Action Committee in Los Angeles operating a working farm on land it owned in then-rural Los Angeles County in the 1960s) using agriculture as a community development device, but nothing on the scale of Growing Power. Another example of urban agriculture that promotes community development is Growing Home (http://www.growinghomeinc.org) (accessed March 17, 2009), which provides homeless and low-income people with job training based on urban agriculture. Also, the partnership of Market Umbrella in New Orleans and the Federation of Southern Cooperatives shows a new dimension of agriculture and community and economic development. The Federation is made up of African American farmers who supply part of their production to an urban community market in New Orleans managed by Market Umbrella. Market Umbrella also helps the farmers supply their produce to restaurants in New Orleans. See http://www.marke tumbrella.org/ and http://www.federatio nsoutherncoop.com/.

70. Community gardens have become an important tool to get neighbors in challenged urban neighborhoods to come out and reclaim fallow land and plant flowers and vegetables. The perception of their community and their sense of each other changes for the better. Land values go up and community security improves because residents are out of their homes, showing drug dealers and others who would do harm in a com-

munity that there are those who care about it. See, for example, the City of Chicago's CitySpace Program (http://egov.cityofchicago.org) (accessed March 20, 2009), and Casillas (2009).

71 Greasley and Stoker (2008).

Chapter 7

Assets and Agency

Promoting individual and collective agency and self-determination is a central community economic development goal. But agency and self-determination cannot prosper in circumstances where the community, neighborhood, and regional economy are weak and residents are unable to earn livelihoods.[1]

Government policy has promoted individual asset accumulation in poor and minority communities over the years through supporting small businesses and increasing home ownership.[2] Recently, the influence of ideas putting wealth or asset building at the center of community and economic development has called into question past economic development strategies.[3]

This chapter looks at recent attempts to enhance or build individual and community assets in places with limited resources. Business development has been a public policy tool for asset building; however, new ideas and trends such as microenterprise development, supported savings accounts, and efforts to increase self-employment have made inroads as strategies. Asset-building strategies can potentially be important in reducing poverty when complemented by the built capacity of the community economic development industry.

Economic development policies specifically targeting minority and poor communities originated during the Great Society years. Interestingly, minority economic development gained added currency during the Nixon administration through President Nixon's effort to promote "Black Capitalism" as a successor to the Great Society.[4]

Nixon's Black Capitalism instituted set-aside programs giving minority- and women-owned businesses priority access to government contracts. In addition, minority entrepreneurs gained access to a host of small business assistance services from the Small Business Administration such as entrepreneurship training and low-interest loans.[5] Although scaled back, many of these programs still exist, and supporters hold that these policies have been a powerful tool for economic development.

Evidence suggests that the programs helped create minority entrepreneurs but played a mixed role in creating jobs in minority communities.[6] One of the criticisms has been that minority business development is less useful as a device for capital formation at the lower end of the income spectrum than it is for creating a middle class for a small number of people in minority communities.[7] In fact, encouraging self-employment through public policy for the poor has been an elusive goal in the United States. The question is whether emerging asset-building strategies can do much better

In the last 15 years, asset building has become the umbrella term for a set of policies and practices aimed at increasing capital for the poor and other marginalized groups. As Oliver (2001) describes the importance of assets thinking:

> An "asset" in this paradigm is a special kind of resource that an individual, organization, or entire community can use to reduce or prevent poverty and injustice. An asset is usually a "stock" that can be drawn upon, built upon, or developed, as well as a resource that can be shared or transferred across generations. Because all societies' assets are unevenly distributed, their distribution is highly related to both public policy decisions and cultural traditions and forces.[8]

Oliver goes on to say that these

> policies and traditions have affected the ways in which society structures ownership of assets and investments in assets. These structures have often affected women and members of ethnic minorities in particular by excluding them from asset building activities. As the poor gain access to assets, they're more likely to take control of important aspects of their lives, to plan for their future and deal with economic uncertainty, to support their children's educational achievements, and to work to ensure that the lives of the next generations are better than their own.[9]

The asset-building paradigm calls much past "asset-building" policy into question, arguing that some of these policies actually keep people in poverty.[10] Federal policy, for example, supported racial segregation through Federal Housing Administration policies that restricted people of color from getting home mortgages. This limited the intergenerational transfer of assets and still contributes to what some term the black/white wealth gap.[11]

Although overt discrimination is less the problem, public policy still has an indirect role in limiting economic opportunity. Sacrosanct policies such as the home mortgage deduction, one of the key policies of the federal government that encourages home ownership...by allowing the marginal tax rate to be deducted from families' income..., are part of the hidden welfare state, which cost the federal government about $94 billion a year in fiscal expenditures. Home ownership may very well be sound policy for many Americans, but it is an uneven process that clearly advantages some groups over others.[12]

It is not that home ownership is bad. Far from it: owning a home is an important way to build assets and escape poverty in the United States. Asset-building proponents, though, point out the obvious: that to take advantage of the mortgage deduction you must already have an asset, a house. Thus the old adage comes into play: "It takes money to make money." What if you do not have the resources to purchase a home?[13] Then you are locked out of not only the benefits of the deduction but also the use of an asset to leverage starting a small business or investing in education for yourself or family members that can increase economic opportunity.

Individual Asset Building

How does an asset-building policy translate into a guide for policy and programs? A number of key innovations in community economic development are being used to build wealth. Individual Development Accounts (IDAs), microenterprise self-employment strategies, and the Earned Income Tax Credit (EITC) are relatively new strategies, in the American context, to develop long-term income-generating capacity.[14]

As some claim, an assets perspective takes a radically different mindset: social science and public policy must incorporate

an assets perspective into its understanding of the structure of social divisions and social equality.... Any fruitful discussion of the social dynamics must take into account both labor market dynamics and the processes by which family wealth is accumulated and must also explore the kinds and amounts of assets that might promote well-being and mobility. Very modest assets can generate large changes: $3,000 of down payment purchases a house by most low- and moderate-income families; $1,500 is the average annual tuition at a community college; and $5000 or less capitalizes most businesses in the United States.[15]

Individual Development Accounts

Savings vehicles such as Individual Development Accounts (IDAs) can build a modest asset base for marginalized communities to leverage upward mobility.[16] IDAs are matched savings accounts for the poor. They entered the policy stream as innovations in the late 1980s and were embraced by all points of the political spectrum.[17] They can be implemented in many forms, but usually a community-based organization or CEDI hosts an IDA program with support from a federally sponsored program originating from HUD, Health and Human Services, and now the Department of Labor.[18]

The federal government's Department of Health and Human Services offers the Assets for Independence Program (AFI), which enables community-based non-profits and government agencies to pursue an assets-based approach to poverty reduction.[19] AFI projects help participants save earned income through IDAs.[20] Every dollar in savings deposited into an IDA by participants is matched (from $1 to $8 combined federal and nonfederal funds). AFI project families use their IDA savings, including the matching funds, toward acquiring a first home, capitalizing a small business, or enrolling in postsecondary education or training.[21]

The Department of Housing and Urban Development's Family Self-Sufficiency (FSS) initiative has much the same underlying concept as AFI but is targeted toward residents of public housing and those receiving housing supplements such as the Housing Choice Voucher (HCV) program (formerly called Section 8). Created by Congress in 1990, the FSS increases the incentive for seeking and staying employed and saving by public housing residents.[22] Those living in public housing must pay 30 percent of their adjusted income for rent and utilities. This fixed rate keeps housing cost reasonable for those with low incomes; however, it creates a disincentive for seeking better-paying jobs or saving money. Through the FSS program, residents still pay higher rents as their income increases, but the FSS program deposits an amount equal to the increase in rent each month. Public housing authorities (PHAs) create escrow accounts in which residents can deposit their savings.[23] Figure 7.1 provides spending totals for the FSS program from 2004 to 2009.[24]

The FSS initiative comes with a system of support to help PHA residents save enough to leave public assistance. Participating families work with counselors who help them take stock and put in place a personal plan to earn their way off public assistance. The plan is constructed in the form of a five-year plan that serves as a contract with the program. Counselors help participants find relevant support services such as financial literacy, child care, transportation, and employment training. On graduation from FSS, participants can use their saved resources for any purpose including a down payment on a home.

One evaluation of the FSS concluded that

> consistent with the goals of the FSS program, the results of the…analysis showed that program participants derived considerable benefits from their enrollment. FSS participants' income rose substantially over time, compared to non-FSS participants, and the escrow accounts provided often-sizable cash disbursements for education, transportation, and other uses. As a benefit to the PHAs as well as participants, FSS

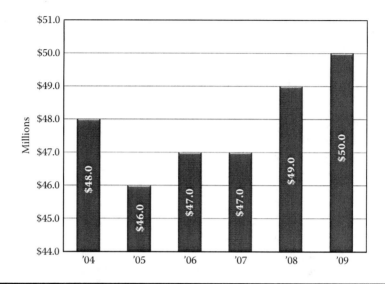

Figure 7.1   HUD Family-Self-Sufficiency Program (2004–2009).

programs encouraged the development of community partnerships that helped address a range of tenant needs beyond the provision of affordable housing.[25]

Without doubt, supported savings is now a mainstream policy strategy. Of course there are limitations. IDA programs are expensive to operate and not very profitable for the financial institutions that host them.[26] It is estimated that it costs about $64 per participant per month, excluding the cost of the match but including costs of recruitment, financial education, monitoring accounts, and providing other financial services.[27]

Overall, the evidence suggests that IDAs do have an impact. Another study, *Saving Performance in the American Dream Demonstration,* related outcomes among 2634 participants who contributed to 13 IDA programs over two years. Researchers found that "participants do use IDAs to purchase assets expected to have high enough returns and that mark key steps in the life course" and that "what matters is not only the amount, but the existence of accumulation."[28] Furthermore, they argue that assets "are associated with household economic stability, education attainment, lower rates of intergenerational poverty transmission, local civic involvement, and other positive effects."[29]

Efforts to collaborate between the private and public sectors to finance matching funds are a recent innovation in IDA administration. Recipients of federal grants to provide IDA deposits are required to obtain an equal amount of funding from a private source. This requirement for both public and private sector funding helps one build on the other and therefore makes more capital available to administer the IDA funds. In addition, many financial institutions are creating collaboratives among banks to pool funds.

Nevada, the state with the highest percentage of households with zero net worth, created the Nevada Individual Development Account Collaborative.[30] The Nevada collaborative has encouraged smaller banks to become involved in the IDA program. The collaborative also helps to centralize resources for banks that are looking for IDA program support.

In another example of collaboration around IDAs, the United Way of Metropolitan Atlanta administers three IDA programs for home ownership, microenterprise, and youth.[31] Several community-based organizations, financial institutions, and education organizations established the IDA for Home Ownership Program. Through this program, participants are enrolled in a 6- to 24-month saving period, during which they attend financial literacy courses to learn saving strategies, repair credit or debt issues, and understand the responsibilities that come with home ownership.[32]

The United Way IDA for Microenterprise Development benefits low-income entrepreneurs who need assistance starting or expanding their business with equipment or inventory (microenterprise is discussed below). The IDA Microenterprise Development program participants must attend 12 hours of economic education classes and receive one-on-one credit/debt repair counseling from Consumer Credit Counseling Services. Some of their partners include Business NOW of Goodwill Industries of North Georgia, Consumer Credit Counseling Services, and Wachovia (now part of Wells Fargo).

The United Way's Youth IDA program is also helping to build assets in young men and women from low- to moderate-income families in Atlanta. This program supports young adults by emphasizing financial literacy education, the importance of saving and establishing relationships with financial institutions, community service, and investing in future entrepreneurial or educational endeavors.[33]

Hidden Gold: Earned Income Tax Credits

The Earned Income Tax Credit (EITC) is an income tax credit benefiting low-income workers who have incomes that fall below $30,000–$36,000, based on the number of dependent children. One of the most important innovations of the EITC is its refundability as "taxpayers receive the full amount they are eligible for, even if the amount exceeds their tax liability."[34]

Many families use refunds from the tax credit to pay off existing debt or to satisfy immediate needs. As such, the EITC may not be the best asset-building approach, but it is an important source of income for those who want to start saving.[35]

In 2003, 19.3 million families received $34.4 billion from the EITC.[36] Since its inception in 1975, under the Ford administration, the EITC has expanded from a tax credit benefiting 6.2 million families claiming $1.25 billion in credits to more than 20 million families claiming $40 billion. Because of its expansion and the creation of local and state EITC, this federal policy is well known, studied, and cited as an effective antipoverty strategy. Annually, the credit lifts nearly 5 million Americans above the poverty line.[37]

The EITC phases in, peaks, and then phases out as a benefit. Those eligible for the credit receive it for each additional dollar earned to a certain level. The EITC rules maintain the maximum credit payment until the taxpayer earns additional income, and then phases the credit out at higher income levels up to a cap on eligibility.[38] Some have argued that this may cause a dependency on the credit and dissuade low-income people from earning more than the allotted amount, but studies show that the EITC has actually encouraged employment among single women.[39] For example, the labor force participation rate for single women increased by 2.8 percent between 1984 and 1990, and it is estimated that EITC and other tax incentives resulted in more than a 60 percent increase in single mothers participating in the labor force.[40]

In an effort to publicize the availability of EITC to low-income populations, many municipalities including San Antonio, Chicago, New York City (see Chapter 2), Baltimore, and San Francisco have created campaigns to aid families with the tools necessary to benefit from low-cost bank accounts, EITC, and financial counseling.[41] In 2005, the city of San Antonio filed nearly 25,000 tax returns for free through its municipal EITC outreach campaign. Furthermore, the San Antonio Department of Community Initiatives also combines the EITC with IDAs to promote a powerful asset-building opportunity for the poor.[42]

Similarly, the state, city, philanthropy, and other CED stakeholders in Baltimore support the Baltimore CASH Campaign in an effort to increase EITC use in the city. The CASH Campaign has many locations in Baltimore, including community centers owned by the city where low-income families and individuals can have their taxes prepared free of charge. Many are able to claim the EITC, which in 2007 averaged $1500 for qualified Baltimore residents.[43] The Campaign prepared 13,200 tax returns over the 2007–2008 tax season, claiming more than $18 million in state and federal tax refunds, and saving families an estimated $1,986,450 in tax preparation costs. Since 2001, the Campaign has helped city residents claim over $20 million in EITC payments.

Twenty-four states (counting the District of Columbia) have created state EITC programs to complement and enhance the federal effort. Similar to the federal EITC, the state programs refund money if the size of the taxpayer's credit exceeds the amount of state income tax owed.[44]

The question is why there is such strong public sector support for the EITC, which has been called the most effective antipoverty program tried by government. No question that the EITC is a very strong program. Millions are lifted across the poverty line each year, and because the credit goes to individuals and families who are working, it supports labor force participation, especially those transitioning out of welfare. But as Alan Berube notes, the EITC is more than a people-focused policy: it is also a place enhancing policy.

The EITC represents a particular boon to urban areas. An above-average share of central city taxpayers (20 percent) benefit from the credit. What's more, on average, their credits tend to be larger than credits received by taxpayers in most other locations. In 2002, when the EITC was worth $32 billion nationwide, families in large cities (those with populations over 100,000) received $8.1 billion; families in older suburbs, $5.1billion.[45]

Berube goes on to note that for all jurisdictions,

[I]n 2004 the Community Development Block Grant and HOME programs (which provide cities and states with flexible funds for affordable housing and community economic development) awarded roughly $3.1 billion to nearly 1,000 municipal governments nationwide. That same year, residents of those same cities and towns received over $20 billion from the EITC. Both programs contribute to urban and suburban health, of course, but until recently the tax code's tremendous boost to local economies was overlooked. [46]

The point is not without irony. Many place analysts have long maintained that the poor are a drain on a local economy struggling to revitalize. They note that it is rational for elected officials to resist welfare or income transfer policies that attract the poor.[47] Yet here is a policy, known but little heralded in relation to its impact and power, that bridges the divide between people and place policy. The fact that local governments see a benefit for their taxable revenue and can use the EITC along with IDAs and community-based partners to help the working poor speaks volumes about our learning how to calibrate community economic development.

Access to Credit for Self-Employment and Human Capital Development

IDAs and other savings vehicles such as the very innovative EITC are not the only programmatic form on which asset-building policy rests. Many working in this field of practice saw the powerful transformation of the poor in developing nations through microenterprise development and access to microcredit. Both grow out of the pathbreaking work of the Grameen Bank in Bangladesh and its founder, Muhammad Yunus. Starting with a university-based action research project in 1976, Dr. Yunus wanted to see how the provision of small amounts of credit at reasonable lending rates for purchase of farm implements, seed, or livestock would assist rural development.[48]

The experiment found that the poor, especially women, have high repayment rates and that microloans of $25 (U.S.) make a significant difference in increasing family income and asset accumulation. Borrowers tend to reinvest profits in farm equipment and livestock that increase crop yield.

Beyond the lending, the Grameen model also incorporates peer lending as a component. The idea is that in any community your neighbors are apt to know your personal habits and how they influence the potential to repay a loan. In peer lending, your reputation is a key form of collateral.[49] Peers decide if an individual receives a loan. The peer-lending model also incorporates support and technical assistance as an important facet. Borrowers meet periodically to provide advice and support for each other in their business ventures. The model is both a capital formation strategy and a way to build more social capital in poor communities.

Microenterprise and peer lending have experienced mixed success in the United States. The personal mobility that is a staple of U.S. society works against strict application of the peer-lending model. Nonetheless, the model, or a homegrown variant, has made its way into the policy mainstream here in the United States.

The Small Business Administration (SBA) has offered a microloan program since 1992. The SBA uses nonprofit CDFIs to make loans to new or existing borrowers. Important to this program model is the ability of the CDFIs to provide organizational and technical assistance to entrepreneurs. Small businesses needing small-scale financing and technical assistance for startup or expansion may be able to obtain up to $35,000 through short-term loans of public money called microloans, which average about $13,000. These loans are administered through local CDFIs or state finance authorities that are selected and approved by the SBA. The SBA loans the money to the nonprofit organization, which then pools the funds with local money and administers direct loans to small businesses.[50]

The microloan program is an important innovation, especially given that the SBA's other loan efforts (administered through mainstream lending institutions) are (1) not viewed as priced for entrepreneurs with a small capital base and (2) require a great deal of paperwork to get a loan.[51] Yet it is unclear that microloans boost self-employment rates among the poor in the United States. The reason for the mixed result in the United States is complicated. The problem is not so much capital access. There are simply limitations to the supply of good ideas that turn into viable self-employment opportunities, despite how the ingenuity of small business owners is lauded in myth and legend.[52] Then again, not everyone should be self-employed, and no amount of training and capital is going to change that. It takes a level of dedication and sacrifice that not many of us have, much less people on the margins engaged in a day-to-day struggle for survival.

The question of self-employment and how many capital resources (and public attention) should be put behind such a strategy for poverty reduction goes beyond the SBA and is a continuing question for all CEDIs and CDFIs. Any community would take people who are productively engaged in work and enterprise, but public policy must ask for some threshold to assure that the effort and transaction costs involved in pursuing microscale self-employment strategies are worth public support. I would not throw it out as a strategy just yet, however.

Microenterprise should be reconceived as a human capital development strategy just as one would think of workforce development. In fact, in cases such as training businesses (see the example of Homeboy Industries), they can be combined. Conceived as simply another skill, microbusiness ownership takes the onus off microenterprise, producing widespread economic development and alleviating poverty. This is an expensive human development strategy to be sure, but properly executed it may yield a complement of micro- and small businesses that contribute to the community's quality of life.

The type of entrepreneur who can help a community rebuild and rebound probably has some level of capacity and experience. These entrepreneurs may be locked out of a market such as construction by barriers to entry such as limited personal networks and access to financing, but once supported they can compete.

There are now many models using the basics, access to capital coupled with dedicated mentorship, to increase the survival of minority and disadvantaged companies. One example that stands out is the Neighborhood Builder Program run by the New York City Housing Partnership in close concert with the New York City Department of Housing and Preservation. The Partnership was and still is one of the leading public/private partnerships that helped to revive housing in economically depressed communities over the last 30 years. Using a combination of private and public financing, the Housing Partnership, along with LISC and Enterprise, helped to take the enormous inventory of abandoned buildings that had built up in the 1970s and 1980s and return those buildings to the tax rolls with the help of nonprofit developers.

The Housing Partnership realized that although revitalizing housing was great and its main mission, it could also build a base of minority entrepreneurs in the communities in which it was rebuilding housing and housing markets. In 1983, the Partnership launched a decade-long demonstration program to build the capacity of minority construction firms to become "prime contractors" on construction work in their home communities. Qualified minority contractors were provided access to capital, industry expertise, and mentorship to complete projects commissioned by the New York City Partnership.

The minority contractors were deliberately given prime status, which in turn provided a way for them to establish a track record for subsequent projects and additional access to capital (loans). Homes built by these contractors were sold to community residents at an affordable price so a class of home owners with a deep stake in the community could be established. Assessment of the project showed a highly successful program that built the capacity of an entire generation of small minority contractors who went on to complete projects in and beyond their communities. Since 1983, locally based minority-owned contractors working through this program have developed affordable housing valued at well over $100 million.[53]

Mentorship, focused financial resources, and access to partnerships on projects are key tools in promoting self-employment with those poised for success. The Enterprise

Center (TEC) in West Philadelphia uses this model, not focused on housing, to help build entrepreneurial capacity in a tough part of the city. Started in 1989 as a project of the Wharton School's Small Business Development Center, the Enterprise Center's mission is to provide "access to capital, building capacity, business education and economic development opportunities to high-potential, minority entrepreneurs. Through our portfolio of business-acceleration initiatives, TEC seeks to better position minority enterprises to compete in the local, regional, and global economies."[54]

Standing the test of time, including economic downturns and change of administrations (local, state, and national), TEC has endured, offering critical support services to their target community. First, TEC has a subsidiary CDFI called the Enterprise Center-Capital Corporation (TEC-CC), which provides financing and technical assistance to minority- and women-owned businesses located in Philadelphia's low-income communities. In addition to debt financing, the Capital Corporation assists small businesses in attaining grant and equity funding. TEC-CC loan programs are designed to finance minority businesses that are challenged in obtaining funds for startup capital and business growth. The Capital Corporation makes loans of between $5000 and $35,000 to entrepreneurs through its role as a U.S. Small Business Administration co-lender.

TEC is a federally qualified Minority Business Enterprise Center, which allows it to provide technical consulting services to its client companies in addition to information about public sector contracting at all levels of government. But the TEC does more than provide capital and technical assistance. It is a full-fledged CEDI that uses business development to approach the larger project of place and people development.

If this were not enough, TEC also has an affiliate CDC called the Enterprise Center Community Development Corporation that tries to support the physical redevelopment around its catchment area. Recently, TEC has partnered with LISC and three CDCs, The People's Emergency Center CDC, the University City District, and The Partnership CDC, to form the Sustainable Communities Initiative–West Philadelphia (SCI–West). SCI–West seeks to improve communities in West Philadelphia by making them healthier, more competitive, and better connected with the economic mainstream through investments in physical development and social services. SCI–West also plans to work with local schools to improve student performance.

This initiative illustrates a point I have made throughout this book: that CEDIs cannot do everything and must do one thing well before branching out. Without question, TEC's main function is enterprise development, but its expertise has allowed it to go into areas less familiar to the organization. Although SCI–West is still at an early stage of development, it is just the type of diverse collaboration needed to shift thinking, making CED more expansive and outward looking without losing the core competencies that CEDIs have built.

Collective Asset Building

Individual asset building has become a central focus of community economic development policy in the United States. Place development, although not totally out of fashion, is increasingly being reconceptualized as collective asset building. What does that mean? There is a bit of forcing the old wine into not so new bottles here, but the reworking of categories is not important enough to put up a fuss. The infrastructure in a community, the homes, parks, even the reputation of a community, are shared assets. Of course these items are not public goods in the traditional sense, but the condition of these assets often determines how individual assets can be enhanced. As such, there is a theoretical and applied interest in seeing the community as a "commons" where the actions of individual actors can have negative or positive consequences depending on the context.[55]

Stabilizing the Commons

Typical causes of destabilization include a decrease in the level of property investment, abandonment, and crime.[56] Recently, the fraudulent practices of predatory subprime lenders have sent many homes into foreclosure, leading to widespread vacancy and abandonment. Vacant homes become places for crime when, for example, they are stripped of copper piping; they also create public health issues ranging from pest infestation to becoming havens for drug use. Vacant properties also create downward pressure on neighboring home values, limiting neighbors' ability to refinance into more affordable loan terms or restricting their ability to move, which can lead to additional foreclosures and continuance of the cycle.[57]

CEDIs have been working to assist homeowners through credit counseling or helping them negotiate with their lenders to modify loan terms.[58] Unfortunately, for many other homeowners who are too far along in the foreclosure process, relocation assistance is the only recourse.[59] In addition to the strong need to stop the vacancies before they occur, there is also a need to deal with the growing foreclosed housing stock.[60]

CEDIs are addressing these new challenges by adapting their traditional neighborhood stabilization strategies such as land banking.[61] This concept of buying up distressed properties and holding on to them as a way of stemming the tide of blight was first used in the 1960s by CDCs. Properties were bought, renovated, and put back on the market either as rental units or for home ownership. In fact, land banking and subsequent renovation became one of the few ways that CDCs could earn substantial income. The key to land banking is market timing: with enough resources the organization running the land bank can remove blighted properties from the market in the hope of stemming a free fall in land prices. In some cases with CDCs the land banking worked well enough to reignite the neighborhood market, bringing in higher-income individuals. Now the concept is being reused to help staunch the fallout from the subprime crisis but with some unique variations on the model.

Operation Neighborhood Recovery

Housing and Neighborhood Development Services, Incorporated (HANDS) is a CEDI working in and around Essex County, New Jersey, specifically the towns of Orange and East Orange. HANDS tries to stop the spread of vacant properties in its catchment area, serving a population of about 100,000 people.[62]

In 2000, HANDS began an annual inventory of all vacant properties in its service area as a measure of need and as a basis for development of the best strategies for reducing the area vacancies and ultimately eliminating the problem. After identifying the total vacancies, HANDS analyzed each property and decided whether HANDS or the local government would be best suited to intervene. The organization was very successful in Orange; in 2001 there were 372 problem properties in Orange and in 2006 there were fewer than 40. In 2007, the subprime crisis destroyed the organization's hard work.[63]

In response, HANDS helped start Operation Neighborhood Recovery (ONR), whose aim is to secure at-risk properties by buying them from lenders before they become blighted. HANDS incorporated a nonprofit collaborative of other local and statewide CEDIs called the Community Asset Preservation Corporation (CAPC) to implement Operation Neighborhood Recovery.[64] Initially, 47 properties were purchased from a pool of nonperforming mortgages from a lending institution.

The properties had been defaulted as a result of risky lending practices by one mortgage lender. The properties were vandalized, their boilers and copper stripped and carted away because the properties had not been well secured.[65] Instead of waiting for the lending institution to take the properties through the foreclosure process, ONR wanted to obtain the properties quickly to forestall blight.

Because of its previous work buying tax lien properties, HANDS adapted its work to combat the results of predatory lending. All of the mortgages were in the lender's portfolio, not securitized or owned by many lenders. If that had not been the case, the process would have become much more difficult, if not impossible. The complexity that comes from collateralized debt obligations and similar investment vehicles makes it difficult to establish who owns the properties and who has the authority to negotiate the sale.[66] Although this is the case for many mortgages throughout the country, fortunately it was not so for ONR.

After months of negotiation and right before HANDS was about to purchase the properties, the bank filed for bankruptcy and was taken over by the FDIC. In March 2009, the Community Asset Preservation Corporation closed on the portfolio for about 23.5 cents on the dollar.[67]

Because HANDS agreed to take the entire pool of mortgages from the bank and did not pick and choose the specific properties to include, some of the properties were located outside its neighborhood of Orange. Because of this, HANDS decided to partner with CEDIs from the surrounding areas. HANDS will be partnering with six other CDCs that will purchase the properties in their areas after the titles have been cleared, rehabilitate the properties, and place them with homeowners. Because of CAPC, the CDCs will receive the properties in better condition, at a good price, and avoiding negotiation with the bank.

Financing Innovation

One of the innovations of ONR is that it is purchasing bulk mortgages, also referred to as Real Estate Owned (REO) on the bank's balance sheet. In essence, CAPC is purchasing a piece of paper before the property has been taken through foreclosure, instead of waiting to purchase a discounted property from the bank after it is taken through the foreclosure process. See Figure 7.2 for an example of a foreclosed property acquired by HANDS. The purchase of REOs will save time as well as money, especially because CAPC has foreclosure lawyers who are offering free services and are working to hasten the foreclosure process down to only a few months. With this process comes a financing risk for investors. The risk is because they are purchasing a mortgage and not the property, so there is no actual collateral to back up a loan until the property is through foreclosure. In the time

Figure 7.2   Foreclosed property in Newark, New Jersey, bought under Operation Neighborhood Recovery by HANDS. Photo courtesy of HANDS.

it takes to finish the foreclosure process the property could deteriorate and lose value. Because of this risk, there is a lack of available financing options.

New Jersey Community Capital, a community development financial institution based in New Jersey, is the lead lender for ONR. Other participating investors include the Prudential Foundation and the local office of LISC. Financing from community development financial institutions and foundations offers both a good rate and flexible terms, inasmuch as they are not bound to the strict underwriting parameters used by traditional banks and are interested in a double bottom line of a lower financial return coupled with a social return on their investments.[68]

CAPC did not receive any below-market financing, and all debt was priced to risk. Equity was raised for the transaction, and dividends will be paid on those investments. The pilot project of Operation Neighborhood Recovery models what CAPC wants to achieve on a national scale. Instead of focusing only on performing bulk acquisitions of distressed inventory, the larger goal of the Community Asset Preservation Corporation is to expand the access to capital to make future large projects such as ONR easier to complete.

What Can Be Done Nationally: The National Community Stabilization Trust

The National Community Stabilization Trust (NCST) was incorporated in October 2008 in response to the national foreclosure crisis. Five national CEDI intermediaries started NCST in reaction to the crisis, which keenly challenges their CED work; they came together to act as an intermediary between the banks that hold the foreclosed mortgages and the organizations on the ground that can rehabilitate the houses and restore them to usable status. Enterprise Community Partners, the Housing Partnership Network, the Local Initiatives Support Corporation (LISC), National Urban League, and NeighborWorks America make up this unprecedented partnership. Working together across the nation, NCST helps facilitate the interaction between financial institutions and housing developers. To do this, NCST standardized the brokerage process, leveraged its power to negotiate with many leading banks, and utilized current federal program dollars to fund the acquisitions and rehabilitations of the properties.

Before NCST, there had been a lack of collaboration and information sharing on a national scale. As Operation Neighborhood Recovery demonstrated, local CEDIs focused on their local area and generally lacked the expertise or interest in expanding their efforts across the country. In addition, local CEDIs lacked the power to negotiate with the banks, whose negotiations, paperwork, and processes differed from each other. By joining together, the partnership is able to work with the range of financial institutions that hold the majority of the nonperforming mortgages.

Operation Neighborhood Recovery and the National Community Stabilization Trust have four themes in common: (1) information, (2) collaboration, (3) fast action, and (4) access to capital and financial relationships. Although these concepts may not be new ideas for community economic development, they are necessary now more than ever to help preserve and stabilize local economies. It is extremely important to know and understand local housing markets and local communities. This information requires collaboration among all the stakeholders. By utilizing partnerships with organizations versed in local conditions and equipped to actually facilitate action, the process can manage threats to neighborhood stability.

Summary

Community economic development finance is here to stay as a key innovation and adjunct of community economic development. Efforts to build individual assets and stabilize community assets have developed expansively over the last 20 years. Assets and agency support the renewed focus on people and building their ability and assets to make choices about their future. Key innovations are as follows:

- *Supported savings.* Pilot projects in housing projects have demonstrated the usefulness of tools such as Individual Development Accounts in helping low-income families save. IDAs have also been used effectively with job training and other specialized antipoverty strategies. IDAs are an innovation, but the transaction costs are high, and public policy needs to find ways of lowering these costs to make them widespread. The other sobering note is that on average, the matched saving totals about $5,000. This is not going to raise families across the poverty line, but it can be the base for transformation through an investment in education, the purchase of a car to get to work, or a microbusiness.
- *Increase the use of the Earned Income Tax Credit.* The EITC has become a tried and true antipoverty tool. Use of the EITC is now spreading beyond the federal level to states that are implanting their own version of the federal credit. This expansion is welcome, and used in conjunction with the federal credit will only expand coverage to more qualified individuals and families.
- *Self-employment as a poverty-reduction strategy should be promoted with care.* Microenterprise and microcredit are important innovations in the worldwide battle against poverty. There is limited evidence in the United States to say that microenterprise can generate significant self-employment among the poor. Our learning, thus far, points in the direction of circumspection and the use of layered technical and organizational development assistance if the strategy is used on a wide scale.
  - Rethink homeownership as the primary vehicle for building assets. Before the recent financial crisis, calls for long-term saving were almost antithetical to the pervasive culture of consumption. Policy analysts might not want to admit that encouraging home ownership policies supported the

culture of consumption and also the short-term thinking that if we can find ways to put the poor into home ownership we could increase asset building for the poor. Yes, predatory lenders wreaked havoc in the housing market at all levels of income, including the working poor who had built equity over a number of years. But there is no denying that policy was a driving force in trying to get more people into home ownership than were ready for such a significant undertaking.

For many years, each administration or government-sponsored enterprise such as Fannie Mae and Freddie Mac would announce targets in the million for new (minority) home owners.

Encouraging home ownership under the right circumstances is laudable. The time horizon was wrong, and it is easy to understand why. No politician is going to support a program that says we are going to reduce poverty by building the savings of the poor over a 10- to 15-year period. It was much easier to turn a blind eye to zero-down mortgages with the hope that the majority of new homeowners would fare well when given the chance. We now know that they did not fare well. The choice, though, was never between renting or home ownership. There are in-between strategies that can help build solid low-income home ownership without unnecessary risk to the individual and the system.

One example of an innovation in mortgage lending popular in the United Kingdom and Australia is shared-equity mortgages (SEM). This type of lending, also known as equity finance, partnership, and shared appreciation mortgages, attempts to share the costs and risks of the housing market with lenders and homeowners. A private or public partner invests along with the homeowner to make the initial purchase more affordable, and continues to own a portion of the property. These mortgages make it easier for first-time and low-income buyers to own a house, although they also reduce the returns when the home appreciates. Partners also share in the downside, reducing the risk to homeowners whose largest asset is at risk.

In Australia, the Equity Finance Mortgage (EFM) allows the homeowner to borrow up to 20 percent of the property's value as a second mortgage without monthly payments. When the owner sells the property, the buyer repays the bank, in addition to a predetermined percentage of the appreciation in the value of the home. The risk, however, is borne by the bank, as the homeowner does not have to pay the full value of the EFM in the event that the property depreciates.

Community land trusts come from the environmental sector, where development easements are often sold to nonprofit entities, preserving land in perpetuity while reducing the cost burden of conservation for homeowners. With community land trusts, a CEDI owns the land and enters into a ground lease with the buyer, who owns the house itself. There are over 200 community land trusts nationwide, and the system has proven to be a successful mechanism to achieve low-income home ownership, preserve assets, and stabilize neighborhoods.

These are similar in concept to shared equity mortgages; buyers are essentially partnering with a nonprofit entity that covers some of the cost of the initial investment. The result is that appreciation is also shared, meaning that in an upmarket homeowners do not capture the full value of their investments. The reverse side is that homeowners have more protection from economic downturns.

Endnotes

1. Arrow, Sen, and Suzumuro (1997).
2. Lowry (2005).
3. In my mind, economic development as a substantive term is the same as asset building.
4. Kotlowski (2001).
5. Bendick and Egan (1991); Doctors (1974).
6. Bendick and Egan (1991); Lowry (2005).
7. Another criticism is that minority firms tend to be isolated and develop without the networks necessary to create a multiplier effect and are thus limited in their market penetration. Without such an effect, minority firms are vulnerable and tied to their proximate geographical market. That is fine if we are speaking about a grocery store; it is less good if we are talking about, say a construction company.
8. Oliver (2001, p. xii).
9. Ibid.
10. Many working in the asset-building field take the "welfare state" to task, asserting that supplementing or enhancing incomes has failed as an antipoverty strategy. Income strategies, or income transfer programs, are posed as a counterdistinction to policies that build or enhance assets. The charge is posed in a way that makes it seem that government has pursued income transfers as the only antipoverty policy. American government, though, has always supported individual and place economic development (asset building by another name). This is an important point, because it harkens back to my point about how government learns. There are always antecedents to any given policy strategy. Whether the strategy is effective is another matter, but we have to acknowledge them or run the risk of making the same mistakes.
11. Oliver and Shapiro (2006).
12. Shapiro (2001, p. 16).
13. Belsky and Calder (2004) found that one-third of all homeowners and two-thirds of renters in the bottom quintile have $500 or less in savings and other liquid assets. They cite Caner and Wolff (2001), who found that "as many as 41 percent of households had inadequate savings or other liquid assets to cover three months of expenses at the poverty level." (p. 2)
14. Sherraden (1991); McKernan and Sherraden (2008).
15. Shapiro (2001, p. 31).
16. Oliver and Shapiro (2006).
17. Sherraden (1991); McKernan and Sherraden (2008); see also http://www.cfed.org/focus .m?parentid=2&siteid=374&id=374. (accessed March 27, 2009)

18. Currently, IDAs are a supported strategy in several federal programs, like the Workforce Investment Act (WIA), the Temporary Assistance for Needy Families (TANF) programs, and the Assets for Independence Act (AFIA).
19. Eligible hosts for the AFI are nonprofit organizations, including faith-based and community groups, state, local, and tribal government agencies applying jointly with nonprofits, and, lastly, community development financial institutions partnering with a community-based antipoverty group.
20. Assets for Independence is authorized under the Assets for Independence Act in Title IV of the Community Opportunities, Accountability, and Training and Educational Services Human Services Reauthorization Act of 1998, P.L. 105-285.
21. Individuals and families eligible for the AFI include those whose household assets do not exceed $10,000 in value (excluding a residence and one car) and who are either eligible for the Earned Income Tax Credit or have total household income of less than two times the federal poverty line. Additionally, all AFI projects provide basic financial literacy, credit counseling and repair, and guidance in accessing refundable tax credits, including the Earned Income Tax Credit and the Child Tax Credit.
22. FSS was enacted in 1990 as part of the Cranston-Gonzalez National Affordable Housing Act of 1990.
23. The matched savings do not come from PHA budgets. As noted at the HUD FSS Web site: "For the most part, PHAs must rely on their own or other local resources to operate FSS programs. However, under the authority of annual appropriations acts, HUD has been able to provide some funding for FSS program coordinators to assist PHAs in operating housing choice voucher FSS programs." http://www.hud.gov/offices/pih/programs/hcv/fss.cfm. (accessed March 27, 2009)
24. Data for this figure was taken from the following: http://wyomca ses.courts.state.wy.us/applications/oscn/DeliverDocument.asp?CiteID=398364; FY 1996: http://bulk.resource.org/gpo.gov/register/1996/1996_39262.pdf; FY 1997: http://ftp.resource.org/gpo.gov/register/1997/1997_17673.pdf; FY 2000: http://ftp.resource.org/gpo.gov/register/2000/2000_17114.pdf; FY 2001: http://www.cbpp.org/cms/?fa=view&id=346; FY 2004-FY 2009 Info: http://www.nlihc.org/doc/FY10-presidents-request33.pdf; This federal Web site shows slightly different numbers for FY 2007-FY 2009: http://www.whitehouse.gov/omb/rewrite/assets/omb/expectmore/detail/10002188.2004.html. (accessed March 30, 2009)
25. Ficke and Piesse (2005, pp. xv–xvi); see also Sard (2001).
26. Cytron and Reid (2005, p. 12).
27. Boshara (2003, p. 4).
28. Schreiner, Clancy, and Sherraden (2002, p. 56).
29. Boshara (2003, p. 5).
30. Cytron and Reid (2005, p. 14).
31. See "Individual Development Accounts," *United Way of Metropolitan Atlanta*, February 2009. http://www.unitedwayatlanta.org/e0-ida.asp. (accessd April 8, 2009)
32. The United Way not only provides an eligible match of 5:1 but also a $1,500 emergency reserve fund that can be applied to the principal of a mortgage if not used within two years of ownership.
33. The Youth IDA program targets youth between the ages of 14 and18. They enroll in the program for 12 to 24 months and receive a match of a 2:1 ratio up to $1,000.
34. Berube (2006, p. 2).
35. Holt (2006, p. 18).

36. Ibid.
37. Berube (2006).
38. Holt (2006, p. 11).
39. Ibid., p. 13.
40. Ibid., p. 14.
41. Berube (2006, p. 5).
42. Ibid.
43. The Campaign tries to steer its low-income clients away from the Refund Anticipation Loans offered by many commercial tax preparers. These products encourage consumption, not savings.
44. The state EITCs use the same eligibility rules as the federal EITC with state EITCs set at a fixed percentage of the federal credit.
45. Berube (2006, p. 2).
46. Ibid.
47. Tiebout (1956); Peterson (1985).
48. Yunus and Jolis (1999).
49. http://www.grameenfoundation.org. (accessed April 19, 2009) Other variants of peer lending include the very interesting Kiva model in which use of the Internet makes possible small investments in the projects of microentrepreneurs in the developing world. See http://www.kiva.org/.
50. These loans are administered much like a line of credit and are intended for the purchase of machinery and equipment, furniture and fixtures, inventory, supplies, and working capital. The maximum maturity for a microloan is six years and cannot be used to pay existing debts.
51. U.S. Congress. House Small Business Subcommittee on Finance and Tax, Testimony. (2007).
52. Bendick and Egan (1991).
53. http://www.nyc.gov/html/hpd/html/developers/partnership-new-homes.shtml. (accessed April 19, 2009).
54. http://www.theenterprisecenter.com/about/history.php. (accessed April 18, 2009)
55. Of course the use of the commons as a metaphor for how we can collectively destroy the ecology by pursuing rational self-interest is well known from the work of Hardin (1968).
56. Gass (2008).
57. Ibid.
58. Ibid., p. 2.
59. Ibid.
60. Ibid.
61. See Alexander (2009).
62. Marissa Myers played a major role in developing this case study.
63. Beyond the rise in properties, it became apparent that the properties were all from the same lender. The portfolio lender held the 47 mortgages that were located mostly throughout Essex County, New Jersey. As detailed in a 2008 report done by NeighborWorks America, Essex County was a former "hot" housing market that experienced rapid escalation in housing prices followed by sharp declines due to overheated markets.

64. The Community Asset Preservation Corporation of New Jersey is a public-purpose, nonprofit organization whose mission is to stabilize neighborhoods made at risk by mortgage foreclosures, help homeowners avoid foreclosure, return vacant foreclosed property to productive reuse efficiently, and equitably, and increase the availability of affordable housing.
65. Gass (2008, p. 26).
66. Ibid.
67. Many of the owners still owed a lot of money that they couldn't repay, and the homes had dropped so much in value that they owed hundreds of thousands of dollars on home that were almost worthless. Those debts will be forgiven and the mortgage holders will be released from the loan. One month after the closing, 25 of the 47 owners wanted out of their mortgage.
68. Rubin (2007, pp. 123–124).

Chapter 8

Innovations in Community-Based Workforce Development

The term "workforce development" describes the coordination of a broad array of programs and policies designed to increase the skills of those who are in or want to enter the workforce.[1] Practically speaking, this usually refers to preparing workers for employment, connecting them to employment opportunities, and ensuring their upward movement once employed.

Workforce development seeks to create not only benefits for workers who are gainfully employed but also for employers. The benefit for employers follows from the logic that human capital investment leads to worker productivity, resulting in more profitable, successful businesses. The targets of these policies vary, yet are consistently those groups that are most in need, including low-income communities, youth, ex-offenders, and dislocated workers. Those who direct such efforts can also vary, from the government and businesses to CEDIs. This chapter focuses on the efforts of CEDIs to construct and implement innovative programs to effectively promote employment.

In order to best understand the challenges faced by these organizations in carrying out their own workforce development efforts, it is useful to examine how their particular role has emerged, especially in relation to the government's own influential initiatives. From the 1970s to the 1990s, a highly centralized federal workforce development policy emphasized job training and skills development, focusing heavily on the needs of workers. Community-based organizations responded to the availability of funds supporting these objectives and directed their own efforts toward related activities, with the presumed advantage of possessing an intimate knowledge of specific local needs.[2]

By the 1990s, however, through a series of significant legislative reforms, the public sector began its transition toward what was hoped would be a more effective, work-first emphasis with a greater balance between the needs of both employers and workers. Welfare reform, spurred by the Personal Responsibility and Work Opportunity Reconciliation Act (PRWOA) of 1996, with its explicit promotion of on-the-job learning over training, led to a growth of community-based initiatives to assist workers, especially welfare recipients, through job-placement activities.[3]

The subsequent federal workforce development reform, embodied by the Workforce Investment Act (WIA) of 1998, was equally catalytic. It decentralized federal workforce development authority, demanding a greater role for community colleges and giving local authorities greater flexibility over the design and implementation of federal efforts in their communities, in many cases essentially replicating the activities performed by community-based organizations.[4] Whereas the effect of the PRWOA was to provide community-based organizations with an opportunity to be a critical partner with the government, the WIA appeared to be a clear step into territory previously dominated by these local organizations.

CEDIs were thus forced to re-evaluate their relationship to these new federal policies, a process that continues today. Sometimes there has been a natural supporting role for these local organizations to play; in other instances, given the federal government's intention to decentralize public sector workforce development efforts through more empowered local offices, CEDIs have found themselves acting in direct competition with public sector efforts. A central challenge for community-based groups now is to maintain their relevance by seeking out new roles and potential collaborations with the public sector, community colleges, and other community-level actors. Furthermore, these groups must do so in a more financially competitive environment in which social interventions are increasingly evaluated with performance-based indicators.

A number of key questions underpin this struggle to define a role for community-based workforce development efforts. How can community-based groups continue to demonstrate their utility in light of increased emphasis on performance-based evaluations? Are community-based organizations partners or competitors with public sector efforts? Should these groups look locally or regionally in planning their activities? These issues will not be easily resolved, yet many community-based groups have been working on new ways of confronting them. Efforts in the areas of sectoral employment, career ladders, temporary staffing, network building, and community college partnerships all indicate that there is and will continue to be a critical role for community-based organizations in local workforce development efforts.

Sectoral Employment

Recognizing the great need of low-income workers to acquire employment that allows them to provide for families and the need of employers in high-growth sectors for a labor force that meets the requirements of their industries, many community-based organizations have gravitated toward the concept of sectoral employment. Initiatives based on this concept are "regional, industry-specific approaches to workforce needs, implemented by an employer-driven partnership of relevant systems and stakeholders."[5] These efforts focus "on multiple employers in [an] industry, over a sustained period of time," seeking to meet the labor needs of these employers through the relevant training of local workers.[6] In this sense, facilitators of such initiatives work to close the gap between supply and demand in the labor market of a specific industry with real benefits for both workers and employers.

The efforts of one organization in South Los Angeles, AGENDA, exemplify this goal of deriving local benefits from industry growth.[7] On learning that Los Angeles was in the process of awarding a $70 million subsidy to DreamWorks Studio to locate facilities in already well-invested West Los Angeles, AGENDA, from a more economically distressed end of the city, took a proactive approach in organizing churches, labor, community, and social service providers to demand a commitment on the part of the studios and the city to train students from inner-city communities for jobs in the region's film industry. Both sides preferred collaboration to conflict, and discussions resulted in a multimillion-dollar training program conducted in conjunction with local community colleges. From there, the initiative transformed into Workplace Hollywood, a much expanded program in which numerous studios from the region participate. This collaborative effort has clearly borne benefits for both workers and employers, generating access to the region's most prominent industry for youth who might not otherwise enjoy such opportunity and increasing the labor pool for studios that now have more options when seeking qualified workers.

No contemporary discussion of sectoral employment would be complete, however, without mention of "green jobs." Billed as possessing the potential to be a massive job generator as the world moves toward more Earth-friendly means of living, the green job sector generally refers to any number of professions—especially in manufacturing and construction—that offer access to entry-level workers, offer family-sustaining wages, and benefit the environment.[8] Although it is a relatively new sector, community-based organizations have already begun to tap its potential.

In December 2007, Congress passed the Green Jobs Act of 2007, creating a pilot program between the U.S. Department of Labor and the U.S. Department of Energy.[9] With a large annual budget, the program awards grants to training partnerships and community groups that provide green jobs. Priority is given to partnerships that target low-income adults and youth.

President Barack Obama has pledged even more support for green jobs. Along with $70 billion of the stimulus package directed toward green jobs, Obama pledged to spend $150 billion in the next decade to stimulate millions of new jobs.

It is important to understand how green jobs are innovative. Innovation is implicit in creating new ideas that can move us forward as a nation. Although in the past companies may have paid attention to their effect on the environment, today there is clearly a much stronger effort made by almost every industry to limit its impact on the environment.[10]

Raquel Pinderhughes, the director of the Urban Studies Program at San Francisco State University, defines green-collar jobs as "blue-collar work force opportunities created by firms and organizations whose mission is to improve environmental quality."[11] Examples of green jobs include recycling and reuse, hazardous material cleanup, building retrofits to increase energy efficiency and conservation, housing deconstruction, solar installation, urban agriculture, and manufacturing items related to the green economy.

This definition is important: instead of simply providing low-skill jobs to those seeking new careers, the overriding theme of many green industries is to provide careers with room for growth and the potential to be part of America's middle class. Most of these jobs have limited educational requirements and help fill the void left by vanishing low-skilled jobs. Still, there is a path for job development in these fields that provides not only low-paying jobs to those who need employment but also a way for people to build wealth and assets to help them to move out of poverty.

Those new jobs may provide help to many Americans seeking employment in this challenging employment environment. In addition, they attempt to provide more sustainable opportunities for advancement than traditional occupations. Although we have lost many of America's manufacturing jobs to those overseas, many green jobs are place-based, meaning they cannot be outsourced.

One creative partnership in this emerging sector is that between Homeboy Industries (discussed in Chapter 6), which offers employment assistance to people in the Los Angeles area with criminal histories, and the East Los Angeles Skills Center, which, among many vocational programs, teaches solar panel design, construction, and installation.[12] With the strengths of each of these partners, the two came together to create a new program tailored specifically to individuals seeking a new start to life outside of the corrections system.

The course is free to participants sponsored by Homeboy Industries, which even pays them a small stipend, and it has already drawn praise from regional employers, who appear to be eager to hire its graduates to fill their increasing labor needs. In fact, the program has built such a positive reputation that organizers have begun to expand its availability to those without criminal histories, further increasing the employment potential of people seeking opportunities while broadening the labor pool for this rapidly growing sector.

Second Chance, Inc.

Second Chance, Inc. is a community-based nonprofit in Baltimore that defies easy categorization. In simple terms, the organization methodically takes old homes apart, while keeping architectural elements intact so they can resell the items to give them their second chance. As the mission statement reads,

> In our throw-away world, buildings are only meant to last for 20 years, shingles are plastic and old-world craftsmanship is nearly impossible to find. Second Chance gives old buildings new life. We work with local and regional architects, builders and contractors to search out old buildings which are entering the demolition phase. We rescue the wood, metal, marble, plaster, stone and other architectural elements that make the building special. We give these pieces new lives, in new homes, in new ways, with new uses. It's a Second Chance.[13]

Second Chance, Inc. sends trained people into buildings that are ready to be demolished where they remove "specific usable elements" from the buildings.[14] This kind of "deconstruction" is time-consuming and exacting, because Second Chance needs to ensure that the architectural elements are removed without being damaged.

Often, larger elements must be removed in pieces to be reassembled later, outside the building. The workers remove everything, from kitchen cabinets to wood paneling, from hardwood floors to marble fireplaces, and store these items in the warehouses until they are "ready to bring life to another home."[15] To Second Chance, this process is the "ultimate in recycling": the organization uses elements from the past to enrich future homes and developments.

One of the organization's key goals is to train low-income unemployed and underemployed people from Baltimore, giving them the skills and experience they need to help them find rewarding employment opportunities either at Second Chance or elsewhere. Many of these individuals are ex-offenders. They are trained in a variety of skills sets, from carpentry to craftsmanship, with the goal of creating a pool of proficient workers who can make a living wage with benefits for themselves and their families.

The organization receives public and private money to support its operations. The retail arm (selling building elements) of the organization also supports the organization. It works with the city of Baltimore to find qualified underemployed people with the right basic skills to go through its structured interview process. Those selected from the interviews then go through a paid 16-week training period with at least one week of "soft skills," where the trainees are taught "people skills" and how best to work alongside others. They work on diverse issues ranging from anger management to organizational skills.

Second Chance prides itself on its ability to build a structure for its trainees to step forward on their own accord. It takes a chance with a small group of under-employed people (mostly men) and helps them grow into careers. At the end of the training session, the trainees are guaranteed a job with Second Chance.

Second Chance also opens the doors to a world beyond its employees' "six square blocks of Baltimore." Workers take trips to deconstruct homes in other states throughout the country. Many of these men have never before left Baltimore, and this gives them the opportunity to see other parts of the country while providing them with the chance to talk about Second Chance in front of a new audience, an excellent skill they can apply to future employment.

Beyond what Second Chance does for its employees and trainees, it also provides a service to the community. Its warehouses are a source of inexpensive building material, giving community members access to high-quality architectural fixtures to refurbish existing homes in Baltimore. The retail portion of the company funds a large portion of its business and training expenses. A portion of its customer base is low-income, too. It is far less expensive to purchase previously used building materials than to buy brand-new items.

Still, it takes more effort for a person to turn to Second Chance for "deconstructing" and reclaiming services or to shop there instead of buying new products. The organization works with area contractors as donors and intermediaries: they donate materials and purchase recycled elements for reuse. Both the donors and Second Chance benefit from the relationship: Second Chance is paid to remove materials, earning funding as well as elements to sell, and donors benefit by earning tax benefits. Moreover, there is a decreased need for new products and more people are able to reclaim and recycle items for their homes. Green building is still nascent; it is far more expensive than traditional building, but the story of Second Chance goes a long way in illustrating the possible links between the green economy and community-based economic development.

Career Ladders

Closely related to sectoral employment strategies, but with a more specific focus on intrasector advancement, is the concept of career ladders. As upward mobility in the transforming American workplace has diminished in many sectors, workers with a high school diploma or less have experienced major declines in real wages over the past several decades.[16] By 1988, more than half of U.S. families with incomes in the lowest quintile remained in the lowest quintile ten years later.[17] In the past, especially because of the wider availability of manufacturing and other unionized jobs, promotion ladders within firms facilitated the advancement and increased wages of workers. These mechanisms have now become less common, with the effect of this change being especially pronounced for lower-skilled workers, "who have fewer points of entry to jobs that offer the potential for advancement."[18] Worse still, employers provide the least amount of training to workers with the lowest levels of education, the lowest salaries, and the lowest job positions within their companies.[19]

To confront this reality, many community-based organizations have developed initiatives to encourage the employment of local residents in fields that offer the greatest potential for advancement. These sectors are identified as possessing points of entry for those with both the most basic level of skills and a continuum of incrementally more technical positions that are obtainable through supplemental education or, better yet, on-the-job training. These elements combine to form what is known as a career ladder.

Community-based agencies can help build career ladders through working with area employers, providing specific training and wraparound support services.[20] Project QUEST of San Antonio, Texas, for example, serves as something of a labor market broker by connecting the city's low-income residents to job training, placement, and supportive services through the Alamo Community College District, the University of Texas Health Science Center, and several related programs. Noting the area's robust health care field, organizers of this initiative sought to train participants for industry positions such as registered nurses and surgical technicians. In addition to paying for students' tuition and helping them apply for grants to cover personal expenses, project counselors hosted group support meetings each week to prepare students for job searches. Seeking to build a reputation as a partner to participating workers as well as to health care employers, initiative organizers developed in-house mobility programs for local employers to move their current entry-level workers into higher-level nursing positions, thus creating openings for new incoming workers.[21]

Temporary Staffing

In the contemporary business environment, marked by unpredictability and turbulence, the American temporary staffing sector is growing as companies realize the benefit of "testing workers out or shielding themselves from the risks associated with a permanent hire."[22] In fact, it has been estimated that 90 percent of U.S. employers now use some type of temporary workers. Meanwhile, funding for traditional community-based workforce development efforts has been limited in recent years, forcing local groups to seek alternative means of supporting their operations.[23] In order to confront these business realities as well as meet the needs of local residents for gainful employment, especially welfare recipients whose government assistance mandates rapid employment placement, some workforce development organizations have begun operating temporary staffing ventures, becoming what are otherwise known as Alternative Staffing Organizations (ASOs).

These programs, usually directed toward entry-level and low-skilled workers, not only help disadvantaged participants secure temporary employment positions but also can provide retention and support services for workers while on a placement, access to continually better jobs for those returning from fulfilled placements, assistance in obtaining full-time permanent employment, and support for partnering organizations as they leverage employer relationships and diversify funding. Beyond meeting the needs of employers and workers, these programs can be much more financially sustainable than traditional service provider models, as the fees that are charged to participating employers mostly cover the cost of the support systems, helping free the organization from the constraints of foundation grants or public contracts.

One such organization, FirstSource Staffing, was founded in Brooklyn, New York, in 1998 as a collaborative with the Fifth Avenue Committee, Good Shepherd Services, and the ICA Group.[24] Identifying itself as a "social purpose staffing company," the organization focuses on providing temporary placements and temporary-to-permanent arrangements as well as a host of free supportive services including child care, elder care, remedial training, counseling, and financial management.

Network Building

Another area of workforce development efforts that has received increasing attention from community-based organizations in recent years is network building. There has been a realization that the varied social connections among individuals have value in themselves. Relatives, friends, and acquaintances can pass along information about job opportunities, for example, or exert influence over hiring decisions and promotions. On the other hand, in the modern economy, job transitions and changes are expected and common. Workers must be prepared to search for jobs frequently, and networks—the collection of those social connections—help provide a web of information and assistance for individual job seekers.

Practically speaking, networking is simply the process of making connections with other workers, who can then provide help and insight as one looks for job opportunities. For low-income workers, it is the process of recognizing one's employed friends and families as sources of information, as well as striving to meet workers in higher-income positions who can help the worker obtain job mobility and recognize opportunities for advancement.

Local initiatives such as the Job Network Program based at the Community College of Baltimore County in Baltimore County, Maryland, have drawn upon this knowledge for the benefit of low-income individuals.[25] During a required four-week job-readiness training program for residents who apply for or are receiving welfare, program operators offer intensive case management services as well as job development assistance, which primarily seeks to build awareness of the existing networks that program participants possess as well as foster a new peer network. The initiative helps participants network with each other, as well as realize their connections with friends and family to whom they might reach out for assistance in finding a job.

Partnerships with Community Colleges

Community colleges and community-based organizations have worked together with employers to create educational curricula, job-training programs, and supportive services that reflect the skills and experiences needed in growing industries. As a result, students can be effectively prepared for jobs that offer meaningful career potential. Community colleges, for their part, adopt cluster approaches and adapt their programs to the skill needs of local employers. Higher-quality programs and services can develop because community colleges can use their resources more efficiently.[26] For many families, the community college is still an affordable, accessible option to obtain an advanced education or qualifications for living-wage jobs. Some community colleges concentrate on preparing students to transfer to a four-year college or university; however, many have developed career-focused education, which includes customized training for local businesses, dislocated worker training programs, welfare-to-work initiatives, and a multitude of career-oriented certificate programs.[27]

Community colleges recognize their limitations in implementing comprehensive training programs to serve low-income workers. The schools are challenged by issues of recruitment, pretraining preparation, support during training, and postplacement job retention, and lack the experience, staff, or resources to address these needs. However, community colleges do have the resources to support skills upgrading and continuing education.[28] They have the means to hire faculty and outside experts and to maintain and update the facilities necessary to provide participants with realistic exposure to the workforce environment. Their resources are further leveraged by collaborating with local groups who possess extensive experience working with low-income populations and thus a sensitivity to what support services are needed. Community-based organizations also maintain far-ranging outreach and communication mechanisms in neighborhoods, while possessing credibility among residents.

An example of one such partnership is that between the Instituto del Progreso Latino (IPL) and the West Side Technical Institute of Richard J. Daley Community College in Chicago, which prepares low-income inner-city populations for metalworking jobs in skilled manufacturing. The IPL offers a variety of educational and support services to more than 2,000 students each year. Since 1997, the IPL has developed a collaborative partnership with Daley Community College to run a 16-week intensive training program with more than 200 participants and a graduation rate of 65 percent. Approximately 70 percent of graduates obtained manufacturing jobs with an average starting wage of $9.60 an hour. The IPL also established a preparatory program to help develop math, enhanced English, and introductory computer skills. In addition to counseling, case management, paid internships during training, job placement assistance, and continuing technical training, the IPL offers students instruction in industry-specific English and basic math, and more than 80 hours of practical training in the machine shop at Daley Community College's

West Side Technical Institute. "By receiving instruction in blueprint reading, quality control, computer applications, and applied physics, as well as taking machining and welding classes, students receive five college credits that can be applied toward an advanced machining certificate as well as an associate's degree."[29]

Another unique collaborative, Gateway to Health Careers, came about as an initiative of the Jewish Vocational Service (JVS), City College of San Francisco (CCSF), and Visitacion Valley Jobs, Education and Training (VVJET) in San Francisco to prepare and connect low-income workers to skilled positions in health care. In San Francisco, as in many parts of the country, the growth of the health care industry has generated new openings and higher wages. Through this initiative, recent immigrants already trained as health care professionals in their countries of origin are aided in obtaining appropriate American certifications. The local community groups, JVS and VVJET, are responsible for recruiting participants and providing program support and job retention services. The two groups host a 12-week preparatory program to help participants improve their basic literacy skills, and provide job shadowing experiences to prepare them for the health-occupation training programs at CCSF.

CSSF supports the preparatory program by providing instructors for the program and placement opportunities with local employers. Course offerings are scheduled at times accessible to program participants, and participants are able to apply credits earned in the preparatory program toward a program certificate. JVS and VVJET provide support for students in the preparatory program and health programs at CCSF to address issues such as transportation, child care, career planning, and counseling.[30] In 1999, 75 percent of participants entering a CCSF program completed their course of study and 87 percent of these individuals were placed in a related job. At the start of placement, the average wage was $10.75 an hour and involved a full-time position with health care benefits.

Summary

Through the use of these inventive strategies, community-based organizations are actively seeking to confront the changing needs of workers and employers in today's economy as well as adapt to the public sector's own efforts in workforce development.

Sectoral strategies key in on growing industries, and, given the right research and institutional capacity, CEDIs can work with employers in growing fields to create a winning relationship for employers and job seekers. Sectoral strategies should be used with a great deal of forethought and research. Investment in any given sector should be predicated on evidence that the sector can support employment growth in the long term (ten years and beyond). The attention to "green jobs" presents a case study in caution with sectoral strategies. The hope that solar panels and other green initiatives will become a significant job generator is welcomed. Despite hopes, we have to acknowledge that any predictors of growth in this part of the

American economy are quite fluid. We do know, however, that brownfield development in the past 20 years has opened up jobs in site remediation, and Second Chance shows us that taking apart buildings and mining fixtures, wood, and other building materials offers an intriguing way to link workforce development to environmental sustainability.

Career ladders represent an important way of helping low-income workers proceed along the path of upward mobility. CEDIs are now proactively working with local employers who will hire skilled workers (despite challenges such as a prison record or past addiction) if the CEDI can deliver such workers. A mature example of such an innovation is the Automotive Technician Training Center run by the New Community Corporation in Newark, New Jersey. The program, run in partnership with the Ford Motor Company, prepares adults for high-paying (often starting at $25 an hour) positions as auto technicians. The program is operated out of a 12,000-square-foot state-of-the-art facility in Newark and uses a Ford-designed curriculum for training. The trainees come with challenging backgrounds and the Center has to put in place wraparound services, including help with paying back child support and assisting in the process of reversing suspended licenses that often prevent participation in the program. Success is measured by acknowledgment by the main client, Ford, that even with the added cost of services built into the partnership, the net is a reliable workforce that helps resolve a chronic shortage in the industry.[31]

Networks and Partnerships:

Low-skilled workers need key supportive services to increase the likelihood of successful job placement.

Although lack of experience is a challenge, getting the low-skilled worker ready for a specific sector or job increases the probability that that worker will be retained or choose to stay.

Supported work and benefits greatly increase the chances that low-skilled workers will stay in the job for any length of time after placement.

"Soft skills" are important, but possessing a skill in demand is key to long-term participation in the labor force.

One thread that emerges is the consistent use of collaboration to leverage resources.

As Giloth (2009) notes:

> Because such a wide range of interventions are needed, the most promising models of workforce development today involve partnerships among industry and employer groups, community colleges, state and local agencies (including workforce boards), community groups, and intermediary organizations, such as community development corporations (CDCs)….These partnerships are also critical to breaking down traditional workforce silos.[32]

In workforce development, partnership creates a win–win situation. Institutions partner to engender new initiatives that combine comprehensive support services with temporary hard-skills training to produce qualified workers to meet the workforce needs of employers. In this sense, the pieces to the workforce development puzzle already exist; we know what works. The problem may rest more with the age-old question: "How do you get elephants to dance?"

Endnotes

1. Jacobs (2002).
2. Burwick et al. (2007), Roberts (2002).
3. Melendez (2004).
4. Ibid.
5. http://www.sectorstrategies.org/. (accessed April 16, 2009)
6. Ibid.
7. Pastor et al, (2004).
8. Walsh (2008).
9. H.R. 2847 [110th Congress].
10. Langer (2008).
11. See her definition at "Green Collar Jobs." *Urban Habitat: Race, Poverty & the Environment.* http://www.urbanhabitat.org/node/528. (accessed April 16, 2009)
12. Jordan (2009).
13. http://www.secondchanceinc.org/. (accessed April 16, 2009)
14. Ibid.
15. Ibid.
16. Bradbury and Katz (2002).
17. Ibid.
18. Osterman (1999).
19. Bradbury and Katz (2002, pp. 19–46).
20. Sheridan (2002).
21. Roder (2008).
22. http://www.ppv.org/p pv/initiative.asp?section_id=26&i nitiative_id=3.
23. Spaulding, Freely, and Maguire (2009).
24. http://www.fssny.com/index.cfm. (accessed May 5, 2009)
25. Spaulding, Freely, and Maguire (2009).
26. Rosenfeld, Jacobs, and Liston (2003).
27. Elling (2009).
28. Roberts (2002).
29. Ibid.
30. Ibid.
31. http://www2.newcommunity.org/services/workforce/automotive/. (accessed May 6, 2009)
32. Giloth (2009, p. 7).

Chapter 9

Reforming Schools and Strengthening Community Economic Development

Of all the things that can limit the impact of community economic development, none presents more of a test than the lack of good schools in a community. Good schools provide the foundation for young people to become good citizens and learn the basic skills to earn a livelihood. Alternatively, the perception or reality that a community's schools are not functioning undermines efforts to improve the income mix in poor communities.

What role can community economic development play given that the field's primary function and strategies are toward building assets? This chapter presents the case that community building and community economic development encourage the rise of good schools in different ways, but the reverse is also true. School reform efforts influence the practice of both community building and community economic development for the better.[1] Some of the strategies involve galvanizing community voice; other strategies involve the use of planning and development to act as a spark for reinventing local schools. Still other efforts are changing the scope of financing and programmatic strategies for community economic development institutions.

Whatever the programmatic thrust, the emerging relationship between education reform and community building—and ultimately community economic development—is a much-needed change from the former standard where the link was acknowledged but not widely acted upon. Now we have a wide range of experiments and innovations, many experiencing scholastic gains, some other results very mixed.[2]

The inevitable question is whether we have to make choices between the many experiments. The answer here is that we do not have enough information and data to make final choices. There is no magic educational reform bullet that will help all communities in all circumstances. We do have enough information to say that the innovations look promising, and as they are replicated and improved upon, we can see a level of standardization that will sustain empirical testing of impact. There Is now a wide variety of educational reforms that either indirectly or directly help community economic development. The examples in this chapter are promising, but they are context-specific, and the lessons must be tailored for local circumstances.

Linking Community Building and Education

Perhaps the most successful models connecting schools to community economic developments are community schools. As defined by Abrams and Gibbs (2000), the full-service community school is a recent school reform model that is growing in its scope and popularity.[3] Full-service schools seek to integrate programs such as health care, mental health services, parent education, or after-school care into a schoolwide change process that encompasses the surrounding community.[4] Community schools strive to improve the educational quality of urban schools by increasing the focus not only on the academic program but also on other community problems, such as violence, lack of access to health care, and poverty.[5]

Community schools, sometimes called full-service or extended-service schools, seek to alleviate this problem through transforming the school building into a one-stop center for community services. By incorporating these services into the school, the school potentially becomes the center of community activity.[6] A community school is characterized by hours extended beyond the conventional school day, expanded services, and relationships among agencies serving students and families. Community schools employ strategies that expand the role of the school to provide nonacademic supports that encourage students and families to make education a priority in their lives.[7]

Many suggest that community schools build social capital along with providing these services. Moreover, schools cannot hope to succeed without addressing the challenges brought to the schools by students and the surrounding community. Community schools affect community building and community economic development in a number of positive ways. The most obvious of these is simply providing needed social services in disadvantaged communities.[8] Other services typically include job training, access to recreation facilities to reduce youth violence and gang activity, and supporting life-skills training for students.[9] Adding social services in economically challenged communities is essential both for community economic development and the emerging practice of community schools.[10]

A second effect of the community school model is community building. Community schools can provide a central location for increasingly fragmented communities. They offer places for community residents and groups to meet and interact, places where increased dialogue and connection can happen. This centeredness develops networks that can, in turn, grow social and political capital.

Community schools are not without critics. Merseth and colleagues (2000) argue that providing social services at public schools may divert educators' attention from the central goal of schools: teaching and learning. Teachers in a community school may become overly involved in managing and providing social services to the point of neglecting student academic achievement.

This criticism highlights one significant barrier to linking education, community building, and community economic development: clearly aligning mission, goals, and function. Although there is little agreement on the primary goal of education in the United States, the current trend is toward increased focus on student academic achievement. Many testing and accountability advocates argue that schooling should be removed from pursuits that may detract from student learning. This is not an insignificant concern, but there is no inherent reason why community schools, or any other alternatives to traditional education, cannot also produce academic achievement.[11]

One such effort that is closing the gap between traditional educational achievement and supporting services is the Harlem Children's Zone. This is a well-regarded antipoverty effort centered on education and wraparound services for children and their families in a 97-block area of central Harlem in the borough of Manhattan in New York City. Founded by a brilliant social entrepreneur named Geoffrey Canada, the Harlem Children's Zone uses a holistic approach, providing educational and social services for children beginning even before birth.[12] Zone community organizers actively search out and encourage young teen parents and others in the community to sign up for parenting classes in a program called Baby College. The program stresses early educational exposure of children along with stressing the role of discipline in children's lives.

About 8,000 children a year are served by the Harlem Children's Zone. Through a lottery, children are picked to attend a rigorous K–12 charter school called the Promise Academy, where students have access to a free health clinic, extended-day instruction, and a drop-in arts center for teenagers. The various schools in the Promise Academy operate on a rigorous curriculum, and educational outcomes are measured by standardized testing. Children born in the Zone receive access to prekindergarten programming that promotes intensive language development. This emphasis is a reaction to studies indicating that poor children lack breadth of vocabulary when compared to middle-class children of the same age. Zone children regularly test above New York City averages for their grade level.[13]

The Harlem Children's Zone is one of the best examples of what a well-funded, community-based, school-centered effort can accomplish. Academic achievement is not compromised by adding on social services; in fact, the educational thrust, in the case of the Harlem Children's Zone, becomes more significant.

The Harlem Children's Zone is one example, in one city, and some may view it as unique. It is well funded and supported by government and the private sector; the Harlem Children's Zone is a wonderful example of what works.[14] Emerging evidence shows significant positive impact in the lives of children living in the Zone.[15] Other examples of community schools are springing up and are more in the realm of possibility for jurisdictions and communities to support. The city of Baltimore, for example, has embarked on an initiative to coordinate social and community development services in over 35 community schools.[16] One of the major innovations in Baltimore's community schools is the scale of involvement. Often community schools struggle as unique entities, either as charter schools or as part of the regular school system. Baltimore has made a statement that community schools will be more than small-scale experiments and that the efforts will be scaled up over the next few years.

The schools involved in Baltimore encompass kindergarten through twelfth grade, and each school is paired with a community partner such as the YMCA or a community development corporation. Like many community schools, these schools work to provide support services across youth development, health, family support, workforce, and community development.[17]

An important focus in the Baltimore project deals with direct service delivery for community economic development. By partnering with development organizations such as CDCs, Baltimore's community schools have more structured ties to the actual work of community economic development.[18] It may be argued that the focus of schools may be drawn away from education by the apparently outward-looking stance of Baltimore's community schools; however, the vision that is imparted constitutes an important shift in the operations of community schools. By creating a vision aligning schooling with community building and economic development, Baltimore's community school initiative has established a standard that bears watching.

Lincoln, Nebraska: Leadership Makes a Difference

Lincoln, Nebraska is approaching governance of its community schools in a unique way. Fifteen elementary and middle schools are branded as community learning centers (CLCs). On the surface, programmatically, they look like other community schools across the country. Program objectives include:

- Increasing academic achievement of students in math and reading
- Providing students access to positive enriching activities during out-of-school hours and helping them avoid substance abuse and violence while building personal, social, and leadership skills

- Serving as a resource for parents and other community members to improve literacy skills, parenting skills, and family well-being, and develop computer technology skills
- Providing academic, social, and family support to students transitioning from elementary to middle school, from middle school to high school, and beyond
- Increasing capacity of schools, staff, parents, students, and community partners to plan, implement, and sustain neighborhood-based community learning center activities[19]

These goals are typical for community schools and do not constitute innovation by themselves. The leadership structure of CLCs, however, blends several levels of input into developing a cohesive community feel for these schools. This structure revolves around five groups that function together to provide guidance and leadership for CLCs. The Leadership Council is made up of stakeholders from the community and acts as a steering committee for funding and development of long-term goals for the CLC project across Lincoln.

Individual schools also have a School Neighborhood Advisory Committee (SNAC), which has "active participation from parents, youth, neighborhood residents, educators, community based organizations and service providers."[20] This group oversees planning and communication for individual schools. The CLC project has also made a commitment that SNACs will reflect the diversity of the neighborhoods they serve. This helps to ensure equitable access to school governance and change.

The third prong of CLC leadership is Action Teams, which address specific issues important to school functioning. Examples of Action Teams include teams for Evaluation and Leadership Development. The CLC Management Team brings together Lincoln public schools, the city of Lincoln, the University of Nebraska, and other community interests to develop research, leverage resources, and increase the functioning of the Lincoln CLCs.

Finally, each CLC is assigned a site supervisor tied to one of several community organizations such as parks and recreation, youth services, or the YMCA. These supervisors work to ensure successful collaboration between schools and the community.

Although the goals of Lincoln's community schools project focus squarely on the success of students, unlike the more community-oriented projects of Baltimore, the combination of many different facets of the community provides a new look at including all stakeholders in developing successful school and community ties. Parents, students, business, community developers, the school district, and university scholars all invest in leading these schools. The use of these varied stakeholders increases the likelihood of community unity and organizational strength. This model has the potential to develop a great deal of social and political capital, as networks are already in place connecting members of all levels of the community.

Innovation in community schools may also be seen in refinements to the existing models. Varying communities have different needs, and community schools often vary by services offered to adapt to local needs. Certainly community schools have significantly changed the way community development and education are viewed.

Smart Education Systems

Elaborating on the community school model, Smart Education Systems (SES), developed by the Annenberg Institute, utilize community resources to improve public schools. This model functions as a community-to-school initiative, encouraging action from outside agencies to support improved schooling. Although by Annenberg's own admission no schools have successfully implemented a complete SES, the overarching vision constitutes a significant thrust in joining education and community.[21]

Smart Education Systems are envisioned to encompass five significant dimensions:

■ Build substantial cross-sector partnerships that can provide a broad range of services to young people and their families.

■ Specify a broad set of positive outcomes, including but not limited to academic achievement, for students, families, and communities.

■ Put students, families, and communities at the center of the work with shared accountability across the system.

■ Any given SES has a systematic approach for bringing reforms to scale.

■ Put strategies in place for managing power differentials, for example, by creating clear meaningful roles for all stakeholders.[22]

Clearly these goals represent a substantial undertaking for a school district or community. It is the comprehensive networked nature of the SES outline that makes it an interesting wrinkle on standard practice. The Smart Education Systems initiative takes steps forward in setting a vision for how communities and school districts can work to improve local schools. These systems will require an enormous use of social and political will to achieve the ambitious goals of the vision, but having that vision in place provides a reference point for building successful community-to-school relationships. A number of schools and districts across the country have received Annenberg funding and are building components of smart systems in novel ways.

Chicago: Logan Square Neighborhood Association

Annenberg funded the Logan School District and a community partner, the Logan School Neighborhood Association (LSNA) to illustrate what a "loosely coupled network" can accomplish not only in school improvement but also in community economic development. The innovation in the Logan School story lies in its "grow your own" bilingual teacher-training program. The idea of the program is refreshingly simple. The Logan Square community numbers approximately 85,000 residents, two-thirds of whom are Latino. Bilingual educators are in short supply across the country, and Logan Square is no exception.[23] A lower-income community, Logan

Square faced challenges similar to urban districts across the country, namely, lack of funds or other enticements to attract qualified teachers.

LSNA solved this problem by creating training programs for local residents interested in becoming teachers. This mobilized community members in a number of ways. For the schools of Logan Square, it meant that there was an almost in-house supply of teachers, and teachers who lived in the very community in which they taught. In addition, having teachers who were community members created a greater connection between students and teachers. The teachers are representative of the neighborhoods that students live in; they understand the conditions and situations students face.

Furthermore, the jobs were intended to stay within the community, raising the income and education levels of Logan Square. Urban and rural areas often experience a "brain drain" of educated members leaving for less-challenged neighborhoods or suburbs, but the Logan Square programs kept jobs in the neighborhoods. In all, the program has provided significant benefit to both school and community. So successful was the program that in 2006 the Illinois legislature passed funding to replicate the Logan Square model.[24]

Logan Square is an innovation within an innovation and has to be mentioned in context. For many years, Chicago has been focusing its school reform efforts on Local School Councils (LSCs). Local control of schools has been a foundation of schooling dating back to the first common schools movements of the mid-nineteenth century, but Chicago's mandated LSCs ensure community influence over schools in a time of increasingly centralized administration. First established in 1989, Local School Councils are elected officials working in the schools. Each school has its own council, made up of the principal, two teachers, six parents, two community residents, and, in high schools, one student.[25] Parents and community members are elected at large; teachers and students are appointed by school boards.

LSCs are given significant authority in participating in school direction and personnel including hiring and firing the principal. This authority supports a strong community link to school and educational direction in general. In addition to handing over these authorities to parents and community members in partnership with school officials, LSC training sessions are provided in order to develop administrative capacity in the community.

The innovation of the LSC lies in the mandated nature of the reform. Each school *must* have a council, with the only exceptions being designated small or alternative schools.[26] This means that schools are linked to community, thereby reducing mistrust and misunderstanding. The experiment seems to be working; LSCs are generally highly functional entities.[27] The educational effects of LSCs are not necessarily continuously upward, but drawing the community into school affairs provides greater local power to residents in controlling their own communities.

Many of the schools working toward Smart Education Systems have adopted more traditional methods of connecting the educational system to the community; however, the variety of new approaches illustrates a great deal of innovation at work in these models.

Parent Involvement and Organizing

Another significant push in connecting the school to the surrounding community is reflected in efforts to increase parent involvement in schools.[28] As students grow older, entering middle and upper grades, parent involvement in schools generally decreases. Increasing parent involvement helps schools become more central to community life. Students benefit from greater local control of schools by those local stakeholders; communities benefit from the broader community networks developed by contact through the schools.[29]

Advocates of increased parental involvement cite the need to draw parents into schools both to combat the continuing cycles of mistrust between schools and communities and to increase social and political capital in the community.[30] Other analysts see building strong parental ties to the community as a way of overcoming a system designed to relegate the poor to continued poverty.[31]

A unique and powerful example of mobilized parent power is the Alliance School model in Texas, organized by the Industrial Areas Foundation (IAF), a long-standing, successful community-organizing group. In 1992, the IAF proposed to the Texas Education Agency that it try to use its community-organizing skills to improve low-performing schools. The state of Texas allocated $350,000 for an Alliance Schools network composed of 22 low-performing member schools.[32]

The IAF then harnessed the energy of parents in its faith-based organizing network, many in local neighborhood parishes, to work with willing school administrators to practice a variation of school-based management. Parents and school administrators in individual Alliance schools developed principles and plans with measurable outcomes. School management and parents hold each other accountable for promises made and for meeting or not meeting goals on test scores. The results have been mixed, as is the case with many efforts at school reform. Alliance Schools are able to raise scores over time, eliminating the achievement gap between Latino students and whites in most of the schools, but not all. Schools that did not see a rise in test scores were characterized by an inability to overcome teachers' fears and concerns that they were being pulled out of their comfort zones.[33] The problem partly reflects failure to break down the barriers to increased parental participation in school management (which are inherently laden with conflict). Studies also document that it takes a different mindset for teachers to see beyond their roles as educators to include the roles of community builders, which in turn support their roles as educators.

Linking Community Economic Development and Educational Reform

Charter schools have become a part of community economic development in two significant ways. A growing number of CEDIs, especially large organizations with

resources and administrative capacity, have taken on the implementation of charter schools. In many respects, they are well positioned to do so: many have run or
managed large facilities such as supermarkets or industrial parks. There are several
challenges in managing a charter school; one top challenge is the acquisition and
maintenance of the school facility.

Many CEDIs with charter schools see these schools as an important and necessary adjunct to their primary community economic development activities, such as
housing development and business development. New Community Corporation
(NCC), one of the most successful and well-regarded CDCs in the country, saw
charter schools as a natural outgrowth of its mission. It had spent 30 years building
housing, running job-training programs, creating day care centers, and providing a
wide range of social services for low-income people in Newark, New Jersey.

Over the years, the organization also raised funds for and helped administer
after-school and summer programs for local public and Catholic schools. The organization's senior leadership has been publicly vocal about the need to improve local
schools as the linchpin of revitalizing Newark and especially the Central Ward,
NCC's home community. When a charter school law was passed in New Jersey in
1996, NCC realized it finally had a chance to control the day-to-day operations of
a school.

In 1997 the organization used its experience in purchasing and financing facilities to acquire a building for the North Star Academy Charter School in downtown
Newark. The founders of the new charter school did not know anything about
facility purchase and management, so the partnership with NCC made perfect
sense. An NCC board member also became a board member of the new charter
school, cementing the relationship between the organizations. In the process, NCC
learned a great deal about managing a charter school.

By 1998 NCC was ready to open its own charter school, New Horizons
Community Charter School.[34] It approached the Prudential Financial Services
Corporation, headquartered in Newark, for a low-interest loan to finance the construction of the building.[35] NCC built a brand-new three-story facility on a site that
had been a crack house and a neighborhood eyesore. New Horizons opened as a
K–5 school in autumn 1998 with almost 500 students, after turning away another
500 students who had applied for a slot.

New Horizons Charter School, seen in Figure 9.1, was built as a community
school. The cafeteria was designed specifically as a multipurpose facility that could
be sealed off from the rest of the school and used in the evenings and on weekends
for community events. The new school was built without a gymnasium in order to
encourage student participation in NCC's youth-support activities: New Horizons
children use NCC's full-scale recreation center across the street from the school for
gym class and after-school programs. A local library, also across the street from the
school, rounds out the block.

Despite New Community's years of working with children and youth, running a school presented a unique challenge. The school parted ways with the

Figure 9.1   New Horizons Charter School, Newark, New Jersey. Courtesy of the author.

education management organization by year three after a series of challenges with principals and efforts at different educational strategies. The school opened with 27 students per class but soon realized it needed to decrease that number and over time reduced to 21 to 22 students per class. Test scores rose very slowly, as it became increasingly clear that educating low-income children from communities marked by concentrated poverty presented unique challenges. Most children came to the school several years below their grade level in reading and math. More of the school's students brought more special needs challenges than originally anticipated. Still, the school serves as an important anchor in the community and continues to provide choice and educate children from the Central Ward community.

Community development corporations starting charter schools will not solve the problems brought by concentrated poverty.[36] Macro public policy at the state and federal levels must lessen the destructive impacts of segregated poverty by enforcing open housing laws that disperse low-income families close to jobs and affordable housing. That said, linking charter schools to the work of community development corporations and community economic development is an important innovation in two ways. The CED field is already using its expertise in managing and financing facilities to help connected (to CDCs) and stand-alone charter schools survive.[37] This linkage is natural and to be promoted given similar field values such as local control and self-determination. Emerging evidence is showing that charter schools can help educate low-income minority kids.[38] Public policy may be able to incentivize CDCs with administrative capacity to host charters, but this should be done with great care and more documentation of best practices for CDCs to manage and operate charters.

Community Economic Development Partnerships for Educational Reform

McCormack Baron Salazar, generally known as McCormack Baron, is a leading for-profit developer of housing in inner-city markets.[39] Seeing opportunity in tangible, equitable community partnerships, McCormack Baron has a long-standing development method of partnering with existing CDCs on projects and sharing developer fees. This makes good business sense and builds capacity in the CDCs, who gain experience working with a large developer. On occasion, McCormack Baron has helped neighborhood residents start a CDC to bring the community into the development process of a project on which they are working.

At times McCormack Baron has gone beyond bricks-and-mortar development to assure the long-term success of a project. This was the case in North St. Louis, Missouri. McCormack Baron built The Residences at Murphy Park, a mixed-income development, in 1996. The developers had a broad vision for contributing to a healthy community, and this vision was aided by the federal government's Hope VI program designed to encourage mixed-income housing development in communities with a high concentration of public housing.[40]

The development, made up of low-rise townhouses, included 413 units for existing public housing residents. Another 10 percent of the units were built with Low Income Housing Tax credits, which limit resident income to 60 percent of area median income, and 40 percent have market-determined rents.[41] Knowing that attracting moderate- and middle-income families to the project would be a challenge, McCormack Baron chose to address the schools by working with the community to improve the Jefferson Elementary School, located in the neighborhood. No institutional partnership was in place to do this, so McCormack Baron sought out the Danforth Foundation, which had been working on developing CED programs in a neighboring community. A team of civic leaders and the St. Louis Public School District rounded out the network necessary to begin the ambitious effort to help the school.[42]

Support from HUD and $3.5 million in private funds allowed them to begin their extensive reform program.[43] The team conducted a nationwide search for a new principal, who came to the school during the 1998–1999 school year. The principal instituted a new instructional program, including an after-school arts program known as Urban Arts. Summer school was instituted, and teachers were trained to incorporate technology in the classroom. The school building was renovated with new wiring, a fiber optic cable for Internet access, and two computer labs, one for children and one for adults. A parent liaison works to involve parents by visiting homes to discuss the children's academic development.[44]

The reform initiative network has also worked to spread improvements beyond Jefferson School. The partners have worked together to form the Vashon Education Compact (VEC) to connect the feeder elementary school and middle schools to Vashon High School, the public school that students from Murphy Park attend. The VEC uses donations to fund enhanced educational and teacher training opportunities, focusing on science, technology, and the arts. It also monitors performance of these programs.[45] This effort has attempted to broaden the scope of education reform beyond Jefferson School so that children can continue to benefit after they finish elementary school.

Although a private developer interested in housing development played a key role in the school reform initiative, the residents, through their COVAM CDC, had an important voice in the process.[46] COVAM CDC coordinates residents from Carr Square Village, O'Fallon Place, Vaughn, Cahill House, and Falstaff Brewery, the different developments that make up Murphy Park, and it works to connect them to Jefferson School. The CDC's board of directors includes neighborhood residents, church leaders, investors in Murphy Park, managers of other housing developments, and the Jefferson School principal.

Using funding from public and private sources, the CDC engages in support programs and links residents to health care, child care, education, and employment training.[47] Some of these programs include summer youth employment programs; the St. Louis Cardinals-funded Redbird Rookies baseball league, which resulted in the construction of a local baseball field; the construction of a walking/jogging path around a playground; and a technology project for children and parents.[48] Furthermore, the developer of Murphy Park now runs the health center across the street from Jefferson School. Plans are also underway for an early childhood center at the school that is linked to the senior housing in Murphy Park. A resident liaison works to connect the school and the community by supporting these activities and advocating for residents.

The reform program has been relatively successful. Despite changes in school leadership, the effort has not changed significantly over time. Test scores have increased and enrollment is strong. The arts programming and adult computer training have also been successful. Unfortunately, the local school district still faces many problems, and many children face limited options once they move beyond elementary school.[49]

One important sign of progress is that prior to the reform initiative, 80 percent of Murphy Park elementary schoolchildren went to school outside the area, and children from different parts of the city were bused to Jefferson. Today, almost 75 percent of the school's students live in the surrounding neighborhoods, allowing the school and the community to be much more strongly linked.[50]

The initiative draws its strength from the connections formed between the school and the community and the different partners involved. They exemplify the multilayered partnerships and connections that encompass CDCs (but are not necessarily driven by them) and can push innovative projects and transform communities.

Enterprise Community Partners and New Compact School

In Chapter 5, I discussed the role of Enterprise Community Partners as one of the larger, successful community economic development intermediaries. For many years the organization has been working in the Baltimore neighborhood of Sandtown–Winchester. The demonstration of how to change opportunity systems in a neighborhood has simultaneously yielded important lessons for sustainable community economic development. As part of the initiative, Enterprise worked closely to change target schools in the community. Over the course of its work in Sandtown, its engagement with the schools intensified partly as a result of community partners' insistence that schools in this challenged community needed immediate attention.

The project is dubbed the New Compact Schools, and Enterprise, the City of Baltimore, and the residents of Sandtown agreed to concentrate time and resources in three elementary schools in the neighborhood. First the physical infrastructure of the schools was overhauled and modernized. Interestingly, Enterprise steered this effort, using its linkages in the private development community to do the work at a reduced cost. But it is the next leg of the journey that established a new link between the CED world and education. Enterprise went in search of curricula that would improve performance in the targeted schools. As noted in one report of the initiative:

> But beyond fixing the building and its grounds, the deeper challenge would be choosing and implementing that new curriculum. Wading into the whirlpool of competing theories of pedagogy and negotiating changes with lifelong educators in the school system would take deep expertise both in teaching and educational management. For that, Enterprise turned to Sylvia Peters, an award-winning principal in Chicago who had created and led an organization of reformist school leaders in that city. Working with Muriel Berkeley of the Baltimore-based Abel Foundation, a prominent education philanthropy, Peters surveyed curriculum models from around the country, visiting centers of research and experimentation as far away as Oregon. Peters and Berkeley were drawn particularly to two models that seemed to

fit together: Direct Instruction, a highly scripted system for teaching elementary-level spelling, reading, language arts and math; and Core Knowledge, a basic curriculum in the arts and letters, humanities and sciences covering the fundamentals of what it means to be educated.[51]

Enterprise and its community partners implemented both curricula, which from the onset they acknowledge were very different educational strategies and could potentially cause tension during implementation. But implementation was closely monitored by school leadership and consultants paid by Enterprise to come in and provide assistance to teachers. The intense nature of the instruction and the support for teachers resulted in significant gains for the two schools that remained in the Compact.

It should be noted that beyond introducing a new curricula, the New Compact schools became community schools. The initiative deployed experienced parents in the community who had undergone training to mentor younger parents. Armed with educational toys, books, and proven learning games and activities, these community "advocates" helped parents become more confident in child rearing. The outreach effort also drew them into overall support of the initiative and their neighborhood school.[52]

Summary

Education, community building, and community economic development are working together in productive ways to assist poor communities and their residents in their search for community viability. They may pursue different paths, but these fields are inextricably linked. Some samples of interesting programs and linkages across fields were presented here. Are they the most effective at raising test scores and overall school performance? The evidence is mixed. Are they the best at community building and community economic development? That depends on your criteria. Within the limits of resources and time, all of these programs are innovative attempts to build community wrapped in education and development. It would be wrong to say that we have a template for how to link access to good educational opportunities in poor communities to economic development, but the innovations here illustrate the importance of the following points.

Linking Schools to Community

Local schools are community institutions and can with careful thought, design, and support help play a role in community development and community economic development. As an active agent in the latter, the model is heavily reliant on the perception and acceptance of school-based administrators and the host district. A fully integrated economic development and educational system has not been reached, and these conceptions ultimately fall into one of two categories.[53] To date, practitioners and researchers have proposed plans in which community development is used to improve local schools or models in which schools are used to serve community needs. Depending on the circumstances, both frameworks can provide benefits and challenges to the fields of education and community building. For instance, communities focused on improving schools may forgo other essential development opportunities, leaving adult education or economic improvements without considerable attention. This will do little to improve conditions in the community, and successful students will find little enticement to remain in these neighborhoods.

A second issue constraining innovation in this field deals with the lack of diverse program examples. The most promising seems to be the service model, those schools that are essentially community or full-service schools. However, the development model (using community development for school reform or new schools) and the organizing model (using schools for community organizing) have also made inroads. Each model has seen success and failure, positive and negative outcomes.

Linking Education and Development

Innovation in this arena is limited by the lack of a framework in which both education and development are coproductive. Coproductivity simply means developing a system in which education serves its students and provides community building and development without sacrificing education, and a community development process in which education is a key feature of the plan and not an afterthought. Although some argue that the community school can be this model, evidence shows that this has yet to be achieved.

In large measure, the community partnership examples presented in this chapter address coproductivity, but it is a model in which the moving parts determine success; if one part is missing, the model may not work. Here the examples rest on the presence of an engaged private developer with broad and deep experience in urban real estate markets or a CED intermediary with historic interest in Baltimore.[54] This intensity of effort is not usual, nor is the government support that helped make this happen on solid ground.[55]

Although limited at present, this type of private, public sector, and community partnership linking development and education must increase. Now the effort must support the clear value and integration of development and education. Community schools, parental involvement, and charter schools are potentially effective tools, but unless the power and force of partnership can be brought to bear in charting a new course we may not see sustained changes in poor communities.

More Effective Mobility Policies

There is no avoiding the fact that although innovative tools and partnerships are emerging, regional policies that thin out the concentration of poverty have to be pursued simultaneously. This does not mean that any one community or any one partnership must take on the issue of regional dispersal of poverty.

Significant movement on better schools and better economic opportunities is a function of public policies that (1) encourage regional mobility along with (2) local efforts that organize parents for change and (3) alternative schools, such as charters, that offer a community-based alternative to poor schools, and organizing can play an advocacy role in change.

Endnotes

1. Crowson and Boyd (2001).
2. See Payne (2008) for a sobering portrait of how difficult school reform is to do in practice.
3. Beck (2006); Crowson and Boyd (2001); Dryfoos (1995); O'Looney (1996).
4. Abrams and Gibbs (2000, p. 80).
5. Rothstein (2004) argues that although urban schools must improve the education of inner-city students, schools alone cannot defeat the harmful effects of poverty. Furthermore, school reform without associated community development may be difficult to carry out (Warren 2005). This is because students cannot perform academically when affected by outside issues such as violence, lack of housing, poor nutrition, lack of health care, and stress induced by family issues such as low wages or unemployment Duncan and Brooks-Gunn (1997).
6. Dryfoos (1995).
7. Each community school is unique and tailored to the needs of its community, but common elements include: (1) a site coordinator who manages the acquisition and maintenance of programs and services; (2) extended hours, including evenings, weekends, and summers; (3) shared governance among school administrators and community through the development of a school coordinating council; (4) health, mental health, and other wraparound social services; (5) programs for community members such as adult education, parenting classes, job training, and entrepreneurial training.
8. Roby (2004); Dekalb (1999); and Robins and Ratcliff (1978).
9. Howell and Hawkins (1998) and Kellerman et al. (1998).
10. Knitzer and Fida (2002).
11. Abrams and Gibbs (2000).
12. Harlem Children's Zone has a close working relationship with the New York City Board of Education and the city's political, financial, and philanthropic establishment, so it enjoys the type of support (an annual budget of $68 million) necessary for a significant experiment such as this undertaking. See also Tough (2008).
13. Tough (2008).

14. The Harlem Children's Zone has been singled out by President Barack Obama as an important program to replicate as part of his domestic initiatives. See Shulman (2009).
15. Brooks (2009); Dobbie and Fryer (2009).
16. Baltimore Coalition for Community Schools (2008).
17. Ibid.
18. Ibid.
19. Lincoln Community Learning Centers (2008).
20. Ibid., p. 3.
21. Annenberg Institute for School Reform (2008).
22. Ibid., p. 1.
23. See Emerging Knowledge Forum (2007); U. S. Department of Education (2004).
24. Guajardo, Guajardo, and Casaperalta (2008); Emerging Knowledge Forum (2007).
25. Catalyst Chicago (2008).
26. Bowker (2008).
27. Moore and Merritt (2002); Ryan et al. (1997).
28. Comer (1991).
29. This sort of community/school improvement has been supported by philanthropic organizations such as the Ford Foundation since the mid-1960s, when the Foundation's president at the time, McGeorge Bundy, headed a panel advocating for greater parental involvement in New York City schools that promoted decentralization as an antidote to the "spiral of decline" of big city schools. See Petrovich (2008, p. 14) for more on this historical reference.
30. Abrams and Gibbs (2000); Stone et al. (1999); and Smylie and Evans (2006).
31. Fine (1991); Bowles and Gintis (1976).
32. The Alliance would come to be known as the Texas Alliance School Initiative and includes well over 100 schools in Texas. The model is now being tried in Arizona and Los Angeles.
33. Shirley (1997, 2002).
34. A second charter school, the K–8 Lady Liberty Charter School, opened in 2001 in a converted Catholic school building.
35. After working with NCC, Prudential went on to provide low-interest loans for a number of charter schools. The school was the first school built by Kullman Industries, known primarily for building diners and embassies. To reduce costs, the modular building was built in the Kullman factory and assembled on-site in Newark. As more and more CDCs embrace charter schools, the community economic development intermediaries and the CFDIs have all learned how to finance charter school facilities at the local level. The question of whether the charter school model is the most efficacious way to go pales in comparison to the emerging trend that sees community economic development embrace education reform using the standard tools in the field such as community-based management and financing.
36. See Knitzer and Fida (2002) for an interesting discussion of the role CDCs can play in promoting better outcomes for children in partnership with other key stakeholders and partners.
37. Halsband (2003).
38. Hoxby, Murarka, and Kang (2009).
39. See www.mccormackbaron.com. (accessed May 12, 2009)

40. The Hope VI is one of the most innovative ideas to address concentrated poverty in public housing. The outcome after a decade and more of implementation is still a question for many analysts. See Popkin et al. (2004).
41. Khadduri, Schwartz, and Turnham (2007).
42. Moore and Glassman (2007).
43. Chung (2002).
44. Khadduri, Schwartz, and Turnham (2007, p.28).
45. Moore and Glassman (2007, pp. 54–55).
46. COVAM is not an acronym.
47. McCormack Baron Salazar, Inc. (2008).
48. Moore and Glassman (2007, p. 55).
49. Khadduri, Schwartz, and Turnham (2007, pp. 28–29).
50. McCormack Baron Salazar, Inc. (2008). (accessed March 12, 2009)
51. Proscio (2004, p. 9).
52. Ibid., p. 14.
53. Schorr (1997).
54. McCormack Baron Salazar, Inc. wanted to build community economic development capacity so that the community could be a strong partner, but it also wanted to build a sustainable local economy to ensure the project's long-term success.
55. Many are now questioning the federal government's Hope VI effort to promote mixed-income communities on the basis that (1) the effects are not that evident and (2) it is not clear that mixed communities are really the key to fighting poverty.

Chapter 10

Higher Education as a Partner in Development

Universities, colleges, and community colleges play an important role not only in education but also in the lives of those living near these institutions. Institutions of higher education are economic engines, using goods and services; their very presence dictates the type of available cultural amenities, homes, and often the quality of local schools. However, higher education's involvement in the direct development of local communities has a complicated history. A number of colleges and universities have service built into their mission statements, ranging from professional and scientific partnerships to more focused missions where universities offer their resources, faculty, and students for community improvement and development.

Yet for all the important things higher educational institutions do for their surrounding communities and regions, effective partnership is often elusive unless defined carefully with thought for the core reason for the relationship. Higher educational institutions have, at times, been criticized as disengaged from the community. In other instances they have been criticized for seeing their surrounding communities as laboratories serving as objects of study. Higher educational institutions often respond by reminding critics that their role, above all else, is to serve tuition-paying students, and in the case of research institutions, to serve as important institutions of learning and investigation.

Urban institutions of higher learning have less choice in the matter whatever their primary mission. People and families can move from cities to other places when they feel threatened. Colleges and universities located in urban centers cannot simply sell their property and move. Instead, they are bound to their location. And although some colleges try to wall out the city around them, preserving the ivory tower in the face of crumbling neighborhoods, others recognize that improving their surrounding community benefits the university as well.

Many urban and nonurban institutions choose to engage in community economic development in order to make themselves more attractive. Potential students are less likely to attend a university or college located in a dilapidated or unsafe neighborhood. That is one of the main reasons schools work to improve not only the neighboring community but also their own image as responsive institutions.

As we see from other examples in this book, public and private higher educational institutions are lending support and partnership to all types of economic development. This chapter shows the increasing comfort level and cooperation between higher education and community economic development. This level of cooperation is often driven by public sector support and policy. The result is a set of innovative strategies benefiting communities and regions while showing the possibilities for diverse institutions working toward sustainable community economic development.

Successful University–Community Partnerships

A number of factors undergird successful university–community partnerships. Among the most important is establishing productive relationships in the community. Economic development, although carried out by CEDIs, often hinges on the strength of social capital between higher education institutions and their surrounding community. Without this foundation of trust, the relationship between partners will be neither a lasting nor healthy one.

In addition, partnerships, although driven by relationships, are not likely to go forward without defining clear goals, agreements, and purpose. The success of partnerships between community and higher education rests on the partners' ability to develop a common vision. This may seem obvious, but too often university–community partnerships do not achieve solid outcomes because goals are nonspecific. Without this, the various partners may find themselves acting at cross-purposes. Creating a concise shared vision helps to prevent misunderstandings and allows for forward progress.

"Mutuality" implies the involvement of both sides of the collaboration throughout the project and should be viewed as a primary outcome as well as a starting point for partnership. As Maurrasse explains, "Mutual gain is the optimum goal because it produces incentives on both sides. However, many are beginning to realize that institutions of higher education are beginning to gain more mileage out of community partnerships than are communities. The institutions of higher education tend to have more power than other neighborhood based entities, allowing them to drive the agenda."[1]

In working out the partnership, success can also be measured by success indicators developed by the partners. Furthermore, both sides should feel that they gained from the experience.

Building Community Capacity

The most direct support for university–community partnerships has come from the Department of Housing and Urban Development. The goal of HUD's Office of University Partnerships (OUP) is to increase university involvement in local community revitalization. The OUP supports nine different programs that promote university engagement in community economic development through research, outreach, or a combination of both.

The Community Outreach Partnership Centers (COPC) program, the one that most concerns us here, has since 1994 provided funding to colleges and universities to operate centers that engage in outreach (community capacity building) and applied research activities (knowledge building).

The COPC program did not receive funding in FY 2008, and grants have not been awarded since 2005.[2] Until that time, grants lasted two to three years and provided universities with funding of up to $400,000 for each grant round. At the time of this writing, the status of the COPC program is seriously in doubt. The reasons are unclear, but the most likely explanation is shifting priorities rather than any groundswell against the program. To restate a point made in Chapter 3, "innovations can last a short time (for any number of reasons, including timing and cost) and disappear. The question is how much we can learn from the innovation's impact and the potential to change outcomes at some later date." That is exactly the case here. The COPC program supported a remarkable body of work, often fostering the best in higher education–community partnerships. Rather that mourn the possible death of a program, what can we say about its legacy?

Seventy-five percent of COPC funding supported outreach efforts, and no more than 25 percent could be used for research. Universities had to match at least 50 percent of the cost of research activities and 25 percent of the cost of outreach activities through contributions from private sources or state and local governments. "New Grants" went to first-time grantees and "New Directions" grants were awarded to grantees who previously received COPC funding and aimed to engage in new efforts or expand their activities to other neighborhoods. OUP has awarded 59 COPC grants to colleges, universities, and consortia since the program began.[3]

COPC grants had to be used in urban areas and address three of the following issues: local housing, infrastructure, economic development, neighborhood revitalization, health care, crime, or planning. Supported activities included job training and counseling, fair and affordable housing efforts, youth programs, support for entrepreneurs, capacity-building efforts for community organizations, public health, safety, and environmental projects, activities to increase local access to information, and university coursework.

Despite the current lack of support, the program created a great deal of capacity and learning about fostering partnerships between communities and universities. The University of Maine–Bangor (UMB) is one legacy. Awarded a COPC New Grant of $396,278 in 2005, with matching community funds of $219,886 and university funds of $828,866, UMB established its COPC in 2006; its three focus areas centered on community inclusion, youth empowerment, and affordable housing. These issues had become significant problems in Bangor over the last 30 years. Large numbers of middle-class residents left the city for the suburbs, businesses relocated to a retail mall outside the downtown area, and a major U.S. Air Force base closed, all of which have resulted in a decline of the urban community surrounding the university.

Community-based efforts such as The Bridges to a Better Community Advisory Council and the Our Neighborhood, Our Homes Planning Coalition guided the efforts to plan and build partnerships in order to establish the UMB-COPC. In addition, teams involving both university and community partners spearheaded each of the projects. UMB-COPC is based at the Margaret Chase Smith Policy Center, but overall the program includes 27 faculty, staff, and administrators representing four colleges and four interdisciplinary centers, the Center for Teaching Excellence, and the Office of Research at UMB. Through these efforts, "UMB-COPC establishes a front door to UMaine for community partnership building."[4] It seems that by providing a specific location where university and community partners can convene and work on efforts to improve their communities, COPCs serve this function not only at UMB but at other universities as well.

Addressing community inclusion, two projects reached out to "disconnected" young adults in the Bangor region in the effort to increase their employment and higher education opportunities. Community Dialogues facilitates conversations between young adults, merchants in downtown Bangor, and local residents, supplying them with a venue for discussing the issue of "'noninclusion.'" By allowing these groups to hear each other's perspectives, the project fosters understanding among them. In turn, the goal is that they will explore efforts together to make the downtown area a more open and inviting place.

The second project, entitled New Media & Life Planning, connects young adults to formal education or work training while motivating them to pursue higher education. It does so with the CYBER (Connecting Youth to Bangor and Electronic Resources) project, an "experiential education program." Local youth participate in workshops that the University of Maine New Media Department and the Center for Community Inclusion and Disability Studies developed. Through this program, graduate students train teens and preteens to use new interactive media, including imaging, Web design, and video. The projects also involve career and life planning while helping youth to develop work skills.

The University of Nebraska at Lincoln (UNL) is a second example of a COPC used to build community capacity. In 2001, the university received a new grant from HUD. The UNL-COPC was initially established as a center for community development activities that focused on addressing issues of inadequate housing, school dropouts, and high morbidity in ten low-income neighborhoods in Lincoln. It collaborates with community partners such as the Cooper Foundation, the Foundation for Educational Funding, Inc., Woods Charitable Fund, Hispanic Community

Center, Asian Community and Cultural Center, Clyde Malone Community Center, and the Indian Center, Inc. With funding provided by the HUD's New Directions Grant (an exit strategy for HUD's COPC grantees), the UNL-COPC has continued its efforts to work specifically on enhancing the leadership capacity of Latino parents so they can advocate for their children in the public schools.[5]

During the New Grant phase, from 2001 to 2005, main accomplishments included five efforts. First, UNL faculty and staff established the UNL-COPC to provide a concrete location from which outreach activities with surrounding neighborhoods could be conducted. The center allowed community members to define and initiate research and community efforts and encouraged university faculty and students to work with neighborhood residents and organizations toward achieving these goals.

Second, the Neighbors Working Together project focused on building community capacity through leadership workshops. Activities included monthly meetings, training for neighborhood residents, political forums, and needs assessments. These sessions also enabled residents from different neighborhoods to form collaborations and share ideas and resources. NWT has worked on strengthening the relationship between university and community partners to help the projects run more smoothly, allowing the project to continue beyond the initial four-year COPC grant.

As a third, ongoing longer-term effort, students from UNL, Nebraska Wesleyan University, and Union College mentor local Latino youth aged 12 to 18 through the Latino Achievement Mentoring Program (LAMP). They provide academic, emotional, psychological, and social support in the effort to address language, cultural adjustment, and identity issues, along with preventing problems related to low academic achievement. This program seeks both to address the issue of youth development among Latinos enrolled in Lincoln public schools and to train college student mentors to work in community-related activities.

UNL-COPC was also involved in a fourth activity, creating a community-based database with the Neighborhood Geographic Information System program. UNL faculty and staff trained staff from Lincoln's four community cultural centers, Lincoln Indian Center, Hispanic Community Center, Malone Center, and Asian Community and Cultural Center, to use census data when necessary for writing grants. They also worked to develop the system, provide technical support, and identify and examine pressing issues in the neighborhood. Enabling access to local data regarding their communities, the GIS effort sought to help residents be better able to engage in public debates and have more leverage in influencing local policy.

Finally, the Partnership to Revitalize the Heart of Lincoln's Neighborhoods (PRHOL) addressed issues related to housing and community leadership. Neighborhood residents, private partners, nonprofit organizations, and UNL faculty, staff, and students worked together to provide community service and promote homeownership and leadership in the target neighborhoods. They also worked on beautification efforts, with students volunteering to rebuild or repair front porches in various neighborhoods, for example. Residents benefited through their efforts by earning recycled computers for contributing 100 hours of service in their neighborhoods. University–community partnerships, centered at the UNL-COPC, have provided the foundation for these accomplishments. In turn, their success continues to strengthen the community economic development network in Lincoln.[6]

A positive cyclical relationship evolves between this type of partnership and community economic development efforts. The reciprocal involvement of both university and community partners has been necessary for UNL-COPC's programs to have an impact, and the results they have achieved have in turn reinforced their partnership.

Overall, the Office of University Partnerships, and more broadly, the federal government, have played a key role in providing funding to support collaborations between university and community partners. The COPC program encouraged strong partnerships that provided a base for community economic development activities. The collaborative work of university and community partners helps to expand the community economic development network so that it can have a wider impact. In turn, this helps to further strengthen the partnerships that are central to achieving results. OUP's programs suggest that the federal government recognized, at least for a time, this power and potential, causing them to support these programs and partnerships.

The University as Developer

The second avenue of community partnership is the one that is growing rapidly. Universities around the world are entering into development of their surrounding cities and neighborhoods directly, whether by buying property and renovating or working on economic development programs with commercial interests. In the United States this strategy has become popular because colleges can often gain access to HUD funding or other dedicated sources for the purpose of land development. Throughout the country, a number of examples illustrate the various approaches to this type of community collaboration.

At St. Mary's University in San Antonio, Texas, the college developed a comprehensive plan for urban renewal.[7] This proposal, entitled *Vision 2012*, received a $600,000 grant from HUD to begin building a new community resource center designed to "deliver to residents those housing, economic development and volunteer resources they themselves have identified as most needed in their neighborhood."[8] This initial phase is also a good example of investment driving investment, as St. Mary's has obtained funding beyond the HUD grant from both public and private sources to continue into further development.

In addition, this method of opening a resource or community center as an entry point to deeper community development seems to be a common thread among development partnerships.[9] It may be that community resource centers provide immediate service to the community without forcing conflict over agenda or residents' potential fears of gentrification or university takeover.

Even grander in scale, the College of St. Rose in Albany, New York, has purchased over 50 homes in its neighborhood.[10] These homes have been renovated for resale, turned into community buildings, or used for university purposes but also designed for community events. This more aggressive purchasing strategy can show great impact over a short period of time and is becoming more common as universities begin to get more involved in development. Again, it is imperative that true partnership occurs when developing plans for this type of project. Colleges that fail to address the needs of the community will face resistance and mistrust. Relationship building and mutuality are exceedingly important. One way of establishing trust when the university acts in the role of a developer is to establish a community development corporation that brokers the interests of the university and the community.

In 1995, Coppin State University (a historically black institution) in Baltimore, Maryland, established the Coppin Heights Community Development Corporation (CHCDC) to "advance the broader community improvement/ neighborhood revitalization agenda for the Greater Coppin Heights/Rosemont Community."[11] The CHCDC works on coordinating partnerships among the university, government agencies, elected officials, and those in the neighborhood, including public schools, social and community service organizations, businesses, and residents. From there, the CHCDC works to develop and improve upon affordable housing options in the Greater Coppin Heights/Rosemont community. With this, it also seeks to foster economic and business development in the neighborhood.

Next, the CHCDC strengthens existing relationships between Coppin State University and the community around it through the Greater Coppin Heights/ Rosemont Alliance Steering Committee, which is a community-based collaborative established by the CHCDC to consider input from residents on questions of slum and blight removal, community safety, and the elimination of known health and educational disparities.

To aid residents seeking to become homeowners, the CHCDC provides home ownership counseling services to members of the community.[12] It also holds an annual Community Housing Fair to provide services and resources for community residents. In addition, the CHCDC provides tenants' services, including tenant–landlord mediation.

These programs provide an important service to the neighborhood around Coppin State University. CHCDC bridges the gap between the university and the neighborhood so that everyone benefits. The CDC has given the university political capital to use when it pursues physical development projects in the community that might otherwise be a point of conflict.

Knowledge Generation, Geographical Information Systems, and Community Economic Development

Promoting the use of geographic information systems (GIS) is a key point of entry used by universities to become involved in their surrounding communities. As technology has improved, GIS has become an innovative tool in planning and community development. Programs at universities across the country have worked to make it more accessible to individual citizens and community organizations working in CED.

Minnesota 3-D (M3D), started at the University of Minnesota, and the University of Washington's Community GIS, show how universities take part in knowledge generation by using GIS technology and promoting it in their communities. They often also contribute their own funds or organize outside grants to support these projects, particularly to provide training and support for community organizations. Furthermore, M3D and Community GIS have created opportunities for students to become involved through assistantships and coursework. Community organizations also play significant roles in such projects. Working with their university partners, they become the primary users of these tools, which in turn help them to generate new data about their communities and provide feedback for improvement of the programs themselves. These partnerships often also include different government actors, who provide various degrees of funding and support. By engaging with their communities and working with government in a variety of ways, universities help to forge dynamic partnerships that promote innovative uses of technology in community economic development.

Minnesota 3D

M3D, originally based at the University of Minnesota, is one example of a program started at the university level with a focus on benefiting the community. The Center for Urban and Regional Affairs (CURA) was awarded a three-year Technology Opportunity Program (TOP) grant, lasting from October 1, 2004, to September 30, 2007.[13] The project aimed to address the spatial mismatch resulting from the increased separation between job growth and housing for low-income families as a result of metropolitan development in the Minneapolis–St. Paul area.

Using GIS technology, the project centered around creating an online mapping tool geared toward various target groups, including neighborhoods, community development corporations, employment trainers, businesses, central cities, suburbs, counties of the Twin Cities metropolitan region, and the state of Minnesota. M3D allows interested individuals and practitioners to gain access to information about the region's affordable housing, economy, and job market, commuting and transportation issues, and development opportunities. It expanded existing GIS infrastructure in the region by combining statewide data on employment and demographic statistics with regionwide housing data.[14]

Key data, for example, includes information on laborsheds (where people live) and commutesheds (where they work) so that economic travel patterns can be assessed. In turn, M3D seeks to make the link among housing, economic development, and transportation more visible in the effort to promote greater coordination between planning in these different areas.[15] Practical applications of the maps generated from the online tool include the more efficient placement of affordable housing and job development projects and more cost-effective public and private investments in housing and economic development projects in order to expand economic opportunities in the region.[16]

Various university, community, and government partners have played significant roles in this effort. As the official grantee, CURA has acted as a central facilitator. It has used its purchasing power, generated knowledge, and developed opportunities for graduate students to become involved through assistantships and coursework. The center has served as the overall project manager, responsible for the reporting, accounting, and quality control of M3D. It also contributed financially to the project by matching the funds initially provided by the TOP grant. University resources have helped to provide support and training to community organizations. Knowledge generation at the university, through faculty and student research, has also resulted in a compilation of best practices and public policy options. CURA has also been responsible for dissemination of M3D among university, community, and public and private partners.

Community organizations have also been important players. A collaborative network of CDCs in Minneapolis and St. Paul participates in the project. Staff and volunteers work to increase GIS capacity in their organizations through workshops and training. These groups are also some of the key targets of M3D. As a result, their use of the online tool in planning, development, and evaluation of their projects contributes to the continued effort for M3D to have an impact in communities throughout the region. Because they explore the practical applications of the online tool, community organizations also provide feedback on the integrity of the current data and generate new data.

Some specific examples of community organizations working with M3D include the Edge Project and the Fort Road Foundation. The Edge Project addresses issues among communities in the Twin Cities region. M3D has become an important part of their technical assistance to community members with a better understanding of the issues that affect their communities, particularly in relation to the surrounding area. This knowledge in turn plays an important role in the organization's effort to promote local citizens' involvement in their communities. The Ford Road Foundation, which serves the West End community of St. Paul, has also benefited from the comparisons enabled by the varied and timely data that M3D provides.

GIS mapping has shown that West End is a mixed residential–small business community. The foundation used this information to promote mixed-use, mixed-income property developments in order to meet community members' needs. Because they reflect the current status of the community, M3D maps have also helped the Fort Road Foundation to lobby for or against certain development projects. Information provided by GIS technology has played a significant role in influencing the ways that community organizations engage with their constituents and work to improve their neighborhoods.

Different levels of government have also acted as key players in the network that makes up M3D. The federal government provided the main initial grant for the program under the rubric of the Technology Opportunities Program (TOP).[17] The federal government has also made a significant contribution to M3D's database through an agreement with the U.S. Bureau of Labor Statistics, the Social Security Administration, and the Census Bureau. These efforts have helped make M3D a comprehensive and useful online tool.

County, regional, and state entities have also contributed existing data and supported the creation of new data. In addition, they have worked to promote M3D among their existing partners. The Labor Market Information Office at Minnesota's Department of Employment and Economic Development (LMI/DEED) acted as CURA's primary partner during the initial three-year grant period, also providing matching funds. At the end of the grant period, the office took on the main responsibility of developing and maintaining the online tool. CURA continues to promote M3D through its Web site, provide user support, and participate in developing the application further. In key ways, however, the operation of M3D has shifted within the public sector from a university to a government agency.

At the local level, cities and suburbs, like community organizations, have both contributed to and benefited from M3D. Support of strategic development projects that link jobs and housing is just one way local governments have used M3D data in decision making and policy concerning housing and economic development. The comparison between towns provided by GIS maps has also highlighted their interconnections within the region, leading to more partnerships between municipalities in development projects.[18]

The city of Chaska, for example, has used GIS data provided by M3D to improve public transportation. Recognizing that this effort would be more effective if it involved its neighbors, the city has worked with other communities to improve infrastructure beyond its own borders. Local government in Chaska has also used M3D to contribute a regional perspective to its city-planning efforts. Specifically, it has analyzed housing and industrial strategies in other communities so that they could potentially be applied in Chaska. The city has made a pointed effort, in the spirit of M3D, to simultaneously promote developments and job growth in order to allow people to live close to where they work. The development of the Chaska Biotech Center is a prime example of this endeavor. A manufacturing site for over 5000 workers, the center seeks to provide people with both jobs and housing. The use of M3D in Chaska acts as a case in point, showing how the online tool provides the information necessary for local places to focus on cohesive improvements that simultaneously address housing, economic development, and transportation.

Overall, M3D represents an example of systems innovation in two key ways. University, community, and government actors have formed a dynamic partnership that works to promote the development, maintenance, use, and application of M3D and its data. Moreover, the project's integration of various types of data serves to highlight the inextricable links among housing, economic development, and transportation. In other words, through M3D, a network of partners works to maintain a network of data. An open-access philosophy connects these two aspects, resulting in "a multi-layered information environment with a public entry point."[19]

Matson and his colleagues sum up the incentive for data providers to contribute to M3D: "Ultimately they recognized that integrating their data with other data sets made the collective data more useful and that making these data available through a single portal means that people are more likely to find them and use them."[20] This has been useful for specific projects, such as grant applications, that show area building locations, housing analyses, business financing purposes, and projections of employment in various cities. It has also more generally resulted in a deeper understanding of single communities and their position within a regional context. As a result, the involvement of various actors who have access to different types of information encourages the support for projects that combine a variety of problem areas in their efforts to promote community economic development.

The Special Role of Community Colleges as CEDIs

The community college system in the United States was created with the intention that these institutions would, among other goals, serve as engines of economic development both for people and places. This is why many of these institutions emphasize sectoral training that can directly place their graduates into the local and regional economy. Their primary role is training, rather than community capacity building, physical development, or knowledge generation. Their comparative advantage in generating innovation is hosting interesting efforts such as the Florida Solar Energy Center/University of Central Florida.[21]

The Employ Florida Banner Center for Alternative Energy was created by Workforce Florida, Inc. and is made up of a partnership of universities, community colleges, technical institutions, workforce agencies, and the industries themselves. It strives to provide training for workers in sustainable and growing industries in Florida, specifically alternative energy. The Alternative Energy Banner Center was created in February 2008 to make training in the field of alternative energy available throughout Florida.

The Banner Center's goal is to supply education, training, and workforce placement in alternative energy technologies for students, initially focusing on solar thermal (solar water heating) and photovoltaics (solar electricity). Workforce training for alternative energy is not traditionally available at vocational schools, community colleges, or universities. In addition to the statewide training for photovoltaics and solar water heating, the Banner Center also provides coursework in alternative fuel vehicle technology, building science training and certification, training in disaster relief, fuel cell technology, a training course in home energy rating, and professional development for teachers.

The Employ Florida Banner Center was created to increase economic development in Florida by providing entry-level, advanced, and skilled training for workers in alternative energy. The collaborative effort between industry experts, community colleges and universities, and industry forces as well as local business development councils and regional workforce boards is vital to its success.

The training program is set up so that instructors can first be taught the program; then these trained instructors can turn around and teach students the curriculum. If successful, they hope to create an associate of science degree in alternative energy as well as a certificate in training.

This is one example of the tremendous work performed by community colleges in partnership with others. Community colleges are nimble and can adapt quickly to the needs of local labor markets quite well. In this case the institutions are exploring the case for alternative energy as a growth sector. The effort might yield marginal results. We should acknowledge the reality of this and see it as forward progress in helping define sustainable community economic development even if the results are less than spectacular. But there is another role for community colleges that has yet to be explored fully.

Community colleges have grown so much in their ability to reach important segments of the poor (see New York City's initiative in Chapter 2) that perhaps we should ask more of them. Certainly in the area of enhancing community capacity, urban community colleges could become leadership development engines by training more residents to work in community development and community economic development.

This is more than social work, which has evolved into a profession to cope with the dysfunctions of the poor rather than a developmental role. Community work encompasses everything from community organizing to the management of community institutions that train people and develop jobs. There are very few examples of community colleges taking up this management training for residents, the effort at Trade-Tech (see discussion in Chapter 1) being the notable example. Despite the lack of plural examples, one can only hope that this becomes a new arena for community colleges where they increase their direct role in helping increase the impact of CED. No other set of institutions can make the claim that they have the expertise to venture into this complicated arena.

Summary

Community–university partnerships aimed at CED have grown in popularity, number, and impact over the past 20 years. Higher education partnerships fall into four categories: developer, building community capacity, knowledge building, and trainer. The categories are permeable, and rightfully so, to better address the multiple challenges facing poor communities. The discussion and examples here show that higher education institutions can address some of the big problems facing communities in the search for sustainability and economic development.

Effective Partnerships

First and foremost, CED partnerships between higher education and communities are based on relationships, and universities must ensure that any effort incorporates the needs and desires of neighborhood residents. Higher educational institutions have approached these partnerships in many ways, generally including knowledge dissemination, development efforts, and program provision, but the most successful partnerships have incorporated all of these models in increasing capacity for residents. These multifaceted plans require a great deal of planning commitment and support, but they also provide significant impact.

Public Sector Support

The COPC and TOP programs show that higher educational institutions are extremely important for sustainable community economic development, but the weakness of the model is also in evidence. Many higher educational institutions in challenged communities may not take on the direct expansive work supported in the past by the federal government. Most will support an ad hoc number of programs for a time, but the full power of institutions of higher education in community economic development may not be realized.

This is not an easy challenge to meet. Institutions of higher education have to evolve new ways of aligning the academic needs (rigor, investigation, rewards) to the needs of the communities in which they are embedded, and philanthropy and government have to find sustainable ways of supporting these institutions when they create innovative partnerships. The question is not whether diverse institutions of higher education can be partners in community economic development, but how long they can stay in the process without support.

Endnotes

1. Maurrasse (2002, p. 134).
2. http://www.oup.org/programs/aboutCOPC.asp (accessed June 22, 2009).
3. http://www.hud.gov/progdesc/copc.cfm (accessed June 22, 2009).
4. www.umaine.edu/mainecenteronaging/documents/HUD_COPC_overview.pdf (accessed June 17, 2009).

5. http://www.oup.org/grantee/orgDetail.asp?orgid=341&myHeadID=COPC+New+Dir&yr=2005 (accessed June 22, 2009).
6. Baker (2006).
7. Ramey (2008).
8. Nivin, as cited by Ramey (2008).
9. Miller (2008); Nye and Schramm (1999).
10. Fischer (2008).
11. http://www.coppin.edu/chcdc/. The CHCDC aims to "be a catalyst for suitable and affordable housing for low to moderate income residents and to stimulate economic development within neighborhoods immediately adjacent to CSU" by establishing social, economic, educational, and affordable housing development initiatives that seek to increase the stability and sustainability of the neighborhood.
12. http://www.coppin.edu/CHCDC/HealthyNeighborhoods/Homebuying101.pdf. (accessed May 27, 2009)
13. The Technology Opportunity Program was started in the Clinton administration to address the "digital divide." A part of the National Telecommunications and Information Administration (NTIA) of the U.S. Department of Commerce, TOP supported innovative uses of technology by providing grants to nonprofit and public organizations engaged in promoting access to and use of them. From 1994 to 2004, the program made 610 matching grants to state, local, and tribal governments, health care providers, schools, libraries, police departments, and community-based nonprofit organizations. It has left a rich legacy of learning and impact that deserves study and analysis.
14. http://ntiaotiant2.ntia.doc.gov/top/details.cfm?oeam=276004024 (accessed May 27, 2009). Programs in place prior to M3D include the Minneapolis Neighborhood Information System and the St. Paul Community GIS Consortium. The Twin Cities region has also been recognized as a leader in public GIS.
15. http://www.cura.umn.edu/reporter/07-Wint/Matson_et_al.pdf (accessed May 27, 2009), 37.
16. http://ntiaotiant2.ntia.doc.gov/top/docs/nar/pdf/276 004024n.pdf (accessed May 27, 2009), 6.
17. http://www.ntia.doc.gov/otiahome/top/about.html (accessed May 22, 2009).
18. http://ntiaotiant2.ntia.doc.gov/top/docs/nar/pdf/276004024n.pdf (accessed May 27, 2009), 5.
19. Ibid., 4.
20. http://www.cura.umn.edu/reporter/07-Wint/Matson_et_al.pdf (accessed May 27, 2009), 39.
21. http://www.fsec.ucf.edu/en/. (accessed May 27, 2009)

Chapter 11

Looking Forward: Promise and Hope

For more than 40 years, public, private, and nonprofit community organizations have worked collaboratively to revitalize distressed neighborhoods and communities through the practice of community economic development. Increasingly, however, community economic development has been challenged by economic and social trends that limit the viability of neighborhood and community economies. The result is a period of flux: many urban and rural communities have been pushed deeper into economic distress and their community development and community economic development institutions are operating with outdated information and tools.

At the same time that community economic development faces significant challenges, the field possesses rich resources from which to draw on and innovate. This book's overriding argument suggests that the United States has created a framework that helps economically marginalized groups participate in the broader process of economic development.

Community economic development began as a specialized, but loosely coupled set of institutional and programmatic strategies allowing people in urban and rural places to develop or redevelop their community's economic base. More than an economic development subfield, CED creates an institutional bridge between mainstream communities and marginalized communities on issues of development both local and regional. Community economic development continues to exist, in part, because it is embedded in a web of public policies whose general goals are poverty reduction and asset building for economically marginalized individuals and communities.

Public policy has nurtured different sides of CED, such as community capacity building, asset building, and workforce development. Taken in total, these sub-fields, along with innovation and learning in fields such as education, higher education, and sustainable development, are playing an important cross-sector role in the evolving development of sustainable places and regions.

The CED principles and strategies described in this book now make up a coherent framework. That framework is graphically represented in Figure 11.1. The examples of institutions and strategies presented throughout this book all address some part of the policy value propositions identifying sustainable places of opportunity in the rightmost column of the figure. Of course, no single place or example fits the framework completely, and probably one never will. Ongoing innovation and impact rest not on paradigm shifts in thinking but on policies and strategies that enhance the possibilities that existing CED strategies can be further networked or connected.

Major trends and ideas have emerged in efforts to reinvigorate community and local economic development. One such trend focuses on enhancing the livability of economically challenged places along with building the workforce skills and asset base of low-income people. Another local development trend uses the overlay of sustainability to inform the future needs of community economic development. Here, sustainability or sustainable development is defined as (1) adaptively and productively using existing resources (land, structures, and other assets) to further build livelihoods without destroying the environment and (2) supporting locally based development organizations that are well managed, use available information to adapt to new trends, and can participate in the economic development process over time by effectively husbanding available resources.

This is not to say that community economic development stakeholders have not built a structure that supports and builds the capacity of community-based development institutions. In fact, the opposite is true. A rather remarkable infrastructure that includes local and national intermediaries has developed to support locally based community economic development. But even this support structure faces limits in its collective ability to enhance the internal capacity of CEDIs. The result is that many CEDIs are accomplishing a great deal and others are marginal at best. There is an uneven quality to locally based development that limits how much even staunch supporters can argue for their use as partners in the local and regional economic development process.

Addressing the Organizational and Institutional Challenge

It is not impossible to address the challenge of CEDIs' uneven capacity to transition toward sustainable community economic development, but it will take a concerted

Community Economic Development Capacity Building	CED Innovation Strategies	Sustainable Places of Opportunity and Hope

Locally-Based Community Economic
Development Institutions
    Community Development Corporations
    Community Development Credit Unions
    Local Community Development Loan Funds
    Local Organizations Focused on Workforce
    Development
    Community Colleges

Community Development***
    Role of Information Technology
      Geographical Information Systems
      CEDI Knowledge Development
      Performance Measures/Indicators
    Neighborhood Security and Economic
    Development
      Community Mobilization for
      Crime Reduction
    Youth Development
      Involvement in Physical and Economic
      Development
      Gang Diversion through Employment
      Arts and Cultural Development

Communities have access
to functioning schools,
health care, neighborhood
security and an overall
good quality of life

CEDI Intermediaries
    National Community Community
    Capacity-Building Intermediaries
    National Community Development
    Finance Institutions
    Regional/Local Community
    Capacity-Building Intermediaries
    Regional/Local Community Development
    Finance Institutions

Local School Reform
    Community Schools
    Parent Organizing/Community
    Mobilization
    Smart Education Systems
    Charter Schools
    CEDI Co-Productivity Partnerships

The economic base of the
community is diverse and
open and promotes access
to social and economic
integration in and to a
wider city and regional
economy

Assets and Agency
    Micro Credit/Micro Finance
    Supported Savings
    Community Asset Stabilization
      Land Trusts
      Shared Equity Mortgages

Support Institutions
    Banks and other Financial Institutions
    Private Sector Firms (General)
    National Foundations
    Community and Regional Foundations
    Public Sector (Federal, State and Local)

Changes in Workforce Development
    Career Ladders
    Sectoral Employment
    Temporary Staffing
    Building Networks
    Institutional Partnerships

Existing assets such as
land, buildings, and other
resources to base
development that is
sustainable over time.

Federal Policies
    AmeriCorps
    Brownfield Redevelopment
    Community Development Block Grant
    Community Development Financial Institutions Fund
    Community Outreach Partnership Program*
    Community Reinvestment Act
    Earned Income Tax Credits
    Low Income Housing Tax Credit
    Rural Housing and Economic Development Grant
    Rural Cooperative Development Grants
    Rural Business Opportunity Grants
    Home investment Partnership
    Technology Opportunities Program**
    Weed and Seed
    Youth Build

Sustainable Development
    Building Internally Strong
    Local CEDIs
    Adaptive Reuse of Land,
    Physical Structures,
    Fabricated Material
    Rural to Urban Food Markets
    Urban Farming
    Green Jobs

Development incorporates
a range of capable
institutions that can
contribute to community
building and sustainable
community economic
development

Federal Institutions
    Federal Home Loan Banks
    United States Treasury
    Various Cabinet Agencies

Local Public Sector Agencies
    State home mortgage and finance agencies
    State economic development agencies
    Local community and economic development
    departments

* Though the COPP's funding is in doubt, the need for the program as part of an intergovernmental support base for CED is critical, and so I retain it as part of the summary model.

** Although the Technology Opportunity Program ceased funding in 2004, a similar version was resurrected under the American Recovery and Reinvestment Act of 2009. The Recovery Act appropriated $7.2 billion and directed the Department of Agriculture's Rural Utilities Service (RUS) and The Department of Commerce's National Telecommunications Information Administration (NTIA) to expand broadband access to unserved and underserved communities across the U.S., increase jobs, spur investments in technology and infrastructure, and provide long-term economic benefits. BIP will make loans and grants for broadband infrastructure projects in rural areas. BTOP will provide grants to fund broadband infrastructure, public computer centers and sustainable broadband adoption projects.

*** The innovations discussed in this book and this figure comprise a subset of possible CED strategies to improve outcomes for people and places.

Figure 11.1 Mapping sustainable community economic development.

response and reorientation of all the stakeholders in the present community economic development infrastructure.[1] But can this be done within the existing CED structure, or is this a case where we need to go beyond the structure?

The community economic development field must expand its capacity to develop and train new managers and practitioners. Leaders now managing community-based development organizations come from diverse backgrounds and have a wide range of ability and experience. Well-designed training opportunities are available through the national intermediaries and dedicated leadership development organizations to increase CED leadership capacity.[2]

This mode of leadership development supports those who are already in leadership positions (one or two levels deep in a CEDI), and this support is important and necessary. The ability to improve community economic development knowledge and leadership is needed throughout the expanse of the CED network. We must focus on the management capacity of local community-based development organizations; however, we need to do so in conjunction with educating new staff members at any given city's community and economic development office, county economic development officials, or even local foundation officials. In short, we must provide a common education for anyone who wishes to enter the field of community economic development.[3]

Promoting this type of inclusive training and education lessens the separation in knowledge and experience between those on the ground and the support organizations. This accomplishes two additional things: (1) creating a shared information base so that stakeholders and practitioners can further refine and agree on what we might term a "CED body of knowledge" and (2) building career opportunities through common training and education that do not lock practitioners and others into one track. For many in government, training in a CED body of knowledge not only improves their own skills for government work but also holds out the possibility of working in a local CEDI. This type of circularity already happens, but preparation for different roles is often ad hoc, which can limit the chance for individual success in any given role.[4] Thus, training is a crucial first step in advancing the professionalization and ultimate sustainability of community economic development.

The challenge is how to provide not only management training for individuals in the CED network but also exposure to technical economic and housing development skills needed to work in CED, while promoting skills that encourage strategic thinking on the challenges facing the field. Although there are many ways to grow management and strategic capacity in the field, I offer the following suggestions.

Resources providers (those in the lower-left quadrant of Figure 11.1) should:

■ Increase the number of public–private support collaborations in cities and regions. Local and regional support collaborations made up of government, foundations, and the private sector are key pieces in building a CED infrastructure. They provide resources for community and organizational capacity building. As examples such as the North Carolina Community Development Initiative, the Atlanta Neighborhood Development Partnership, and

Cleveland Neighborhood Progress Inc. show, these partnerships can act as bellwethers for local change and innovation.

■ State and federal governments must find ways of directly supporting the public–private funder partnerships. At present, many of these partnerships can only access resources that flow through their organizations for programming. Federal support should be redirected to provide (1) resources to build core operations of CEDIs and (2) some level of support to build the public–private partnership as a local and regional entity. Some precedent exists for state government funding these partnerships (see the North Carolina example), but government recognition and support of these partnerships in general has been slow.

■ Rethink the demise of the Community Outreach Partnership program. Universities and colleges are integral to CED training and capacity-building efforts. The program was eliminated without a thorough review of its accomplishments or challenges. Going forward, university–community linkages are needed if we are to help CED transition to a new level of effectiveness.

■ Encourage the development of curricula and training modules for sustainable community-based development. We must go beyond the very good curricula and training efforts provided by the local, regional, and national CED intermediaries. This suggestion recommends the funded development of an extensive systematized curriculum to train and educate a broad range of CED practitioners.

■ Resource providers should focus on supporting community colleges and engaged institutions of higher learning through funding to develop CED curricula that institutionalize the field and help improve impact and sustainable development. Such curricula should show the linkages between local and regional development through improving primary education, workforce development, environmental sustainability, transportation, and building community capacity.

■ In conjunction with evolving a curriculum for sustainable community economic development, the field must work with thought leaders, universities, and practitioners to increase the number of evidenced-based studies that help the CED learn and calibrate overall impact and training need on more than an ad hoc basis.

Expanding the Planning and Implementation Capacity for Innovation

Many examples in this book show a range of CEDIs involved in innovative work beyond prevailing expectations. To truly move to sustainable community economic development, we have to encourage CEDIs to become learning, planning, and implementation organizations instead of simply being used as implementers of strategies emanating from the resource providers in the CED network.

The Unity Council building the Fruitvale BART project in Oakland, California, (see discussion in Chapter 4) is a good example of learning, planning, and implementation, but it took time and support from nontraditional funders (the Department of Transportation providing a planning grant) and partners taking a chance on an innovation. The question is whether we can be more intentional about supporting innovation.

There are federal and many more local programs that move us toward strategic inclusiveness and organizational diversity in focusing on CED challenges. Weed and Seed is instructive here (see discussion in Chapter 6). Grants, in relative terms, are not huge. The most important product of the Weed and Seed program is the deliberation, planning, and local support each application has to establish before submission. The process involves planning and developing programs on the part of a multiplicity of local actors, youth-serving agencies, faith institutions, local law enforcement, and, increasingly, CED institutions before resources are granted.

Such dedicated planning may not be possible on a grand scale, but we have to further encourage a local community and regional planning regime where functional areas are connected through the power of the purse and agency coordination at the federal and local levels. The challenges to both propositions are numerous. Our federal system of government is predicated on multiple lines of support, many of them overlapping, for any given policy problem. As a report by President George W. Bush's Strengthening America's Communities Initiative concluded:

> [W]hile the drivers of economic growth have changed, our nation continues with policies, organizational structures, and investment strategies built for an economic era that is gone. It is time to align our federal economic and community development policy with the new paradigm for regional economic growth and competitiveness. Federal policy must recognize that growth is likely to be driven at the regional level, beyond the local jurisdictions that have prescribed past efforts—and, indeed, beyond state lines. Every region of the United States must craft a regional economic and community development strategy to build and sustain a competitive edge in a rapidly changing global marketplace.[5]

The report goes on to discuss local and economic development programs and expenditures that have not been adapted to the times:

> Significant amounts of federal community and economic development assistance are allocated with formulas that have not changed over the years. This has resulted in inequitable distributions of federal assistance based upon need.... In reviewing this problem with the current targeting

formulas, the Committee concluded that traditional indicators of community need (age of housing stock, population growth, overcrowding, and unemployment) are not always reliable. Current formulas do not fully represent the economic health of a community.[6]

The problem with formulas represents a more systemic problem with federal expenditures for regional and community development: they are not coordinated or targeted based on local and regional strategies. Rather, important resources are still allocated on the basis of formulas that are driven by the need to spread resources in a competitive electoral system. This is not the age-old problem of "pork-barrel" politics; it is an administratively sophisticated way of automatically spreading the wealth by formula.

The authors of the Strengthening America's Communities initiative are right to say that we have to target our resources in this new economic environment, but we cannot neglect the reality of politics. We have to find ways of including new measures that encourage sustainable regional development, as they recommend, but we must also calibrate formulas and programs that provide a cross-section of communities (not just poor communities) with support to explore community and regional economic sustainability. Part of the solution may well be to try to improve the targeting of allocations, while recognizing that silos are always going to exist. The goal should not be to replace them but to construct active and engaged ways to network public agencies.

Modeling Innovation

The City of New York's Center for Economic Opportunity, examined in Chapter 3, is an intriguing concept to consider at a national level as an administrative and strategic force for innovation. The Center does not redirect the expenditures of New York's line agencies with the most impact on poverty reduction by fiat. Rather, incentives to innovate are encouraged by enhancing agency resources when stakeholders can make the argument for (1) a new direction in policy and (2) collaboration. Experimentation that creates "an evidence-based foundation from which we can build the next generation of government-funded, anti-poverty policies" is encouraged.[7]

New York Mayor Michael Bloomberg has suggested that in the case of increasing economic opportunity, the federal government ought to build on the many promising local experiments on engaging disconnected youth, providing incentives for work, and building human capital by ensuring "that our local efforts advance one another." Bloomberg's suggestion is an urban innovation fund administered by the White House. Leaders of the fund would then coordinate and galvanize other federal agencies into supporting innovation at the local level.

Nationally, public policy should consider an initiative that sees program staff detailed from key federal line agencies to a program within HUD. Each functional area, such as linking education to development, should have associated resources in which to support regional and community economic development innovations on the ground. This lessens but does not eliminate the problem of getting established programs and bureaucracies to share power, resources, and territory. To summarize, the nationwide goal should be to:

■ Create a program in the Department of Housing and Urban Development called the Program for Regional and Community Economic Development. The program should be composed of staff with expertise in key areas touching on sustainable local and regional development, detailed from other federal agencies. Staff positions must come with a set line-agency allocation where funding decisions on local innovation have to be done in concert with home agency priorities but also with commonly determined criteria for promoting local innovation and collaboration. Internal decisions on funding local and regional innovations must be pursued in a non-silo way that encourages program staff to work jointly on supporting complex, cross-silo programs and strategies. The program should be given latitude and resources to promote regional competitiveness as a key goal of economic development policy.

■ More than a funding entity, the Program for Regional and Community Economic Development should be charged with producing evidence-based research that shows the potential of funded innovations based on program context.

■ The program should be charged with reviewing key federal programs and then recommending how they can be better calibrated to improve sustainable development for communities and regions. Such a review should examine federal expenditure allocation formulas for opportunities to improve relevance to sustainable local and community development. Additionally, the program should take responsibility for understanding how federal expenditure supports or affects the work of CEDIs.

■ The program should increase the leadership networking and capacity of regional leaders by working with local public and private–nonprofit partnerships to engender conversation around innovation and best practices for economic development.

The Program for Regional and Community Economic Development is one way to move toward sustainable regional and local development. Whether or not it becomes a reality, here are some additional recommendations based on discussions in this book and summarized in Figure 11.1.

Community Development

■ Revive the Technology Opportunities Program that resided in the Department of Commerce in another form but with a similar goal of supporting the innovative use of information technology in broad areas of economic and community development. The TOP program helped community-based agencies and local public sector organizations use technology to improve impact and coordination. The need to use technology in community development is still critical if we want CEDIs to become learning organizations. We see what the use of technology married to accountability measures can accomplish in neighborhood planning and neighborhood security, but it is also extremely useful in planning for workforce and economic development.

■ Highlight the work of Weed and Seed and Youth Build in the public imagination, but also find ways to build on the significant outcomes both are accomplishing, sometimes in the same jurisdiction, but never coordinated. This is also true for other youth crime prevention work such as the Office of Juvenile Justice and Delinquency Prevention (OJJDP) in the Department of Justice. OJJDP, Weed and Seed, and Youth Build often target the same population, and encouraging local program operators and recipients of the grants to network and find ways to collaborate would increase local impact.

■ Encourage the Endowment for the Arts to work with state and local partners to inventory innovative programs highlighting the link between the arts and community development. These model programs should be developed as case studies to base a short-term effort to lift awareness of the important link between the fields. This pilot should base a beginning conversation with the CED infrastructure on best ways to infuse the arts into community and economic development in a sustainable way.

■ Create a small support program linking the Department of Agriculture and HUD that supports urban gardens and urban farming, with the proviso that the core thrust of the program is youth development. The hosting agency for any such program should be a CDEDI.

Local School Reform

■ The Department of Education should work with HUD to study the impact of CEDIs hosting or working with charter schools with other types of school reform models. Although many of the models are promising, we do not yet have evidence-based knowledge of what works and in what circumstances. If the initial scan shows a positive role for CEDIs, consider focusing existing resources on supporting a set of pilot projects for further study. This recommendation might seem incremental, but this is unfamiliar territory for both fields, and a rush to judgment could prove disastrous for a potential important working partnership between education and CED.

Assets and Agency

■ The nation must build on the promise of the Individual Development Account (IDA) model and find ways to increase the average match, while lowering the transaction costs for financial institutions. In the latter case, the viability of providing a type of "good behavior" credit (much like the Community Reinvestment Act) to mainstream institutions that absorb the transaction cost of IDAs might help increase the use of IDAs.

■ Strengthen the Community Reinvestment Act (CRA). Weak implementation and oversight have steadily eroded the CRA's impact, not to mention that CRA only covers one sector of the financial system: banks. The Act must be expanded to cover, as Immergluck argues, "[a]ny financial institution that makes a housing or small business loans should be subject to the Act, regardless of its status as a depository institution."[8]

■ Expand the use of the Earned Income Tax Credit. This is an easy recommendation to make inasmuch as there is solid evidence that the credits help the working poor. A more original recommendation, on my part, is to encourage direct support for CEDIs to use this as a tool for economic organizing in their communities.

■ Explore new ways of gradually increasing home ownership. My recommendation is to continue strengthening antipredatory lending laws and to look at existing tools, such as limited equity home mortgages and cooperatives, as a way to transition low-income individuals (in this case through a longer savings horizon) to traditional mortgages.

Workforce Development

■ Emerging strategies such as career ladders, sectoral employment, temporary staffing, and establishing regional employment networks are showing promise in placing low-income workers. Public sector support and resources must explore ways of bringing the CED intermediaries directly into the workforce development field. The larger national and regional intermediaries have the administrative capacity to use innovative workforce development strategies in their CED work (see the Working Families Initiative in Chicago with LISC as the coordinating agent). Centralizing workforce development within the work of CED takes advantage of existing capacity and directly addresses the now emerging focus on building the individual out of poverty, not just homes.

Sustainable Development

Earlier I discussed the need to strengthen organizational effectiveness in the CED field as part of sustainable development. Strong local and regional institutions are the foundation for a shift in the CED direction, augmenting the more familiar sustainability strategies such as brownfield development, housing preservation, and green jobs. Many long-standing models combine facilities and housing development with workforce development. There are always opportunities for positive cross-fertilization. Brownfield development began in the Department of Environmental Protection; now HUD offers a supplemental program for states and localities to use in their development work. I see this as additive, not redundant, in an effort to provide resources to capable organizations and jurisdiction.

There is a body of tried ideas and methods in this area. The emerging paradigm linking environmental sustainability to regional and community development is exciting, although incipient, and it needs much more definition. There are evident opportunities for green building, linking food systems across a region. What we need now is field definition based on models that can in turn be evaluated for their effectiveness. This means supporting small-scale programs and pilots that link environmental sustainability to regional and community development. These programs and pilots should be assessed in due course to determine their ability to build individual and community assets and their cost effectiveness in the mainstream development process. Doing so will indicate whether this is a positive long-term direction for our society or a fad destined for obscurity. My sense is that the former is the case, but we do not yet have evidence to stem the inevitable and appropriate question of how and if sustainability adds value in framing economic development.

Public Sector Involvement in Sustainable Community Economic Development

The local public sector, city governments, county governments, and other area governments are critical forces in the widespread use and support of community economic development.[9] Far too many local governments see the business attraction model as the definition of economic development. Trying to change that is a less productive use of time than efforts that encourage the use of mixed strategies, CED being one of those strategies.

To make the case, we need documentation and administrative analysis of innovative local governments actively seeking to link people and place development. The cases are growing, but lack of a complementary language and framework limits the comparison and utility of emerging cases. The recommendation is that resource providers and state and local peer associations call for increased assemblage of knowledge that will help articulate and frame emerging trends linking people and place development. It is only by further articulating categories describing the work and assessment of impact that we can truly know what works or does not work and why. This book has tried to start the discussion on what a framework looks like, but much more work needs to be done.

Summary

I hope the reader takes away from this book the knowledge that the United States has accomplished much in addressing the combination of poverty and place decay. There is enormous work yet to be done, but we have tried (and are still trying) much as a nation. We should value experimentation and not call it government failure when a program or strategy is less than effective. Within national values of local democracy, economic opportunity, and community self-determination we now have a community economic development movement that is evolving, albeit slowly at times; nevertheless, progress is being made in understanding the complexities of community and regional economic development.[10]

Stemming poverty and building sustainable regional and local economies is not for those expecting short-term change. We have the base on which to grow the field. We should do so with all deliberate speed, but with an objective eye for what works. The promise of hope is not that we can eliminate blight and poverty tomorrow, but that we can learn to make important changes based on thoughtful strategies, strong institutions, and evidence. Combined, the prospects for building strong communities and regions should give us all reason to hope.

Endnotes

1. McNeely (2004).
2. Ibid.
3. N. S. Mayer (2004); McNeely (2004); Zdenek and Steinbach (2000).
4. Zdenek and Steinbach (2000); N. S. Mayer (2004).
5. U.S. Department of Commerce (2005, p. 7).
6. Ibid., p. 25.
7. See   http://www.nyc.gov/html/ceo/downloads/pdf/innovation_fund_january_2009. pdf. (accessed June 1, 2009)
8. Immergluck (2004, p. 249).
9. Catlaw (2009); Hall (2008).
10. Hall (2008); Howell-Moroney (2008); Savoie (2008).

References

Abrams, Laura S., and Jewelle Taylor Gibbs. 2000. Planning for school change: School-community collaboration in a full-service elementary school. *Urban Education* 35(1) (March).

Abramson, Mark A., and Ian D. Littman, Eds. 2002. *Innovation*. Lanham, MD: Rowman & Littlefield.

Agranoff, Robert. 2003. *Leveraging networks: A guide for public managers working across organizations*. Washington, DC: IBM Center for the Business of Government.

Alexander, Frank. 2009. Neighborhood stabilization and land banking. *Boston Federal Reserve Bank, Community Banking*. Summer. Available at http://www.bos.frb.org/commdev/c&b/2009/summer/Frank_Alexander_land_banks.pdf. (accessed November 1, 2009).

Alford, John, and Owen Hughes. 2008. Public value pragmatism as the next phase of public management. *American Review of Public Administration* 38(2).

Allen, Molly, Nick Lienesch, Nancy Rosenbaum, and Sandra Jamet. 2008. *Project reach out*. New York: Seedco. Available at http://www.seedco.org/pro_toolkit/ (accessed November 3, 2009).

Almer, Ellen. 2000. Chicago journal: "The romance is back" along a revitalized river. *New York Times*. Available at http://www.nytimes.com/2000/08/20/us/chicago-journal-the-romance-is-back-along-a-revitalized-river.html (accessed April 1, 2009).

Altshuler, Alan A., and Robert D. Behn. 1997, eds. The dilemmas of innovation in American government. In *Innovation in American Government*. Washington, DC: Brookings Institution Press.

Anglin, Roland V. 1990. Diminishing utility: The effect on citizen preferences for local growth. *Urban Affairs Review* 25(4).

——. 1994. Searching for justice: Court-inspired housing policy as a mechanism for social and economic mobility. *Urban Affairs Quarterly* 29(3).

——. 2000. Stakeholder community development. *National Housing Institute*. Available at http://www.nhi.org/online/issues/114/anglin.html (accessed October 12, 2008).

——. ed. 2004. *Building the organizations that build communities: Strengthening the capacity of faith- and community-based development organizations*. Washington, DC: U.S. Department of Housing and Urban Development, Office of Policy Development and Research.

Annenberg Institute for School Reform. 2008. AISR: Our Vision. Available at http://www.annenberginstitute.org/Idea/index.php. (accessed June 1, 2009).

Annie E. Casey Foundation. 2007. *LISC and Centers for Working Families help Chicago families to stabilize their finances and move ahead*. Available at http://www.aecf.org/MajorInitiatives/FamilyEconomicSuccess/FESinAction/LISC.aspx (accessed May 6, 2009).

Arigoni, Danielle. 2001. *Affordable housing and smart growth: Making the connection.* Washington, DC: National Neighborhood Coalition.

Armistead, P. Jefferson. 2005. *New markets tax credits: Issues and opportunities.* Brooklyn, NY: Pratt Center.

Armstrong, Jim, and Robin Ford. 2002. Public sector innovations and public interest issues. *The Innovation Journal.* March 13. Available at http://www.innovation.cc/discussion-papers/ps-innovation-public-interest.html (accessed June 2, 2008).

Arrow, Kenneth Joseph, Amartya Kumar Sen, and Kaotarao Suzumuro. 1997. *Social choice re-examined.* New York, Macmillan.

Atlanta Neighborhood Development Partnership. 2004. *Making the case for mixed income and mixed use communities: An executive summary.* Atlanta Neighborhood Development Partnership. Available at http://www.andpi.org/mici.html (accessed November 3, 2009).

———. *Making the case for housing choices and complete communities: The next generation.* 2007. Atlanta: Atlanta Neighborhood Development Partnership. Available at www.andpi.org/MTCNG.pdf (accessed November 3, 2009).

Baker, Sarah. 2006. Second grant keeps outreach center rolling, *The Scarlet,* February 9, 2006, University of Nebraska-Lincoln. (http://www.unl.edu/scarlet/archive/2006/02/09/story2.html) (accessed June 22, 2009).

Baltimore City Public School System. 2008 *Baltimore's community school initiative fact sheet.* Available at http://www.baltimoreconnections.org/bcpssfact.pdf (accessed August 5, 2008).

Baltimore Coalition for Community Schools. 2008. *Baltimore coalition for community schools.* Available at http://www.baltimorecoalition.org/ (accessed August 26, 2008).

Baltimore Community School Connections. *Baltimore city community school initiative shool year 2007–2008.* Available at http://www.baltimoreconnections.org/cs0708SN.html (accessed August 26, 2008).

Barlow, Andrew L. 2003. *Between fear and hope: Globalization and race in the United States.* Lanham, MD, Oxford: Rowman & Littlefield.

Barnes, William R., and Larry C. Ledebur. 1998. *The new regional economies: The U.S. common market and the global economy.* Cities and planning series. Thousand Oaks, CA: Sage.

Baumgartner, Frank R., and Bryan D. Jones. 1991. Agenda dynamics and policy subsystems. *The Journal of Politics* 53(4).

Beck, Christine S. 2006. Redefining "community" to benefit inner-city students. *Momentum* 37(4).

Behn, Robert. 1995. Creating an innovative organization: Ten hints for involving frontline workers. *State and Local Government Review* 27(3) (Fall).

Belluck, Pam. 1999. In Chicago, the story behind the rising test scores. *New York Times* 1999. Available at http://www.nytimes.com/1999/01/21/us/state-union-education-programs-chicago-story-behind-rising-test-scores.html (accessed April 1, 2009).

Belsky, Eric, and Allegra Calder. 2004. *Credit matters: Low-income asset building challenges in a dual financial service system.* Cambridge, MA: Joint Center for Housing Studies, Harvard University.

Bendick, Marc, Jr., and Mary Lou Eagan. 1991. *Business development in the inner-city: Enterprise with community links.* New York: Community Development Research Center, New School for Social Research.

Bennett, Michael I. J., and Robert Giloth. 2007. *Economic development in American cities: The pursuit of an equity agenda.* SUNY Series in Urban Public Policy. Albany: State University of New York Press.

Berry, Jeffrey M., Kent E. Portney, and Ken Thomson. 1993. *The rebirth of urban democracy.* Washington, DC: Brookings Institution.

Berube, Alan. 2006. *Using the earned income tax credit to stimulate local economies.* Washington, DC: Brookings Institution. Available at http://www3.brookings.edu/metro/pubs/Berube20061101eitc.pdf.

Bingham, Lisa Blomgren, Tina Nabatchi, and Rosemary O'Leary. 2005. The new governance: Practices and processes for stakeholder and citizen participation in the work of government. *Public Administration Review* 65(5).

Borins, Sandford F. 1998. *Innovating with integrity: How local heroes are transforming American government.* Washington, DC: Georgetown University Press.

Borts, George H., and Jerome L. Stein. 1964. *Economic growth in a free market.* New York: Columbia University Press.

Boshara, Ray. 2003. The $6,000 solution. *Atlantic Monthly* 291(1): 91–95

Bourn, John. 2006. *Achieving innovation in central government organizations.* London: National Audit Office.

Bovaird, Tony. 2007. Beyond engagement and participation: User and community coproduction of public services export. *Public Administration Review* 67(5).

Bowker, Paul D., 2008 , Judge rules against local school councils. *Chi*Town Daily News,* April 11.

Bowles, Samuel, and Herbert Gintis. 1976. *Schooling in capitalist America: Educational reform and the contradictions of economic life.* New York: Basic Books.

Bradbury, Katherine L., and Jane Katz. 2002. Are lifetime incomes growing more unequal? Looking at new evidence on family income mobility. *Boston Federal Reserve Regional Review 2.*

Bradbury, Katharine L., Anthony Downs, and Kenneth A. Small. 1982. *Urban decline and the future of American cities.* Washington, DC: Brookings Institution.

Bratt, Rachel G., and William M. Rohe. 2007. Challenges and dilemmas facing community development corporations in the United States. *Community Development Journal* 42(1).

Bratt, Rachel G., Langley C. Keyes, Alex Schwartz, and Avis C. Vidal. 1995. *Confronting the management challenge: Affordable housing in the nonprofit sector.* New York: Community Development Research Center, Graduate School of Management and Urban Policy, New School for Social Research.

Brière, Bénédicte de la, and Laura B. Rawlings, 2006. Examining conditional cash transfer programs: A role for increased social inclusion? The World Bank. Available at http://siteresources.worldbank.org/SOCIALPROTECTION/Resources/SP-Discussion-papers/Safety-Nets-DP/0603.pdf (accessed June 17, 2009).

Brooke-Weiss, Blair, Kevin P. Haggerty, Abigall A. Fagan, J. D. Hawkins, and Rick Cady. 2008. Creating community change to improve youth development. *The Prevention Researcher* 15(2).

Brooks, David. 2009. The Harlem miracle. *New York Times.* Available at http://www.nytimes.com/2009/05/08/opinion/08brooks.html?em=&pagewanted=print (accessed May 10, 2009).

Brown, Helen. 2007. *Knowledge and innovation: A comparative study of the USA, the UK, and Japan.* New York: Routledge.

Brown, Pamela M. 2006. Municipally operated charter schools: A new trend in community services. *Education & Urban Society* 39(1).

Brown, Prudence. 1996. Comprehensive neighborhood-based initiatives. *Cityscape: A Journal of Policy Development and Research* 2(2).

Bullard, Robert D. 2007. *The black metropolis in the twenty-first century: Race, power, and politics of place.* Lanham, MA: Rowman & Littlefield.

Burwick, Andrew, Michelle Derr, Jeffrey Max, and Diane Paulsell. 2007. *Collaborating with faith and community-based organizations: Lessons learned from 12 workforce investment boards.* Princeton, NJ: Mathematica Policy Research.

Businessweek. An inner city renaissance. October 27, 2003. http://www.businessweek.com/@@JXi1OYQQdP6jnA0A/magazine/content/03_43/b3855110_mz021.htm (accessed March 29, 2008)

Buss, Terry F., F. Stevens Redburn, and Kristina Guo. 2006. *Modernizing democracy: Innovations in citizen participation.* Armonk, NY: M.E. Sharpe.

Calestous, Juma, and Yee-Cheong Lee. 2005. UN Millennium Project 2005. *Innovation: Applying knowledge to development.* Available at http://www.unmillenniumproject.org/documents/Science-complete.pdf. (Accessed July 1, 2009)

Calthorpe, Peter. 1993. *The next American metropolis: Ecology, community, and the American dream.* New York: Princeton Architectural Press.

Caner, Asena and Edward Wolff. 2002. *Asset poverty in the United States, 1984–1999: Evidence from the panel study of income dynamics.* New York: Levy Economics Institute Working Paper No. 356.

Capuzzo, Jill P. 2001. Mount Laurel: A battle that won't go away. *New York Times* (November 25, 2001). Available at http://www.nytimes.com/2001/11/25/nyregion/mount-laurel-a-battle-that-won-t-go-away.html?n=Top/Reference/TimesTopics/Subjects/S/SuitsandLitigation&scp=19&sq=mt.laurellitigation&st=cse&pagewanted=all (accessed April 2, 2009).

Carayannis, Elias G., and David F. J. Campbell. 2006. *Knowledge creation, diffusion, and use in Innovation networks and knowledge clusters: A comparative systems approach across the United States, Europe, and Asia. Technology, innovation, and knowledge management.* Westport, CT: Praeger.

Carlson, David, and Arabella Martinez. 1988. *The Economics of Community Change.* Unpublished manuscript. Washington, DC: Center for Policy Development.

Caro, Robert A. 1974. *The Power Broker: Robert Moses and the fall of New York.* New York: Knopf.

Carty, Winthrop. 2003. *Findings of the workshop on innovation and quality* (delivered at the Fifth Global Forum on Reinventing Government). Mexico City. Available at http://www.innovations.harvard.edu/showdoc.html?id=8064 (accessed November 2, 2009).

Casillas, Ofelia I. 2009. Urban gardening finds a home on Leclaire Ave. *Chicago Tribune.* April 15. Available at http://archives.chicagotribune.com/2009/apr/15/local/chi-leclaire-gardens-zone-city-1apr15 (accessed November 2, 2009).

Catalyst Chicago. 2008. *Local school councils.* Available at Catalyst Chicago: http://www.catalyst-chicago.org/guides/?id=77 (accessed August 12, 2008).

Catlaw, Thomas J. 2009. Governance and networks at the limits of representation. *The American Review of Public Administration.* 39(5).

Cervero, Robert. 2004. *Transit-oriented development in the United States: Experiences, challenges, and prospects.* TCRP report. Vol. 102. Washington, DC: Transportation Research Board.

Chaskin, Robert J. 2001. *Building community capacity.* New York: A. de Gruyter.

Christian Science Monitor. 2009. Milwaukee's urban farmer. January 28. Available at http://features.csmonitor.com/gardening/2009/01/28/milwaukees-urban-farmer/ (accessed May 25, 2009).

Chung, Connie. 2002. *Using public schools as community development tools: Strategies for community-based developers.* Joint Center for Housing Studies, Harvard University, Neighborhood Reinvestment Corporation.

Clear, Todd R. 2007. *Imprisoning communities: How mass incarceration makes disadvantaged neighborhoods worse.* New York: Oxford University Press.

Cohen, Adam, and Elizabeth Taylor. 2000. *American pharaoh: Mayor Richard J. Daley, his battle for Chicago and the nation.* First ed. Boston: Little, Brown.

Cohen, Mark, A. and Alex R. Piquero. 2008. *Costs and benefits of a targeted intervention program for youthful offenders: The YouthBuild USA offender project.* Available at SSRN: http://ssrn.com/abstract=1154055 (accessed April 11, 2009).

Cohen, Rick. 2003. The United Way's new business plan for community development. *Shelterforce* (January/February). Available at http://www.shelterforce.org/online/issues/127/fundraising.html (accessed November 2, 2009).

Comer, James P. 1991. Parent participation: Fad or function? *Educational Horizons* 69(4).

Condon, Tom. 2003. The art of renewal: Can putting the country's largest modern-art center in an abandoned mill save a beleaguered factory town? So far, it's working in North Adams, Mass. *Hartford Courant* (September 14). Available at http://infoweb.newsbank.com/iw-search/we/InfoWeb?p_product=AWNB&p_theme=aggregated5&p_action=doc&p_docid=0FD9844024C5EAEE&d_place=HRCB&f_subsection=sARTS&f_issue=2003-09-14&f_publisher= (accessed April 1, 2009).

Crowson, Robert L., and William Lowe Boyd. 2001. The new role of community development in educational reform. *Peabody Journal of Education* 76(2) (April).

Cuciti, Peggy L., and Marshall Kaplan. 1986. *The Great Society and its legacy: Twenty years of U.S. social policy.* Durham, NC: Duke University Press.

Cunningham, Kiran, Phyllis A. Furdell, and Hannah J. McKinney. 2007. *Tapping the power of city hall to build equitable communities: 10 city profiles.* Washington, DC: National League of Cities.

Cytron, Naomi, and Carolina Reid. 2005. *Engaging the financial services industry in asset building individual development accounts.* Federal Reserve Bank of San Francisco. Available at http://www.frbsf.org/publications/community/investments/0505/individual.pdf (accessed June 23, 2009).

Dangler, David. 2007. Beyond the farm. *Shelterforce* (Winter). Available at http://www.shelterforce.org/article/227/beyond_the_farm/ (accessed June 26, 2009)

de Souza Briggs, Xavier. 2007. Networks, power, and a dual agenda: New lessons and strategies for old community building dilemmas. Available at http://web.mit.edu/workingsmarter/media/pdf-ws-kia-brief-0703.pdf (accessed May 11, 2009).

DeFilippis, James, and Susan Saegert. 2007. *The community development reader.* New York: Routledge.

Dekalb, Jay. 1999. *Student truancy.* Eugene, OR: ERIC Clearinghouse on Educational Management.

Dionne, Eugene J. 1998. *Community works: The revival of civil society in America.* Washington, DC: Brookings Institution Press.

Dobbie, Will, and Roland G. Fryer, Jr. 2009. *Are high-quality schools enough to close the achievement gap? Evidence from a bold social experiment in Harlem.* Cambridge, MA: Harvard University. Available at http://www.economics.harvard.edu/faculty/fryer/files/hcz%204.15.2009.pdf. (accessed April 23, 2009)

Doctors, Samuel I. 1974. *Whatever happened to minority economic development.* Hindsdale, IL: Dryden Press.

Donahue, John D. 2005. *Government innovators network: Dynamics of diffusion: Conceptions of American federalism and public-sector innovation*, March 11. Available at http://www.innovations.harvard.edu/showdoc.html?id=6771 (accessed April 11, 2008).

Dreier, Peter, John H. Mollenkopf, and Todd Swanstrom. 2004. Place matters: Metro politics for the twenty-first century. *Studies in Government and Public Policy*. University Press of Kansas.

Drucker, Peter. *Workforce development 101: Workforce development in support of economic development*. Slideshow Presentation Ed. Available at staging.okcommerce.gov/.../Workforce_Development_101_1305051490.ppt (accessed November 3, 2009).

Dryfoos, Joy G. 1995. Full service schools: Revolution or fad? *Journal of Research on Adolescence*. 5(2).

Duncan, Cynthia M. 1986. *Coal and economic development in Central Appalachia: A new framework for policy*. Coal and Economic Development, 1. Berea, KY: Mountain Association for Community Economic Development.

————. 1992. *Rural poverty in America*. New York: Auburn House.

Duncan, Greg J., and Jeanne Brooks-Gunn. 1997. *Consequences of growing up poor*. New York: Russell Sage Foundation.

Eggers William, D. 2008. Innovation: Beyond the Big Bang Theory. *Governing.Com* Available at http://www.governing.com/mgmt_insight.aspx?id=5026 (accessed April 5, 2008).

Eichner, Alfred S. 1970. State development agencies and employment expansion. *Policy Papers in Human Resources and Industrial Relations*, vol. 18. Ann Arbor: Institute of Labor and Industrial Relations, University of Michigan–Wayne State University.

Elling, M. Duane. 2009. Community colleges at forefront of workforce development in the U.S. *Mott Mosaic* 7(2), Available at http://www.mott.org/~/media/pdfs/Current/Mott%20Mosaic/MosaicV7N2low.ashx (accessed September 23, 2009).

Emerging Knowledge Forum. 2007. *Logan Square, Chicago*. Providence, RI: Annenberg Institute for School Reform.

Feehan, David, and Marvin D. Feit. 2006. *Making business districts work: Leadership and management of downtown, main street, business district, and community development organizations*. New York: Haworth Press.

Feiock, Richard C., Annette Steinacker, and Jun Hyung. 2009. Institutional collective action and economic development joint ventures. *Public Administration* Review. 69(2).

Ferguson, Ronald F., and William T. Dickens. 1999. *Urban problems and community development*. Washington, DC: Brookings Institution Press.

Ficke, Robert C., and Andrea Piesse. 2005. *Evaluation of the family self-sufficiency program: Retrospective analysis, 1996 to 2000*. Washington, DC: U.S. Department of Housing and Urban Development.

Fine, Michelle. 1991. *Framing dropouts: Notes on the politics of an urban public high school*. SUNY Series, Teacher Empowerment and School Reform. Albany: State University of New York Press.

Fischer, Karen. 2008, May 16. Struggling communities turn to colleges. *The Chronicle of Higher Education* , pp. 1-7.

Flint, Anthony. 2006. *This land: The battle over sprawl and the future of America*. Baltimore: Johns Hopkins University Press.

Florida, Richard L. 2005. *Cities and the creative class*. New York: Routledge.

Ford Foundation. 1979. *Communities and neighborhood: A possible private sector initiative for the 1980s*. New York: Ford Foundation Archives.

———. 1987. *Leadership in affecting poverty: A Report for the mid-decade review of the Ford Foundation's programs on persistent poverty*. New York: Ford Foundation Archive.

Freudenburg, William R. 1992. Addictive economies: Extractive industries and vulnerable localities in a changing world economy. *Rural Sociology* 57(3).

Friedman, Thomas L. 2000. *The Lexus and the olive tree*. New York: Anchor Books.

———. 2007. *The world is flat: A brief history of the twenty-first century*. New York: Farrar, Straus and Giroux.

Gale, William G. and Janet Rothenberg Pack. 2000. Brookings Papers on Brookings Institution, Center on Urban and Metropolitan Policy. Samuel Zell and Robert Lurie Real Estate Center. Brookings-Wharton Papers on Urban Affairs.

Garmise, Shari. 2006. *People and the competitive advantage of place: Building a workforce for the 21st century*. Armonk, NY: M.E. Sharpe.

Gass, Anne. 2008. Post-foreclosure community stabilization strategies: Case studies and early lessons. Available at http://neighborworks.issuelab.org/research/listing/post-foreclosure_community_stabilization_strategies_case_studies_and_early_lessons_2008 (accessed June 29, 2009).

Gazley, Beth. 2008. Beyond the contract: The scope and nature of informal government-nonprofit relationships. *Public Administration Review* 68(1).

General Accountability Office. 2007a. *Nonprofit sector: Increasing numbers and key role in delivering federal services*. Washington, DC: United States Government Accountability Office, GAO-07-1-84.

———. 2007b. *New markets tax credit appears to increase investment by investors in low-income communities, but opportunities exist to better monitor compliance*. Washington DC: United States Government Accountability Office, GAO-07-296.

Geoghegan, Martin, and Fred Powell. 2006. Community development, partnership governance and dilemmas of professionalization: Profiling and assessing the case of Ireland. *British Journal of Social Work* 36(5).

Gibson, James O., G. Thomas Kingsley, and Joseph B. McNeely. 1997. *Community building: Coming of age*. The Urban Institute. Available at http://www.urban.org/Publications/307016.html (accessed May 11, 2009).

Giloth, Robert. 1998. *Jobs & economic development: Strategies and practice*. Thousand Oaks, CA: Sage.

———. 2009. Lessons for a new context: workforce development in an era of economic challenge. Federal Reserve Bank of San Francisco. *Community Investments*. v. 21, no. 1. Spr, 2009 - p. 8-13

Gittell, Ross J., and Avis Vidal. 1998. *Community organizing: Building social capital as a development strategy*. Thousand Oaks, CA: Sage.

Gonzalez, David. 1993. In the South Bronx, the grass roots grow up: Organizations born in protest uncomfortably find they're now the establishment. *New York Times* (January 7, 1993). Available at http://query.nytimes.com/gst/fullpage.html?res=9F0CE7DC103FF934A35752C0A965958260&sec=&spon=&pagewanted=all (accessed March 30, 2008).

Goodman, Robert. 1979. *The last entrepreneurs: America's regional wars for jobs and dollars*. New York: Simon and Schuster.

Gottlieb, Paul. 1994. Amenities as an economic development tool: Is there enough evidence? *Economic Development Quarterly* 8(3).

Greasley, Stephen, and Gerry Stoker. 2008. Mayors and urban governance: Developing a facilitative leadership style. *Public Administration Review* 68(4).

Green, Gary P., and Anna Haines. 2008. *Asset building & community development.* Second ed. Los Angeles: Sage.

Greenstein, Rosalind, and Yesim Sungu-Eryilmaz. 2004. *Recycling the city: The use and reuse of urban land.* Cambridge, MA: Lincoln Institute of Land Policy.

Grizzard, Mike. 2008. *The daily reflector. Community development initiative goes green.* Available at http://www.reflector.com/business/community-development-initiative-goes-green-140.html (accessed April 14, 2009).

Grogan, Paul S., and Tony Proscio. 2001. *Comeback cities: A blueprint for urban neighborhood revival.* Boulder, CO: Westview Press.

Guajardo, Miguel, Francisco Guajardo, and Edyael Del Carmen Casaperalta. 2008. Transformative education: Chronicling a pedagogy for social change. *Anthropology & Education Quarterly* 39(1).

Hall, Jeremy L. 2008. The forgotten regional organizations: Creating capacity for economic development. *Public Administration Review* 68(1).

Halpern, Robert. 1995. *Rebuilding the inner city: A history of neighborhood initiatives to address poverty in the United States.* New York. Columbia University Press.

Halsband, Robin. 2003. Charter schools benefit community economic development. *Journal of Housing & Community Development.* November/December, pp.34–38.

Hamilton, David K., and Patricia Sue Atkins. 2008. *Urban and Regional Policies for Metropolitan Livability.* Armonk, NY: M.E. Sharpe.

Hardin, Garrett. 1968. The tragedy of the commons. *Science* (162) December.

Harrison, Bennett, and Sandra Kanter. 1978. The political economy of states' job-creation business incentives. *Journal of the American Planning Association* 44(4).

Harrison, Bennett, and Marcus Weiss. 1998. Labor market restructuring and workforce development: The changing dynamics of earnings, job security, and training opportunities in the United States. In *Jobs & Economic Development: Strategies and Practice,* ed. Robert Giloth. Thousand Oaks, CA: Sage.

Harvey, David. 2005. *A brief history of neoliberalism.* New York: Oxford University Press.

Henson, Eric C. 2008. *The state of the native nations: Conditions under U.S. policies of self-determination: The Harvard Project on American Indian Economic Development.* New York: Oxford University Press.

Henton, Douglas C., John Melville, and Kimberly Walesh. 1997. *Grassroots leaders for a new economy: How civic entrepreneurs are building prosperous communities.* A joint publication in the Jossey-Bass Public Administration Series and the Jossey-Bass Nonprofit Sector Series. San Francisco: Jossey-Bass.

Herbers, John. 1983. Cities turn to private groups to administer local services. *New York Times.* May 23.

Holt, Stephen. 2006. *The earned income tax credit at age 30: What we know.* Washington, DC: The Brookings Institution. Available at http://www.brookings.edu/~/media/Files/rc/reports/2006/02childrenfamilies_holt/20060209Holt.pdf. (accessed June 3, 2009).

Howell, James. C., and David J. Hawkins. 1998. Prevention of youth violence. *Crime and Justice: A Review of Research* 24.

Howell-Moroney, Michael. 2008. The Tiebout hypothesis 50 years later: Lessons and lingering challenges for metropolitan governance in the 21st century. *Public Administration Review* 68(1).

Howlett, Michael. 1999. Rejoinder to Stuart Soroka, Policy agenda-setting theory revisited: A critique of Howlett on Downs, Baumgartner and Jones, and Kingdon. *Canadian Journal of Political Science/Revue Canadienne de Science Politique* 32(4).

Hoxby, Caroline M., Sonali Murarka, and Jenny Kang. 2009. The New York City charter school evaluation project. Available at www.nber.org/.../how_NYC_charter_schools_affect_achievement_sept2009.pdf (accessed November 3, 2009).

Hughes, Mark A. 1994. A mobility atrategy offers real choices: A response to the myth of community development. *Shelterforce.* Available at http://www.nhi.org/online/issues/74/hughes.html (accessed April 2, 2009).

Hula, Richard C., and Cynthia Jackson-Elmoore. 2000. *Nonprofits in urban America.* Westport, CT: Quorum.

Immergluck, Daniel. 2004. *Credit to the community: Community reinvestment and fair lending policy in the United States.* Cities and Contemporary Society series. Armonk, NY: M.E. Sharpe.

Insight Center for Community Economic Development. 2008. *What is a sector initiative?.* Available at http://www.insightcced.org/index.php?page=what-is-sector-initiative (accessed May 27, 2009).

Jackson, Pamela J. 2007. *The low-income housing tax credit: A framework for evaluation.* Washington DC: Congressional Research Service, RL33904.

Jacobs, Ronald. 2002. Understanding workforce development: Definition, conceptual boundaries, and future perspectives. Paper presented at the International Conference on Technical and Vocational Education and Training, Winnipeg, Manitoba, October 17–19.

James, Franklin. 1984. *Urban economic development: A zero sum game?* Beverly Hills, CA: Sage.

Jargowsky, Paul A. 1997. *Poverty and place: Ghettos, barrios, and the American city.* New York: Russell Sage Foundation.

———. 2003. *Stunning progress, hidden problems: The dramatic decline of concentrated poverty in the 1990s.* Washington, DC: Brookings Institution, Available from http://www.brookings.edu/reports/2003/05demographics_jargowsky.aspx (accessed April 5, 2009).

Johnson, Dirk. 1999. With black support, Daley seems sure of re-election. *New York Times.* February 23, 1999. Available at http://www.nytimes.com/1999/02/23/us/with-black-support-daley-seems-sure-of-re-election.html (accessed April 1, 2009).

———. 2008. Chicago unveils multifaceted plan to curb emissions of heat-trapping gases. *New York Times.* September 18, 2008. Available at http://www.nytimes.com/2008/09/19/us/19chicago.html?_r=1 (accessed April 1, 2009).

Johnson, Martin. 2005. Isles adopts regional focus for greater impact. *Cascade* 58 (Summer). Available at http://www.philadelphiafed.org/community-development/publications/cascade/58/01_isles-adopts-regional-focus.cfm (accessed June 11, 2009).

Jonnes, Jill. 2002. *South Bronx rising: The rise, fall, and resurrection of an American city.* New York: Fordham University Press.

Jordan, Miriam. 2009. A new gang comes to Los Angeles: Solar-panel installers. *Wall Street Journal.* February 17.

Kamarck, Elaine C. 2003. *Government innovation around the world.* Ash Institute for Democratic Governance and Innovation, John F. Kennedy School of Government, Harvard University. Available at http://www.innovations.harvard.edu/showdoc.html?id=2551 (accessed June 8, 2009).

Kanter, Rosabeth Moss. 1995. *World class: Thriving locally in the global economy.* New York: Simon and Schuster.

Karlinsky, Sarah. 2000. *Community development corporations and smart growth: Putting policy into practice.* Cambridge, MA: Joint Center for Housing Studies of Harvard University and Neighborhood Reinvestment Corporation.

Katz, Bruce. 2003. Cities and suburbs need to forge alliances in light of new metropolitan reality. *Cascade* 53 (Winter). Available at http://www.philadelphiafed.org/community-development/publications/cascade/53/cascade53.pdf (accessed June 8, 2009).

Kellermann, Arthur L., Dawna Fuqua-Whitley, Frederick P. Rivara, and James Mercy. 1998. Preventing youth violence: What works? *Annual Review of Public Health* 19(1).

Khadduri, Jill, Heather Schwartz and Jennifer Turnham. 2007. *Reconnecting schools and neighborhoods: An introduction to school-centered community revitalization.* Enterprise Community Partners Inc.

Kingdon, John W. 2003. *Agendas, alternatives, and public policies.* Longman Classics in Political Science. New York: Longman.

Klein, Katherine J., and J. Speer Sorra. 1996. The challenge of innovation implementation. *Academy of Management Review* 21(4).

Knitzer Jane, and Adely Fida. 2002. *The role of community development corporations in promoting the well-being of young children.* New York: National Center for Children in Poverty, Columbia University.

Kotkin, Joel. 2007. Opportunity urbanism: An emerging paradigm for the 21st century. Houston, TX: Greater Houston Partnership.

Kotlowski, Dean J. 2001. *Nixon's civil rights: Politics, principle, and policy.* Cambridge, MA: Harvard University Press.

Kromer, John. 2000. *Neighborhood recovery: Reinvestment policy for the new hometown.* New Brunswick, NJ: Rutgers University Press.

———. 2009. *Fixing broken cities: The implementation of urban development strategies.* New York: Routledge.

Kuttner, Robert. 1990. The poverty of neoliberalism. *The American Prospect.* Available at http://www.prospect.org/cs/articles?article=the_poverty_of_neoliberalism (accessed June 22, 2009).

Langer, Gary. 2008. Fuel costs boost conservation efforts; 7 in 10 reducing 'carbon footprint'. *ABC News.* August 9.

Lemann, Nicholas. 1992. *The promised land: The great black migration and how it changed America.* New York: Vintage.

———. 1994. The myth of community development. *New York Times.* January 9, 1994. Available at http://query.nytimes.com/gst/fullpage.html?res=9F0CEEDB153EF93AA35752C0A962958260&sec=&spon=&pagewanted=print (accessed March 30, 2008).

Lewis, Dan A. 1996. Crime and community: Continuities, contradictions, and complexities. *Cityscape: A Journal of Policy Development and Research* 2(2).

Lincoln Community Learning Centers. 2008. *Welcome to Lincoln Community Learning Centers.* Lincoln Community Learning Centers: http://www.lincolnclc.org/who/clc_overview.html (accessed August 26, 2008).

Lindblom, Charles E. 1977. *Politics and mrkets: The world's political economic systems.* New York: Basic Books.

Liou, Thomas Y., and Robert C. Stroh. 1998. Community development intermediary systems in the United States: Origins and evolution. *Housing Policy Debate* 9.

Lowry, James H. 2005. *Realizing the new agenda for minority business development.* Boston, MA: Boston Consulting Group.

Lueck, Thomas J. 2007. From database to crime scene: Network is potent police weapon. *New York Times.* June 7, 2007. Available at http://www.nytimes.com/2007/06/07/nyregion/07real.html?_r=1&sq=comstat&st=cse&scp=4&pagewanted=all (accessed May 25, 2009).

Magat, Richard. 1979. *The Ford Foundation at work, philanthropic choices, methods, and styles.* New York: Plenum Press.

Maguire, Sheila, Joshua Freely, Carol Clymer, and Maureen Conway. 2009. Job training that works: Findings from the sectoral employment impact study. *Public/Private Ventures,* 7 (May).

Markusen, Ann R. 2007. *Reining in the competition for capital.* Kalamazoo, MI: W.E. Upjohn Institute for Employment Research.

Martinac, Paula. 2009. East End groups partner to bring jobs, training "on the road"! *Weed and Seed Neighborhood Newsletter.* 34(5). Available at http://www.bloomfield-garfield.org/pages/documents/may2009.pdf (accessed June 21, 2009).

Martinson, Karin, and Pamela Holcomb. 2007. *Innovative employment approaches and programs for low-income families.* Washington, DC: Urban Institute, 2009.

Maurrasse, David J. 2001. *Beyond the campus: How colleges and universities form partnerships with their communities.* New York: Routledge.

Mayer, Neil S. 1984. *Neighborhood organizations and community development: Making revitalization work.* Washington, DC: Urban Institute Press.

———. 2004. Education and training for community development. In *Building the organizations that build communities: Strengthening the capacity of faith- and community-based development organizations,* ed. Roland V. Anglin. Washington, DC: U.S. Department of Housing and Urban Development, Office of Policy Development and Research.

Mayer, Steven E. 1994. *Building community capacity: The potential of community foundations.* Minneapolis: Rainbow Research.

McCormack Baron Salazar. 2008. Community Initiatives.

McClure, Kirk. 2000. The low-income housing tax credit as an aid to housing finance: How well has it worked? *Housing Policy Debate* 11(1).

McKernan, Signe-Mary, and Michael W. Sherraden. 2008. *Asset building and low-income families.* Washington, DC: Urban Institute Press.

McLinden, Steve. 2006. A second look: Nonprofits reveal urban opportunities missed by the U.S. Census. *Shopping Centers Today.* July. Available at http://www.icsc.org/srch/sct/sct0706/worth_second_look.php (accessed November 2, 2009).

McNeely Joseph B. 2004. The history and future of training and education for faith-based and community development. In *Building the organizations that build communities: Strengthening the capacity of faith- and community-based development organizations,* ed. Roland V. Anglin. Washington, DC: U.S. Department of Housing and Urban Development, Office of Policy Development and Research.

Melendez, Edwin, ed. 2004. *Communities and workforce development in the era of devolution.* Kalamazoo, MI: Upjohn Institute Press.

Melendez, Edwin, and Lisa J. Servon. 2007. Reassessing the role of housing in community-based urban development. *Housing Policy Debate* 18(4).

Merseth, K. K., L. B. Schorr, and R. F. Elmore. 2000. Schools, community-based interventions, and children's learning development: What's the connect? In M. C. Wang, & W. L. Boyd (Eds.), *Improving results for children and families: Linking collaborative services with school reform efforts.* Greenwich, CT: Information Age.

Metropolitan Area Research Corporation. 2003. Atlanta metro patterns: A regional agenda for community stability. Ameregis, Minneapolis. Available at http://www.metroresearch.org/projects/region_maps.asp (accessed April 5, 2009).

Miller, Peter. 2008. Neighbors engage in dialogue: A university-community partnership. *Catholic Education: A Journal of Inquiry and Practice ,* 12 (1), 71-95.

Moore, Donald R., and Gail Merritt. 2002. *Local school councils: What the research says.* Chicago: Designs for Change.

Moore, Sandra, and Susan Glassman. 2007 The neighborhood and its school in community revitalization: Tools for developers of mixed income housing communities. *Urban Strategies.* 53

Morse, Ricardo S., Terry F. Buss, and Morgan C. Kinghorn. 2007. *Transforming public leadership for the 21st century.* Armonk, NY: M.E. Sharpe.

Mueller, Elizabeth J., and Alex Schwartz. 1998. Why local economic development and employment training fail for low-income communities. In *Jobs & economic development: Strategies and practice.*, ed. Robert Giloth. Thousand Oaks, CA: Sage.

Nambisan, Satish. 2008. *Transforming government through collaborative innovation.* Washington, DC: IBM Center for the Business of Government.

National Alliance of Gang Investigators Associations. 2005. *National gang assessment.* Washington, DC: Bureau of Justice Assistance. Available at http://www.ojp.usdoj.gov/ BJA/what/2005_threat_assesment.pdf (May 14, 2009).

Nelson, Mary. 2005. How one CDC is changing neighborhoods with NMTC. *Community Development Investment Review.* Available at www.frbsf.org/publications/community/ review/122005/article8.pdf (accessed November 3, 2009).

Neustadt, Richard E., and Ernest R. May. 1986. *Thinking in time: The uses of history for decision-makers.* New York: Free Press; Collier Macmillan.

New Urban News. 2000. New urbanism and traditional neighborhood development: Comprehensive report & best practices guide. Ithaca, NY: New Urban News.

New York Times. 2007. Can cities save the earth? Available at http://www.nytimes. com/2007/05/19/opinion/19sat4.html (accessed April 1, 2009).

———. 2001a, Community leader to head economic group in Bed-Stuy" Available at http://www.nytimes.com/2001/03/22/nyregion/community-leader-to-head-economic-group-in-bed-stuy.html?scp=29&sq=community+economic+development&st =nyt (accessed April 26, 2009).

———. 2001b. Mount Laurel: A battle that wont go away Available at http://www.nytimes. com/2001/11/25/nyregion/mount-laurel-a-battle-that-won-t-go-away.html?n=Top/ Reference/Times (accessed April 28, 2009).

———. 1990. Chicago studies plan to spur industry revival. Available at http://www. nytimes.com/1990/05/27/us/chicago-studies-plan-to-spur-industry-revival.html (accessed April 1, 2009).

North Carolina Community Development Initiative. 2009. *Fifteen years of innovation.* Raleigh, NC.

Nowak, Jeremy. 1998. Expanding the scope of community development. *Shelterforce* (January/February).

———. 2003. The reinvestment fund pursues smart-growth agenda. *Cascade* 53 (Winter). Available at http://www.philadelphiafed.org/community-development/publications/ cascade/53/cascade53.pdf (accessed July 1, 2009).

Nye, Nancy, and Richard Schramm. 1999. Building higher education-community development corporation partnerships. New York: Seedco.

Ocasio, Ray. (Executive director, La Casa de Don Pedro). In interview with the author. September 13, 2008.,

O'Connor, Alice. 2000. *Poverty knowledge: Social science, social policy, and the poor in twentieth-century U.S. history.* (Politics and Society in Twentieth-Century America). Princeton, NJ: Princeton University Press.

Okun, Arthur M. 1975. *Equality and efficiency, the big tradeoff.* Washington, DC: Brookings Institution.

Oliver, Melvin L. 2001. Introduction. In *Assets for the poor: The benefits of spreading asset ownership,* ed. Thomas M. Shapiro and Edward N. Wolff. New York: Russell Sage Foundation.

Oliver, Melvin L., and Thomas M. Shapiro. 2006. *Black wealth, white wealth: A new perspective on racial inequality.* 10th anniversary ed. New York: Routledge.

O'Looney, John. 1996. Full service schools: A revolution in health and social services for children, youth, and families. *Social Service Review* 70(1).

Olson, Mancur. 1965. *The logic of collective action: Public goods and the theory of groups.* Cambridge, MA: Harvard University Press.

O'Neill, Karen M. 2006. *Rivers by design: State power and the origins of U.S. flood control.* Durham NC: Duke University Press.

Orfield, Myron. 2002. *American metropolitics: The new suburban reality.* Washington, DC: Brookings Institution Press.

Organisation for Economic Co-operation and Development. 1999. *Managing national innovation systems.* Paris: Organisation for Economic Co-operation and Development.

Orlebeke, Charles J. 1997. *New life at ground zero: New York, home ownership, and the future of American cities.* First ed. Washington, DC: Brookings Institution Press.

Osborne, David, and Ted Gaebler. 1993. *Reinventing government: How the entrepreneurial spirit is transforming the public sector.* New York: Plume.

Osterman, Paul. 1999. *Securing prosperity: The American labor market: How it has changed and what to do about it.* Princeton, NJ: Princeton University Press.

Pastor, Manuel Jr., Chris Benner, Rachel Rosner, Martha Matsuoka, and Julie Jacobs. 1997. *Growing together: Linking regional and community development in a changing economy: Summary report.* Los Angeles: International & Public Affairs Center, Occidental College.

———. 2004. *Community building, community bridging: Linking neighborhood improvement initiatives and the new regionalism in the San Francisco Bay area.* Santa Cruz, CA: Center for Justice, Tolerance and Community.

Payne, Charles M. 2008. *So much reform, so little change: The persistence of failure in urban schools.* Cambridge, MA: Harvard Education Press.

Perez, Teresita and Reece Rushing. 2007. *The CitiStat model: How data-driven government can increase effeciency and effectiveness.* Washington DC. The Center for the American Progress.

Perri 6. 2004. Joined-up government in the western world in comparative perspective: A preliminary literature review and exploration. *Journal of Public Administration Research and Theory* 14(1).

Peterson, Paul E. 1985. *The new urban reality.* Washington, DC: The Brookings Institution.

Petrovich, Janice. 2008. *A foundation returns to school: Strategies for improving public education.* New York: Ford Foundation.

Pinderhughes, Raquel. Green collar jobs. *Urban habitat: Race, poverty & the environment.* Available at http://www.urbanhabitat.org/node/528 (accessed May 27, 2009).

Pitcoff, Winton. 1996. *Comprehensive community initiatives: Redefining community development.* Available from http://www.nhi.org/online/issues/96/ccis.html (accessed April 2, 2009).

———. 1997. *Developing workers: Community-based job training brings families out of poverty.* Available from http://www.nhi.org/online/issues/102/jobs.html (accessed April 2, 2009).

———. 1998. *Comprehensive community initiatives: Redefining community development.* Available from http://www.nhi.org/online/issues/97/ccis.html (accessed April 17, 2009).

Popkin, Susan J., Bruce Katz, Mary K. Cunningham, Karen D. Brown, Jeremy Gustafson, and Margery Austin Turner. 2004. *A decade of HOPE VI: Research findings and policy challenges.* Available at http://www.urban.org/publications/411002.html (accessed March 17, 2009).

Porter, Michael E. 1995. The competitive advantage of the inner city. *Harvard Business Review* 73.

Poverty & Race Research Action Council and the Lawyers' Committee for Civil Rights Under Law. 2008. *Building opportunity: Civil rights best practices in the low income housing tax credit program: An updated fifty-state review of LIHTC "qualified allocation plans."* Washington, DC, October.

Project for Public Spaces. 2001. *Revitalizing Chicago through parks and public spaces.* Available at http://www.pps.org/topics/whats_new/daley_speech (accessed April 1, 2009).

Proscio, Tony. 2004. Schools, Community and Development. The Enterprise Foundation. Available at http://www.practitionerresources.org/cache/documents/56274.pdf (accessed March 12, 2009).

Quigley, John M. 1999. *A decent home: Housing policy in perspective.* Berkeley Program on Housing and Urban Policy Working Papers, Paper W99-007.

Ramey, Lucha. 2008. *News Center at St. Mary's University.* St. Mary's University. Available at http://www.stmarytx.edu/news/?go=community&id=1892 (accessed October 30, 2008).

Ramsay, Meredith. 1996. *Community, culture, and economic development: The social roots of local action.* Democracy in American Politics. Albany: State University of New York Press.

Reisman, David A. 1990. *Theories of collective action: Downs, Olson and Hirsch.* Basingstoke, UK: Macmillan.

Rich, Michael J. 1993. *Federal policy-making and the poor: National goals, local choices, and distributional outcome.* Princeton, NJ: Princeton University Press.

Rivlin, Alice M. 1992. *Reviving the American dream: The economy, the states & the federal government.* Washington, DC: Brookings Institution.

Roberts, Brandon. 2002. *The best of both: Community colleges and community-based organizations partner to better serve low-Income workers and employers.* New York: Public/Private Ventures.

Robins, Lee Nelken, and Katherine Strother Ratcliff. 1978. *Long range outcomes associated with school truancy.* Washington, DC: Public Health Service.

Roby, Douglas E. 2004. Research on school attendance and student achievement: A study of Ohio schools. *Educational Research Quarterly* 28(1).

Roder, Anne. 2008. *Targeting industries, training workers and improving opportunities.* New York: Public/Private Ventures.

Rosenfeld, Stuart, Jim Jacobs, and Cynthia Liston. 2003. *Cluster-based workforce development: A community college approach.* Carrboro, NC: Regional Technology Strategies. Available at file:///Users/ResearchAsst/Downloads/cluster_wf.pdf.

Rothstein, Richard. 2004. *Class and schools: Using social, economic, and educational reform to close the black-white achievement gap.* New York: Teachers College, Columbia University.

Rubin, Julia Sass. 2007. *Financing low-income communities: Models, obstacles, and future directions.* New York: Russell Sage Foundation.

Rusk, David. 1999. *Inside game/outside game: Winning strategies for saving urban America.* Washington, DC: Brookings Institution.

Ryan, Susan, Anthony Byrk, Gudelia Lopez, Kimberly Williams, Kathleen Hall, and Stuart Luppescu. 1997. *Charting reform: LSCs—local leadership at work.* Chicago: Consortium for Chicago School Research.

Safford, Sean. 2009. *Why the garden club couldn't save Youngstown: The transformation of the Rust Belt.* Cambridge, MA: Harvard University Press.

Salamon, Lester M. 1995. *Partners in public service: Government-nonprofit relations in the modern welfare state.* Baltimore: Johns Hopkins University Press.

Samberg, Laura, and Melyssa Sheeran. 2000. Community school models. *Coalition for community schools.* Working Draft. Available at http://www.eric.ed.gov:80/ERICDocs/data/ericdocs2sql/content_storage_01/0000019b/80/1a/3f/41.pdf. (accessed March 21, 2009)

Sard, Barbara. 2001. Housing vouchers should be a major component of future housing policy for the lowest income families. *Cityscape: A Journal of Policy Development and Research* 5(2).

Sassen, Saskia. 2006. *Cities in a world economy. Sociology for a new century.* Thousand Oaks, CA: Pine Forge Press.

Saulny, Susan. 2007. In miles of alleys, Chicago finds its next environmental frontier. *New York Times.* November 26, 2007. Available at http://www.nytimes.com/2007/11/26/us/26chicago.html?scp=25&sq=mayor+daley&st=nyt (accessed May 13, 2008).

Savoie, Donald J. 2008. Searching for answers by retracting the roots of public administration and looking to economics. *Public Administration Review* 68(1).

Schorr, Lisbeth B. 1997. *Common purposes: Strengthening families and neighborhoods to rebuild America.* New York: Anchor.

Schneider, Keith. 2006. To revitalize a city, try spreading some mulch. *New York Times.* May 17, 2006. Available at http://www.nytimes.com/2006/05/17/business/businessspecial2/17chicago.html?sq=mayor daley gardens&st=nyt&scp=1&pagewanted=all (accessed May 13, 2008).

Schreiner, Mark, Margaret Clancy, and Michael Sherraden. 2002. *Final report. Saving performance in the American dream demonstration: A national demonstration of Individual development accounts.* St. Louis: Center for Social Development Center for Community Capitalism.

Schwartz, Alex. 1998. From confrontation to collaboration? Banks, community groups, and the implementation of community reinvestment agreements. *Housing Policy Debate* 9(3).

Shapiro, Thomas M. 2001. The importance of assets. In *Assets for the poor: The benefits of spreading asset ownership*, ed. Thomas M. Shapiro and Edward N. Wolff. New York: Russell Sage Foundation.

Sheridan, Laurie. 2002. *Career ladders in Boston: A summary of recent progress.* Boston: Boston Workforce Development Coalition.

Sherraden, Michael W. 1991. *Assets and the poor: A new American welfare policy.* Armonk, NY: M.E. Sharpe.

Shirley, Dennis. 1997. *Community organizing for urban school reform.* First ed. Austin: University of Texas Press.

———. 2002. *Valley interfaith and school reform: Organizing for power in South Texas.* Joe R. and Teresa Lozano Long Series in Latin American and Latino Art and Culture. First ed. Austin: University of Texas Press.

Shulman, Robin. 2009. Harlem program singled out as standard to improve children's lives. *Washington Post.* August 2, 2009. Available at http://www.washingtonpost.com/wp-dyn/content/article/2009/08/01/AR2009080102297.html (accessed November 3, 2009).

Shuman, Michael. 1998. *Going local: Creating self-reliant communities in a global age.* New York: Free Press.

Silberstein, Jane, and Chris Maser. 2000. *Land-use planning for sustainable development.* Sustainable Community Development Series. Boca Raton, FL: Lewis.

Silverman, Robert M. 2008. The influence of nonprofit networks on local affordable housing funding: Findings from a national survey of local public administrators. *Urban Affairs Review* 44(1).

———. 2009. Sandwiched between patronage and bureaucracy: The plight of citizen participation in community-based housing organizations in the US. *Urban Studies* 46(1).

Simon, William H. 2001. *The community economic development movement: Law, business, and the new social policy.* Durham, NC: Duke University Press.

Singer, Audrey. 2009. *The new geography of United States immigration.* Washington, DC: Brookings Institution.

Smylie, Mark A., & Andrea E. Evans. 2006. Social capital and the problem of implementation. In Meredith I. Honig (Ed.) *New directions in education policy implementation: Confronting complexity.* Albany, NY: State University of New York Press.

Snyder, William M., and Xavier de Souza Briggs. 2003. *Communities of practice: A new tool for government managers.* Washington, DC: IBM Center for the Business of Government.

Spaulding, Shayne. 2005. *Getting connected: Strategies for expanding the employment networks of low-income people.* New York: Public/Private Ventures.

Spaulding, Shayne, Joshua Freely, and Sheila Maguire. 2009. *A foot in the door: Using alternative staffing organizations to open up opportunities for disadvantaged workers.* New York: Public/Private Ventures.

Squires, Gregory D. 2002. *Urban sprawl: Causes, consequences & policy responses.* Washington, DC: Urban Institute Press.

Staples, Brent. 1996. The second Daley's legacy. July 14,. *New York Times.* Available at http://www.nytimes.com/1996/07/14/opinion/editorial-notebook-the-second-daley-s-legacy.html (accessed April 1, 2009).

State Sector Strategies. 2008. *Welcome.* Available at http://www.sectorstrategies.org/.

Stegman, Michael A. 1991. New markets tax credit appears to increase investment by investors in low-income communities, but opportunities exist to better monitor compliance. *Housing Policy Debate* 2(2).

Stoecker, Randy. 1996. Community development and community organizing. *Shelterforce.* May/June 1996. Available at http://www.nhi.org/online/issues/87/cdcmodel.html (accessed April 2, 2009).

Stone, Clarence, Kathryn Doherty, Cheryl Jones, and Timothy Ross 1999. Schools and disadvantaged neighborhoods: The community development challenge. In R. F. Ferguson, & W. T. Dickens (Eds.), *Urban problems and community development* pp. 339-380. Washington, DC: Brookings Institution Press.

———. 1997. The CDC model of urban redevelopment: A critique and alternative. *Journal of Urban Affairs* 19 (1).

Sviridoff, Mitchell, and William P. Ryan. 1996. *Investing in community: Lessons and implications of the comprehensive community revitalization program.* Chicago, IL: Institute for Comprehensive Community Development. Available at http://www.instituteccd.org/library/1385 (Accessed March 10, 2009).

Sviridoff, Mitchell, Franklin Thomas, Louis Winnick, Robert Cohen, and William P. Ryan, eds. 2004. *Inventing community renewal: The trials and errors that shaped the modern community development corporation.* New York: Milano Graduate School, New School University.

Tansey, Charles D. 2009. *Community development credit unions: An emerging player in low-income communities.* Available at http://www.brookings.edu/articles/2001/09metropolitanpolicy_tansey.aspx (accessed June 22, 2009).

Taub, Richard P. 1994. *Community capitalism.* Boston: Harvard Business School Press.

Taveras, Barbara A. 1998. Transforming public schools. *Shelterforce.* September/October 1999. Available at http://www.nhi.org/online/issues/99/taveras.html (accessed April 2, 2009).

Teaford, Jon C. 1993. *Cities of the heartland: The rise and fall of the industrial midwest.* Bloomington: Indiana University Press.

———. 2006. *The metropolitan revolution: The rise of post-urban America.* New York: Columbia University Press.

The Economist. 2008. Rise of the super-mayor. Available at http://www.economist.com/world/na/displaystory.cfm?story_id=10809127 (accessed April 1, 2008).

Tiebout, Charles. 1956. A pure theory of local public expenditures. *Journal of Political Economy* 64.

Tocqueville, Alexis de. 1945. *Democracy in America,* New York: Knopf.

Tough, Paul. 2008. *Whatever it takes: Geoffrey Canada's quest to change Harlem and America.* Boston: Houghton Mifflin.

Twelvetrees, Alan C. 1996. *Organizing for neighborhood development: A comparative study of community based development organizations.* Second ed. Aldershot, UK; Brookfield, VT: Avebury.

United Nations. 1959. *Public administration aspects of community development programmes.* No. St/TAO/M/14. New York: United Nations.

United Nations General Assembly. 1987. *Report of the world commission on environment and development.* New York: United Nations.

United States Congress. 2007. *H.R. 2847—110th Congress: Green Jobs Act of 2007.* Available at http://www.govtrack.us/congress/bill.xpd?bill=h110-2847 (accessed May 26, 2009).

———. House Committee on Government Reform, Subcommittee on Federalism and the Census. 2005. *A Top to Bottom Review of the Three-Decades-Old Community Development Block Grant Program: Is the CDBG Program Still Targeting the Needs of Our Communities?: Hearings Before the Subcommittee on Federalism and the Census of the Committee on Government Reform, House of Representatives, One Hundred Ninth Congress, First Session, March 1, April 26, and May 24, 2005.* Washington, DC: U.S. Government Printing Office.

———. Joint Economic Committee. 1993. *Reinventing Government: Restructuring the Public Sector to Deliver More or Less: Hearing Before the Joint Economic Committee, Congress of the United States, One Hundred Second Congress, Second Session, March 5, 1992.* Washington, DC: U.S. Government Printing Office.

———. House Small Business Subcommittee on Finance and Tax. Testimony. 2007. *Hearing on Improving the SBA's Access to Capital Programs for Our Nation's Small Businesses.* Testimony of Daniel Bentancourt. 110th Congress. June 14, 2007. Available at: http://www.house.gov/smbiz/test/hearings/testimony/06-14-07-microloan/testimony-06-14-07-betancourt.pdf (accessed October 20 2009).

———. Millennial Housing Commission. 2002. *Meeting Our Nation's Housing Challenges: Report of the Bipartisan Millennial Housing Commission.* Washington, DC.

United States Department of Commerce. 2005. *Strengthening America's communities advisory committee.* Available from www.eda.gov/PDF/EDAmericaSummer05.pdf (accessed November 3, 2009).

United States Department of Education. 2004. *List of teacher shortage areas as of April 30, 2004.* Available at http://www.ed.gov/about/offices/list/ope/pol/list.doc (accessed November 3, 2009).

United States Department of the Treasury, ed. 2008. *CDFI Fund-U.S. Treasury. new markets tax program.* U.S. Department of the Treasury. September 12, 2008.

Unity Council. *Welcome to Fruitvale Village.* Available at http://www.unitycouncil.org/fruitvale/index.html (accessed May 6, 2009).

Vidal, Avis, and Langley Keys. 2005. *Beyond housing: Growing the community development system*. Washington, DC: The Urban Institute. Available at http://www.urban.org/uploadedPDF/311219_beyond_housing.pdf (accessed May 6, 2008).

Wachter, Susan M., R. Leo Penne, and Arthur C. Nelson. 2000. *Bridging the divide: Making regions work for everyone*. Washington, DC: U.S. Department of Housing and Urban Development.

Wagner, Fritz W. 2005. *Revitalizing the city: Strategies to contain sprawl and revive the core*. Cities and Contemporary Society. Armonk, NY: M.E. Sharpe.

Walker, Christopher. 2002. Community *development corporations and their changing support systems*. Washington, DC: The Urban Institute. Available at http://www.urban.org/UploadedPDF/310638_ChangingSupportSystems.pdf (accessed October 11, 12009).

Walker, Christopher, and Mark Weinheimer. 1998. *Community development in the 1990s*. Washington, DC: The Urban Institute. Available at http://www.urban.org/books/comdev90/ (accessed June 11, 2008).

Walsh, Bryan. 2008. What is a green-collar job, exactly? *Time*. May 26. Available at http://www.time.com/time/health/article/0,8599,1809506,00.html (accessed April 8, 2009).

Walters, Jonathon. 2001. Understanding innovation: What inspires it? What makes it successful? *Governing Magazine*. December.

Wang, Margaret C., and William Lowe Boyd. 2000. *Improving results for children and families: Linking collaborative services with school reform efforts*. Research in Educational Policy. Greenwich, CT: Information Age.

Warren, Mark R. 2005. Communities and schools: A new view of urban education reform. *Harvard Education Review* 75.

Weber, Edward P., and Anne M. Khademian. 2008. Wicked problems, knowledge challenges, and collaborative capacity builders in network settings. *Public Administration Review*. 68(2).

Wikstrom, Nelson. 2008. Central city policy issues in a regional context. In David K. Hamilton and Patricia Sue Atkins (eds.) *Urban and regional policies for metropolitan livability*, Armonk, NY: M.E. Sharpe.

Williamson, Thad, David Imbroscio, and Gar Alperovitz. 2002. *Making a place for community: Local democracy in a global era*. New York: Routledge.

Wilson, William J. 1996. *When work disappears: The world of the new urban poor*. New York: Knopf.

Wolf-Powers, Laura. 2004. Beyond the first job: Career ladder initiatives in telecommunications and related information technology industries. In Edwin Melendez *(ed.) Communities and workforce development*, , pp. 253–290. Kalamazoo, MI: W.E. Upjohn Institute for Employment Research.

World Bank. 2003. *World development report: Sustainable development in a dynamic world*. Washington, DC: World Bank.

Worth, Robert. 1999. Guess who saved the South Bronx. *Washington Monthly*. April. Available at http://www.washingtonmonthly.com/features/1999/9904.worth.bronx.html (accessed December 22, 2008).

Wright, David J., Ingrid Gould Ellen, and Michael H. Schill. 2001. *Community development corporations and welfare reform: Linkages, roles, and impacts*. Albany: Nelson A. Rockefeller Institute of Government, State University of New York.

Yunus, Muhammad, and Alan Jolis. 1999. *Banker to the poor: Micro-lending and the battle against world poverty*. New York: Public Affairs.

Zdenek, Robert O., and Carol Steinbach. 2000. The leadership challenge. *National Housing Institute.* Available at http://www.nhi.org/online/issues/114/zdenek.html (accessed October 12, 2008).

Resource Guide

Further Reading: Public Sector Innovation

Abramson, Mark A., and Paul R. Lawrence. 2001. *Transforming organizations*. Lanham, MD: Rowman & Littlefield.

Abramson, Mark A., and Ian D. Littman. 2002. *What do we know about innovation?* Lanham, MD: Rowman & Littlefield.

Allen Consulting Group. 1999. *Stakeholder relations in the public sector: Innovation in management: A collaborative study*. Melbourne: Allen Consulting Group.

Ball, Stephen J. 2007. *Education: Understanding private sector participation in public sector education*. New York: Routledge.

Behn, Robert D. 2008. The replication challenge. www.Governing.com. http://www.governing.com/mgmt_insight.aspx?id=3160 (accessed January 6, 2009).

———. 1995. Creating an innovative organization: Ten hints for involving frontline workers. *State and Local Government Review* 27(3), Fall.

Cavanagh, Thomas E. 1999. *Community connections: Strategic partnerships in the digital industries*. Research report. Vol. 1254-99-RR. New York: Conference Board.

Cleveland, Harlan. 1972. *The future executive: A guide for tomorrow's managers*. New York: Harper & Row.

Cohen, Steven, William B. Eimicke, and Tanya Heikkila. 2008. *The effective public manager: Achieving success in a changing government*. San Francisco: Jossey-Bass.

Collin, Robert W. 2006. *The environmental protection agency: Cleaning up America's act. (Understanding Our Government)*. Westport, CT: Greenwood Press.

Collins, Paul. 2000. *Applying public administration in development: Guideposts to the future*. New York: Wiley.

Donahue, John D. 2005. Government innovators network: Dynamics of diffusion: Conceptions of American federalism and public-sector innovation, March 11, 2005. Available at http://www.innovations.harvard.edu/showdoc.html?id=6771 (accessed April 11, 2008)

Downey, Edward H., and Walter L. Balk. 1976. *Employee innovation and government productivity: A Study of suggestion systems in the public sector*. Personnel report. Vol. 763. Chicago: International Personnel Management Association.

Eggers, William D. 2008. Innovation: Beyond the big bang theory. *Governing.Com* http://www.governing.com/mgmt_insight.aspx?id=5026 (accessed April 5, 2008).

Farazmand, Ali. 2004. *Sound Governance: Policy and Administrative Innovations*. Westport, CT: Praeger.

Frederickson, H. G. 2007. Why the management of innovation may be an oxymoron. Governing.com. http://www.governing.com/mgmt_insight.aspx?id=4070 (accessed April 5, 2008).

Gallaher, Michael P., Albert N. Link, and Jeffrey E. Petrusa. 2006. *Innovation in the U.S. service sector*. New York: Routledge.

General Accounting Office. 2008. Forces that will shape America's future: Themes from GAO's strategic plan 2007-2012. www.GAO.com, http://www.gao.gov/new.items/d07467sp.pdf (accessed April 5, 2008).

Glor, Eleanor D., 1996. *Policy innovation in the Saskatchewan public sector, 1971-82*. Ontario: Captus Press.

Goldsmith, Stephen. 2008. Governing.com/Innovative Mayors: Introduction. http://www.governing.com/articles/mayors.htm (accessed April 11, 2008).

————, and William D. Eggers. 2004. *Governing by network: The new shape of the public sector*. Washington, DC: Brookings Institution Press.

————, and Donald F. Kettl. 2009. *Unlocking the power of networks: Keys to high-performance government.(Innovative Governance in the 21st Century)*. Washington, DC: Brookings Institution Press.

Hanna, Nagy. 2008. *Transforming government and empowering communities: The Sri Lankan experience with e-development*. Washington DC: World Bank.

Hartwich, Frank, and International Food Policy Research Institute. 2007. *Building public-private partnerships for agricultural innovation in Latin America: Lessons from capacity strengthening*. IFPRI Discussion Paper. Vol. 00699. Washington, DC: International Food Policy Research Institute.

Johnston, Van R. 2008. *Entrepreneurial management and public policy*. New York: Nova Science.

Kaplan, Robert S., and David P. Norton. 2004. *Strategy maps: Converting intangible assets into tangible outcomes*. Boston: Harvard Business School Press.

Kaul, Inge, and Pedro Conceição. 2006. *The new public finance: Responding to global challenges*. New York: Oxford University Press.

Keehley, Patricia. 1997. *Benchmarking for best practices in the public sector: Achieving performance breakthroughs in federal, state, and local agencies*. San Francisco: Jossey-Bass.

Klein, K.J., and J. Speer Sorra. 1996. The challenge of innovation implementation. *Academy of Management Review* 21(4).

Kortelainen, Sami. 2005. *Innovating at the interface: A comparative case study of innovation process dynamics and outcomes in the public-private context*. Acta Universitatis Oeconomicae Helsingiensis. Vol. 260. Helsinki: Helsinki School of Economics.

Kraemer, Kenneth L., and James L. Perry. 1999. Innovation and computing in the public sector: A review of research. *Knowledge, Technology & Policy* 12(1).

Link, Albert N. 2006. *Public private partnerships: Innovation strategies and policy alternatives*. New York: Springer.

Lips, Miriam, John A. Taylor, and Frank Bannister. 2005. *Public administration in the information society: Essays on risk and trust*. (Innovation and the Public Sector). Vol. 11. Amsterdam; Washington, DC: IOS Press.

McNabb, David E. 2007. *Knowledge management in the public sector: A blueprint for innovation in government*. Armonk, NY: M.E. Sharpe.

Mulgan, Geoff. 2009. *The Art of public strategy: Mobilizing power and knowledge for the common good*. Oxford; New York: Oxford University Press.

Murray, John A., Constantinos Markides, and Robert Galavan. 2008. *Strategy, innovation, and change: Challenges for management.* Oxford; New York: Oxford University Press.

Nadol, Michael. 2005. *Management innovation in U.S. public water and wastewater systems.* Hoboken, NJ: John Wiley.

Naschold, Frieder, and Casten von Otter. 1996. *Public sector transformation: Rethinking markets and hierarchies in government.* (Dialogues on Work and Innovation). Amsterdam: J. Benjamins.

O'Neill Jr., Robert J. 2008. Trust, leadership, and courage: Keys to local innovation. www. Governing.com. 2006. http://www.governing.com/mgmt_insight.aspx?id=3188 (accessed April 5, 2008).

Organisation for Economic Co-operation and Development. 2006. *OECD reviews of innovation policy. Switzerland.* Paris: OECD.

———. 2008. *OECD reviews of innovation policy. China.* Paris: OECD.

Sagawa, Shirley, and Eli Segal. 2000. *Common interest, common good: Creating value through business and social sector partnerships.* Cambridge MA: Harvard University Press.

Salamon, Lester M. 1995. *Partners in public service: Government-nonprofit relations in the modern welfare state.* Baltimore, MD: Johns Hopkins University Press.

Schall, Ellen. 1997. Public-sector succession: A strategic approach to sustaining innovation. *Public Administration Review* 57(1): 4.

Schmandt, Jurgen, Lyndon B. Johnson School of Public Affairs, and University of Texas at Austin. Center for Research on Communication Technology and Society. 1991. *Telecommunications and rural development: A study of private and public sector innovation.* New York: Praeger.

Stein, Janice Gross. 2001. *Networks of knowledge: Collaborative innovation in international learning.* Institute of Public Administration of Canada Series in Public Management and Governance. Toronto: University of Toronto Press.

United States. Congress. Joint Economic Committee. 1993. *Reinventing Government: Restructuring the Public Sector to Deliver More for Less: Hearing Before the Joint Economic Committee, Congress of the United States, One Hundred Second Congress, Second Session, March 5, 1992.* S. Hrg. Vol. 102–1077. Washington: U.S. G.P.O.; for sale by the U.S. G.P.O., Supt. of Docs., Congressional Sales Office.

United States Government Accountability Office. 2007. Forces that will shape America's future: Themes from GAO's accounting plan 2007-2012. http://www.gao.gov/new.items/d07467sp.pdf (accessed April 11, 2008).

University of Melbourne. Centre for Public Policy. 2008. *Strategic issues for the not-for-profit sector.* New Governance. Sydney, N.S.W.: UNSW Press.

Veenswijk, Marcel. 2006. *Organizing innovation: New approaches to cultural change and intervention in public sector organizations.* (Innovation and the Public Sector). Washington, DC: IOS Press.

Vigoda-Gadot, Eran. 2009. *Building strong nations: Improving governability and public management.* Farnham, Surrey, UK; Burlington, VT: Ashgate.

Walters, Jonathan. 2008. Understanding innovation: What inspires it? What makes It successful? http://unpan1.un.org/intradoc/groups/public/documents/un/unpan011090.pdf (accessed April 11, 2008).

West, Darrell M. 2005. *Digital government: Technology and public sector performance.* Princeton, NJ: Princeton University Press.

Wong, Poh Kam, and World Bank. 2005. *Singapore as an innovative city in East Asia.* Policy Research Working Paper. Vol. 3568. Washington, DC: World Bank.

Further Reading: Sustainable, Community, and Economic Development

Andrew E.G. Jonas, and Kevin Ward. 2002. A world of regionalisms? Towards a US–UK urban and regional policy framework comparison. *Journal of Urban Affairs* 24(4).

Annarino, Alex, and National Business Incubation Association. 1998. *The complete guide to federal & state support of business incubation.* Athens, OH: National Business Incubation Association.

Armour, John, Douglas Cumming, and ESRC Centre for Business Research. 2004. *The legal road to replicating silicon valley.* Working Paper. Vol. 281. Cambridge, UK: ESRC Centre for Business Research, University of Cambridge.

Arzeni, Sergio. 2004. *Entrepreneurship: A catalyst for urban regeneration.* Local Economic and Employment Development. Paris: Organization for Economic Co-operation and Development.

Atkinson, Giles, Simon Dietz, and Eric Neumayer. 2007. *Handbook of sustainable development.* Elgar Original Reference. Cheltenham, UK; Northampton, MA: Edward Elgar.

Barrowclough, Diana, and Zeljka Kozul-Wright. 2007. *Creative industries and developing countries: Voice, choice and economic growth.* New York: Routledge.

Becattini, Giacomo. 2003. *From industrial districts to local development: An itinerary of research.* Northhampton, MA: Edward Elgar.

Beer, Andrew, Graham Haughton, and Alaric Maude. 2003. *Developing locally: An international comparison of local and regional economic development.* Bristol, UK: The Policy Press.

Blakely, Edward James, and Ted K. Bradshaw. 2002. *Planning local economic development: Theory and practice.* Thousand Oaks, CA: Sage.

Brown, Helen. 2007. *Knowledge and innovation: A comparative study of the USA, the UK, and Japan.* Routledge (Studies in Innovation, Organizations and Technology). Vol. 6. New York: Routledge.

Clark, Gordon L. 1983. *Interregional migration, national policy, and social justice.* Totowa, NJ: Rowman & Allanheld.

Collins, Thomas W., and John Davis Wingard. 2000. *Communities and capital: Local struggles against corporate power and privatization.* Southern Anthropological Society Proceedings. Vol. 33. Athens: University of Georgia Press.

Cooke, Philip. 2002. *Knowledge cconomies: Clusters, learning and co-operative advantage.* Routledge (Studies in International Business). Vol. 26. New York: Routledge.

———, and Luciana Lazzeretti. 2008. *Creative cities, cultural clusters and local Economic development.* New Horizons in Regional Science. Northampton, MA: Edward Elgar.

D'Costa, Anthony P., and World Bank. Development Research Group. 2006. *Exports, university-industry linkages, and Innovation challenges in Bangalore, India.* Policy Research Working Paper. Vol. 3887. Washington, DC: World Bank.

Deichmann, Uwe. 2005. *Agglomeration, transport, and regional development in Indonesia.* Policy Research Working Paper. Vol. 3477. Washington, DC: World Bank.

Development Bank of Southern Africa. 2000. *Building developmental local government.* Development Report/DBSA. Halfway House, South Africa: Development Bank of Southern Africa.

Drabenstott, Mark. 2005. *A review of the federal role in regional economic development.* Kansas City: Federal Reserve Bank of Kansas City.

European Commission. 1998. *The era of tailor-made jobs: Second report on local development and employment initiatives.* Luxembourg: European Commission.

European Commission, Directorate-General for Regional Policy and Cohesion. 2000. *Inclusive cities: Building local capacity for development.* Vol. 32. Luxembourg: Office for Official Publications of the European Community; Bernan.

Fasenfest, David. 1993. *Community economic development: Policy development in the US and UK.* (Policy Studies Organization Series). New York: St. Martin's Press.

Galston, William A., and Karen J. Baehler. 1995. *Rural development in the United States: Connecting theory, practice, and possibilities.* Washington, DC: Island Press.

General Accounting Office. 1998. *Community development progress on economic activities varies among the empowerment zones.* Report to the Subcommittee on Human Resources, Committee on Government Reform and Oversight, House of Representatives. Washington, DC.

Geoghegan, Martin, and Fred Powell. 2006. Community development, partnership governance and dilemmas of professionalization: Profiling and assessing the case of Ireland. *British Journal of Social Work* 36(5).

George, Michael L., James Works, and Kimberly Watson-Hemphill. 2005. *Fast innovation: Achieving superior differentiation, speed to market, and increased profitability.* New York; London: McGraw-Hill.

Gersovitz, Mark, and W. Arthur Lewis. 1982. *The theory and experience of economic development: Essays in honor of Sir W. Arthur Lewis.* London: Allen & Unwin.

Goldman, Benjamin A., and Judith Shapiro. Economic Development Administration. 1996. *Sustainable America: New public policy for the 21st century.* Cambridge, MA; Washington, DC: U.S. Dept. of Commerce, Economic Development Administration.

Greenstein, Rosalind, and Yesim Sungu-Eryilmaz. 2004. *Recycling the City: The Use and Reuse of Urban Land.* Cambridge, MA: Lincoln Institute of Land Policy.

Halpern, Robert. 1995. *Rebuilding the inner city: A history of neighborhood initiatives to address poverty in the United States.* New York: Columbia University Press.

Hamilton, David K., and Patricia Sue Atkins. 2008. *Urban and regional policies for metropolitan livability.* (Cities and Contemporary Society). Armonk, NY: M.E. Sharpe.

Hanson, Royce. 1983. *Rethinking urban policy: Urban development in an advanced economy.* Washington, DC: National Academy Press.

Higgins, John. 1996. *The Kiltimagh renewal: Best practice in community enterprise.* Dublin: Oak Tree Press.

Hill, Paul Thomas, and James Harvey. 2004. *Making school reform work: New partnerships for real change.* Washington, DC: Brookings Institution Press.

Kemp, Roger L. 2001. *The inner city: A handbook for renewal.* Jefferson, NC: McFarland.

———. 1995. *Economic development in local government: A handbook for public officials and citizens.* Jefferson, NC: McFarland.

Kozmetsky, George, Frederick Williams, and Victoria Williams. 2004. *New wealth: Commercialization of science and technology for business and economic development.* Westport, CT: Praeger.

Lewis, W. Arthur. 1970. *Tropical development, 1880-1913: Studies in economic progress.* London: Allen & Unwin.

———. 1966. *Development planning; The essentials of economic policy.* New York: Harper & Row.

———. 1955. *The theory of economic growth.* Homewood, IL: R. D. Irwin.

Mawdsley, Nick. 2005. *Building sustainable peace: Local economic development, natural resources, and livelihoods, North Maluku, Maluku, and Central Sulawesi.* Jakarta: United Nations Development Programs.

Mazama, Ama. 2007. *Africa in the 21st century: Toward a new future.* (African Studies: History, Politics, Economics, and Culture). New York: Routledge.

McCann, Philip, and Stephen Sheppard. 2003. The rise, fall and rise again of industrial location theory. *Regional Studies* 3(6): 649.

Menon, Vineetha, P.R. Gopinathan Nair, K.N. Nair, Kerala Research Programme on Local Level Development, and Centre for Development Studies. 2005. *Alleviating poverty: Case studies of local-level linkages and processes in the developing world.* Noida, UP: Rainbow.

Merrett, Christopher D., and Norman Walzer. 2001. *A cooperative approach to local economic development.* Westport, CT: Quorum Books.

Meyer, Peter B. 1993. *Comparative studies in local economic development: Problems in policy implementation.* Westport, CT: Greenwood Press.

Möhring, Johanna. 2005. *Business clusters: Promoting enterprise in Central and Eastern Europe.* Local Economic and Employment Development. Paris: OECD LEED Programme.

Moll, Henk A. J. 2004. *Agrarian institutions between policies and local action: Experiences from Zimbabwe.* Harare, Zimbabwe: Weaver Press.

Mourdoukoutas, Panos, and Stratos Papadēmētriou. 2002. *Nurturing entrepreneurship: Institutions and policies.* Westport, CT: Quorum Books.

Natural Sciences and Engineering Research Council of Canada. 2002. *Research means business: A directory of companies built on NSERC-supported university research.* Ottawa, Ont.: Natural Sciences and Engineering Research Council of Canada.

Nolan, Alistair, and Ging Wong. 2004. *Evaluating local economic and employment development: How to assess what works among programmes and policies.* Paris: Organization for Economic Co-Operation and Development.

Noya, Antonella, and Organization for Economic Co-Operation and Development. 2009. *The changing boundaries of social enterprises.* Local Economic and Employment Development. Paris: OECD.

Organization for Economic Co-Operation and Development.1996. *Networks of enterprises and local development: Competing and co-operating in local productive systems.* Paris: OECD

———. 1999. *Business incubation: International case studies.* Paris: OECD

———. 2009. *China: Defining the boundary between the market and the state.* OECD Reviews of Regulatory Reform. Paris: OECD.

O'Riordan, Timothy. 2001. *Globalism, localism, and identity: Fresh perspectives on the transition to sustainability.* Sterling, VA: Earthscan.

Phillips, Fred. 2006. *Social culture and high-tech economic development: The technopolis columns.* New York: Palgrave Macmillan.

Plummer, Janelle, and John G. Taylor. 2004. *Community participation in China: Issues and processes for capacity building.* Sterling, VA: Earthscan.

Potter, Jonathan, and Gabriela Miranda. 2009. *Clusters, innovation and entrepreneurship.* Paris: OECD.

Pyke, F., and Werner Sengenberger. 1992. *Industrial districts and local economic regeneration.* Geneva: International Institute for Labour Studies.

Quadrio Curzio, Alberto, and Marco Fortis. 2002. *Complexity and industrial clusters: Dynamics and models in theory and practice.* New York: Physica-Verlag.

Raines, Philip. 2002. *Cluster development and policy.* EPRC Studies in European Policy. Burlington, VT: Ashgate.

Reese, Laura A. 1997. *Local economic development Policy in the United States and Canada.* London: Garland.

Reese, Laura A., and David Fasenfest. 2004. *Critical evaluations of economic development policies.* Detroit: Wayne State University Press.

Reese, Laura A., and Raymond A. Rosenfeld. 2002. *The civic culture of local economic development.* Thousand Oaks, CA: Sage.

Rice, Mark P., Jana B. Matthews, Laura Kilcrease, and Center for Entrepreneurial Leadership, Inc. 1995. *Growing new ventures, creating new jobs: Principles and practices of successful business incubation.* Westport, CT: Quorum.

Richards, Sally. 2002. *Inside business incubators and corporate ventures.* New York: Wiley.

Salet, W.G.M., and Enrico Gualini. 2007. *Framing strategic urban projects: Learning from current experiences in European urban regions.* New York: Routledge.

Sawhney, Mohanbir S. 2001. *TechVenture: New rules on value and profit from silicon valley.* New York: John Wiley.

Scott, Allen John, and Gioacchino Garofoli. 2007. *Development on the ground: Clusters, networks and regions in emerging economies.* New York: Routledge.

Scott, Michael, Peter Rosa, and Heinz Klandt. 1998. *Educating entrepreneurs for wealth creation.* Brookfield, VT: Ashgate.

Seers, Dudley. 1981. *Dependency theory: A critical reassessment.* London: F. Pinter.

Servon, Lisa J., and Jeffrey P. Doshna. 1999. *Making microenterprise development a part of the economic development toolkit.* Washington, DC: U.S. Dept. of Commerce, Economic Development Administration.

Soussan, John, Anjan Kumar Datta, and Netherlands Directoraat-Generaal Internationale Samenwerking. 1998. *Community partnership for sustainable water management: Experiences of the BWDB systems rehabilitation project.* Dhaka: University Press Ltd.

Thomas, June Manning. 1997. *Redevelopment and race: Planning a finer city in postwar Detroit.* Creating the North American Landscape. Baltimore; London: Johns Hopkins University Press.

Tiffin, Scott. 2004. *Entrepreneurship in Latin America: Perspectives on education and innovation.* Westport, CT: Praeger.

United States Congress. House Committee on Banking Finance and Urban Affairs. Subcommittee on Economic Growth and Credit Formation. 1994. *Job Development and the Economic Future of the Southern Tier: Field Hearing Before the Subcommittee on Economic Growth and Credit Formation of the Committee on Banking, Finance, and Urban Affairs, House of Representatives, One Hundred Third Congress, Second Session, July 8, 1994.* Washington: U.S. Government Printing Office.

———. 1994. *Legislative Proposals to Provide Financing Assistance for Projects Fostering Economic Development and Job Creation: Hearing Before the Subcommittee on Economic Growth and Credit Formation of the Committee on Banking, Finance, and Urban Affairs, House of Representatives, One Hundred Third Congress, Second Session, June 22, 1994.* Washington: U.S. Government Printing Office.

———. 1994. *Renewing the Economic Development Administration: New Approaches to Economic Development: Hearings Before the Subcommittee on Economic Growth and Credit Formation of the Committee on Banking, Finance, and Urban Affairs, House of Representatives, One Hundred Third Congress, Second Session, March 15, 17, and 22, 1994.* Washington: U.S. Government Printing Office.

————. 1992. *Small Business Incubators: Field Hearing Before the Subcommittee on Policy Research and Insurance of the Committee on Banking, Finance, and Urban Affairs, House of Representatives, One Hundred Second Congress, Second Session, May 11, 1992.* Washington: U.S. Government Printing Office.

United States Congress. House Committee on Public Works and Transportation. Subcommittee on Economic Development. 1994. *1993 Empowerment Zone and Enterprise Community Program: Hearing Before the Subcommittee on Economic Development of the Committee on Public Works and Transportation, House of Representatives, One Hundred Third Congress, Second Session, February 7, 1994.* Washington: U.S. Government Printing Office.

United States Congress. House Committee on Small Business. 1998. *Revitalizing America's Economically-Distressed Communities Hearing: Hearing Before the Committee on Small Business, House of Representatives, One Hundred Fifth Congress, Second Session, Washington, DC, May 19, 1998.* Washington: U.S. Government Printing Office.

————. Subcommittee on Empowerment. 1997. *Urban Empowerment: Hearing Before the Subcommittee on Empowerment of the Committee on Small Business, House Of Representatives, One Hundred Fifth Congress, First Session, Washington, DC, May 13, 1997.* Washington: U.S. Government Printing Office.

United States Congress. House Committee on Transportation and Infrastructure. Subcommittee on Public Buildings and Economic Development. 1998. *Reauthorization of the Economic Development Administration and the Appalachian Regional Commission: Hearings Before the Subcommittee on Public Buildings and Economic Development of the Committee on Transportation and Infrastructure, House of Representatives, One Hundred Fifth Congress, First Session, July 10 and 17, 1997.* Washington: U.S. Government Printing Office.

United States Congress. Dept. of Housing and Urban Development. 1998. *Building Communities, Together: Performance Measurement System Guide.* Washington, DC: U.S. Dept. of Housing and Urban Development.

————. United States Dept. of Agriculture, and United States President's Community Empowerment Board. 1997. *What Works! In The Empowerment Zones and Enterprise Communities.* Washington, DC: U.S. Dept. of Housing and Urban Development.

United States Congress. Economic Development Administration. 1995. *Investing in America's Communities.* Washington, D.C.: U.S. Dept. of Commerce, Economic Development Administration.

Van Donk, Mirjam. 2008. *Consolidating developmental local government: Lessons from the South African experience.* Cape Town: UCT Press.

Walzer, Norman. 2007. *Entrepreneurship and local economic development.* Lanham, MA: Lexington Books.

Warburton, Diane. 2009. *Community and sustainable development: Participation in the future.* Sterling, VA: Earthscan.

Watson, Douglas J., and John C. Morris. 2008. *Building the local economy: Cases in economic development.* Athens: Carl Vinson Institute of Government, The University of Georgia.

Wolfe, David A., and Matthew Lucas. 2005. *Global networks and local linkages: The paradox of cluster development in an open economy.* (The Innovation Systems Research Series). Montreal; Ithaca, NY: McGill-Queen's University Press.

Wood, Andrew, and David Valler. 2004. *Governing local and regional economies: Institutions, politics, and economic development.* Burlington, VT: Ashgate.

Wu, Weiping. 2005. *Dynamic cities and creative clusters.* Washington, DC: World Bank, Development Research Group.

Xue, Fengxuan, and Dadao Lu. 2001. *China's regional disparities: Issues and policies.* Huntington, NY: Nova Science.

Yarwood, John R. 2006. *The Dublin–Belfast development corridor: Ireland's mega-city region?* Burlington, VT: Ashgate.

Yusuf, Shahid, Simon J. Evenett, and Weiping Wu. 2001. *Facets of globalization: International and local dimensions of development.* World Bank Discussion Paper. Vol. 415. Washington, DC: World Bank.

Community Economic Development Institutions and Stakeholders

The Public Sector Institutions, Strategies, and Programs

Board of Governors of the Federal Reserve System: www.federalreserve.gov/communitydev/default.htm

The Federal Reserve System acts as the nation's central bank. The institution has become heavily invested in community economic development over the last few years. Its Web site includes helpful information on community economic development topics such as the Community Reinvestment Act, stabilizing communities, and poverty reduction.

Community Development Financial Institutions Fund – US Department of Treasury: www.cdfi-fund.gov

The CDFI Fund's mission is to expand the capacity of financial institutions to provide credit, capital, and financial services to underserved populations and communities in the United States. The CDFI Fund was created for the purpose of promoting economic revitalization and community development through investment in and assistance to community development financial institutions (CDFIs). Since its creation in 1994, the CDFI Fund has awarded $1.11 billion to community development organizations and financial institutions; it has awarded allocations of New Markets Tax Credits that will attract private-sector investments totaling $26 billion, including $1 billion of special allocation authority to be used for the recovery and redevelopment of the Gulf Opportunity Zone.

Community Reinvestment Act: www.ffiec.gov/cra/

The Community Reinvestment Act of 1977 encourages depository institutions to help meet the credit needs of the communities in which they operate. This Web site explains the regulations, and tracks the CRA performance of lending institutions.

Empowerment Zone and Enterprise Community Program (EZ/EC): http://www.ezec.gov/

EZ/EC works with rural communities in particular to give them opportunities for growth and revitalization. Specifically, they work with communities to create economic opportunities for all residents, creating communities by supporting local plans that coordinate economic, physical, environmental, community, and human development, and provide a pathway of communication with the federal government for an easier transition with the right community designs. Since it has been created in 1993, 57 rural empowerment zones and enterprise communities have been established and nearly 28,000 jobs have been created or saved. This Web site provides the resources that can help rural communities enhance their future and also lists the accomplishments and activities of the EZ/EC.

Federal Housing Finance Agency: www.fhfa.gov

The Federal Housing Finance Agency (FHFA) was created on July 30, 2008, when the President signed into law the Housing and Economic Recovery Act of 2008. The Act created an empowered regulator with all of the authorities necessary to oversee vital components of the U.S. secondary mortgage markets: Fannie Mae, Freddie Mac, and the Federal Home Loan Banks. In addition, this law combined the staffs of the Office of Federal Housing Enterprise Oversight (OFHEO), the Federal Housing Finance Board (FHFB), and the GSE mission office at the Department of Housing and Urban Development (HUD).

Mayors Innovation Project: http://www.mayorsinnovation.org/index.asp

The Mayors Innovation Project (MIP) is a learning network among American mayors committed to "high road" policy and governance: shared prosperity, environmental sustainability, and efficient democratic government. MIP participants believe that building high road cities and metropolitan regions is both good for their residents and a key way to move the country to the high road nationally. They also believe that cities have enormous untapped assets and political strengths that can now be better organized. Already a leading source of policy innovation, cities can now do more to improve education and lifelong learning, promote high road economic and workforce development efforts, expand housing and transit availability, develop the opportunities of the clean energy economy while combating climate change, and model advanced government administration. MIP exists to help its member participants lead by example, share their experiences with peers, and make this argument for cities nationally.

New York City Center for Economic Opportunity: http://www.nyc.gov/html/ceo/html/home/home.shtml

The Center for Economic Opportunity (CEO) works with city agencies to design and implement evidence-based initiatives aimed at poverty reduction. The Center also manages an Innovation Fund through which it provides city agencies annual funding to implement such initiatives. CEO oversees a rigorous evaluation of each program to determine which are successful in demonstrating results toward reducing poverty and increasing self-sufficiency among New Yorkers.

Office of the Comptroller of the Currency, Financial Literacy Resource Directory: http://www.occ.treas.gov/cdd/finlitresdir.htm

This directory provides information on financial literacy resources, issues, and events that are important to bankers, organizations, and consumers of all ages. The directory includes descriptions and contact information for a sampling of organizations that have undertaken financial literacy initiatives as a primary mission, government programs, fact sheets, newsletters, conference materials, publications, and links to websites.

Portland Economic Development Commission: http://www.pdc.us/bus_serv/economic-op.asp

In 2004, Portland launched the Economic Opportunity Initiative, grounded in best practices and driven by measurable outcomes to help propel people out of poverty. The Initiative supports a coordinated portfolio of 33 workforce and microenterprise projects for adults and youth ages 18 to 25. There are multiple routes to success because one size does not fit all. Each project is tailored to a specific group of participants, is intensive, long-term, and provides comprehensive supports to give participants a real shot at success. The overriding goal of the Initiative is to increase the income and assets of low-income participants by at least 25 percent within three years of their enrollment in the Initiative.

U.S. Department of Agriculture, Rural Development: http://www.rurdev.usda.gov/
Rural Development is working to eliminate substandard housing from rural America by helping rural people buy, build, or rent decent housing. They also create jobs by funding the growth and creation of rural businesses and cooperatives. Other Rural Development programs help rural communities build or improve community facilities, such as schools, health clinics, and fire stations. Additional programs help build or extend utilities, including water, electricity, and telecommunications services. The agency provides direct or guaranteed loans, grants, technical assistance, research, and educational materials, and works in partnership with state, local, and tribal governments, as well as rural businesses, co-operatives, and nonprofit agencies.

U.S. Department of Commerce, Economic Development Administration: http://www.eda.gov/
EDA aims to attract private capital investment and create higher-skill, higher-wage jobs in those communities and regions that are suffering from economic distress. EDA investments are focused on locally developed, regionally based economic development initiatives that achieve the highest return on the taxpayers' investment and that directly contribute to economic growth. EDA is authorized to partner with nonprofit organizations and units of local government.

Community Economic Development Support, Advocacy and Learning Resources

The Catholic Campaign for Human Development: http://www.usccb.org/cchd/mission.shtml
The Catholic Campaign for Human Development is the domestic antipoverty, social justice program of the U.S. Catholic bishops. Its mission is to address the root causes of poverty in America through promotion and support of community-controlled, self-help organizations and through transformative education.

Center for Economic Progress: http://www.economicprogress.org/
The Center for Economic Progress provides direct assistance, including free tax preparation and a tax clinic, and also offers financial counseling to empower people to make economic progress.

Center for Neighborhood Technology: www.cnt.org
CNT is a nongovernmental organization that combines rigorous research with effective solutions. CNT works across disciplines and issues, including transportation and community development, energy, natural resources, and climate change. Since 1978, CNT has been a leader in promoting urban sustainability, the more effective use of existing resources and community assets to improve the health of natural systems and the wealth of people, today and in the future.

The Center for Responsible Lending: www.responsiblelending.org
The Center for Responsible Lending is a nonprofit, nonpartisan research and policy organization dedicated to protecting homeownership and family wealth by working to eliminate abusive financial practices. CRL is affiliated with Self-Help, one of the nation's largest community development financial institutions.

Center for Rural Affairs: http://www.cfra.org
> The Center for Rural Affairs mission is to establish strong rural communities, social and economic justice, environmental stewardship, and genuine opportunity for all while engaging people in decisions that affect the quality of their lives and the future of their communities.

The Center for Social Development (Washington University, St. Louis): http://csd.wustl.edu
> The Center for Social Development conducts research that informs how individuals, families, and communities increase capacity, formulate and reach life goals, and contribute to the economy and society. Major areas of work include Asset Building and Civic Engagement & Service.

The CitiStates Group: http://citistates.com
> Formed in 1995, the CitiStates Group is a network of journalists, speakers, and civic leaders focused on building competitive, equitable, and sustainable twenty-first century cities and metropolitan regions.

CLASP: http://www.clasp.org/
> CLASP's mission is to develop and advocate for policies at the federal, state, and local levels that improve the lives of low-income people. In particular, CLASP seeks policies that work to strengthen families and create pathways to education and work.

Coalition of Community Development Financial Institutions: www.cdfi.org/
> The CDFI Coalition is the unified national voice of community development financial institutions (CDFIs). Its mission is to encourage fair access to financial resources for America's underserved people and communities.

Community and Economic Development Toolbox: http://www.cdtoolbox.org
> Cornell University and Penn State University have combined their efforts to maintain this Web site, which provides tools to "local community and economic development practitioners, such as community leaders, newly elected officials, extension educators, and community technical assistance providers." It gives them information about basic community and economic development issues to assist them in decision making and determining the future of their communities.

Community Development Banking List Forum: http://www.communityinvestmentnetwork. org/CDB-L/index.php
> Community Development Banking List Forum is a free ongoing clearinghouse of news, discussions, and information about the community development finance industry. The list serves as a resource to credit unions, banks, CDCs, loan funds, trade associations, regulators, governments, and nonprofits. Discussion topics range from the practical (construction, mortgage, and small business lending; job opportunities; conferences; fundraising) to legislative (CRA, HMDA, and CDFI) to the cutting edge (microloan funds, peer lending, local currency, targeting social impact).

Community Development Society: www.comm-dev.org
> The Community Development Society provides leadership to professionals and citizens across the spectrum of community development. Members are offered opportunities to learn about new developments in the profession, to exchange ideas, to obtain the most current research and reference information available, and to share professional expertise. CDS's annual conference, publications, and listservs offer professional development, networks, information on initiatives and job opportunities, recognition for outstanding contributions and achievements, and opportunities for discussion and debate.

Community-Wealth.org: www.community-wealth.org/
> This Web site is dedicated to providing the Internet's most comprehensive and up-to-date information resource on state-of-the-art strategies for democratic community-based economic development. Resources include directories, breaking news, publications, and conference information. The site also provides information about cutting-edge initiatives from cities, states, CDCs, land trusts, universities, and the like.

Corporation for Enterprise Development: http://www.cfed.org/
> CFED expands economic opportunity by helping Americans start and grow microenterprises. They conduct research, partner with others in the field to create, pilot, and fund programs, and advocate for federal and state policies and private sector innovations that lead toward a more equitable economy. CFED's research papers are available on its Web site. The Web site also contains legislative updates, comment letters, listservs and more.

EnterWeb: www.enterweb.org/communty.htm
> This Web site lists and rates web resources related to community development in general and community economic development in particular.

Initiative for a Competitive Inner City: http://www.icic.org
> ICIC was founded on the conviction that the only sustainable path out of economic distress is to leverage the existing assets in inner cities to enable them to participate in the market economy. ICIC's mission is to promote economic prosperity in America's inner cities through business development and private sector engagement that leads to jobs, income, and wealth creation for local residents.

Innovating Networks: www.innovatingnetworks.net/
> Innovating Networks is a community development blog site with information on economic development, education, entrepreneurship, and more. Individuals must join the space to have full access to information on the site.

The Insight Center for Community Economic Development: www.insightcced.org
> A national research, consulting, and legal organization dedicated to building economic health opportunities in vulnerable communities, the Insight Center works with foundations, nonprofits, educational institutions, government, and businesses to develop, strengthen, and promote programs and public policy that lead to good jobs, strengthen early care and education systems, and enable people and communities to build financial and educational assets.

Institute for Social and Economic Development (ISED): http://www.ised.org/
> This Web site provides two more Web sites with two goals. One is a solutions Web site that consults and evaluates organizations that specialize in refugee and immigrant services, economic and asset development, organizational capacity building, performance measurement, program evaluation and public policy analysis. The ventures Web site helps people start a business, obtain a good job, and build financial assets.

KnowledgePlex: www.knowledgeplex.org
> KnowledgePlex is an online resource center for affordable housing and community development. The site includes relevant news and research, collaboration tools, events and chats, and special reports.

Living Cities: http://www.livingcities.org
> Living Cities is a philanthropic collaborative made up of 22 of the world's largest foundations and financial institutions. Living Cities focuses on improving the lives of low-income people and the urban areas in which they live.

The National Alliance of Community Economic Development Association: http://www.naceda.org/
NACEDA is a national organization created to support the work of community economic development (CED) associations, local Community Development Corporations (CDCs), and practitioners nationwide. The goal of NACEDA is to be a strong support vehicle and a national voice for local community development organizations, practitioners, and their associations.

The National Association of Development Organizations: http://www.nado.org/
The National Association of Development Organizations (NADO) provides advocacy, education, research, and training for the nation"s regional development organizations. Building on nearly four decades of experience, the association offers its members exclusive access to a variety of services and benefits, all of which are designed to enhance the ability of regional development organizations to foster "regional solutions" to local government, business, and community needs.

National Civic League: http://www.ncl.org
The National Civic League (NCL) is America's original advocate for community democracy. It is a nonprofit, non-partisan, membership organization dedicated to strengthening citizen democracy by transforming democratic institutions. NCL fosters innovative community building and political reform, assists local governments, and recognizes collaborative community achievement.

The National Community Reinvestment Coalition: http://www.fairlending.com/
The National Community Reinvestment Coalition (NCRC) is an association of more than 600 community-based organizations that promote access to basic banking services, including credit and savings, to create and sustain affordable housing, job development and vibrant communities for America's working families.

National Housing Institute: http://www.nhi.org
NHI is an independent nonprofit organization dedicated to fostering decent affordable housing and a vibrant community for everyone. NHI focuses attention and encourages action on progressive, high-impact housing and community development policies and practices through the lens of such subjects as economic equity, racism, poverty, health, the environment, education, and sustainability. NHI is the publisher of *Shelterforce* magazine and Rooflines blog.

National Low Income Housing Coalition: http://www.nlihc.org
The National Low Income Housing Coalition is dedicated to achieving socially just public policy that assures people with the lowest incomes in the United States have affordable and decent homes.

National Tribal Environmental Council (NTEC): http://www.ntec.org/
NTEC works with Indian tribes and Alaskan Native villages. This council attempts to integrate traditional teachings and values into modern-day practices. Its mission is to enhance each tribe's ability to protect, preserve, and promote the management of air, land, and water for the benefit of current and future generations. It consists of 184 tribes.

Neighborhoods Online: National: http://neighborhoodsonline.net/
Neighborhoods Online was created in 1995 by the Institute for the Study of Civic Values as an online resource center for America's neighborhood builders, people who work through grassroots organizations as volunteers, and in government to build strong neighborhoods and communities throughout the country.

The Next American Opportunity: http://www.nextamericanopportunity.org

The Next American Opportunity is where you can explore the possibilities of innovative policy solutions to foster small business and entrepreneurship, promote affordable housing, protect the environment, build national savings, revitalize rural America, strengthen the nonprofit sector, and maximize the leverage of public investment.

Partners for Livable Communities: http://www.livable.com

Partners for Livable Communities is a nonprofit leadership organization working to improve the livability of communities by promoting quality of life, economic development, and social equity.

PolicyLink: www.policylink.org

PolicyLink is a national research and action institute advancing economic and social equity by "Lifting Up What Works." Their focus areas include health and community, infrastructure equity, leadership and civic engagement, and federal policy. PolicyLink also produces policy papers, links to resources, and provides an online toolkit that includes 28 tools that may be used to reverse patterns of segregation and disinvestment, prevent displacement, and promote equitable revitalization.

Resilience Alliance: http://www.resalliance.org/

The Resilience Alliance is a research organization comprised of scientists and practitioners from many disciplines who collaborate to explore the dynamics of social-ecological systems. The body of knowledge developed by the RA encompasses key concepts of resilience, adaptability, and transformability and provides a foundation for sustainable development policy and practice.

Seva Foundation: http://www.seva.org/

Seva Foundation partners with Native Americans to build healthy communities while preserving their culture and sacred lands and their environment. They help using a Native American Grants Program as well as a Diabetes Wellness Program.

Sustainable Communities Network: www.sustainable.org/

This Web site is dedicated to informing citizens of resources available for creating healthy sustainable communities. It includes information about funding, awards, jobs, and conferences. Case studies and planning tools are also available here.

Sustainable Community Development Group, Inc.: www.sustainablecommunitydevelopment-group.org/

SCDG works with the public, private, and community sectors to advance environmental sustainability, equitable development, and global smart growth. Specializing in programs and public policies that address diverse populations, low-income communities, people of color, and the underserved, SCDG creates strategies that help develop leaders in communities who understand how private redevelopment works and can be used to address health and environmental concerns as well as social and economic issues posed by brownfields, vacant, and other distressed properties. Strategies include education and training, research, strategic planning, stakeholder outreach, coalition building, meetings, and conferences.

Asset Building and Community Development

ACCION International: www.accion.org

A leader in microfinance since 1973, ACCION International is a private nonprofit organization whose mission is giving people the financial tools they need to work their way out of poverty. By providing "micro" loans, business training, and other financial services to poor men and women who start their own businesses, ACCION helps people work their way up the economic ladder with dignity and pride.

Association for Enterprise Opportunity (AEO): www.microenterpriseworks.org/

AEO is a national leadership organization and voice for microenterprise development. It provides cutting-edge training, knowledge sharing, federal and state public policy and advocacy, and communications to its community of nearly 500 member organizations. Its goal is to enable members to be uniquely effective in serving the needs of microentrepreneurs who do not have access to traditional sources of business education or capital.

Certified CDFIs listed by city and state: http://cdfifund.gov/docs/certification/cdfi/CDFIbyState.pdf

The organizations on this list have been certified by the Community Development Financial Institutions Fund (Fund) as Community Development Financial Institutions (CDFIs). The organizations are presented alphabetically by state and city.

Coastal Enterprises Inc.: http://www.ceimaine.org/

CEI is a private nonprofit CDC and CDFI with roots in the civil rights movement. Founded in 1977, the organization provides financing and support in the development of job-creating small businesses, natural resources industries, community facilities, and affordable housing.

Community Builders Inc.: http://www.tcbinc.org/

Community Builders Inc. is one of the largest nonprofit urban housing developers in the United States. The organization uses housing as an entry point for comprehensive community development. Most of their housing projects also include initiatives for training residents, building individual assets, youth development, and opportunities for enhancing education.

Community Development Venture Capital Alliance: www.dcvca.org

CDVCA funds provide equity capital to businesses in underinvested markets, seeking market-rate financial returns, as well as the creation of good jobs, wealth, and entrepreneurial capacity. CDVCA promotes community development through advocacy, education, communications, and best-practice dissemination via conferences and workshops. By promoting use of venture capital tools, CDVCA aims to create jobs, entrepreneurial capacity, and wealth to advance the livelihoods of low-income people and the economies of distressed communities.

Cook Inlet Lending Center: www.cookinlethousing.org/

CILC is a housing CDFI located in Anchorage, Alaska. CILC's mission is to promote community and economic development throughout south-central Alaska by the provision of lending services and products, and increased access to credit markets, particularly for low and moderate-income families, individuals, and minorities. Its primary services include second mortgages, down payment assistance, and financial counseling. CILC serves all residents of the Cook Inlet Region, but 80 percent of its clients are Alaska Natives or Native Americans.

Corporation for Supportive Housing: www.csh.org

> CSH helps communities create permanent housing with services to prevent and bring an end to homelessness. CSH provides high-quality advice and development expertise by making loans and grants to supportive housing sponsors, by strengthening the supportive housing industry, and by reforming public policy to make it easier to create and operate supportive housing.

Enterprise Community Partners, Inc.: www.enterprisecommunity.org

> Formerly called The Enterprise Foundation, Enterprise Community Partners provides capital and expertise for affordable housing and community development. Enterprise uses its resources to bring together private and public organizations toward a shared mission, it pioneers innovative community development solutions, it advocates for federal policy in support of affordable housing and community development, and it offers financial products and services that support affordable housing and community development.

Evergreen Cooperatives: http://www.evergreencoop.com/

> The Evergreen Cooperatives of Cleveland, Ohio are pioneering innovative models of job creation, wealth building, and sustainability. Evergreen's employee-owned, for-profit companies are locally based and hire from the community. Cooperative businesses now include a laundry, a company that installs solar panels, and a hydroponic greengrowers cooperative.

First Nations Development Institute: www.firstnations.org

> First Nations Development Institute educates, advocates for, and capitalizes Indian communities in order to restore Native American control and culturally compatible stewardship of the assets they own—land, human potential, cultural heritage, and natural resources—and to establish new assets for ensuring the long-term vitality of Native communities. First Nations serves rural and reservation-based Native American communities throughout the United States.

Housing Assistance Council & Rural Housing Services, Inc.: www.ruralhome.org

> HAC improves housing conditions for the rural poor, with an emphasis on the poorest of the poor in the most rural places in the United States. Services to public, private, and nonprofit organizations include loans, technical assistance, research and information, and training. HAC maintains a special focus on high-need groups and regions: Indian country, the Mississippi Delta, farmworkers, the Southwest border colonias, and Appalachia.

The ICA Group: www.ica-group.org

> The ICA Group is a national not-for-profit organization that seeks to create and save jobs through the development and strengthening of employee-owned cooperatives and community-based projects. ICA provides a full range of business consulting and technical assistance services, education, and financing to clients working in or seeking to start worker-owned and community-based businesses.

Institute for Community Economics: http://www.iceclt.org/

> The Institute for Community Economics (ICE) is a federally certified Community Development Financial Institution that makes loans for permanently affordable homeownership across the United States. ICE is the originator of the community land trust (CLT), a housing model that develops equity for homeowners while preserving public subsidy and affordability in perpetuity. Since its founding in 1967, ICE has assisted

hundreds of grassroots organizations in building or rehabilitating thousands of units of permanently affordable housing in both rural and urban neighborhoods throughout the country.

Kentucky Highlands Investment Corporation: http://www.khic.org/

KHIC was formed in 1968 to stimulate growth and create employment opportunities in a nine-county region of Southeastern Kentucky. KHIC's mission is to provide and retain employment opportunities in Southeastern Kentucky through sound investments and management assistance.

Local Initiatives Support Corporation: www.lisc.org

LISC connects local organizations and community leaders with resources to revitalize neighborhoods and improve quality of life. LISC mobilizes corporate, government, and philanthropic support to provide local community development organizations with: loans, grants, and equity investments; local, statewide, and national policy support; and technical and management assistance. LISC's Sustainable Communities plan calls for the organization to concentrate not only on its traditional focus of affordable residential development, but also on re-establishing functioning local markets and on improving the quality of life of residents through work in public safety programs, health care and recreation centers, education initiatives, and programs to build family assets.

National Council of La Raza: http://www.nclr.org

The largest national Latino civil rights and advocacy organization in the United States, NCLR works to improve opportunities for Hispanic Americans by conducting applied research, policy analysis, and advocacy. NCLR provides a Latino perspective in five key areas: assets/investments, civil rights/immigration, education, employment and economic status, and health. It also provides capacity-building assistance to its 300 affiliates who work at the state and local level to advance opportunities for individuals and families.

National Federation of Community Development Credit Unions: http://www.natfed.org/

The Federation helps low- and moderate-income people and communities achieve financial independence through credit unions. They carry out their mission by advocating for and providing financial, technical, and human resources to CDCUs.

National Trust for Historic Preservation: http://www.nationaltrust.org/

The National Trust for Historic Preservation is a private, nonprofit membership organization dedicated to saving historic places and revitalizing America's communities. Recipient of the National Humanities Medal, the Trust was founded in 1949 and provides leadership, education, advocacy, and resources to protect the irreplaceable places that tell America's story.

National Urban League: http://www.nul.org/

The National Urban League is a historic civil rights organization dedicated to economic empowerment in historically underserved urban communities. The National Urban League spearheads the efforts of its local affiliates through the development of programs, public policy research, and advocacy. There are more than 100 local affiliates in 36 states and the District of Columbia providing direct services including workforce development, business development, and family support.

NCB Capital Impact: http://www.ncb.coop/

A subsidiary of National Consumer Cooperative Bank, NCB Capital Impact provides innovative community lending, technical assistance, public policy support, and development services. Its areas of focus are affordable housing, community health care, economic development, education, and long-term care.

NeighborWorks America: www.nw.org/

NeighborWorks America is a national nonprofit organization created by Congress to provide financial support, technical assistance, and training for community-based revitalization efforts. NeighborWorks America creates opportunities for people to live in affordable homes, improve their lives, and strengthen their communities.

Nonprofit Finance Fund: http://www.nonprofitfinancefund.org/

This CED intermediary's mission is to build a "strong, well-capitalized and durable nonprofit sector that uses capital effectively to support the highest aspirations and most generous impulses of people and communities." It provides financing and technical assistance to a range of nonprofits, and has also created a strong practice supporting nonprofit arts institutions.

Opportunity Finance Network: www.opportunityfinance.net

Opportunity Finance Network is a network of private financial intermediaries that identifies and invests in opportunities to benefit low-income and low-wealth people in the United States. Opportunity Finance Network originated more than $19.8 billion in financing in urban, rural, and Native communities through 2007. This has generated or maintained 191,381 jobs; 43,050 businesses and microenterprises; 577,736 housing units; and, 9552 community facility projects.

Rural Community Assistance Corporation: http://www.rcac.org/

Rural Community Assistance Corporation provides information and assistance to Native American groups by focusing on drinking water, wastewater, solid waste, housing, and financial services.

Seedco: www.seedco.org

Seedco is a national community development intermediary with expertise in the many facets of economic recovery. Seedco provides business assistance, community financing, and technical assistance to community-based and faith-based organizations and small businesses. It has a long history of creating and implementing workforce development and asset-building initiatives. Through its network of CBOs, Seedco also provides career services and financial counseling to job seekers and workers.

Self-Help: http://www.self-help.org/

Self-Help is a community development lender and real estate developer that works with individuals, organizations, and communities traditionally underserved by conventional markets. The funds that support its work come from deposits, grants, and other investments made by individuals and institutions across the United States.

ShoreBank: http://www.shorebankcorp.com

ShoreBank Corporation is America's first community development and environmental bank holding company. Headquartered in Chicago, ShoreBank is a $2.4 billion company with banks and nonprofits in Chicago, Cleveland, Detroit, Ilwaco, Washington, Portland, Oregon, and Michigan's Upper Peninsula, and consulting services around the world.

The Reinvestment Fund: http://www.trfund.com/
> TRF is a national leader in the financing of neighborhood revitalization. What began in 1985 as a small community development organization working in Greater Philadelphia, has evolved into a progressive, results-oriented, socially responsible community investment group that today works across the Mid-Atlantic region.

The Trust for Public Land: http://www.tpl.org/
> The Trust for Public Land (TPL) is a national, nonprofit, land conservation organization that conserves land for people to enjoy as parks, community gardens, historic sites, rural lands, and other natural places, ensuring livable communities for generations to come.

Workforce Development

The Aspen Institute's Workforce Strategies Initiative: http://www.aspenwsi.org
> Workforce Strategies Initiative (WSI) has been studying sectoral initiatives for more than a decade, with a particular focus on strategies with the potential to positively affect the employment situation of low-income workers. WSI identifies and advances strategies that help low-income Americans gain ground in today's labor market. To that end, WSI engages in applied research, facilitates dialogue, disseminates findings, and shares new ideas.

The Council for Adult and Experiential Learning: http://www.cael.org/
> The Council for Adult and Experiential Learning (CAEL) is a national nonprofit organization whose mission is to expand learning opportunities for adults. CAEL works to remove policy and organizational barriers to learning opportunities, and identifies and disseminates effective practices.

Center for Employment Training (CET): http://www.cet2000.org
> CET is a private, 501(c)(3) nonprofit organization dedicated to fighting poverty and dependence on public aid by making hands-on job training available to youth and adults of all educational levels and backgrounds, but especially to those most in need and hardest to serve.

Jewish Vocational Services: http://www.jvs.org
> JVS was founded in 1973 to aid recent Jewish college graduates who were having trouble finding work. In the 1980s and 1990s, it expanded to meet the needs of both the huge influx of refugees from the former Soviet Union and the workers who had been displaced during turbulent economic times.

Jobs for the Future: http://www.jff.org
> Jobs for the Future identifies, develops, and promotes new education and workforce strategies that help communities, states, and the nation compete in a global economy.

The National Fund for Workforce Solutions: http://www.nfwsolutions.org/
> The mission of the National Fund for Workforce Solutions is to improve employment, training, and labor market outcomes for low-income individuals. The Fund's vision is that its support will improve both the quality of jobs and the capacity of workers. It will promote change at three levels—individual, institution, and system—leading to better jobs, better workers, and a better workforce development system.

Project QUEST: http://www.questsa.com

> Project QUEST, an innovative job training program in San Antonio, Texas, has earned statewide and national attention as a model for local workforce development efforts. Since 1993, Project QUEST has met the needs of San Antonio area businesses by training local residents who would otherwise be on public assistance and not in the local workforce.

Wider Opportunities for Women: http://www.wowonline.org

> Wider Opportunities for Women (WOW) works nationally and in its home community of Washington, DC to build pathways to economic independence for America's families, women, and girls. WOW has a distinctive history in changing the landscape of women and work.

Wildcat Service Corporation: http://www.wildcatnyc.org/index.php

> Wildcat Service Corporation is a nonprofit workforce development organization located in New York City. Wildcat has developed innovative industry-specific workforce and training programs to support both workers and the hiring needs of NYC businesses. With intensive assessment, ongoing coaching, and goal-driven training, Wildcat develops a constant pool of skilled and marketable job candidates.

The Workforce Alliance: http://www.workforcealliance.org

> The Workforce Alliance (TWA) is a national coalition of community-based organizations, community colleges, unions, business leaders, and local officials advocating for public policies that invest in the skills of America's workers, so they can better support their families and help American businesses better compete in today's economy.

Workforce Strategy Center (WSC): http://www.workforcestrategy.org/

> WSC works with state and national leaders to develop effective education and employment policies that work to better align public resources. It conducts research and increases workforce competitiveness. Its mission is to work hand in hand with education, workforce development, and economic development agencies to develop strategies to help students and worker succeed and help provide regional economic growth.

Higher Education and Community Economic Development

Center for Community and Economic Development (Michigan State University): www.cedp.msu.edu

> The Center for Community and Economic Development at Michigan State University in East Lansing operates with the express purpose of developing and applying knowledge to address the needs of society, primarily in distressed urban communities.

Center for Economic and Community Development (Penn State): http://cecd.aers.psu.edu

> The Center works closely with Pennsylvania regions and communities on issues of economic development, land use, local government finance, and community asset building. Posted on its Web site are community profiles of economic and demographic indicators by county.

Center for Urban Initiatives and Research (University of Wisconsin, Milwaukee): www.uwm.edu/Dept/CUIR

> The Center for Urban Initiatives and Research (CUIR) provides research services and technical assistance to public and nonprofit organizations in many areas, including strategic planning facilitation, survey research, and neighborhood analysis and mapping.

Coalition of Urban Serving Universities: www.usucoalition.org/

USU provides a national voice within public higher education to articulate and promote an urban agenda. USU is identifying and expanding innovative models of university–community partnerships across U.S. cities that aim to create a competitive workforce, build strong communities, and improve the health of a diverse population. In an effort to reach these goals USU advocates federal policies that support public urban research universities and create partnerships with them to fuel the development of the nation's cities and metro regions; it collects and analyzes data across a network of public urban research institutions to create a reliable factual foundation for the universities' work in cities and provides the leadership of public urban research universities with a common agenda and the tools to improve urban health, strengthen urban economies, and develop a capable workforce for the twenty-first century.

Community Colleges Central Bridges to Opportunity: http://www.communitycollegecentral.org

The Ford Foundation initiative Bridges to Opportunity has approved multiyear grants to support state-level reform for developing new policy approaches in six states: Colorado, Kentucky, Louisiana, New Mexico, Ohio, and Washington.

Community Outreach (Rutgers University, Camden, NJ campus) http://camden-www.rutgers.edu/community.htm

Rutgers Camden campus has a wide variety of community programs. One of these efforts is the LEAP Academy, a K–12 charter school initiated by the university that is designed to accommodate up to 700 students as well as develop model practices for implementation in surrounding public schools.

Interactive University Project: http://interactiveu.berkeley.edu:8000/IU/

The Interactive University Project uses the Internet to open UC Berkeley's resources and people to California's K–12 schools and citizens. Its goal is to use technology for the improvement of teaching and learning while making accessible the knowledge in universities, museums, and libraries.

Pratt Institute Center for Community and Environment Development (PICCED): http://www.picced.org

As the oldest university-based advocacy planning organization in the United States, PICCED's mission is to enhance the capacity of low- and moderate-income communities to develop innovative solutions to the physical, social, and economic challenges facing them.

Rural Community College Alliance (RCCA): http://www.ruralccalliance.org/

RCCA is an alliance between the rural colleges of America and is a "network and advocacy group that helps build the capacity of member community colleges to improve the educational and economic prospects for rural America."

Southern New Hampshire University School of Community Economic Development: http://www.snhu.edu/388.asp

Founded in 1982, the school trains practitioners from more than 100 countries in the areas of affordable housing, community development finance, commercial development, and small businesses.

University of Illinois, Chicago Neighborhood Initiative: http://www.uicni.org/

The UICNI is a major vehicle through which the university fulfills the mission of the Great Cities Commitment with particular emphasis on the engagement of students, faculty, and staff in long-term meaningful relationships with communities.

University of Pennsylvania, Center for Community Partnerships: http://www.upenn.edu/ccp/
index.php
> Founded in 1992, the Barbara and Edward Netter Center for Community Partnerships
> is the university's primary vehicle for bringing to bear the knowledge and learn-
> ing needed to solve the complex, comprehensive, and interconnected problems of
> the West Philadelphia community (the community surrounding the University of
> Pennsylvania).

Community Building/Development

Arts and Community Economic Development

Americans for the Arts: http://www.americansforthearts.org/
> Americans for the Arts is the nation's leading nonprofit organization for advancing the
> arts in America. With 45 years of service, it is dedicated to representing and serving
> local communities and creating opportunities for every American to participate in and
> appreciate all forms of the arts.

Arts Education Partnership: http://aep-arts.org/
> The Arts Education Partnership (AEP) provides information about current and emerg-
> ing arts education policies, issues, and activities at the national, state, and local levels.
> AEP commissions and disseminates research about critical arts and education issues,
> maintains the linking databases on state-level policies for arts education, and convenes
> national forums around significant themes and issues in the field.

Community Arts Network: http://www.communityarts.net/
> The Community Arts Network (CAN) is a portal to the field of community arts, pro-
> viding news, documentation, theoretical writing, communications, research, and edu-
> cational information. Headquartered at its website on the Internet, CAN is a program
> of Art in the Public Interest (API), a nonprofit organization based in North Carolina.

National Assembly of State Arts Agencies (NASAA): http://nasaa-arts.org/
> The state arts agencies ensure and increase public access to the arts in every community
> in America, including all 50 states and the six U.S. jurisdictions. The agencies provide
> grants, offer training and information, support arts activities for young people, con-
> duct research showing the impact of the arts, educate the public about the necessity
> of the arts, and lead special initiatives that foster economic and civic development
> through the arts.

National Endowment for the Arts: http://www.arts.endow.gov/
> The National Endowment for the Arts is the nation's largest funder of the arts. It is a
> public agency, independent of the federal government, that supports excellence in the
> arts, broadcasting it to Americans and providing leadership in arts education.

President's Committee on the Arts and the Humanities: http://www.pcah.gov/
> The President's Committee is dedicated to arts and humanities education, cultural diplo-
> macy, economic revitalization through the arts and humanities, and special events com-
> mitted to recognizing excellence in these areas. The committee includes government
> agencies as well as private individuals, providing a dynamic link between public and
> private sectors.

Education Reform and Community Development

Annenberg Institute for School Reform: http://www.annenberginstitute.org/
> The Annenberg Institute works with school system central offices and community constituencies to explore and refine the concept of "smart education systems," networks of schools, community organizations, and services that promote high-quality student learning and development inside and outside of schools.

National Center of Education Statistics: http://nces.ed.gov/
> The National Center for Education Statistics (NCES) is the primary federal entity for collecting and analyzing data related to education in the United States and other nations. NCES is located within the U.S. Department of Education and the Institute of Education Sciences.

National Clearinghouse for Educational Facilities (NCEF): http://www.edfacilities.org/
> Created in 1997 by the U.S. Department of Education, the NCEF provides information on planning, designing, funding, building, improving, and maintaining safe, healthy, and high performance schools.

National Community Education Association (NCEA): http://www.ncea.com/
> The NCEA is a nonprofit membership association that provides members with national and regional training conferences, workshops, information and referral services, and specialized periodicals, publications, and products. In addition, the NCEA advocates for parent and community involvement in public education, the formation of community partnerships to address community needs, and the expansion of lifelong learning opportunities for all community residents.

Community Organizing Groups

Center for Community Change: www.communitychange.org
> The mission of the CCC is to build the power and capacity of low-income people, especially low-income people of color, to change their communities and public policies for the better. CCC builds relationships with grassroots community organizations that cross ethnic, geographic, and issue boundaries to change economic and social justice public policies at the local, state, and national levels. Campaign issues focus on health care, housing, immigration, and worker justice. The Center also mentors new community organizers and funds and trains grassroots community organizations to engage in electoral organizing, registering and turning out voters.

The Gamaliel Foundation: http://www.gamaliel.org/
> The Gamaliel Foundation assists local community leaders in creating a network of local organizations, mainly faith institutions, to improve political and economic opportunities for marginalized communities.

Industrial Areas Foundation (IAF): http://www.industrialareasfoundation.org/
> IAF builds organizations that have a primary purpose of acting when necessary for social change. It represents communities and voluntary institutions such as religious congregations, labor locals, homeowner groups, recovery groups, parent associations, settlement houses, immigrant societies, schools, seminaries, and orders of men and women among society's rich and powerful.

Crime Prevention

Community Development & Crime Prevention Institute, LLC: www.cdcpi.us

> CDCPI exists to provide community development and crime prevention-based training and related services to law enforcement, military, government, school, business, and community groups. CDCPI travels across the country to provide crucial training, technical assistance, and subject matter expertise to those needing or requesting it.

National Crime Prevention Council (NCPC): http://www.ncpc.org

> NCPC aims to help keep people and their communities safe from crime by producing tools that communities can use to learn how to prevent crimes, engage community members, and coordinate with local agencies. It provides publications and teaching materials, programs that can be implemented in schools and communities, support for a national coalition of crime prevention practitioners, and local, regional, and national training.

National Criminal Justice Association (NCJA): http://www.ncja.org/

> NCJA represents state, tribal, and local governments on crime prevention and crime control issues. It promotes a balanced approach to communities' public safety and criminal and juvenile justice system programs. It builds relationships among criminal and juvenile justice agencies and the community. It is the formal way to inform the Congress of needs, accomplishments, and opinions on crime prevention and control of the state, tribal, and local justices.

National Criminal Justice Reference Service (NCJRS): http://www.ncjrs.gov/

> NCJRS is a federally funded Web site with sources that offer justice and substance abuse information to support research, policy, and program development. It is a public Web site that has one of the largest criminal and juvenile justice libraries and databases in the world. It has more than 200,000 publications, reports, articles, and audiovisual products containing information on statistics, research findings, program descriptions, congressional hearing transcripts, and training materials, internationally and nationally.

Youth Development

The Children's Partnership: http://www.childrenspartnership.org/

> The Children's Partnership strives to ensure that disadvantaged children have the resources and opportunities needed to succeed, and to build awareness and involve more Americans in their cause. The Children's Partnership conducts research, analysis, and advocates the needs of the over 70 million children and youth in America. The organization works to secure heath coverage and supply the benefits of technology to disadvantaged children and their families.

Find Youth Information from the Government: http://www.findyouthinfo.gov/

> The official U.S. government Web site that provides help in creating, maintaining, and strengthening effective youth programs. The site provides information on youth facts, funding, and tools to help assess community assets and generate maps of local and federal resources. It also supplies the latest youth-related news.

Innovation Center for Community and Youth Development: www.theinnovationcenter.org
The Innovation Center seeks out extraordinary organizations and individuals across the world to build partnerships and create positive change. The organization works with community organizations, researchers, policymakers, and philanthropists to promote youth leadership, youth and civic engagement, youth–adult partnerships, youth development, and community building. The Innovation Center also offers organizational development, consulting services, and program evaluation to youth-oriented organizations.

National Association of Youth Service Consultants: www.naysc.org
NAYSC hosts a directory of consultants, technical assistance providers, nonprofits, and subject matter experts in workforce development, education, juvenile justice, child welfare, foster care, mental health, disabilities, and more. NAYSC also provides a listing of consulting jobs and funding opportunities nationwide.

National Collaboration for Youth: http://www.collab4youth.org
The National Collaboration for Youth (NCY) is a coalition of the National Assembly member organizations that have a significant interest in youth development. Members of the National Collaboration for Youth include more than 50 national, nonprofit, youth development organizations. The mission of NCY is to provide a united voice as an advocate for youth to improve the conditions of young people in America, and to help young people reach their full potential.

The National Foundation for Teaching Entrepreneurship: www.nfte.com
Through entrepreneurship education, the Network for Teaching Entrepreneurship (NFTE) helps young people from low-income communities build skills and unlock their entrepreneurial creativity. Since 1987, NFTE has reached more than 280,000 young people, and currently has programs in 21 states and 12 countries. NFTE has more than 1500 active Certified Entrepreneurship Teachers, and is continually improving its innovative entrepreneurship curriculum.

National Youth Development Information Center: http://www.nydic.org/
The National Youth Development Information Center runs a Web site that provides information on funding, programming, research, policy, job, and training opportunities for youth workers. It also provides current news in the youth development field. It has one of the largest online libraries that provides practice-related information at little to no cost.

National Youth Employment Coalition: http://nyec.org
NYEC offers a range of projects, programs, and activities, including setting and promoting quality standards for the industry, building and increasing the capacity of youth-serving organizations, providing and supporting professional development, and tracking, crafting, and influencing policy.

YouthBuild Rural & Tribal Development Initiative: http://www.youthbuild.org/site/apps/nlnet/content2.aspx?c=htIRI3PIKoG&b=1300085&ct=1694039
YouthBuild's Rural & Tribal Development Initiative provides support to the development of active young rural leaders, and encourages the development of new programs, particularly on tribal lands or those serving tribal youth in the Mississippi Delta, Appalachia, and the borderland/colonias region. YouthBuild aims to "strengthen the capacity of rural communities to support and train their young people for leadership and a meaningful, productive life within their home communities." Today, there are about 60 YouthBuild programs throughout rural America.

YouthBuild USA: www.youthbuild.org/

YouthBuild is a youth and community development program that addresses core issues facing low-income communities: housing, education, employment, crime prevention, and leadership development. In YouthBuild programs, low-income young people ages 16–24 work toward their GEDs or high school diplomas, learn job skills, and serve their communities by building affordable housing, thus transforming their own lives and roles in society.

International CED

The African Safari Lodge Foundation: http://www.asl-foundation.org/

The mission of the African Safari Lodge Foundation is to maximize the pro-poor impacts of nature tourism enterprises by increasing the flow of tangible benefits from these businesses into the households of local residents via wages, supply contracts, equity agreements, and local institutions that encourage fair and equitable distribution of such benefits.

American Jewish World Service: www.ajws.org

American Jewish World Service (AJWS) is an international development organization motivated by Judaism's imperative to pursue justice. AJWS is dedicated to alleviating poverty, hunger, and disease among the people of the developing world regardless of race, religion, or nationality. Through grants to grassroots organizations, volunteer service, advocacy, and education, AJWS fosters civil society, sustainable development, and human rights for all people, while promoting the values and responsibilities of global citizenship within the Jewish community.

AusAID: www.ausaid.gov.au

AusAID is the Australian government agency responsible for managing Australia's overseas aid program. The objective of the aid program is to assist developing countries reduce poverty and achieve sustainable development, in line with Australia's national interest.

Australian Development Studies Network: http://devnet.anu.edu.au/

The Network is an independent organization, which encourages discussion and widespread exchange of knowledge of global, social, and economic development issues, development-related research, and international development assistance policy and practice.

Bangladesh Rural Advancement Committee: www.brac.net

BRAC has established itself as a pioneer in recognizing and tackling the different dimensions of poverty. Its unique holistic approach to poverty alleviation and empowerment of the poor encompasses a range of core programs in economic and social development, health, education, human rights, and legal services.

British Urban Regeneration Association: http://www.bura.org.uk

The British Urban Regeneration Association (BURA) is the leading membership organization championing regeneration. BURA claims its strength is derived from its wide range of members in the private, public, and community sectors.

Calmeadow: http://www.calmeadow.com

Calmeadow's mission is to provide self-employed people in Canada and the developing world with access to credit and savings services.

Canadian Community Reinvestment Coalition: http://www.cancrc.org

The CCRC is a coalition of over 110 antipoverty, consumer, community economic development, labor, and small business groups from across Canada.

Canadian Co-Operative Association: http://www.coopcca.com

The CCA is the national umbrella organization of anglophone co-operatives. The CCA supports and promotes co-operative enterprise in Canada and around the world. Included on this site is an excellent introduction to co-operatives and how they work.

CED Centre – Simon Fraser University: www.sfu.ca/cedc

The CED Centre engages in collaboration with communities in British Columbia and with individuals, institutions, and organizations working in CED. This site also houses an excellent "gateway" to CED resources.

The Center for Development and Population Activities: www.cedpa.org

Founded in 1975, the Centre for Development and Population Activities (CEDPA) is an internationally recognized nonprofit organization that improves the lives of women and girls in developing countries. Their approach is to work hand in hand with women leaders, local partners, and national and international organizations to give women the tools they need to improve their lives, families, and communities.

Centre for Community Enterprise: www.cedworks.com

This British Columbia based center keeps its eye on community economic development know-how. This site is a compilation of their resources, and includes the CED journal *Making Waves*.

Centre for Entrepreneurship Education and Development: http://www.ceed.info/

CEED is devoted to helping people discover and use entrepreneurship as a vehicle to become self-reliant. It has a vision of a vibrant entrepreneurial culture for all of Atlantic Canada.

Colombo Plan for Cooperative Economic and Social Development in Asia and the Pacific: http://www.colombo-plan.org/

The Colombo Plan is a partnership concept of self-help and mutual-help in development aimed at the socioeconomic progress of its member countries.

Communities and Local Government: http://www.communities.gov.uk/

Communities and Local Government is working hard to create thriving, sustainable, vibrant communities that improve everyone's quality of life. Communities and Local Government sets policy on local government, housing, urban regeneration, planning, and fire and rescue.

Community Futures Development Corporations: www.communityfutures.ca

A network of 90 Community Futures Development Corporations (CFDCs) across Western Canada work together to foster entrepreneurship and community economic development in rural areas.

Cooperative for Assistance and Relief Everywhere: www.care.org

CARE is a leading humanitarian organization fighting global poverty. It places special focus on working alongside poor women because, equipped with the proper resources, women have the power to help whole families and entire communities escape poverty.

The Crafts Center: http://www.craftscenter.org/

The Crafts Center is a leading international crafts production, marketing, and design assistance network dedicated to supporting low-income artisans around the world.

Development Gateway: www.developmentgateway.org

Development Gateway is an international nonprofit organization with the mission to reduce poverty and enable change in developing nations through information technology. It envisions a world in which the digital revolution serves people everywhere, creating greater opportunity through increased access to critical information; greater reliance on local capabilities; and more effective, better-coordinated international aid.

The Global Development Research Center: http://www.gdrc.org/

The Global Development Research Center is an independent nonprofit think tank that carries out initiatives in education, research, and practice, in the spheres of environment, urban, community, and information, and at scales that are effective.

Grameen Family of Enterprises: www.grameen-info.org/gfamily.html

The Grameen Bank (and now its affiliate organizations) is a leader in microenterprise lending. Grameen has expanded to include social enterprises in many sectors, including clothing production, cellular telephone service, information technology services, rural education, and energy production.

Improvement and Development Agency: http://www.idea.gov.uk/

The IDeA supports improvement and innovation in local government, focusing on the issues that are important to councils and using tried and tested ways of working. It works with councils in developing good practice, supporting them in their partnerships. The organization does this through networks, online communities of practice and Web resources, and through the support and challenges provided by councilor and officer peers.

Institute for Development Studies: http://www.ids.ac.uk/go/home

The Institute of Development Studies is a leading global organization for research, teaching, and communications on international development. IDS was founded in 1966 and has built a solid reputation based on the quality of its work applying academic skills to development practice all over the world.

International Community Development Society: http://comm-dev.org

The international Community Development Society is a professional association for community development practitioners and citizen leaders around the world.

International Development Exchange: http://www.idex.org/

IDEX is a San Francisco-based nonprofit organization that promotes sustainable solutions to poverty by providing long-term grants and access to resources to locally run organizations in Africa, Asia, and Latin America.

International Foundation for Education and Self-Help: http://www.ifesh.org/

Founded in 1981, IFESH helps improve the lives of people in sub-Saharan Africa by addressing the problems of poverty and illiteracy. Through self-help programs, it specializes in education systems, health, community development, and conflict mitigation. The work of IFESH supports the efforts of the eight United Nations Millennium Development Goals, particularly the eradication of poverty and hunger, achieving universal education, combating HIV/AIDS, promoting gender equality, and maternal health.

International Fund for Agricultural Development: www.ifad.org

IFAD is dedicated to eradicating rural poverty in developing countries. Working with rural poor people, governments, donors, nongovernmental organizations, and many other partners, IFAD focuses on country-specific solutions, which can involve increasing rural poor peoples' access to financial services, markets, technology, land, and other natural resources

International Institute for Sustainable Development: http://iwww.isd.org

The International Institute for Sustainable Development advances policy recommendations on international trade, economic instruments, climate change, and natural resource management to make development sustainable. Using Internet communications, it covers and reports on international negotiations and broker knowledge gained through collaborative projects with global partners.

Policy Innovations: http://www.policyinnovations.org/

The Global Policy Innovations program provides a forum for pragmatic alternatives to the current global economic order. A growing body of innovative scholarship offers promising strategies for sustainable development and a fairer globalization. Yet, these proposals have not been disseminated in a coordinated fashion. The Global Policy Innovations program provides a central address for a fairer globalization.

Rural and Small Town Programme – Mount Allison University: www.mta.ca/rstp/rstpmain.html

The Rural and Small Town Programme (RSTP) is an independent university-based research center dedicated to exploring and resolving social, environmental, and economic issues facing small communities in Canada.

Trickle Up: www.trickleup.org

Trickle Up empowers people living on less than $1 a day to take the first steps out of poverty, providing them with resources to build microenterprises for a better quality of life. In partnership with local agencies, it provides business training and seed capital to launch or expand a microenterprise, and savings support to build assets.

The Trust for the Americas: www.trustfortheamericas.org

The mission of the Trust is to execute capacity-building programs, both for individuals and organizations. The Trust implements its programs through local partner organizations, with support from over 200 public and private sector partners in more than 21 countries throughout Latin America and the Caribbean.

United Nations Development Programme: http://www.undp.org/

UNDP is the UN's global development network, an organization advocating for change and connecting countries to knowledge, experience, and resources to help people build a better life. It is on the ground in 166 countries, working with them on their own solutions to global and national development challenges.

United States Agency for International Development: http://www.usaid.gov

U.S. foreign assistance has always had the twofold purpose of furthering America's foreign policy interests in expanding democracy and free markets while improving the lives of the citizens of the developing world. USAID works around the world to achieve these goals. USAID has been the principal U.S. agency to extend assistance to countries recovering from disaster, trying to escape poverty, and engaging in democratic reforms.

World Bank: http://www.worldbank.org/

The World Bank provides financial and technical assistance to developing countries around the world. Its mission is to fight poverty through helping people help themselves and their environment by providing resources, sharing knowledge, building capacity, and forging partnerships in the public and private sectors.

World Learning – International Development Program: www.worldlearning.org

In 20 countries World Learning works with communities to design and implement development programs that address some of the main obstacles to human development, such as the spread of HIV/AIDS, the marginalization of children, the global education crisis, and the widespread need for government accountability and an active civil society.

Index

A

AAMU. *see* Alabama A&M University Community Development Corporation (AAMU CDC)
Affordable housing, 26
AFI. *see* Assets for Independence Program (AFI)
AGENDA, 157
Alabama A&M University Community Development Corporation (AAMU CDC), 56
Allen, Will, 124
Alternative Energy Banner Center, 195
Alternative Staffing Organizations (ASOs), 161
ANDP. *see* Atlanta Neighborhood Development Partnership (ANDP)
Anti-Graffiti Network, 123
Arts
    community building and development, 121–23
    resource guide, 153, 253–54
    youth, 123
Ash Institute for Democratic Practice, xxv
ASOs. *see* Alternative Staffing Organizations (ASOs)
Asset building
    poverty, 134
    resource guide, 246–48
Assets and agency, 133–54
    collective asset building, 144–54
    commons stabilization, 144
    earned income tax credits, 138–39
    financing innovation, 146
    human capital development, 140–43
    individual asset building, 135–39
    individual development accounts, 135–37
    National Community Stabilization Trust, 147
    Operation Neighborhood Recovery, 145
    self-employment credit, 140–43
Assets for Independence Program (AFI), 136
Asset thinking, 134
Atlanta Neighborhood Development Partnership (ANDP), 9
    CDCs, 18
    Metro Atlanta Chamber of Commerce, 10
Australia, 149
Automobile steel reuse in building affordable housing, 34–35

B

Baltimore, Maryland
    CED, 170
    CitiStat, 110
    COMSTAT, 109
    Job Network Program, 162
    Second Chance, Inc., 159
    YMCA, 170
Baltimore CASH Campaign, 139
Baltimore Neighborhood Indicators alliance (BNIA), 110, 125
    CitiStat, 111
Bank(s)
    community development, 13
    records, 69
    requirements, 68
Bank Enterprise Award (BEA) Program, 89
BART. *see* Bay Area Rapid Transit (BART)
Bay Area Rapid Transit (BART), 76
BEA. *see* Bank Enterprise Award (BEA) Program
Bedford Stuyvesant Restoration Corporation, 27
BGC. *see* Bloomfield-Garfield Corporation (BGC)
Black Arts Movement, 121
Black Capitalism, 133
Bloomfield-Garfield Corporation (BGC), 113

BNIA. *see* Baltimore Neighborhood Indicators alliance (BNIA)
Brownfield Redevelopment Act, xxii, 33
Building community capacity, 187–89
Business and Enterprise Development Program, 79
Business attraction, xx
Buss, Terry, 39

C

California, 157
CAPC. *see* Community Asset Preservation Corporation (CAPC)
Capital deployment, xix
Capital-intensive industries, 90
Career development, 32
Career ladders
    community-based agencies, 161
    community-based workforce development innovations, 160–61
    low-income workers, 165
    on-the-job training, 161
    sectoral employment, 160
Carolina Steel Construction LLC, 35
Carter, Jimmy, xxii
CBO. *see* Community-Based Organization (CBO) Outreach program
CCDO. *see* Community Capacity Development Office (CCDO)
CCIs. *see* Comprehensive community initiatives (CCIs)
CCSF. *see* City College of San Francisco (CCSF)
CCT. *see* Conditional Cash Transfer (CCT) program
CDBG. *see* Community Development Block Grant (CDBG)
CDCs. *see* Community development corporations (CDCs)
CDCUs. *see* Community development credit unions (CDCUs)
CDEs. *see* Community development entities (CDEs)
CDFIs. *see* Community development financial institutions (CDFIs)
CDLFs. *see* Community development loan funds (CDLFs)
CDPs. *see* Community development partnerships (CDPs)
CED. *see* Community economic development (CED)

CEDIs. *see* Community economic development institutions (CEDIs)
Census Bureau, 194
Center for Urban and Regional Affairs (CURA)
    community organizations, 193
    LMI/DEED, 194
    M3D, 192
Centers for Working Families (CWF), 95
    CDCs, 96
Charter schools, 174–75
    CDCs, 176
    New Jersey laws, 175
    poverty, 176
    public sector innovation, 40
CHCDC. *see* Coppin Heights Community Development Corporation (CHCDC)
Chicago, Illinois
    CDBG program, 34
    efforts to reinvent itself, xxi–xxii
    LCDC, 34
    public art, xxiii
    South Shore Bank, 13, 88
CitiStat, 110
    Baltimore, Maryland, 110
    BNIA, 111
City College of San Francisco (CCSF), 164
City governments, 209
City of New York's Center for Economic Opportunity, 205
City University of New York (CUNY), 45
CLCs. *see* Community learning centers (CLCs)
Cleveland Neighborhood Progress, 98–101, 104, 203
Clinton, Bill, 88
CMN. *see* College of Menominee Nation (CMN)
Coal industry employment, 78
Collective asset building, 144–54
College of Menominee Nation (CMN), 51
    community services, 52
    Education Outreach Department, 52
    HUD, 51
    Transportation alliance for New Solutions, 52
Colleges, 203. *see also* Community colleges; Higher education; University
Commission for Economic Opportunity, 41
Community Arts Movement, 121
Community Asset Preservation Corporation (CAPC), 145
    CDC, 146

Operation Neighborhood Recovery, 147
Community based agencies, 161
Community based developers, xxiii
Community based development institutions, 68
Community based economic development, 32
        organizations, 26
Community based nonprofit organizations, 29
Community-Based Organization (CBO)
        Outreach program, 45
Community based organizations, 156
    community colleges, 163
    network building, 162
    sectoral employment, 157
Community based partner arguments, 88
Community based workforce development, 156
    career ladders, 160–61
    community colleges partnerships, 163
    innovations, 155–66
    network building, 162
    Second Chance, Inc., 159
    sectoral employment, 157–59
    temporary staffing, 161
Community building, 108
    CED, 105–6, 180
    education, 168–73, 181
Community building and development, 105–32
    arts and culture, 121–23
    community development *vs.* community
        building, 106–9
    food and community development, 124
    gang diversion, 114–15
    graffiti, 122–23
    Homeboy Industries, 114–15
    Mural Arts Program in Philadelphia,
        122–23
    Neighborhood Security and CED, 109–10
    partnering, 114
    planning, information management and
        development, 109–10
    public sector innovation and CED, 50–51
    resource guide, 153, 253–54
    Weed and Seed, 112–14
    YouthBuild, 116–20
    youth development, 116–20
Community Capacity Development Office
        (CCDO), 112
Community colleges
    CED, 203
    CEDIs, 195
    comprehensive training programs, 163
    higher education as development partner,
        195

systems in United States, 195
    training programs, 196
Community development, 108–9
    activities, 188
    banks, 13
    CED future with promise and hope, 206
    vs. community building, 106–9
    community institutions, 180
    GIS, 192
    intermediaries, 9
    learning inhibitions, 108
    LISC, 94
    philanthropy, 111
    political participation, 50
    programming, 3
    public sectors, 111
    school reform, 181
    United States policy, 50
    UNL-COPC, 188
    venture capital funds, 13
Community Development Block Grant
        (CDBG), 63, 74, 76
    accomplishments, 65–68
    CEDIs, 64
    Chicago and LCDC, 34
    economic planning, 64
    expenditures, 63
    HOME program, 140
    jurisdiction plans, 64
    local planning, 64
Community development corporations (CDCs),
        2
    ANDP, 18
    bank records, 69
    benefits, 178
    bilingual education, 5
    CAPC, 146
    CCIs, 107
    CED, 75
    CEDIs, 61
    charter schools, 176
    child are, 4–5
    community barriers, 74
    community-based development institutions,
        68
    CSI, 114
    CWF, 96
    direction, 8
    divisions, 4–5
    economic development, 9
    effectiveness, 4
    example, 4

geographic targets, 99
GIS, 193
government support, 62
housing development, 107
isolation, 81
LISC, 95
local governments, 8
locally based CED institutions, 62
MacArthur Foundation, 96
nonprofit organizations, 62
NPI, 99
real estate development, 8
regional goals, 31
SIP, 62
size, 4
Spanish Speaking Unity Council, 75
staffing, 100
state governments, 9
Strategic Investment Initiative, 99
UDI Community Development
    Corporation, 35
United States, 62
Unity Council, 75
workforce development, 165
Community development credit unions
    (CDCUs), 11
Community development entities (CDEs), 72,
    89
    NMTC, 72
Community development financial institutions
    (CDFIs), 11, 71, 87
    CED, 12, 50
    CEDIs, 56
    direct investments, 89
    for-profit, 73
    for-profit subsidiaries, 73
    Maine, 90
    1995-2009, 89
    poverty, 88
    SBA, 141
    Self-Help, 13
    TEC-CC, 143
Community Development Financial
    Institutions Fund, 12, 71
Community development loan funds (CDLFs),
    11, 20
    microenterprise funds, 13
Community development partnerships (CDPs),
    98
Community economic development (CED),
    xi, 1–22
    accomplishments, xi

addressing organizational and institutional
    challenge, 200–202
affordable housing, 26
assets and agency, 207
Baltimore, Maryland, 170
barriers, 109
bridging regional divide, 76–80
building strong communities, 93–96
capacity, 47–49
capital supply expansion, 88–89
CDC, 62, 75
CDFI, 50
CED, 47–49
CED intermediaries, 9–10
challenges, 199
charter schools, 174–75, 176
city governments, 209
colleges, 203
communities' capital, 52
community building, 105–6, 180
community colleges, 203
community development, 105–6, 206
Community Reinvestment Act, 64–68
community side building capacity, 90–91
community-university partnerships, 196–97
components, 57
connecting basics, 95
COPC, 197
county governments, 209
economic development programs, 204
education, 179, 180
enhancing effectiveness, xxiv
enterprise community partners, 96
evolution, 47
expanding capital access, 11–13
experimentation and innovation, 97–98
federal government, 205
federal government support, 15
federal programs' support, 16–17
framework, 201
future with promise and hope, 199–210
GIS, 192
government support, 62–73
higher education as development partner,
    192
higher learning institutions, 203
innovation, 203–9
innovations, 148
institutional strategy, 11
institutions, 14
institutions and stakeholders resource guide,
    239–52

intermediaries, 87–104, 88–89
international resource guide, 257–61
jurisdiction, 48–49
knowledge generation, geographical
    information systems, 192
leadership development, 202
LIHTC, 69–71
limitations, 167
linking to educational reform, 174–76
LISC, 94, 95, 208
local development programs, 204
local intermediaries, 200
locally based CED institutions, 61–83,
    76–78
local school reform, 207
Low Income Housing Tax Credit, 69–70
management challenge, 74
management training, 202
metropolitan development, 28
modeling innovation, 205
Mountain Association for CED, 76–78
national intermediaries, 200
Neighborhood Partnership Inc., 98–99
Neighborhood Security, 109–10
NeighborWorks America, 91–92
network, 48–49
new Markets Tax Credit Program, 71–73
nonurban institutions, 186
origin, 199
philanthropy, 15
place-based development, 28
policy goals, 29
policy in United States, 144
policy network components, 40
poverty, 1
practices, xx
practitioners, 36
practitioner training, 202
preserving individual assets, 79
principles, 200
public leadership, 41
public policy, 36, 82, 199–200
public sector, 16–18
public sector innovation, 39–60
public sector involvement, 209
public sector support, 88–89, 208
reforming schools, 167–82
regional and local, 98
research and policy, 80
sector, 48–49
state government, 203
strategy and CDFIs, 12

support, 14
support, and advocacy and learning
    resources guide, 241–45
sustainable, 23–38, 208
TOP, 197
training, 203
trends, 200
United States, 1, 80
Unity Council transit-oriented development,
    75
universities, 203
urban institutions, 186
values, xx, 29
workforce development, 53, 208
youth development, 126
Community economic development institutions
    (CEDIs)
    accomplishments, 102
    bank records, 69
    CDBG, 64
    CDCs, 61
    CDFIs, 56
    charter schools, 174–75
    community-based partner arguments, 88
    community colleges, 14, 195
    definition, 2, 61
    diversity, 82
    EITC, 208
    employers, 164
    Enterprise Community Partners, 179
    failure, 47
    function, 3
    government support, 62
    HANDS, 145–46
    higher education as development partner,
        195
    IDA, 136
    isolation, 81
    job seekers, 164
    leadership development, 75
    MACED, 80
    MBC, 122
    neighborhood stabilization, 144
    organization class, 88
    poverty, 27
    public sector, 18
    Self-Help, 11
    skilled workers, 165
    STRIVE, 34
    types, 2–3
Community Employment Alliance, 96
Community gardens, 124–125

Community groups, xxii–xxiii
Community Housing Fair, 191
Community institutions, 180
Community learning centers (CLCs), 170
 program objectives, 170–71
 YMCA, 171
Community organizations, 193
Community organizing groups resource guide,
  254–55
Community Outreach Partnership Center
  (COPC), 187
 CED, 197
 funding, 187
 University of Nebraska, 188
Community Outreach Partnership program,
  203
Community Reinvestment Act (CRA), xxii, 53,
  64, 74, 208
 bank requirements, 68
 investment, 53
 LIHTC, 69
 locally based CED institutions, 64–68
 obligations 1996-2007, 69
Community Renewal Tax Relief Act, 71
Community Safety Initiative (CSI), 114
Community schools
 criticism, 169
 Lincoln, Nebraska, 170
Community-university partnerships, 196–97
Comprehensive community initiatives (CCIs),
  107
Computer Statistics (COMSTAT), 109
COMSTAT. *see* Computer Statistics
  (COMSTAT)
Conditional Cash Transfer (CCT) program, 44
Connecting Youth to Bangor and Electronic
  Resources (CYBER), 188
Conservation-based affordable housing, 35
COPC. *see* Community Outreach Partnership
  Center (COPC)
Coppin Heights Community Development
  Corporation (CHCDC), 191
County governments, 209
CRA. *see* Community Reinvestment Act (CRA)
Crime
 COMSTAT, 109
 poverty, 14, 26
 prevention resource guide, 255
 rates, 14, 109
 vacant homes, 144
CSI. *see* Community Safety Initiative (CSI)

CUNY. *see* City University of New York
  (CUNY)
CURA. *see* Center for Urban and Regional
  Affairs (CURA)
CWF. *see* Centers for Working Families (CWF)
CYBER. *see* Connecting Youth to Bangor and
  Electronic Resources (CYBER)

D

Daley, Richard, xxi
DEED. *see* Department of Employment and
  Economic Development (DEED)
Department of Agriculture, 207
Department of Education, 207
Department of Employment and Economic
  Development (DEED), 194
Department of Energy (DOE), 157
Department of Housing, 116–17
Department of Housing and Urban
  Development, xxii. *see also* Housing
  and Urban Development (HUD)
Department of Labor (DOL), 117, 118, 157
Department of Environmental Protection,
  208–9
Diversity, 82
DOE. *see* Department of Energy (DOE)
DOL. *see* Department of Labor (DOL)
Don Pedro Development Corporation, 6
Durham, North Carolina, 11

E

Earned income tax credit (EITC), 135
 assets and agency, 138–39
 Baltimore CASH Campaign, 139
 CEDIs, 208
 definition, 139
 forms, 44
 IDAs, 140
 low-cost bank accounts, 139
 poverty, 148
Eastside Neighborhood Employment Center
  (ENEC), 113
Economic development
 business loans, 79
 New Jersey Performing Arts Center, 121
 organization, 46
 philanthropy, 111
 poverty, 61
 programs, 204
 public sectors, 111

strategies, 80
Economic planning, 64
Education
    CED, 179, 180
    community building, 181
    and development, 181
Educational coproductivity, 181
Educational reform, 55
    partnerships, 174–76
    poverty, 55
    resource guide, 254
Education Outreach Department, 52
EFM. *see* Equity Finance Mortgage (EFM)
EITC. *see* Earned income tax credit (EITC)
Employee Florida Banner Center, 196
Employers, 164
ENEC. *see* Eastside Neighborhood Employment
    Center (ENEC)
Enterprise Community Partners, 179
Enterprise Foundation, 96
Enterprise Social Investment Corporation
    (ESIC), 73, 97
Environmental Protection Agency (EPA)
    Illinois, 34
    United States Brownfields Program, 33
EOWS. *see* Executive Office for Weed and Seed
    (EOWS)
EPA. *see* Environmental Protection Agency
    (EPA)
Equity Finance Mortgage (EFM), 149
ESIC. *see* Enterprise Social Investment
    Corporation (ESIC)
Ethnicity, 28
    poverty, 28
Executive Office for Weed and Seed (EOWS),
    112
Extended service schools, 168

F

Family dissolution
    poverty, 26
Family Self-Sufficiency (FSS) program, 44
FDC. *see* Fruitvale Development Corporation
    (FDC)
Federal government
    CED, 205
    support of CED, 15
    TOP, 194
Federal Home Loan Bank of Atlanta, 57
Federal Housing Administration, 134
Federal policies, 134

Financial institutions, 137
Financing innovation, 146
Fishing, 90
Florida, 118
    Employ Florida Banner Center for
        Alternative Energy, 195
    YBUSA, 118
Food and community development, 124
Ford Foundation, 95
Foreclosure property, 146
For-profit community development financial
    institutions, 73
For-profit subsidiaries of community
    development corporations, 73
Fort Road Foundation, 193
Fruitvale Development Corporation (FDC), 76
Fruitvale Transit Village, 77–78
FSS. *see* Family Self-Sufficiency (FSS) program
Full-service schools, 168
Funding, 187

G

Gang diversion
    community building and development,
        114–15
    community support, 116
    programs, 115
GAO. *see* Government Accountability Office
    (GAO)
GED. *see* Graduation Equivalency Degree
    (GED)
Geographical information systems (GIS)
    CED, 192
    community development, 192
    M3D, 194
GIS. *see* Geographical information systems
    (GIS)
Globalization, xix
Golden, Jane, 123
Government Accountability Office (GAO), 73
    NMTC, 74
Government support
    CDCs, 62
    CEDIs, 62
    locally based CED institutions, 62–73
    place-based developments, 23
Graduation Equivalency Degree (GED), 6, 45,
    117, 119, 257
Graffiti, 122–23
Green-collar jobs, 32
Green jobs, 158

Green Jobs Act of 2007, 157
Growing Power, 124

H

HANDS. *see* Housing and Neighborhood
    Development Services (HANDS)
Harlem Children's Zone, 169–70
    financial funding, 170
HCAs. *see* Housing credit agencies (HCAs)
HCV. *see* Housing Choice Voucher (HCV)
Higher education
    building community capacity, 187–89
    categories, 196–97
    CED, 203
    community colleges as CEDIs, 195
    community criticisms, 185
    development partner, 185–97
    institutions, 185, 196–97
    knowledge generation, geographical
        information systems and CED, 192
    Minnesota 3D, 192
    public sector innovation and CED, 56
    resource guide, 251–53
    successful university-community
        partnerships, 186
    university as developer, 190–91
Homeboy Industries, 126
    community building and development,
        114–15
Homebuyers Education Club, 56
Home Ownership Program, 138
HOME program, 67
    Community Development Block Grant, 140
Housing
    automobile steel reuse in building, 34–35
    development and CDC, 107
    LCW, 93
    PHAs, 136
    public, 44
Housing and Community Development Act of
        1974, 63
Housing and Neighborhood Development
        Services (HANDS), 145
    CEDIs, 146
Housing and Urban Development (HUD), xxii,
        17, 43, 44, 91, 206
    CMN, 51
    Department of Agriculture, 207
    Department of Education, 207
    Depart of Environmental Protection, 208–9
    family-self-sufficiency program, 136, 137

funding in United States, 190
    New Directions Grant, 189
    OUP, 51, 187
Housing Choice Voucher (HCV), 136
Housing credit agencies (HCAs), 70
HUD. *see* Housing and Urban Development
        (HUD)
Human capital development, 140–43

I

IAF. *see* Industrial Areas Foundation (IAF)
IDAs. *see* Individual Development Accounts
        (IDAs)
Illinois
    CDBG program, 34
    efforts to reinvent itself, xxi–xxii
    EPA, 34
    LCDC, 34
    public art, xxiii
    South Shore Bank, 13, 88
Illinois Facilities Fund, 33
Immigration pattern to United States, xii
Income segregation, 31
Individual asset building, 135–39
Individual Development Accounts (IDAs), 135
    assets and agency, 135–37
    CEDI, 136
    EITC, 140
    financial institutions, 137
    job training, 148
    Microenterprise Development program, 138
    model, 207–8
    public sectors, 137
    United Way, 138
Industrial Areas Foundation (IAF), 174
Industrial Revolution, xx
Innovation in public sector, xxvi, 41–45
*Inside Game/Outside Game: Winning Strategies
        for Saving Urban America*, 26
Institutional strategy, 11
Instituto del Progreso Latino (IPL), 163
International community economic
        development resource guide, 257–61
IPL. *see* Instituto del Progreso Latino (IPL)
Isles Inc.
    North Carolina Community Development
        Initiative, 36
    Trenton, New Jersey, 29
Isles Youth Build Institute (IYI), 30
IYI. *see* Isles Youth Build Institute (IYI)

J

Jacksonville, Florida, 118
Jewish Vocational Service (JVS), 164
Job Network Program, 162
Job seekers, 164
Job training, 148
Johnson, Martin, 30
JVS. *see* Jewish Vocational Service (JVS)

K

Kentucky coal industry employment, 78
Kinghorn, Morgan, 39
Knowledge generation, 192
Koch, Edward, xxii

L

Labor Market Information (LMI), 194
La Casa
    CDC, 8
    CEDI, 8
    decline, 6
    growth, 6
La Casa de Don Pedro child facility, 5
La Casa de Don Pedro housing project, 7
LAMP. *see* Latino Achievement Mentoring
        Program (LAMP)
Land for Tomorrow, 35
Latino Achievement Mentoring Program
        (LAMP), 189
Lawndale Christian Development Corporation
        (LCDC), 33
    Chicago's CDBG program, 34
Lawrence Community Works (LCW), 93
LCDC. *see* Lawndale Christian Development
        Corporation (LCDC)
LCW. *see* Lawrence Community Works (LCW)
Leadership
    CED, 41
    CEDIs, 75
    development, 75, 202
    public sector innovation and CED, 41–45
    skills, 41
LIHTC. *see* Low Income Housing Tax Credit
        (LIHTC)
Lincoln, Nebraska
    community schools, 170
    leadership in reforming schools, 170–71
Linking community building and education,
        168–73

Linking education and development, 181
Linking schools to community, 180
LISC. *see* Local Initiatives Support Corporation
        (LISC)
Livable and sustainable communities, 32
LMI. *see* Labor Market Information (LMI)
Local development programs, 204
Local economic development, xi
Local Initiatives Support Corporation (LISC),
        91
    CDCs, 95
    CED, 95, 208
    CED intermediaries, 94
    community development, 94
    CSI, 114
    Ford Foundation, 95
    workforce development, 96
Local planning, 64
Local School Councils (LSCs), 173
Logan School Neighborhood Association
        (LSNA), 172
    training programs, 173
Logan Square Neighborhood Association in
        Chicago, 172–73
Los Angeles, California, 157
Low-cost bank accounts, 139
Low Income Housing Tax Credit (LIHTC),
        74, 102
    administration, 71
    CED, 71
    CRA, 69
    HCAs, 70
    locally based CED institutions, 69–70
    1987-2007, 70
Low-income workers, 165
LSCs. *see* Local School Councils (LSCs)
LSNA. *see* Logan School Neighborhood
        Association (LSNA)

M

MacArthur Foundation, 96
MACED. *see* Mountain Association for
        Community Economic Development
        (MACED)
MACF. *see* Metropolitan Atlanta Community
        Foundation (MACF)
Magic bullet, xii
Maine
    CDFL, 90
    fishing, 90
    poverty, 90

Manchester Bidwell Corporation (MBC), 122
Manpower development, 53
MAP. *see* Mural Arts Program (MAP)
Maryland
  CED, 170
  CitiStat, 110
  COMSTAT, 109
  Job Network Program, 162
  Second Chance, Inc., 159
  YMCA, 170
MBC. *see* Manchester Bidwell Corporation
  (MBC)
McCormack Baron, 177
M3D. *see* Minnesota 3D (M3D)
Metro Atlanta Chamber of Commerce
  ANDP, 10
Metropolitan Atlanta Community Foundation
  (MACF), 9
Metropolitan development, xix
  CED, 28
Metropolitan Mayors Caucus (MMC), xxv
MICI. *see* Mixed Income Communities
  Initiative (MICI)
Million Trees NYC Training Program, 45, 46
Minnesota 3D (M3D)
  Census Bureau, 194
  community organizations, 193
  CURA, 192
  Fort Road Foundation, 193
  GIS, 194
  higher education as development partner,
    192
  Social Security Administration, 194
  TOP grant, 192
  United States Bureau of Labor Statistics,
    194
Mixed Income Communities Initiative (MICI),
  10
MMC. *see* Metropolitan Mayors Caucus
  (MMC)
Mobility policies, 182
Morrill Act of 1862, 56
Morse, Ricardo, 39
Mountain Association for Community
  Economic Development (MACED),
    77
  Business and Enterprise Development
    Program, 79
  CEDIs, 80
  economic development strategies, 80
  geographic boundaries, 82
  locally based CED institutions, 76–78

  online application, 80
  regional sustainable development, 79
Mural Arts Program (MAP), 123
Mural Arts Program in Philadelphia, 122–23

N

National Center for Construction Education
  and Research (NCCER), 119
National Community Development Initiative
  (NCDIC), 91
National Community Stabilization Trust
  (NCST), 147
  assets and agency, 147
  themes, 147–48
Natural-resource-extractive industries, 78
NCC. *see* New Community Corporation
  (NCC)
NCCER. *see* National Center for Construction
  Education and Research (NCCER)
NCDIC. *see* National Community
  Development Initiative (NCDIC)
NCST. *see* National Community Stabilization
  Trust (NCST)
Nebraska
  community schools, 170
  leadership in reforming schools, 170–71
Neighborhood Builder Program, 142
Neighborhood Partnership Inc. (NPI), 104, 203
  CDCs, 99
  CED, 98
  CED intermediaries, 98–99
  Cleveland, 98
  staffing, 100
Neighborhood Progress, 98–101, 203
Neighborhood Reinvestment Corporation
  (NRC), 91
Neighborhood Security, 109–10
Neighborhood Transformation Initiative
  (NTI), 97
Neighbors Working Together project, 189
NeighborWorks America (NWA), 47, 91, 101
  CED intermediaries, 91
  training programs, 92
NeighborWorks System, 92
Network building, 162
Nevada Individual Development Account
  Collaborative, 138
Newark, New Jersey
  foreclosure property, 146
  New Horizons Charter school, 176
  North Academy, 175

YBUSA, 118
New Community Corporation (NCC), 175
New Compact School, 179
New Horizons Charter school
  NCC, 175
  Newark, New Jersey, 176
New Jersey
  charter school laws, 175
  foreclosure property, 146
  New Horizons Charter school, 176
  North Academy, 175
  YBUSA, 118
  YouthBuild program, 120
  youth crime prevention, 119
New Jersey Community Capital, 147
New Jersey Core Content Curriculum
        Standards (NJCCCS), 119
New Jersey Performing Arts Center, 121
New Markets Tax Credit (NMTC), 71, 89
  CDEs, 72
  GAO, 74
  locally based CED institutions, 71–73
  program, 89
  2003-2008, 72
New York, 142
New York City Acquisition Fund, 101
New York City Housing Partnership, 142
Nixon, Richard, 133
Nixon administration, 94
NJCCS. *see* New Jersey Core Content
        Curriculum Standards (NJCCCS)
NMTC. *see* New Markets Tax Credit (NMTC)
Nonprofit organizations, 62
Nonurban institutions, 186
North Academy, 175
North Carolina
  development infrastructure, 34
  Self-Help loan fund, 11
North Carolina Community Development
        Initiative, 34
  Isles, 36
NPI. *see* Neighborhood Partnership Inc. (NPI)
NRC. *see* Neighborhood Reinvestment
        Corporation (NRC)
NTI. *see* Neighborhood Transformation
        Initiative (NTI)
NWA. *see* NeighborWorks America (NWA)

O

Obama, Barack, 158

OCC. *see* Office of the Comptroller of the
        Currency (OCC)
OFE. *see* Office of Financial Empowerment
        (OFE)
Office of Financial Empowerment (OFE), 44
Office of Juvenile Justice and Delinquency
        Prevention (OJJDP), 207
Office of the Comptroller of the Currency
        (OCC), 64
Office of University Partnerships (OUP), 187
  HUD, 51
Ohio, 98–101
OJJDP. *see* Office of Juvenile Justice and
        Delinquency Prevention (OJJDP)
ONR. *see* Operation Neighborhood Recovery
        (ONR)
On-the-job training, 161
Operation Neighborhood Recovery
  assets and agency, 145
  CAPC, 147
  themes, 147–48
Operation Neighborhood Recovery (ONR), 145
Operation Weed and Seed, 112
  CSI, 114
  expenditures, 113
  LISC, 114
OUP. *see* Office of University Partnerships
        (OUP)

P

Parent involvement and organizing, 174
Parents Empowering Parents (PEP) program, 30
Partnership to Revitalize the Heart of Lincoln's
        Neighborhoods (PRHOL), 189
Pennsylvania
  Anti-Graffiti Network, 123
  TEC, 142–43
PEP. *see* Parents Empowering Parents (PEP)
        program
Personal Responsibility and Work Opportunity
        Reconciliation Act (PRWOA), 156
PHAs. *see* Public housing authorities (PHAs)
Philadelphia, Pennsylvania
  Anti-Graffiti Network, 123
  TEC, 142–43
Philanthropy
  CED, 15
  community development, 111
  efforts, 23
PICs. *see* Property Improvement Committees
        (PICs)

Place-based developments
CED, 28
government efforts, 23
metropolitan development, 28
philanthropic efforts, 23
Place decay
public policy, xii
Policy network components, 40
Population movement, xix
Poverty
asset-building, 134
bad schools, 26
CDFIs, 88
CEDIs, 27
charter schools, 176
class, 28
community building, 105
community development, 105
community development banks, 13
community economic development, 1
crack cocaine, 112
crime, 26
crime rates, 14
criminal gangs, 26
economic development, 61
educational reform implementation, 55
effective school establishments, 14
EITC, 148
family dissolution, 26
GED, 117
government policy, 133
income segregation, 31
Maine, 90
public policies, 23, 27
public policy, xii
quality of life, 1
race, 28
racial segregation, 31
residence of people, 24–25
Self-Help development projects, 31
teenage childbearing, 26
United States, 23, 134, 209
youth development, 116
PRHOL. *see* Partnership to Revitalize the
Heart of Lincoln's Neighborhoods
(PRHOL)
Program for Regional and Community
Economic development, 206
Project QUEST, 161
Promotion ladders, 160
Property Improvement Committees (PICs), 94

PRWOA. *see* Personal Responsibility and Work
Opportunity Reconciliation Act
(PRWOA)
Public art, xxiii
Public education in United States, 40
Public housing, 44
Public housing authorities (PHAs), 136
Public leadership, 41
Public policy
CED, 36, 82, 199–200
poverty, 23, 27
poverty and place decay, xii
Public sector
CED, 16–18
CED intermediaries, 88–89
CEDIs, 18
community development, 111
IDA, 137
information technology changes, 109
innovative CED, 81
institutions, strategies, and programs
resource guide, 239–41
involvement in sustainable CED, 209
leadership and innovation, xxi–xxiii
support, 88–89, 208
Public sector innovation, xxvi
assets and agency, 52
CED, 39–60
charter schools, 40
community building and development,
50–51
higher education, 56
leadership, 41–45
resource guide, 231–33
school reform for sustainable CED, 55
workforce development changing strategies,
53–54
Public sector institutions, strategies, and
programs, 239–41

Q

Quality of life, 1

R

Race and poverty, 28
Racial segregation
federal policies, 134
poverty, 31
Real Estate Owned (REO), 146

REDI. *see* Regional Economic Development Institute (REDI)
Reflection and learning, xxiv
Reforming schools
    CED strengthening, 167–82
    educational reform partnerships, 174–76
    enterprise community partners and New Compact School, 179
    Lincoln, Nebraska leadership, 170–71
    linking CED and educational reform, 174–76
    linking community building and education, 168–73
    linking education and development, 181
    linking schools to community, 180
    Logan Square Neighborhood Association in Chicago, 172–73
    mobility policies, 182
    parent involvement and organizing, 174
    Smart Education Systems, 172
Regional Economic Development Institute (REDI), 54
    components, 54–55
Relocation policies, xx
REO. *see* Real Estate Owned (REO)
Resource guide, 231–61
    arts, 153, 253–54
    asset building, 246–50
    CED institutions and stakeholders, 239–52
    CED support, advocacy and learning resources, 241–45
    community building and development, 153, 253–54
    community organizing groups, 254–55
    crime prevention, 255
    education reform, 254
    higher education, 251–53
    international CED, 257–61
    public sector innovation, 231–33
    public sector institutions, strategies, and programs, 239–41
    sustainable CED, 234–39
    workforce development, 250–51
    youth development, 255–57
Rural economic development practitioners, 36
Rusk, David, 26
Rust Belt, xxi

S

San Antonio, Texas, 161
SBA. *see* Small Business Administration (SBA)

School(s)
    effective establishments and poverty, 14
    linked to community, 180
    poverty, 26
School Neighborhood Advisory Committee (SNAC), 171
School reform, 167–82
    community development, 181
    sustainable CED, 55
SCI. *see* Sustainable Communities Initiative-West Philadelphia (SCI-West)
Second Chance, Inc., 159
Sectoral employment
    career ladders, 160
    community-based organizations, 157
    community-based workforce development innovations, 157–59
Self-employment credit, 140–43
Self-Help development projects, 31
Self-Help loan fund, 11
SEM. *see* Shared-equity mortgages (SEM)
SES. *see* Smart Education System (SES)
Shared-equity mortgages (SEM), 149
Silo thinking, xxiv
SIP. *see* Special Impact Program (SIP)
Skilled workers, 165
Small Business Administration (SBA), 141
    CDFI, 141
Small Business Liability Relief and Brownfields Revitalization Act, 33
Smart Education System (SES), 172
SNAC. *see* School Neighborhood Advisory Committee (SNAC)
Social development organization, 46
Social Security Administration, 194
South Shore Bank, 88
Spanish Speaking Unity Council, 75
Special Impact Program (SIP), 62
State government, 203. *see also* individual state name
Steel-framed homes, 35
Steel reuse in building affordable housing, 34–35
Strategic Investment Initiative
    CDCs, 99
    NPI, 100
Strategic policies, xxii
STRIVE, 34
Sustainable Communities Initiative-West Philadelphia (SCI-West), 143
Sustainable community economic development actions, 26–27

automobile steel reuse in building affordable housing, 34–35
Brownfield redevelopment, 33
components, 57
livable and sustainable communities, 32
putting people first, 29–31
rethinking people and place development, 28
reusing automobile steel to build affordable, 34–35
search, 23–38

T

TABE. *see* The Adult Basic Education (TABE) locator test
Tapping the Power of City Hall to Build Equitable Communities (Cunningham et al.), xx
Targeted enterprise loans, 79
Tax Reform Act of 1986, 70\
TCUP. *see* Tribal Colleges and Universities Program (TCUP)
TEC. *see* The Enterprise Center (TEC)
Technological integration of world markets, xix
Technology Opportunity Program (TOP) grant, 206–7
    CED, 197
    federal government, 194
    M3D, 192
Teenage childbearing, 26
Texas, 161
The Adult Basic Education (TABE) locator test, 118
The Enterprise Center (TEC)
    CDFI, 143
    definition, 143
    Philadelphia, 142–43
Tools for economic prosperity, xxi–xxii
TOP. *see* Technology Opportunity Program (TOP) grant
Transforming Public Leadership for the 21st Century, 39
Transportation alliance for New Solutions, 52
Traynor, Bill, 93
Trenton, New Jersey
    Isles Inc., 29
Tribal Colleges and Universities Program (TCUP), 51

U

UDI Community Development Corporation, 35
UMB. *see* University of Maine-Bangor (UMB)
UN. *see* University of Nebraska at Lincoln (UNL)
Unionized jobs, 160
United Kingdom, 149
United States. *see also* individual agencies
    CDC, 62
    CED, 80
    CED policy, 144
    community building, 126
    community college systems, 195
    community development, 126
    community development strategy, 204
    community economic development, 1
    Department of Energy, 157
    DOL, 118, 157
    EPA Brownfields Program, 33
    HUD funding, 190
    poverty, 23, 134, 209
    public education, 40
    temporary workers, 161
United States Bureau of Labor Statistics, 194
United Way
    IDAs, 138
    local community foundations, 15
Unity Council
    CDC, 75
    Fruitvale BART transit-oriented project, 82
    locally based CED institutions, 75
    transit-oriented development, 75
University. *see also* Higher education; specific name of university
    CED training, 203
    community partnerships, 186
    as developer, 190–91
    higher education as development partner, 186, 190–91
University of Maine-Bangor (UMB), 187
University of Nebraska at Lincoln (UNL)
    community development activities, 188
    COPC, 188
Urban agriculture, 126
Urban Development, 116–17
    Community Outreach Partnership grants, xxii
Urban economic development, 36
Urban institutions, 185
    CED, 186

Urban poverty, xix
Urban Problems and Community Development,
   106

V

Vacant homes and crime, 144
Vashon Education Compact (VEC), 178
VEC. *see* Vashon Education Compact (VEC)
Venture capital funds, 13
Visitacion Valley Jobs, Education and Training
   (VVJET), 164
VVJET. *see* Visitacion Valley Jobs, Education
   and Training (VVJET)

W

Weed and Seed, 112–14
   CSI, 114
   expenditures, 113
   LISC, 114
WIA. *see* Workforce Investment Act (WIA)
Workforce development
   CDC, 165
   CED, 53
   CED future, 208
   changing strategies, 53–54
   definition, 155
   LISC, 96
   resource guide, 250–51
Workforce Investment Act (WIA), 156
Work Opportunity Reconciliation Act of 1996,
   54

Y

YAIP. *see* Young adult internship program
   (YAIP)
YBUSA. *see* YouthBuild USA (YBUSA)
YMCA. *see* Young Men's Christian Association
   (YMCA)
Young adult internship program (YAIP), 45
Young Men's Christian Association (YMCA)
   Baltimore, Maryland, 170
   CLC, 171
Youth
   CED, 126
   community building and development,
    116–20
   crime prevention in New Jersey, 119
   development, 116–20, 126
   MAP, 123
   poverty, 116
   resource guide, 255–57
YouthBuild
   benefits, 126
   community building and development,
    116–20
   expenditures, 117
   New Jersey, 120
YouthBuild Offender Project, 117
YouthBuild USA (YBUSA), 116, 117
   Department of Labor, 117
   Jacksonville, Fl, 118
   Newark, New Jersey, 118
Youth Crime Prevention Initiative, 121